Seeds *in the* Sand

Noah Dosier

Copyright © 2023 Noah Dosier
All rights reserved
First Edition

PAGE PUBLISHING
Conneaut Lake, PA

First originally published by Page Publishing 2023

ISBN 979-8-88960-728-1 (pbk)
ISBN 979-8-88960-737-3 (digital)

Printed in the United States of America

1

THE SUN'S REFLECTION SHONE blue on the surface of a roadside puddle a moment before the front wheel of a wagon rolled across it, making it shake wildly. The path wound its way through the middle of the vast grassy plains found near the center of Humania. The large swaths of flat ground made the area ideal for farming, although it also meant there was no natural shelter to be found from the region's infrequent storms. There wasn't any need to consider this on that day however since the air was warm and clear and the plains' verdant coverings brightly illuminated.

The nondescript small wagon was driven by a Lormish boy of twelve. He had all the characteristic features of his people—meager stature, light-green scaly skin, a set of gills on each cheek, clawed and webbed hands and feet, and a pair of tiny white horns at the top of his head. His broadsword was long enough that it couldn't be sheathed at his hip, and so he kept it on his back when it wasn't in use. But not wanting cold metal pressing hard against him, he placed it beside him lengthwise when he was sitting, as he had done then.

The boy was lost in thought as he held the reins in both hands and so didn't realize his destination was in view until the kreshes pulling the carriage spotted it and picked up their pace slightly. The path they were on led right to it, a small village and its immediate surroundings ringed by a tall wooden wall. Two armed human soldiers stood atop it and on the side of each of its four gates, keeping watch. Of the two facing the Lormish boy's wagon, the one to his left of the gate saw it first and raised one side of his right hand to his brow as he squinted at the mobile speck in the distance. After a few minutes, it was close enough to make out its details, and the guard staring intently at it lit up.

"He's come," he said with excited reverence as he turned to face his counterpart across the gate. As the carriage approached, it was opened from the inside, the motion timed to allow the kreshes to enter the town limits without breaking pace. The Lormish boy's first impressions of the space within the walls were not overly positive; he found himself surrounded by soldiers' barracks and training grounds after passing the wooden perimeter. However, as he peered into the distance directly ahead of him, he saw that its initial appearances were greatly deceiving; all the guards' premises were directly next to the inside walls, and he could see good ways off that the fields, and houses came next in that order.

When the boy saw an elderly human man walking to the wagon at a brisk pace, he brought the kreshes to a halt, and its only passenger emerged from its innards before stepping down onto one of its footplates. He was a human man in his midtwenties with tanned skin and short blond hair, dressed in armor that was white with gold trim and with a wide sword sheathed at his left hip. His gaze was fixed on the older man as the former descended to the ground, and he flashed the latter a radiant smile immediately upon locking eyes with him.

"Master Arcind!" greeted the older man warmly as he and the blond man came to a halt, a short distance away from each other and touched the backs of their right hands together, the equivalent of a handshake in their world. "Welcome to Gred. My name is Lyndon. I am the village elder. Oh, I cannot tell you how grateful I am that you have come."

"Oh, please, Elder, it's no trouble at all," Arcind replied with even sincerity. "I'm merely glad to have been given an excuse to visit your fair village." He looked side to side without moving his head in search of a specific aspect of his immediate environment to compliment but found nothing and returned his gaze to Lyndon, his smile a little tighter. Arcind looked to his right and gestured toward the lorm who drove his wagon before the air could grow uncomfortable. "This is my apprentice—Matthew." Matthew left his seat at the front of the carriage and approached Lyndon before touching the back of his hand to the latter's own as his master had done a moment prior.

"Matthew," repeated Lyndon, "it is good to meet you."

"Thank you, sir," the boy responded stiffly. "It is good to meet you."

"Ah," exclaimed Lyndon in approval, "a well-mannered youth—it is always good to see."

The older man's continued attentions dismayed Matthew, whose rigid and sore muscles were crying out to be stretched but couldn't engage in such casual behavior until no one of consequence was watching. "Thank you, sir."

Lyndon turned around and began walking away from the master and apprentice, motioning for them to follow as he did so. "I will take you to its lair, if you will follow me."

"Certainly!" Arcind replied brightly as he and Matthew obliged. "We might as well get right to it, I suppose." As the three of them made their way through a frutum field a short while later, he looked around curiously at the sizable sections of the crop that had been forcefully destroyed. "What kind of beast is it?"

"We do not know," called back Lyndon over one shoulder. "None who have seen it still live." Arcind took another step forward with his right foot and started as it sank much lower than he'd planned. "All we know is that it is a *man-eater*"—Arcind looked down at the ground beneath his front before coming to a halt and beginning to stare at it in rapt attention—"and it is *large*." The object of the swordsman's focus, as well as the reason behind his front foot's unexpected descent, was a monstrous footprint many times larger than his own, which had pressed the ground beneath it down by several inches.

"Hmm." Arcind didn't look afraid as he gazed down at it but rather merely pensive and after a moment leveled out his view and resumed course.

Lyndon faced straight ahead and raised his voice as he continued speaking to the swordsman, both because he wanted to watch where he was going and was an old man whose neck would grow sore if he kept his head turned for more than a handful of moments. "When word of your forthcoming arrival spread, there were a few men who asked me to offer to you their assistance, should you desire it."

Arcind shook his head immediately. "It's greatly appreciated, Elder, but that won't be necessary."

Lyndon chuckled once. "That is good to hear." They walked the rest of the way, which took only a few minutes, in silence before the older man stopped at the edge of the field and said, "Well, there it is." Several dozen yards ahead of him, in between the crops and the houses, rested a massive cave within an even larger hill, which extended beyond the walls in one direction. Both men were solemn as they touched the backs of their right hands together once again. "I wish you luck, Cornelius Arcind."

"Thank you, Elder, and thank you for your hospitality."

"Oh, think nothing of it," Lyndon responded sincerely as he pointed ahead and off to one side of himself. "I should tell you before I go that a friend of yours came here a few days ago to spend the night and elected to stay when she heard you would be coming. She is waiting for you there."

"A friend?" repeated Cornelius in puzzlement. He had an innumerable amount of those, but none he could think of who would take up arms beside him other than the apprentice directly behind him. Cornelius followed Lyndon's finger and could make out two figures, adult humans judging from their height, in the distance. He squinted, placing one side of his right hand at his brow. Cornelius was just barely able to make out their features then—one was a woman in her early fifties with short blond hair, tan skin, and a fit physique. She wielded a halberd and was clad in armor from head to toe. The other was just barely a man and had short curly black hair and a lanky frame. He was similarly attired, with a sword sheathed at his right hip, a bow slung around one shoulder and across his torso, and a quiver of arrows on his back.

Cornelius—his right hand returned to his side—smiled radiantly as he and Matthew began making their way to them; he didn't know the man but was very familiar with the woman. By the time the two pairs of fighters met, Lyndon had disappeared back the way he came. "Nadia Torum," Cornelius said to the woman warmly.

"Cornelius Arcind," replied Nadia, her voice as flat as if he were a perfect stranger as they touched the backs of their right hands together. "It is good to see you, sir."

Cornelius winced internally at the honorific but said nothing; he knew from experience nothing would get him on a first-name basis with her. "Likewise. I hope you haven't been staying here on my account though. It's a very simple matter that's brought me here."

"If the beast is as large as its footprints make it seem, slaying it is hardly a simple matter, sir," Nadia pointed out. "I'll be accompanying you on your hunt."

"Hmm"—Cornelius was disappointed but as always didn't let it show—"if you insist, I suppose."

"I do, sir."

Cornelius gestured toward the young man accompanying Nadia with one hand. "And who's this?"

"This is Adam Hefull," answered Nadia as she looked over at him. "He—"

"Hello, sir!" Adam interrupted exuberantly as he stepped forward and shook Cornelius's hand with hasty fervor. "Oh, it is *so* good to meet you! I can't believe my eyes. Destiny's Catalyst standing right here in front of me! Oh, it's almost too much to take. It's just so amazing. I'm Adam...er, I guess she just told you that."

"Ah, yes," said Cornelius, taken aback to the degree that a crack of uncertainty formed in his characteristically sunny disposition. "It's good to meet you too, Adam."

"When you address Master Arcind, you are to *bow*, Soldier," Nadia snapped at Adam harshly. "And you are *not* to *interrupt* your superiors when they are speaking."

Adam's eyes widened as he saw himself, and he bent over toward Cornelius in one swift motion. "Oh! Right, right, of course. M-my deepest apologies to you, madam. And to you too, uh, Master Arcind."

"It's quite all right. No need to apologize," responded Cornelius, a little embarrassed at this, as he raised both hands, palms facing outward, slightly. "No need to bow either." At this, Adam straightened as quickly as he'd bent.

Nadia's demeanor softened slightly. "As I was saying, he intends to become a member of the Cobaltus city guard. Since I am going there myself, it was decided that we would travel together when our paths crossed."

"I see," Cornelius said as he nodded, his gaze having never wavered from the young man's face. "Well, that's excellent! I'm sure they'll be glad to have you."

Adam flushed appreciatively. "Thank you, sir." His eyes fell to the broadsword sheathed at Cornelius's hip and bugged out at the sight of it. "Say, is that…oh, tantus mirus, that's *Kiam* at your hip—the sword of legend!" Adam reached for it readily with his left hand. "You wouldn't mind, would you, if I just give it a little touch?"

"*Don't*—" Cornelius started to turn the hip where he kept his sword at away from the other man, his eyes wide, but he was too late, and the latter's left hand closed around the hilt. After a split second, Adam retracted it as fast as he could, crying out in pain, before beginning to cradle it in his other hand.

"Ooh!" exclaimed Adam as he looked down at his left hand, his face contorted with pain yet glowing all the same. "Aah, it's…ow…just as the legends say! It…burns the flesh of…a-anyone who isn't…worthy of wielding it! That's…a-amazing!"

Cornelius was once again thoroughly disarmed by this incredibly heightened individual. "Ah, indeed. Are you…all right?"

"Oh, I'm fine, sir, absolutely fine." Adam's expression said otherwise. "Ready to take on whatever, ah, comes my way."

Cornelius shifted his look of concern to Nadia. "Hmm, I don't know if—"

"Do you truly believe he would be safer on his own?" she pointed out in a deadpan tone.

"A fair point," admitted Cornelius. He turned to face and started walking toward the cave, looking over one shoulder at Adam as he did so. "All right, everyone. We might as well get to it. Adam, I want you bringing up the rear."

"Yes, sir," Adam replied with an oblivious grin, "with pleasure!"

As the four of them entered the cave, Matthew took out and lit a lantern from the pack on his back. Cornelius slowed his pace to allow Nadia at his side. His apprentice looked over one shoulder at Adam with unease every handful of seconds, and after doing this a few times, his neck, unaccustomed to the motion, began to ache.

"You wear the armor of a fresh recruit," pointed out Cornelius to Nadia playfully as he gestured toward her garb. "Have you been stripped of command?"

When she didn't respond or even meet his gaze for several seconds, he began to worry that the joke had been in poor taste, or she *had* been demoted after all. Just as he was about to begin damage control, Nadia however zoned in and looked over at him distractedly. "No. As you know, it is dangerous to travel in our country's less populous regions with the armament of a warlord."

"It was a jest," Cornelius explained lightly. He studied his friend for a moment before asking in concern, "Are you all right, Nadia? You seem out of sorts."

Nadia frowned. "That I am. I do not believe I have ever been to this village before, and yet I have the strangest feeling of familiarity for reasons I cannot identify."

Cornelius furrowed his brow in puzzlement and opened his mouth to respond when he was interrupted by a thin nasal voice at his back inquiring curiously, "So what kind of creature is it?"

Cornelius looked behind him to find Adam had made his way up to them. Matthew sighed heavily, appearing to do so out of relief, but his master took no notice of this.

Cornelius grimaced slightly at the intrusion for a split second before catching himself as he always did. "The villagers don't know. Based on the size of its footprints and the location, there are two possibilities, one being far more preferable than the other." He shifted his gaze forward just in time to spot and duck under a large web hanging from the ceiling. A moment later, he heard Adam spluttering behind him as he had known the other man would.

"You think it made that web?" asked Adam after hastily wiping it off him and increasing his pace to catch up to Cornelius.

"No, definitely not," the older man replied assuredly. "That's the webbing of an aranic, a much smaller creature that lives in caves like this one." They walked on in silence for some time until Cornelius could just make out what appeared to be a wide stream of daylight coming through a hole in the ceiling. He motioned for Matthew to go on ahead and investigate, an order that was immediately followed by the young lorm. Matthew began examining his surroundings upon stopping short of the light by a great distance and froze after looking below and ahead of himself. After a few seconds, he slowly turned around and beckoned the others to him before putting a finger to his lips in a gesture exaggerated enough for them to see.

"Move as quietly as you possibly can," whispered Cornelius to Nadia and Adam as he began to comply. As the three of them approached Matthew, they came to realize why he hadn't gone up to the light; he couldn't, for it was at the center of a massive tubular chamber that extended both far above and below them. It became evident after some time that it was man-made, with a thin walkway circling its perimeter at the foot of the corridor they were in and another starting along its inside before gently sloping down and around it several times to the chamber's floor. Cornelius, Nadia, and Adam reached Matthew after a few minutes of walking and followed his gaze to the bottom of the room they now found themselves in. There laid a titan of a creature so much so that it was clear it could easily reach them if it had a mind to, asleep on its stomach. Its light-gray skin looked as solid as rock. There were long, sharp nails around the bottom of its four feet, dozens of beady eyes dotted the upper section of its face, and three thorned tails wrapped around its prone body.

"Malun!" Cornelius swore quietly at the sight of it.

"What?" whispered Adam back anxiously. "What is it?"

"You remember that I said one possibility was far more preferable than the other?" Cornelius's gaze never wavered from the beast.

"Yes."

"This is the other one." Adam swallowed loudly as Cornelius turned to face him. "The skin of a duracut is incredibly tough. No weapon can pierce it. Its eyes are its only weak point." The older man shifted his gaze to Nadia. "We have but a single chance at this. What I need you to do is—" Cornelius stopped short when he heard the unmistakable tensing sound of a bow being drawn behind him.

He whipped his head around to find Adam training an arrow on the duracut below them, one eye shut. Cornelius's eyes bugged out. "Adam, what are you *doing*?"

"You said its eyes are its weak points, right?" Adam replied without taking his eyes off his target. "An arrow should do the trick."

"ADAM, NO!" Cornelius reached for the other man's bow hand, but it was a futile gesture; he was too late to prevent the arrow from taking flight. And when it bounced off the duracut's skin, several feet from its intended location, the beast awoke, its multitude of eyes opening all at once. It lifted its head groggily to face Adam and held its position for a moment before shaking the last shreds of sleep, bellowing in thunderous rage. Cornelius sprinted toward Adam as the duracut rose and lifted one of its front feet up, planning to crush the younger man beneath it. The older of the two managed to tackle the younger to the ground in an instant before the beast stomped heavily on the spot they'd both been an instant prior.

"WHAT WERE YOU THINKING?" snapped Cornelius, no longer required to lower his voice, as he and Adam shot up.

"I...I was thinking I could kill it!" the younger man replied defensively. "I'm sorry!"

Cornelius gritted his teeth hard. "Never mind that now! The corridor we were just in is too small for it to get inside. We must"—Cornelius stopped himself. His face fell, and he turned around and saw what he'd just realized, the thought that'd been momentarily muffled by all the commotion; the massive foot that just attempted to squash Adam flat now blocked their way back—"get back to it." He whirled around and began sprinting away from the beast. "This way!" called the older man to the younger as he moved.

Adam was frozen as he stared at Cornelius in confusion. "But you just said—"

Cornelius gestured toward the organic blockade with one jerk of a hand. "IF YOU'D LIKE TO TRY IT, BY ALL MEANS!" Turning around once more while keeping pace in the same direction, he cupped his hands around his mouth and shouted out, "NADIA, TAKE MATTHEW AND GET OUT OF HERE! ADAM AND I WILL FIGURE SOMETHING OUT!" He was heading for the ramp leading to the chamber's floor. As he put distance between himself and the duracut, he spotted something; its bulk had blocked his view for a bit—Nadia and Matthew running from it as well in the opposite direction. "Wait, no! Nadia—" He realized how foolish it was to object before he could finish his sentence. *I didn't become the top warlord of the strongest nation in Samu by running from battle.* "Oh, horb it all," Cornelius grumbled to himself in reluctant concession. He and Adam reached the ramp a little before the others. As he began to descend and Nadia approached it herself, he looked over his right shoulder at her and cried out in frustration, "I told you to get out of here!"

"And *I* told *you* that I will not be allowing you to face this beast without me!" barked back Nadia, throwing Cornelius with her tone's similarity to his own.

"Well, I appreciate the sentiment, but you're not going to be of any use to anyone—" he began upon his recovery.

"Master, look out!" yelped his apprentice from behind him.

Cornelius began shifting his gaze around to his left and, in the process, spotted what he'd been too distracted to register previously— the gargantuan shadow of one of the duracut's feet swallowing up the wall beside him. He threw himself forward and to the ground, and the foot slammed into the length of stone that'd neighbored him a moment prior.

"If you are *dead*!" Cornelius finished as he stood and started running again as fast as he could. Fortunately, it didn't occur to the brute targeting them to simply sweep him and the others off the ramp to their doom with its nearest foot; the duracut instead retracted it entirely in preparation for another assault.

"This situation is dire, isn't it?" asked Adam in panic.

"I've dealt with worse!" Cornelius responded after he and the others had dodged another thrust from the beast.

Adam perked up, forgetting his fear. "*Truly?*"

"*No!*" The younger man had been free of fright for but a fleeting handful of seconds.

The four of them made their way down the majority of the ramp, managing against all odds to keep their innards off the wall beside them.

"So what's the plan?" asked Adam when they were a few feet from the bottom of the chamber.

"I am forming one," Cornelius replied, a little uncharacteristically sheepish.

"You *don't have one?*" said the younger man incredulously, he and the older now running along the room's floor.

"Not anymore!" It was Cornelius's turn to be defensive. "We can't stay here, that much I know!" As he craned his neck to and fro in a frantic attempt to find the means of their salvation, he spotted another corridor across the chamber from him and the others. Ecstasy pumped through his veins at the sight of it, but it was soon well tempered; unlike the one they'd used to arrive here, the second corridor was plenty large enough to accommodate the duracut. There was a saying in Humania however: "When you're falling to your death and see a rope, you can ill afford to inspect its craftsmanship." Cornelius led the others to ring the bottom of the chamber until they reached the exit and then began heading down the subsequent passageway. The duracut roared furiously as it tracked and attempted to attack its prey, though it only did so based on where they were presently instead of where they'd be in the future like a more clever beast would, and all four of its targets found their fear of painful death offset very slightly by irritation at the volume of the beast's protestations.

The second corridor led to another chamber of the same shape as its predecessor and with its own natural skylight. Cornelius's heart dropped to the floor as he scanned the room and found nowhere left to run, and it jumped back up into his chest when his eyes fell on a small cranny atop a tall outcropping of rock along the chamber's perimeter. There was a small opening in one side that would allow him and the others to, just barely, squeeze inside to—temporary—safety. A massive swath of aranic webbing across the room from the small shelter rested in the periphery of Cornelius's view, and he noticed, but given the presence of the murderous goliath doggedly chasing him down from behind, he paid no mind to it. As he led the others to the cranny, he forced himself, with much difficulty, not to steal any glances behind him every time one of the duracut's feet slammed into the ground below, causing the whole cave to quake and its target's ears to ring. If they had a chance, doing so would only slow them down, and if they didn't, well, what was the point in seeing certain death coming?

When Cornelius slipped in snugly between the layers of rock that formed his lifeline, he turned around and found to his elation that everyone else had made it too. Only later would he have the chance to reflect and realize that the duracut, for all its astonishing offensive power, was quite slow on its feet. There was a small nigh circular opening in the front of the cranny that Cornelius bent down before and looked out of. When he found he could make out the beast's expansive face through it, he whirled around to face Adam and snagged an arrow out of the other man's quiver before staring at him expectantly. Cornelius got a blank stare in return, and so barked in exasperation, "Give me your bow!"

That made Adam jump more than the bellows from the duracut's cavernous maw or the pounding of its feet. "Oh, yes, yes, I'm sorry." He moved to shrug his bow off himself as quickly as possible, and his haste paradoxically delayed the action. Cornelius, fuming, began lifting his hands, about to take over, when the younger man finally got free of the string and handed him the weapon.

The older swordsman took the bow in both hands and ran them along the length of its stick before taking a few test pulls of its string. After a handful of precious seconds, satisfied, he told the others, "We'll just have to hope I can hit one of its eyes from here. If not"—everyone looked off into the distance, ruminating on the unspoken, for a moment—"well, let's just hope that I can." Cornelius took aim out of the cranny's front opening and released, but right as he did, the duracut shook its head to and fro several times, and the arrow bounced off its rigid exterior several inches from any of its eyes. "Malun!" he swore in distress as he stared up at it.

The beast, provoked even further by the failed assault, lifted its front feet high into the air, leaving a strong gust of wind to shoot across Cornelius's face as he readied another arrow and kept an eye on his target through the large peephole before him. As it brought them down on the top of the cranny, he saw well in advance what was about to happen, but neither acted on this nor told the others to—purely out of optimism—hope that what would obviously come to pass might not on account of its catastrophic nature. The impact threw all four of them to the ground as chunks of rock, large and small, broke off their shelter's ceiling and fell around their heads.

Cornelius took another arrow from Adam's quiver once he and the others found their feet once again and looked out the hole before him. If a bull's-eye through one of the duracut's minuscule eyes had been a long shot before, it seemed impossible now, with the beast almost directly above him. But as Cornelius tore down a shroud of despair and probed the air above him with his eyes, he saw that, if he could manage to let loose an arrow from an (admittedly extremely awkward) nigh vertical position, he might be able to pierce one of his oil-black targets from below. A duracut's brain was wide but thin and rested right behind its face. If an arrow could strike one of its eyes at the slightest of inward angles…

Cornelius readied Adam's bow and let the second arrow fly. When it struck home and the beast howled in anguish and fury, the older swordsman began to rejoice hopefully in his own measured way, but his celebrations were cut unfortunately short when it stayed standing and its voice did not waver.

"Did you get *it*?" inquired Adam optimistically from his vantage point behind Cornelius.

The other man steeled himself and stuck his head out of the hole to look up at his handiwork. Sure enough, the second arrow hadn't curved toward the duracut's face enough. "*No.*" Cornelius began rummaging blindly through Adam's quiver for another arrow with one hand and frowned when it took a moment to find one. Looking back, he found to his utter dismay that he held in his hand the last one. "You only brought four arrows?" Cornelius spat at Adam as he jerked his head around to face him.

"F-four is *plenty*," countered the younger man weakly, "when you've got good aim!"

"There is *much* combat training in your future, Adam Hefull," Cornelius promised with a huff as he readied the final arrow. *Should you have one,* added the older man grimly to himself. He drew back the bow and fired at one of the duracut's many unsullied eyes. This time, he had no one to blame but himself. Even Destiny's Catalyst suffered from nerves when pushed to the brink, and his hands shook enough for the arrow to land a good ways off from where it needed to. Cornelius swore once more. "*No!*"

All three of the others cracked at the sound of the uncharacteristic panic in his voice.

Adam was the first to respond, as you might expect. "W-what do we do now?"

Cornelius paused as he racked his brain for an answer that, for the first time in his life, didn't come. "I don't know." Dismay was felt all around, naturally, but his anguish was of a special breed. *I'm Destiny's Catalyst. Who will slay the Dark Lord after I die? Who will stop Samu's destruction?* He stared at the duracut before him as if he could burn it alive with naught but his eyes while the others glanced back and forth at each other.

"We could wait here until it falls asleep," suggested Matthew so meekly that Nadia and Adam didn't hear him, and he had to repeat what he'd said at a volume more appropriate for the current situation.

"This structure will not hold long enough for that," Nadia pointed out. The boy's face fell.

Cornelius's gaze drifted from the duracut to the ground beneath it as he pondered how his mangled remains would be buried on its other side by day's end. As he did so, he spotted something he'd missed in the commotion—a sizable patch of aranic webbing stuck flat to the floor just behind one of the beast's hind legs. Just when Cornelius took notice of this, the duracut lifted said leg restlessly before bringing it back down immediately thereafter, but when it did so, it was at a slightly outward angle and the corresponding mammoth foot got stuck in the web.

As the beast pulled itself free of the sticky substance and brought its back foot that had become ensnared in it down a little ways outside its perimeter, Cornelius stared at this, a revelatory expression dawning on his face as it happened. He shifted his gaze to the large wad of webbing on the other side of the chamber. "I have an idea."

Adam's brow shot up in surprise and hope. "Truly?"

Cornelius turned to face his apprentice. "Matthew, when I tell you to, run to where we came from as fast you can, all right?"

"Yes, Master," replied Matthew, readily and in an even tone.

"Wait, what?" Adam spluttered in disbelief.

"You must trust me!" said Cornelius. "You must trust me. Stay here. I know what I am doing, hopefully." Matthew got into position, and his master did the same while keeping an eye on the duracut through the small opening before him. Cornelius counted down from three deliberately, and as he called, "Go!" he and his apprentice did just that, the latter making a beeline for the corridor they'd just come from and the former heading to the giant web.

Though he ran at full tilt, Cornelius never took his eyes off the large head looming over them. There was an anxious split second immediately after the master and apprentice took off where the duracut had not yet registered their movement and chosen a target, but when it was up, its gaze fell on Matthew as Cornelius hoped, and it turned to face the boy before letting loose a thunderous roar and beginning pursuit. Matthew, on the other hand, was less than pleased when he looked over one shoulder to see a creature whose nails were taller than him by an absurd margin barreling toward him in a rage, and he swore in a panic once they'd locked eyes. The boy returned his gaze to the corridor entrance before him, both in an attempt to put a terrifying sight out of mind and because he knew it's what his master would've wanted him to do, and the duracut rapidly gained on him as he ran to it. When the ground beneath Matthew was shaking from the beast's footsteps in so pronounced a way that it was throwing him off balance, he couldn't help but steal another glance backward and saw to his utter dismay that the creature was right behind him. As the duracut reared up to crush him beneath his giant feet, he managed to wrench his head back around. Pride in this was the last thing Matthew felt before it happened.

Clang! The sound of steel striking stone rang out across the chamber. Pain washed over the duracut's face as it paused, its front feet in the air, and shut its still-functioning eyes tight. It roared as it brought its front feet straight down, but now its cry sounded more hurt than angry. The duracut shuffled around to face the direction of the noise, wherein stood Cornelius before the large web and beside the sizable boulder he'd struck with his sheathed sword. In spite of everything, Destiny's Catalyst faced down the beast with unwavering self-confidence. The two combatants stood motionless for a moment as the duracut pondered what to do, with prey so close yet an instrument of agony sitting unopposed close by. When Cornelius slammed his sword into the rock again, however, that was enough to set the creature off, and it charged him as it screamed deep and long.

The older swordsman placed his sword back at his side and bent his legs in preparation for a retreat to one side, but the duracut took no notice of this with its thin, throbbing brain. When the beast was but several yards away, Cornelius turned to face and, for a handful of seconds, dashed to his left before leaping forward. The duracut collided with the swath of webbing behind him, missing its target by mere inches. Cornelius stood ponderously and, as he did so, a roar erupted from the creature's throat while it struggled to break free of its newfound bonds, but it was hopelessly, completely ensnared. Even with the duracut entirely immobile, the fear of it froze the others in place for a few moments, but the bravery of all three overcame it then, and they ran to Cornelius.

"Master, are you all right?" Matthew asked him once the two of them were a pace away from each other, his thin brow wrinkled in concern.

Cornelius grinned triumphantly at the boy as he jerked a thumb back in the direction of the paralyzed duracut. "I'm better off than this poor beast, that's for sure!"

Adam, giddy, laughed once as he stepped around Matthew. "I can hardly believe it! You *are* the greatest warrior in the land, just like the stories say!"

"Well, I'm glad I didn't disappoint, Adam," replied Cornelius with a modest smile.

"How did you know that noise would draw the beast?" Adam inquired curiously.

"A duracut's hearing is quite sharp, more so than ours. Sounds that wouldn't bother us are torturously loud for them. I didn't know for certain it would work however. It was a gamble."

"That was terribly reckless, Master Arcind...but successful, as usual," huffed Nadia.

Cornelius laughed. "Well, I'm sorry if I worried you."

"I suppose I forgive you." She decided reluctantly.

Cornelius turned back to gaze upon the captive duracut and the others followed suit. "At any rate, this beast has had its last taste of flesh."

The four of them made their way back to the surface and found Lyndon, whose eyes sparkled when he was given the news.

"I cannot thank you enough for what you've done, Master Arcind," said the old man while he zestfully shook hands with Cornelius.

"Think nothing of it, Elder," the younger replied evenly. "It was my pleasure." He looked down and over at his apprentice. "Let us depart."

Lyndon followed Cornelius as he and Matthew made for their carriage. "Please if you have the time, you should stay with us for the night."

Cornelius fixed the elder with a slight, regretful grimace. "Ah, I would love to under different circumstances, but I must make haste. The ceremony is quite soon, you know, and there is still much ground for us to cover between ourselves and the capital."

"Ah, yes, of course," said Lyndon as he nodded. "My apologies, I am afraid that it slipped my mind. Well, if there is anything I or anyone else here can do for you before you depart, please let us know."

Cornelius clasped one of the old man's hands with both of his own. "Thank you, Elder, truly." As he watched Lyndon go, he had a thought and turned to Nadia. "I suppose you two will be headed for Cobaltus as well, yes?"

"Yes, of course," she confirmed.

"In that case, why don't we all travel together? Always good to keep as much company as you can."

"Certainly," responded Nadia readily. She glanced at Adam and gestured off to one side. "Master Hefull, fetch my carriage."

Adam moved to obey, a little faster than he should've, and stumbled over his own feet before planting both firmly on the ground and resuming his course. "Yes, ma'am! Right away, ma'am!"

That night, the four of them sat around a campfire atop a large hill nestled among Humania's vast plains and ate a stew that Matthew prepared at a word from his master. "That was truly amazing what you did in that cave," Adam said to Cornelius with his mouth full.

"You flatter me," replied the latter as he flashed the former a light smile.

"No, truly it was!" Adam paused and stared into the flames before him. "I wish I could do things like that. That's why I became a soldier so I could learn how to become a great hero, like you."

"That's very kind of you to say, Adam. With the proper training, I'm sure you will." Cornelius commended himself silently for managing a convincing tone.

"I just wish that I could have been of some help to you back there," Nadia brooded, her eyes downcast. "I did not a thing."

"I know that you would've had you had the chance," assured Cornelius. "If it's any consolation, your presence was very comforting to me. It always is."

Nadia shared a meaningful look with him before turning away and blushing. "Er, well, th-thank you. You are too kind." Adam glanced at Matthew with a bemused look on his face, but the boy neither returned his gaze nor donned a similar expression. Nadia struggled to compose herself. "A-at any rate, are you ready for the ceremony tomorrow?"

"Ready as I'll ever be." Cornelius shifted his gaze to Adam. "Have you ever been to Cobaltus, Adam?"

"I haven't, no," Adam answered a little self-consciously.

Cornelius grinned. "Well, then…you're in for a treat."

2

CORNELIUS COULDN'T HAVE BEEN more right. Cobaltus was the capital of Humania, a towering labyrinth of white stone buildings forming a perfect ring around the broad, decadent royal castle at its center. But none of that even came close to being the fabled city's most arresting attribute. No, what would first grab your attention were you to find yourself within its walls was its location; though connected to the surrounding plains and held still by wide bridges at regular intervals along its perimeter, it all floated atop the country's largest lake. Its structures were all built entirely from natate, a heavy yet paradoxically buoyant variety of rock. So why had Cobaltus been built, how, and where it had? It certainly wasn't for the sake of practicality or ease; though the lake's central location made it ideal for the capital of a nation, its waters couldn't be kept clean when a city as expansive and populous as Cobaltus rested in the middle of it, rendering barren what could've been Humania's biggest source of freshwater fish, and the process of building a floating metropolis had been incredibly difficult and expensive at the time of its creation. No, the reason behind it was simply a royal's desire for grandstanding; when House Roneage took the throne after the country's founder stepped away from it centuries ago, the newly minted King Primos wanted to make a pointed display of power to win over those who were now his subjects and who, for the most part, doubted the legitimacy of his rule as well as find a way to utilize Humania's plentiful natural stores of unused natate. And so the floating city was built.

Matthew yawned deeply as he drove his master's wagon up to the right side of one of the hulking gates that granted entrance to the city; he'd trouble falling asleep the night before, and they'd to rise early that morning to make it to the capital in time for the ceremony, which was set to take place only a few hours after sunrise. Cornelius looked upon the boy with sympathy as he sat beside him. Nadia's carriage was right alongside their own vehicle, and even then, there was enough space on their left for several more going the same way as well as numerous others heading in the opposite direction. Many guards armed with crossbows were stationed atop the wall surrounding the city on either side of each gate, glaring down at the new arrivals suspiciously. There were also fully manned, grounded outposts to the left and right of all the entranceways. One of the soldiers working in the one nearest to Cornelius's wagon spotted and came over to it with a smile of recognition on his face.

"'S that you, Cornelius?" asked the soldier of the man in front. James wasn't much older than Cornelius, and yet like all the soldiers working the streets and perimeter of Cobaltus, he'd aged a few decades before his time. He lost an eye a few years ago and several teeth over the course of his short life, and the near-constant rays of direct sunlight on the exposed sections of his flesh as he stood outside for hours on end to work had made it like leather.

"It certainly is!" Cornelius confirmed warmly, seeing the other man's smile but not the gaps within. He leaned forward to shake James's hand.

"Well, how th' ferm are ya, ya sorry excuse for a man?"

Cornelius sat back up. "Doing well, and you?"

"Oh, 'bout the same, I'd say." On each of the innumerable occasions that Cornelius came to the capital through this gate, he and James exchanged the same word-for-word back and forth, and every time, as the soldier walked up to his wagon, he hoped to himself that the other man's rough life had improved in some way since the last time they'd spoken, and he'd respond accordingly with a new collection of words, but it never came to pass. James looked over one shoulder at the men atop the wall behind him.

"Open the gate! It's Cornelius!" The volume of his raspy voice made the man whose presence he was announcing jump a little. As the air filled with the sounds of turning gears and creaking metal, James began walking backward to his post, raising his right hand in farewell. "Well, I s'pose we shouldn't stand 'round talkin' fer too long, given th' circumstances." He gestured toward the other carriage. "Who's 'at behind ya?"

"Nadia Torum and a future member of the city guard," answered Cornelius.

"Ah, well, I wish ya luck!"

Cornelius smiled back warmly. "Thank you, James, to you as well. It's good to see you."

"Good to see ya as well!" When James beamed as he did then, he looked his age.

The gate closed just behind the twin vehicles as they passed into the city. One of the other soldiers stationed on the ground, who was supposed to alternate duties with James, motioned for him to go on as he sat back in his chair. James huffed in frustration but acquiesced; a man of his meager status hadn't much say in anything at all. However, he brightened up upon spotting the wagon next in line, as he recognized another of his acquaintances. Will was a portly merchant in his midforties who still combed over the few wisps of hair he had left in a comical attempt to defy the aging process and his poor genetics. He stepped off the wagon to meet James as the other man approached it, and though this was odd, the guard was too distracted by the promise of conversation outside the realm of the usual terse, proper exchanges he took part in all day to notice. "Is that you, Will?"

"Y-yes, it is." Will was sweating noticeably and breathing heavily despite the characteristically temperate weather, and he kept glancing behind him anxiously at the back of the wagon, but James still detected nothing amiss. Truth be told, he wasn't very good at his job.

"Well, how th' ferm are ya, ya sorry excuse for a man?"

"I-I'm all right."

"Good, good."

There was an expectant pause, brief yet far too long nonetheless. Will stared blankly at the guard for a moment before seeing himself and responding, "And…y-yourself?"

"'Bout the same." James took another step toward the wagon and examined it appraisingly. "Is this a new wagon?"

Will started as if the other man had inquired about the color of his stool. "Y-yes, I…I bought it several weeks ago."

James turned his head to look back at Will and pointed with his right hand to the wagon's near side, which was intricately carved to resemble broad vistas of Humania's eastern mountains. "Very nice. These patterns carved intuh the wood…did ya buy this 'n Yinit?"

Will blanched, and his eyes darted back and forth a few times. "Ah, yes, I…I did." He shifted his weight to his other foot. "I…I *commissioned* the woodworkers to build it about half a year ago, and they, ah, *finished* their work several weeks ago. That is, ah, *that* is what I meant when I said that I…I bought it…at that time."

James stared back at Will in silence for a moment, visibly taken aback, his right arm still hovering in midair. The other man's gaze struck terror in Will's heart until the guard looked back at the wagon, brought his raised arm down to his side, and chuckled playfully. "Olt must be payin' ya more than ya've let on! A wagon from Yinit, huh!" Will exhaled loudly, his mouth a small ring. "Anyhow, I have tuh *conduct an inspection*, as you know," James continued with mock formality as he walked around to the back of the wagon. "I'll make it quick though. How's that sound?"

A little relief seemed to settle over Will. "It, ah…it sounds good." He followed James, who opened both of the wagon's back doors before stepping inside, still grasping them for leverage.

"Hmm," said James as he looked around with admiration, "it's quite spacious back here, innit?"

That it was. The fruits and vegetables were in boxes, the grains in bags, and the meat hung from large hooks on the ceiling. The wagon was filled to the degree that the only walking space left in the back of it was a walkway only wide enough for one person to walk across comfortably from the doors to the row of supplies lining the far wall. James's gaze drifted indolently across the small room before he turned around to face Will again. "Well, I don't think there's much reason for me to be lookin' in 'n' around every little thing back 'ere. Looks like it's all the same stuff. I'd say I've—" The guard cut himself short as a needle of thought seemed to suddenly puncture his brain, and he whirled about to look down upon an aged, tattered rug rife with discoloration in the middle of the walkway.

"Fer Acris' sake, Will, yer still holdin' ontuh this old, beat-up rug 'f yers?" James asked in exasperation as he made his way to it. "I been tellin' ya, ya need to get rid of the thing. All that coin ya've got tuh buy yer *wagons from* Yinit and yer tryin' tuh tell me ya don't have enough tuh—"

The semblance of relative calm that settled over Will once the guard began to conclude his search had evaporated as soon as the other man stopped himself and complete panic had taken over in its stead. "*James!*" The older man crossed the distance between them in a few swift paces and placed a hand on the younger man's shoulder. James shifted his gaze to the merchant in bewilderment. "*It's*…it's good to see you again, truly, it is, but could we conclude our business here, please? I *r-really* must be on my way."

It was incredibly late in coming, but suspicion finally set in for James right then. He furrowed his brow. "Will, yer not in some kinda…trouble, are ya?" Breath gusted out of the older man's mouth, but no words. He looked as if he couldn't even piece together a handful of letters in a proper sequence, let alone form a whole sentence. "'Cuz if ya are, ya should tell me right now."

Will would've been doomed at that very moment if he hadn't, for the first time in this entire exchange, been able to have a thought, in this case, the idea for a deception and the accompanying relief at the possibility of its success and keep it from rising up to his face. "Uh, no, I'm not in any trouble, no t-trouble at all. It's just…the ceremony that's got me anxious. P-plenty of food to cook for tonight, a lot of work to be done, y-you know. That's all."

Another 'bout of tense silence ensued, and Will fretted to himself all throughout, but then James nodded, a look of acceptance on his face. "Ah, I get ya." He motioned for the other man to walk out of the wagon so he could do the same, and Will readily complied.

"Well, fair enough. *But* the next time ya come through this gate, I expect that godforsaken rug to have been replaced, understand?"

Will chuckled nervously as he and the guard clambered out into the open air; the threat of discovery was gone, but his heart had not yet caught on, ceased its insistent pounding. "I'll c-consider it."

So why had talk of the dirty rug in his wagon sparked such anxiety for the portly merchant? Well, beneath it was a trapdoor, leading to a sizable compartment below the wagon's floor, and within that space, about a dozen people were huddled. Their skin was dark purple, and their hair was a shade of the same color deeper still, and their irises were pure gold. Aside from this, they had the same basic appearance and build as humans…and yet anyone looking as they did would've been beaten until death had they been spotted anywhere in Humania or its eastern neighbor the Lormish Isles.

Two members of the group, a man and a woman, stood out from the rest because of the single line of red paint starting at the bottom of each of their eyes and running down their faces from there.

"Do you think we are safe, Zage?" questioned the woman to the man apprehensively.

"He would not dare give us away, Zuza," Zage whispered back.

They were so tightly packed into the hidden space that they had to address each other by name to make clear who each of them was talking to at any given moment, as they hadn't the room to turn and face or reach out to another.

"He knows what will happen to him if he does." Zage's face was a tableau of grim resolve, as usual. "Everyone, take this time to prepare yourselves. The greatest battle of our lives awaits."

* * * * *

"*Tantus mirus!*" exclaimed Adam in awe as he stood before and stared up at the royal castle along with Cornelius and the others some distance further in. Like the rest of the city, the queen's residence was made of natate, but Primos, the man who first commissioned it to be built, wanted it to have some added flair, to differentiate it from the surrounding shops and commoners' houses. The architects had sculptors brought in to work alongside the stonemasons for the purpose of carving several vast, complex patterns into the walls in response. This still did not fully satisfy the king however, who wanted gold incorporated into the structure in some way. Entire bricks of solid gold could not be used, of course, as it would've weighed the castle down to the bed of the lake, and so a compromise was reached—large swaths of the building's interior and exterior were completely gilded. Even this relatively minuscule amount of weight still lowered the castle grounds by several inches, and so one had to watch their feet when stepping onto the premises.

"Impressive, isn't it?" Cornelius asked the younger man, his voice heavy with pride in his motherland.

The new recruit nodded in a vehement and jerky motion. "I'll say!" By contrast, Nadia's face was completely blank as she regarded the castle, and Matthew's expression was flat as well save for a shine in his eyes he couldn't mask, try as he might.

"Well, then, shall we enter?"

"Y-yes, sir!" answered Adam excitedly.

As they approached the castle's towering front doors, open wide for the ceremony, two guards, one stationed on either side of them, came into view. Each party before them seeking admission was stopped, searched, and questioned, but when the four of them reached the front of the line, the guard there stepped aside at once.

"Good day, Master Arcind," he said, "Lady Torum."

"Good day to you, Byron," replied Cornelius amiably. "How goes it?"

"I'm well, sir."

"Good, good." As Cornelius moved to pass him, the guard pointed at Adam subtly and brought his hand back down to his side at a slight nod from the oldest male arrival.

The immense expanse of the castle's foyer was nonetheless tightly packed that morning with smartly-dressed lords and ladies as well as their retainers, who could be identified as belonging to that last group by their inferior nevertheless lavish attire. The walls were covered in paintings by the finest human artists, and grand sculptures stood atop tall pedestals dotting the room.

When someone a short distance away from Cornelius called out his name, he turned to face the voice's source, a pudgy human man of about fifty-five sitting in a wooden wheelchair. This was Samuel Roneage, the older adoptive brother and head adviser to the queen. His coarse brown hair and beard were long and unkempt, and he wore a strikingly simple loose-fitting robe of a shade just dissimilar enough from that of them for the full picture to upset the eyes.

"Samuel!" Cornelius responded, raising his voice to be heard over the surrounding din. "How are you?"

The cripple stopped before him, and the two shook hands. "Glad that we'll be rid of Zage Batur in short order here! And how are you?" Anyone could see the queen's adviser was in very high spirits.

"Never better."

"Good, good." Samuel turned around and began rolling away from the other man. "Come, I'll show you to our seats."

* * * * *

On the other side of the castle, facing west, there was a large ramp, guarded constantly just like the front, leading to its lower levels. The dungeons stood down there immediately ahead of it, for good reason; Kagloris was immediately west of Humania. But it was also here that the castle's staff lived and worked. Will drove his wagon down the ramp and into a wide tunnel. It led all the way to the front of the castle, but he reined in the kreshes pulling him and his cargo about halfway down, where the kitchen was located. After disembarking, Will looked around anxiously but found no one; all the staff members were too busy with preparations for the festival after the ceremony to mill about in between rooms, and no one in view happened to be cutting their way through the tunnel at that moment either. He clambered into the back of his wagon and pushed the rug away from the trapdoor before knocking on it twice.

Zage opened it and stood, glaring at Will with much suspicion. "Is it safe?"

"Yes!" A little defensiveness slipped through the merchant's nerves.

Zage clenched one hand. "You are certain?"

"Y-yes, I'm certain!"

When Will entered the bustling kitchen, he held in both arms a large crate. It was evident from the strain on his face and throughout his body that it was extremely heavy. Olt, an older Lormish man, looked up from his work at his supplier as he entered the room. "Oh! Hello, Will." The merchant was several hours late in delivering needed stores for the upcoming feast, but Olt didn't feel right chastising a man when sweat was already running down the other person's face.

Will kept his eyes averted from the cook's face as he moved ponderously. "H-hello."

Olt began walking toward the merchant, arms outstretched in the latter's direction. "Here, let me help you with that—"

"No!" Will turned away from the other man in a panic.

Everyone who wasn't already looked over, and all the other people in the room raised their brows at the outburst. Will saw this and restrained himself as much as he could, which was hardly at all, before continuing. "Uh, no, that's all right. I've g-got it. Thank you."

Olt stared back at him in silence for a few seconds, his expression unchanging, and it seemed like he might have been about to object until he finally opened his mouth and responded, "Suit yourself. You won't hear me asking twice, given the face you're making."

Will breathed a heavy sigh of relief and set the box in his arms down to the immediate right of the doorway he'd just passed through. After this, he returned to his wagon to get another box that he placed a little further along the wall from its predecessor and did this ten more times until the boxes completely ringed the room.

"That's more than I ordered, isn't it, Will?" asked Olt as he chopped vegetables with his back to the other man, raising his voice to be heard over the cacophony sounding across the kitchen. When the merchant didn't reply, the lorm paused what he was doing and turned around to find the other man standing still as stone beside the last box and facing away from him. Olt frowned. "Will?"

The merchant didn't move for another moment and then turned to face the lorm in a reticent movement, and it was at that moment that Olt saw the other man's dour expression and the tears streaming down the human's face.

Before the lorm could voice his perplexity and concern, all the newly arrived boxes burst open at the top, and Will's passengers, each fully armed, popped out of them in unison. It was so sudden that Olt didn't have time to be afraid; he was only able to shift his gaze to one of the intruders, a man with a bow, and begin, "What—" before he took an arrow right through the heart and died instantly. As his corpse slumped to the floor, the other cooks cried out in terror and shock. Three of them made for the door single file and hadn't taken but a handful of steps before they were massacred in short order by the people from the boxes; at the front, impaled with a sword; in the middle, slashed across the chest with another; at the back, stabbed from behind with a dagger.

Zage, wielding a knife, backed another three into a corner. Grabbing the closest of them by one shoulder, he stabbed him on the side of the neck before slipping the blade out of his flesh as quickly as it had gone in, uncorking a geyser of blood that sprayed across Olt's cutting board. Zage stepped around his first victim as he fell to his knees, futilely clutching at his mortal wound, and pushed the second cook up against the wall, then slit his throat in one swift horizontal slice. Before this kaglorite shifted his gaze to the final cook, the other man had had the benefit of time his fellows hadn't, and so was able to think long enough to conclude he should fight back in time to try to do so. Stepping forward, his lip curled. The cook punched Zage full in the face. The purple man's head didn't even move. Zage batted his assailant's outstretched arm away and pushed the other man into the wall, hard. The cook fell to the floor with his head in his hands, dazed from the impact. Zage closed the short distance between them and knelt before stabbing his opponent, who grabbed the blade with both hands a second too late, deep in the chest.

Less than a minute after the intruders made their presence known, everyone else in the room had been massacred save for Will, who surveyed the purple people's handiwork in abject horror. *At least I am not dead too*, the merchant thought, hating himself for it.

However, as soon as Zage's prey were gone, he whipped around and fixed Will with a menacing stare.

The merchant recoiled and raised his hands defensively as the man with the knife stood and advanced toward him. "W-wait! You promised—"

Zage flashed him a cruel, slight smile. "And you believed me?"

Will turned and ran for the door, and the man with the knife followed quick as he could. The others were unmoving, knowing from experience not to interfere unnecessarily with their leader's hunt. Zage tackled Will to the ground before the other man could exit the kitchen, and the latter, completely panicked, cried out in terror as he struggled in vain to break free from the former's grip.

"*No!*" whimpered the merchant. "*No!*"

Zage raised his blade and stabbed Will in the back deeply and repeatedly. "*N...ukk!*" Blood poured from the wounds, pooling on the floor below. Will fought to escape even after the kaglorite had ceased his attack but failed to completely, and shortly thereafter, he slumped down, dead.

Zage stood and swiveled to regard with pride the red splatters and bits of gore now covering the room. "Very good," he said to the others. Zage turned to face the door and began walking to it. "Let's go."

* * * * *

The ceremony was to take place in a massive chamber, within which were a large wooden stage resting up against one wall and two columns of several dozen very wide natate pews each before it, all of which were specially made and placed for just this occasion. There was a door on either side of the stage in the wall it butted up against. All but a few of the seats at the very front of the formation, which were all reserved for persons of great importance, were taken, and so many were electing to stand behind the back rows.

"Ah!" called out Samuel over one shoulder as he led the others between the pews to the stage. "There's the queen and the oracle." He gestured toward a pair standing just in front of the stage as the two of them conversed with a small group before them. Queen Coria had long, flowing hair, pure blond, and tan skin over a frame far more muscular than one associated with royalty. Her robe, running down far like the hair on her head, was pure white with light-brown trim and a few small, carefully woven patterns across the chest of the same color. Brown was the color of House Roneage's crest, to signify Humania's fertile earth, the most so of anywhere in Samu. Coria was young, twenty-four, and had only been crowned four years prior, when her mother, Maescha, passed away from illness.

Dekkin Eterden served as the humans' oracle. He appeared, as he had for centuries, just barely older than the queen, but his shoulder-length silver hair gave away, at least partially, his true age. Dekkin's posture was only slightly bent and yet a sizable hump extended outward from the top of his back. No one had ever questioned him about this, as his status ensured others either revered him enough to be blind to the deformity or feared divine reprisal from the immortal man for inquiring about the prominent flaw in his figure. Dekkin was dressed in a brown robe, and while Samuel donned such a garment out of practicality, Coria's attire was accented with the color for tradition's sake. The oracle clearly simply couldn't be bothered to dress up; the fabric was stained, rumpled, or both for nearly its entire length. A dagger rested in a sheath at his left hip.

Cornelius bowed to the queen solemnly when he reached her, and after some time, she was finally free to receive him. "It is very good to see you again, Your Highness."

"Welcome, Destiny's Catalyst," Coria, a tad flushed, replied. Rumor had it that she was considering the vaunted hero as a marriage prospect, and her provocative reactions to him whenever they met in public were regarded as supporting evidence. However, it is worth noting that she also seemed to behave in this way around just about any eligible bachelor of appropriate age and status, and Destiny's Catalyst never seemed to smile any wider than he did with any other member of the court. "We are very glad to have you here."

Cornelius turned to Dekkin and nodded at the other man; the oracle didn't stand on ceremony for anyone and expected similar treatment from any other. "Oracle, how are you?"

"I'm well, thank you." Dekkin's smile was always tight, and his movements slow. There seemed to be a slight sadness to the oracle, but he talked so little and made public appearances so rarely that no one really knew the first thing about it. Cornelius was one of the few who could probably be reasonably expected to know something of the immortal (it was from his lips the prophecy that'd changed the hero's life had come) but had only ever encountered him officially, as had everyone else.

Cornelius smiled. "Good, good."

* * * * *

Cornelius would've had something quite different to say had he been aware of the armed intruders who were at that moment exiting the kitchen and then darting into a corridor adjacent to the large tunnel underneath the castle shortly thereafter. Led by Zage, they made their way to the nearest staircase and ascended for several minutes before zigzagging toward the center of the castle through a maze of hallways. After taking a right, they encountered their first guard. He was looking straight ahead, his body running perpendicular to theirs, and so didn't spot them right away. Soon enough, the sounds of their movements, however slight, were too close to be missed, and the guard turned to face them. When he caught sight of the purple of the intruder's skin and hair and stared into Zage's brilliant gold eyes, his own bugged out to such a degree it honestly looked as if they might pop out of his head.

"H-help!" cried out the guard as he turned to face the approaching crush, his pike gripped tight in one hand and his shield in the other but resting uselessly at his side. "Kaglorites!" It was all he managed to accomplish before one of his attackers shot an arrow clean through his neck. The kaglorites passed him without breaking pace as he collapsed, choking on his own blood.

"Did you say something, Bradley?" a voice from up ahead and around a corner called back. By the time the second soldier rounded the bend, the kaglorites were practically on top of him. Like his predecessor, his eyes responded before any other part of his body could, going wide first with surprise and then horror. Unlike him, this one didn't even try to fight, turning and beginning to run away. He didn't get very far before several of the kaglorites caught up and grabbed his arms and shoulders. The guard cried out as he struggled in vain, and those holding him back, unbeknownst to him, ducked in near-perfect unison as another of their number drew his sword while positioning himself before the soldier. The human found himself so consumed with terror he didn't realize what was about to happen until the kaglorite at his front brought said sword back and to one side. The guard was decapitated in one swift motion, his head falling to the floor in equal fashion.

* * * * *

The last seats to be filled were those in the front, which had sat empty when Cornelius and the others entered the room and were taken by them, save for Adam and Dekkin. Coria stood tall atop the stage and surveyed the imposingly large crowd. She briefly pictured a scenario in which she forgot some part of her prepared speech or even all of it. Coria shuddered imperceptibly; she couldn't imagine anything worse.

3

THE QUEEN FIXED THE audience before her with a bright smile. "Welcome, everyone. It is good to see that so many people have come to witness what will be, years from now, a day of legend." As she continued her speech, Matthew failed to stifle a yawn as he sat in the front row. His master glanced over at him as he did so and saw for the first time how visibly fatigued the boy was.

Cornelius brought his mouth to his apprentice's ear discreetly and whispered to him, "Matthew, why don't you go back to the carriage and get some rest?"

The lorm returned the man's gaze, a guilty look on his face, and replied quickly and unconvincingly, "Oh, uh, I'm not tired, Master."

"You are," insisted Cornelius lightly, "and I don't think a child would much enjoy all the speeches about hope in times of darkness and whatnot that we'll be hearing today. *Go.* It's fine, Matthew, really."

His apprentice balked internally at being called a boy but couldn't deny the relief that flooded through his body at his master's words. "Well…if it's all right—" Matthew began hesitantly.

"It is," reassured Cornelius.

After a moment of silent deliberation, the boy got up and made his way down the aisle between the two columns of pews toward one of the chamber's back exits. Before he was three paces away from Cornelius, the man returned his attention to the queen.

"What has brought us here today began many years ago," Coria said as the beginning of the previous conversation had taken place.

"When our oracle, Dekkin Eterden, received a vision of Samu's destruction at the hands of a single being, who would come to be known as the Arsonist, the one who would set the world ablaze, a search for this Arsonist, one which spanned every corner of the four realms began, to no avail. Their target could not be found. The peoples of Samu fell into collective despair, seemingly unable to escape their impending doom."

A pall fell over the room as the queen told this story, but it was to be lifted immediately when she continued, "But a day soon came in when the oracle received another vision, one foretelling the birth of a child by the light of a blue sun who would be destined to slay the Arsonist and prevent the end of days. The denizens of the four realms rejoiced upon hearing of this. Years passed, and then one day, as a cyanic sun shone brightly in the sky above, a baby boy was born in a small village down by the sea."

Were it not for the formal setting, many in the audience would've cheered.

"And as the boy became a man, a force of great evil arose." For everyone present, it was as if a chill passed through the room. "A small number of kaglorites survived the war that swallowed up the rest of their people, and they were intent on reigniting their plot to destroy the humans. Leading them into battle was a vicious warrior—the Dark Lord Zage Batur. The heinous actions of this Dark Lord made it clear that he is the one who the oracle saw in his vision." The queen grinned assuringly, and the others lightened up as her speech went on.

"Many years passed since the fateful day the coming of Destiny's Catalyst was foretold when the Orb of Desire, a magical artifact capable of granting a single wish, was discovered in the Lormish Isles. Our forebears were naturally greatly tempted to use it. But they remembered the prophecy and knew that it should be given to the one it spoke of, to aid him in his quest to destroy the Arsonist. And so it was sealed away inside the temple it was found in, and a map showing the temple's location and key to unlock it were created and hidden away inside this very castle." Coria gestured toward a soldier sitting in the front row of the left column of pews holding a small black wooden box in both hands. "Now the day has come for Destiny's Catalyst to take the map and key and embark on a journey to the Orb—a journey to find it and, in turn, our deliverance from the Dark Lord's clutches."

A soldier stood guard on the other side of each door neighboring the stage. When a clang rang out from around a corner closest to one, he started and turned to the other, asking, "Did you hear that?"

The second guard frowned at the first. "Hear what?" His senses would've had to have been incredibly dull for him to miss the resounding noise of metal on metal, but alas, they were. Not since the war against the kaglorites had the capital been even remotely threatened, and that conflict ended some time before his birth. The soldier nearest to the earlier one looked back over in its direction as if he could see through the walls between him and its source. The guards' eyes almost popped out of their sockets when the coterie of kaglorites rounded the corner, but on sight, they both unsheathed their swords, their years of intensive training saving them from hysteria. The soldiers got into combat stances and moved to meet the intruders single file; not enough room was afforded them in this narrow corridor to allow for a side-by-side offensive.

The kaglorites recognized this too, and one of them was moving a little ahead of the others, a sword of his own in both hands. The front guard swung his blade mightily at his first opponent's neck in a downward diagonal arc. The kaglorite released his grip on the hilt of his sword with one hand and raised it to block the path of the assault. Luminescent energy, red as blood, coated his hand a second before impact, and a moment later, his glowing flesh bisected the soldier's sword like a knife through butter. As the top half of the guard's weapon clattered loudly to the floor, the kaglorite reached forward with his still-gleaming hand to grip the chain mail about his opponent's neck. The red energy ate through the metal in an instant, leaving the human's neck exposed, but, of course, the man's flesh was unaffected. The kaglorite swung the sword in his other hand at the soldier's neck from one side, and though it didn't completely separate head from body, it lodged inside its target deep enough to ensure the victim's death.

As the violet-skinned invader used his first hand as leverage to rip his blade from the first guard's neck and the latter fell against a nearby wall as blood gushed from his newly formed wound before collapsing entirely, the second turned around and began fleeing in alarm. The kaglorite in front raised his free hand up slightly, palm facing the ceiling, and a small ball of the same red energy he had just used on the other soldier materialized just above it. Pulling back the corresponding arm and taking a moment to aim at his moving target, he launched the red sphere at the small of the retreating guard's back, and it hit home with near-perfect accuracy, boring a hole in the human's armor and clothes there. Another of the kaglorites, armed with a bow, readied an arrow before losing it right into the center of the soldier's exposed flesh. The wounded man fell forward to the ground but, in spite of his injury, held on tightly to life and began crawling away from his attackers and toward the nearest of the doors to the crowded chamber. One of Zage's subordinates quickened his pace to pass his fellows, dagger in hand, and stopped upon reaching the scrabbling guard. Kneeling, he stabbed the soldier repeatedly in the perfect circle of naked skin at his back, killing him before he had the chance to sound the alarm.

"This is it," declared Zage over one shoulder to the others as he walked to one of the doors leading to the packed chamber. "Everyone, get into position."

The queen gestured toward Cornelius with one hand. "Now, Destiny's Catalyst, if you could please come up here to receive the map and key."

The kaglorites split into two groups, one led by Zage and the other by Zuza, each at one of the doors beside the stage.

Cornelius walked to the stage and stepped onto it, his movements measured.

"Now!" Zage barked at the others before bursting into the adjoining chamber in perfect unison with Zuza.

The sound of the twin doors being slammed open seemed, in this deathly quiet chamber, to have the volume of a nearby explosion, and all eyes turned to them at once. As Zage and the others made for the unfortunate soldier holding the map and key, it was not so much the weapons in their grasp but the hue of their skin that made many in the audience cry out in shock and horror. Some of the kaglorites lobbed balls of red energy into the crowd as they ran.

Cornelius put himself between the invaders and the queen, placing one hand on the hilt of his sword and motioning behind him with the other. "YOUR HIGHNESS, GET BACK!" As Zage drew ever closer to the map and key, Destiny's Catalyst unsheathed his sword and moved to intercept the kaglorite only to be cut off himself by a second one wielding a sword. The soldier being targeted by the kaglorites maintained his grip on the small black box with one hand and attempted to punch their leader with the other, but his swing was nimbly dodged. A short distance away from the two of them, Cornelius and his opponent locked blades.

Zage's free hand began glowing red, and he punched the soldier he was facing square in the chest, searing a hole through the other man's armor. After a moment of struggle, Cornelius overpowered his opponent and broke the lock; his blade swung to his left as a result but didn't strike home. In an instant, the dagger in Zage's grasp darted out and sank deeply into the hole in the soldier's defenses. Cornelius swung up and to his right, hitting the kaglorite he found himself fighting over the head with the hilt of his sword and knocking him unconscious. Zage yanked the blade of his weapon out of the chest he'd buried it in and wrenched the box holding the map and key from the soldier still dutifully holding it as the latter fell to the ground.

Cornelius and Zage turned to face each other before the former's opponent even hit the ground. Pure animosity, bred from their long history of life-or-death duels, flared up within both of them and leaked onto their faces. Quick as thought, they rushed toward each other, weapons at the ready.

Elsewhere in the chamber, Nadia, holding her halberd in only one hand and allowing the other to rest at her side, was squaring off with a female kaglorite wielding an axe. The warlord's offensive was so vicious she pushed her opponent back a fair distance from where they'd started. The kaglorite rushed Nadia with the same ferocity she had the last several times, as if she didn't recognize how it'd turned out then. Nadia blocked a swing of the axe from her right with the spear of her halberd and then dodged another from her left. Before her opponent could prepare for a third assault, the warlord sliced open one of the kaglorite's arms, causing the other woman to cry out in pain and drop her weapon. Right as the axe clattered to the ground, Nadia stepped on its blade with one foot and quickly pulled back the corresponding leg, sending the weapon sliding across the floor and well out of its wielder's reach.

The two combatants stood and stared at each other, the eye of the battle storm around them. Nadia took a step forward, and in turn, her opponent went back one step too. The kaglorite raised her left hand, palm up, and placed her right palm down, about a foot and a half above it. Nadia swore as she bounded toward her opponent, but she was too late; bright energy blue as deep sea radiated between the kaglorite's hands, causing a flail to materialize there before disappearing as swiftly as it had come. The violet-skinned woman was clearly a highly skilled magic user based on the speed of the process, which was what the warlord facing her failed to anticipate.

The kaglorite grabbed the handle of the flail out of the air with one hand and, this time, allowed Nadia to approach her. When they were a pace away from each other, both swung their weapons in unison and at the same place, causing them to collide and bounce off each other. Recovering with the speed of one of Humania's finest fighters, Nadia stabbed at the other woman with her halberd's spear, but the kaglorite was able to quickly move to her right, dodging it, and finding herself suddenly right beside it, she swung the flail at it. Its singular tendril wrapped around the spear, just as the kaglorite had planned, and she pulled both of them toward her, dragging Nadia along with them.

Despite all this, the warlord still only held her weapon in one hand and was making no move to change that. Nadia began pulling back, bringing herself to a halt and creating a stalemate between the two of them. When the arm she was using to hold the hilt of her halberd began to shake, however, she placed her other hand with great reluctance around it as well and overpowered her opponent immediately upon doing so, wrenching the flail from the other woman's grasp.

As the kaglorite summoned blue magic between her hands once again, Nadia disentangled the flail from the spear of her halberd. This time it was a bow and arrow that came from the ether, and as before, the warlord was already charging her opponent once the other woman was fully armed. The kaglorite walked backward as she pulled back the string of her bow, took aim, and fired at Nadia only for the warlord to swipe the arrow from the air in one sure motion almost too fast to see. The invader's eyes bugged out as this happened, and as she frantically racked her brain for another plan, she backed into the chamber wall Nadia had caught a glance of a little while ago. The kaglorite instinctively turned her head to look behind her at what had touched her, and the warlord seized that moment, impaling the former through the stomach with the spear of her halberd. Removing it, Nadia scanned the room for her next victim.

Elsewhere in the chamber, Adam was facing down another man, middle-aged, who also wielded a sword, the human holding his own tightly in both hands with an intent look on his face. The young man charged at the older with his weapon raised high over his head. Adam's downward assault was easily avoided, and his blade slammed into the stone below them, hard. His opponent prepared a vertical slash of his own as Adam looked up at him in alarm, as if what had just transpired couldn't have been possible. The young man just barely managed to raise up his own blade, positioned horizontally, to block the swing, but the force of the impact knocked it back, and it came within mere inches of unintendedly scalping its owner.

Adam jumped back, and both he and the kaglorite got back to starting positions. The former was the first to close the distance between them after the brief intermission, following this with a leftward horizontal swing that the latter jumped backward to avoid. As Adam stumbled, thrown off balance (so sure he'd been that his attack would land), the kaglorite slashed at a chink in the human's armor, located over one pectoral, the former had noticed during the standstill. The young man saw this and attempted to rear back, completely losing his footing because of this and falling on his back. Adam swore silently as he hit the floor, but in truth, he should've been praising the gods; the accident was the only reason the cut now adorning his chest was but a shallow one.

The young man scrambled to recover, but in rising to one knee, he left another chink, this one just above it, entirely exposed, and his opponent took advantage of this, stabbing the thigh beneath the gap. This time, the blade sank quite deeply, and on any other occasion, Adam's howls of agony would've startled all those within earshot. However, the human could once again count himself lucky; after all, his opponent was a kaglorite, and they were known to shirk physical training in favor of mastering the mystic arts. An assault from that angle would've completely bisected Adam's leg had he been crossing blades with another human or, gods forbid, an itrasus. The human looked down immediately after his opponent drew his blade out of the other man's leg and began to stare at the newly formed opening in his flesh as if his gaze could halt the flow of blood or knit skin. It would've been the last thing he ever saw if sunlight from one of the chamber's high windows hadn't glinted off the edge of the kaglorite's blade as the violet-skinned man held it aloft in preparation for a beheading, shining brightly in the human's eye. As it was, it did, and Adam had just enough time to look up and block the swing but not to think of gripping the hilt of his sword as tightly as was needed, and so with a resounding clang, it was knocked out of his hands, well beyond reach, while the kaglorite's weapon glanced off it, once again missing its target by the breadth of but a few fingers.

The intruder lifted up his blade once more, and his opponent gazed back at him, first squinting in confusion and disbelief, then raising his brow as high as it could go in utter panic. Adam looked away as if what couldn't be seen couldn't hurt you and closed his eyes. The kaglorite began the final swing, and an instant later, both heard the sound of metal slicing through soft flesh and a loud pained cry. The human lifted his lids, only a little apprehensive (he had to have gone to heaven, right?), to find his life after death appeared identical to that which had come before it. Upon turning his head to face frontward, he saw his former opponent collapse forward to the ground with a long, diagonal slash across his back and Nadia standing a pace behind him, halberd in hand; and suddenly he understood—he'd been saved. Adam despaired to himself for a moment (did great heroes lose fights and require rescue?), but his mood swiftly lifted when he noted silently that the main characters of the epic sagas he'd grown up on were often assisted by an ally at a moment that all seemed lost.

His expression turned sheepish however when Nadia stated flatly, "You have much to learn, Adam Hefull," as she helped him to his feet.

Adam chuckled weakly. "Thank you for saving me."

"*Much.*"

While the warlord and new recruit had begun their respective battles, Cornelius and Zage also locked blades. "Zage Batur!" called out Cornelius over the surrounding din with an easygoing grin. "It has been some time since our last meeting."

Conversely, the look on the kaglorite's face was a deathly serious snarl. "Not long enough." Releasing Kiam's hilt with one hand, Cornelius grabbed the box in Zage's grasp with the other; never in Samu's history had one of its best warriors so detested the idea of a fight and worked each time it was forced on him to end it as quickly as possible. For a moment, the two men each struggled to pull the box to themselves, and it twitched back and forth several times. Zage was of far superior strength even when put up against Destiny's Catalyst, but he also had hands prone to profuse sweating, which betrayed him on this occasion, causing the box to slip from his grip. It happened so quickly however that Cornelius wasn't prepared to hold onto it once it was his, and it flew behind him to land at the feet of a pair of kaglorites that included Zuza. All four of them looked down at the box now resting on the floor before Zage grabbed the hilt of his dagger with his free hand and began pressing against his opponent's blade (forcing the other man to return his gaze to the fight he found himself in and do the same), calling out to his right-hand woman, "Go! I will hold him off!"

Cornelius risked a glance over one shoulder back at the box. "No!" He looked back at Zage just in time to block a swing of the other man's dagger. Zuza's companion stooped to pick up the box and started running for a large door on the chamber's eastern wall with her following close behind. While en route, they were intercepted by a human soldier armed with a sword. He swung at the kaglorite in front, who dodged away without breaking pace, before turning to face Zuza instead. She came to a halt to engage him, letting her companion continue to make for the door; even in a scenario this dangerous, with a plan centered around swift escape, she couldn't pass up the opportunity to spill human blood.

Zuza held one of her hands over the tip of the lance she held in the other and endowed it with red magic. She sought to enhance her weapon, not destroy it, and so the magic burned around its point without dissolving it. With one quick thrust of her mystically strengthened lance at the stomach of the man directly before her, Zuza cut through metal, flesh, and then metal once more, killing her opponent in the blink of an eye. Across the room, her former companion reached the eastern door and shoved it open only to find two armed human soldiers waiting for and sprinting toward him. The kaglorite tried skidding to a halt but was too late and impaled through the chest by one of the humans' blades.

Understandably preoccupied at that moment, the thief released the box, which flew down the hallway from the momentum of its possessor. It landed on the floor with a wooden clack before sliding a short distance and hitting the feet of someone else standing in the corridor, the object coming to an abrupt halt. The two human soldiers turned around, the kaglorite's killer slipping his weapon out of the violet-skinned man's guts as he did so, to find the oracle Dekkin Eterden kneeling to pick up the box.

"Oracle!" one of the soldiers said as he and his fellow's faces flushed with relief. "Thank the gods!" Dekkin stood up, box in hand, and the man who'd just spoken to him took a step forward, one hand outstretched toward the immortal man. "Give that to me, quickly! We must keep it safe from the kaglorites." The oracle didn't move, and his steady gaze upon the kinsmen before him became unnerving to despite the fact he was clearly looking right through them. The soldier who'd spoken lowered his raised hand slightly and stared at Dekkin in perplexity. "Oracle?"

The box's new holder put it inside his tunic before turning around and beginning to sprint away from the human soldiers. The one who'd stabbed the kaglorite just then reached out toward Dekkin with his other hand again, this time as if to hold fast the man with the box rather than the object itself, a look of alarm on his face. "Oracle, wait!" Just as the speaking soldier was about to bound after the fleeing immortal, his partner cried out in torment, making the other man jump and whirl around to face him. It felt for the other soldier like a thunderbolt to his heart as he took in the sight of his companion with a lance, its tip glowing red, poking out his chest. The speaking soldier leaped sideways and rotated his body in midair to face his partner's murderer. It was Zuza who ripped her weapon from the flesh of her victim and stabbed out at the next potential one. The surviving soldier brought his sword up to block the blow, lacking the luxury of time in which to assess his opponent like many of his unfortunate cohorts, and it snapped in two upon colliding with the tip of the lance, which then sailed past it to bury itself in the chest of Zuza's opponent. The human's scream faded to a gurgle as he began choking on a fountain of his own blood.

Zuza ran past her second victim after removing her spear from his chest. Dekkin was still in view when she began her pursuit, but shortly after she did, he reached the end of the corridor, where it forked left and right. He disappeared around the latter after the briefest moment of contemplation as she neared the intersection. Zuza swore emphatically, continuing to follow him at hallway's end. Her expression brightened when she saw he'd come to a halt several yards ahead of her, but a second later, her brain caught up to her eyes and recognized that he didn't appear fatigued and so wouldn't have stopped were it not to his advantage. And sure enough, Dekkin turned to his left and pointed in her direction as he spoke with an initially unseen party, which turned out to be a large group of more human soldiers that unwittingly assisted in the oracle's theft by blocking the way to him.

Zuza came to a halt upon seeing them and stood still for a moment as she weighed her options. After a few seconds, she concluded it would be impossible to carve a path through that many armed, trained adversaries, even for her. "No!" bellowed the kaglorite, visibly enraged and distraught. She turned around and retraced her steps back to the grand chamber.

Cornelius and Zage had each split up to engage a different opponent, and many such battles were playing out across the room's vast expanse. Most of the pews for the ceremony had been toppled in the great commotion.

"Zage!" Zuza called out as she ran to him before stopping herself a few paces away. "We have failed! One of the humans took the map and key, and I was not able to get to him!"

"What?" spat Zage, the news bringing him more distress than the human soldier before him swinging wildly at his neck with a sword.

Dekkin sprinted out of the castle's main entrance amid a crush of panicked nobles. He came to a halt just outside and examined his surroundings hurriedly. An inconspicuous means of transportation carrying supplies enough to last an extended journey would be ideal. After a moment, he spotted a nondescript wagon parked nearby and headed hastily toward it. Hoisting himself up onto the driver's seat, Dekkin grabbed the reins and whipped the kreshes bound to them, calling out, "Yah!" The pair of tamed beasts took off with appropriate urgency.

* * * * *

"You must go," Zuza said to Zage.

"What about you?" replied the latter. "And the others?"

Zuza stepped to his side and blocked a swing of his attacker's sword with the tip of her lance before glancing toward him. "Go. We will hold the soldiers off."

"*What?*" Zage stared at her incredulously, though he put some distance between them so she could fight her newfound opponent unencumbered. "No! I will not leave you behind."

"You are our leader," Zuza pointed out as she stabbed at the soldier before her. "You must live, above all else. You know this to be true. *Go.*"

Zage paused, deep in thought, as she and her opponent continued to clash. A handful of seconds later, a look of resignation took over his face. Strong-willed as he was, he was also a kaglorite, and so was no stranger to loss. "All right. But you must promise me that you will try to escape if you have the chance. Promise me!"

"I promise," assured Zuza.

"All right." Zage stood there a moment longer before turning around and wordlessly making for the nearest exit with great reluctance still.

When Dekkin brought the stolen wagon to a halt before Cobaltus's eastern gate, a soldier began running to it from one of its outposts on the ground but stopped halfway, as soon as he could see clearly who the driver was. "CAN YOU OPEN THE GATE FOR ME, GOOD SIR?" the oracle inquired, raising his voice to be heard across the sizable distance between them and over the frenzied bustle of the surrounding city.

"OF COURSE, ORACLE," replied the soldier readily. He looked up at his compatriots atop the wall. "OPEN THE GATE!" They obeyed with all haste, and Dekkin rode out of Cobaltus.

4

THE REST OF CENTRAL Humania looked for all the world like its capital hadn't come under attack ever, let alone earlier that very same day. There was a sharp contrast between the towering, tightly packed spires of Cobaltus and the surrounding country. Queen Coria's predecessor, her mother, Maescha, turned away proposals to construct similar wens around it, opting instead to award land to small groups of low-caste farmers and craftspeople, much to the discontented grumbling of Humania's elite. This gave the country's poor workers direct access to its main hub of commerce, making them rich after but a season in their new home. And as soon as one of Cobaltus's immediate neighbors amassed what Queen Coria deemed to be an amount of coin sufficient to last a long, prosperous lifetime, she required the landowners to cede it back to the crown so she could repeat the process once again. In this way, she championed equality, her most principal ideal.

The view from Cobaltus' eastern path was, therefore, an idyllic picture of simple rural beauty accented by the expected smells and sounds. Fields of crops ran shoulder-to-shoulder with the dirt road in many places, the wind carrying their earthy musk. At the perimeter of the many mills, there was the heavy scent of flour, baking bread, and sizzling meat in the middle of the villages along the way. The farms were dead silent even in the middle of the day, as one didn't have to work long hours to make their fortune here (and it's also worth noting, neither did they need to enlist the help of their children to do so). And in town, you would hear friendly greetings back and forth and the joyous exclamations of the young as they ran around and played among themselves, reckless with the knowledge that any injury they may incur in the process could be easily healed by a top physician with their parents' bountiful coffers.

Dekkin Eterden saw, heard, and smelled none of this. No matter where he found himself on his eastward trek that morning, he had eyes only for the dark-brown dirt on the path before him. When he was addressed by another, he ignored them, and he inhaled deeply not to take in the aroma of the surrounding area but to sigh pointedly. Dekkin saw through the lithe, majestic frames of the carefully plucked kreshes pulling the carriage as if they were transparent to gaze, his nose wrinkled in disgust, at the rani floundering in the puddles along the sides of the path, with their huge black eyes, bulbous bodies, slimy skin, and webbed appendages.

A few hours after his escape, Dekkin was startled out of his ill-tempered trance by the sudden sound of metal scraping against metal behind and to his right of him. He looked over one shoulder to find that, firstly, there was a large slat in the front of the wagon's body, presumably for people inside it to speak with the driver, and secondly, a pair of eyes was looking back at him through it. Dekkin and his passenger stared at each other in still silence for an instant before both cried out in astonishment.

"What...what are you *doing* here?" the oracle spluttered.

"What...what do you mean?" replied the passenger, only a boy by the sound of it. "This is my carriage."

Dekkin raised his brow in puzzlement and pulled over to the near side of the path they were on. As he stepped down from the driver's seat, the boy in the carriage's body hopped out of it himself. The immortal man rounded its back-left corner to find he'd been unwittingly transporting Cornelius's apprentice, Matthew.

"Oh," Dekkin said as an expression of realization dawned on his face. After a moment, it turned accusatory. "Well, then why are you just now making your presence known? I started driving this wagon hours ago!"

"I...I was asleep," revealed Matthew very sheepishly.

Dekkin narrowed his eyes in suspicion. "You mean to tell me you slept through the attack?"

"The attack?" the boy repeated in confusion as he raised his brow. "What attack?"

The oracle paused to survey the lorm's face for signs of deception. He found none, but he thought then, most likely one had to interact with other people somewhat often in order to read them like that. Nevertheless, concluding he could only work with what he had, Dekkin accepted Matthew's response as genuine. "There was an attack on the castle. Kaglorites, led by Zage Batur. They were trying to obtain the map and key that Cornelius Arcind was to receive today. When the attack began, I ran out of the castle and took the first vehicle I could find out of the city. I'm headed away from it, to wait for things to calm down. Cobaltus isn't safe right now."

The lorm's black eyes widened even further, as far as they could, and his mouth fell open slightly as the oracle spoke. "Really?" Matthew looked down at his feet for a moment as he processed the news before returning his gaze to Dekkin's face. "*Tantus mirus*, that's unbelievable."

"Not so, in these times," countered the immortal man. "I'm surprised the royal guard wasn't more prepared for what happened." His eyes darted away swiftly from the boy. "At any rate, I'm sorry for taking your wagon." Dekkin shifted his view back to where it had been immediately previous to then. "But we can't go back to Cobaltus right now. So how about you come with me to Mester, and there we will part ways?"

Matthew nodded distractedly. "That'd be good." He gave the man a guilty grimace. "I'm s-sorry for startling you earlier."

Dekkin started walking back to his seat before the boy even finished what he was saying. "That's all right." The two of them clambered onto the coach box and got on their way again. Though the lorm was small even by the standards of his diminutive people, and there were several inches between him and Dekkin, the latter felt cramped and uncomfortable from the second the former took his place. Both sat in complete silence for quite some time until Dekkin's luck ran out. They hit a sizable bump in the path, jostling the box in the oracle's tunic enough to dislodge it from its cloth trappings. It fell to its thief's feet, and the sound drew Matthew's gaze to it.

"What's this?" the boy asked with furrowed brow as he picked it up.

Dekkin's blood had frozen the moment he felt the box come loose and his body with it. He couldn't bring himself to move until Matthew was beginning to open the mysterious wooden container. "*No, don't—*" The oracle began reaching out with one hand to keep the black box closed, but he was too late.

The lorm raised the lid and spotted the map and key within. He was a perceptive lad, but the truth of the matter was so implausible that he didn't immediately recognize it as such.

"Why do you—" began Matthew inquisitively as he turned to look at the oracle, confused.

Dekkin hurriedly placed the left rein in his right hand and unsheathed the dagger at his hip with the other, a foreboding expression on his face, before pointing it at an alarmed Matthew. "All right, don't move."

"What...what?" the boy stammered uncomprehendingly. "What are you doing?"

"You're my hostage now."

"I...I don't—" began Matthew meekly, looking at his feet as if this meager attempt at resistance was on the edges of good taste.

"You saw something you shouldn't have. So you must stay with me for a while."

"But..." the boy trailed off, still utterly perplexed by this turn of events for several long moments before finally realizing what was happening. He seemed ready to argue the point further until his eyes fell on the blade at his side. "All right," he concedes with a dejected expression on his face. "I understand."

Dekkin scanned the youth to determine the veracity of his words. Satisfied, he stowed his blade and returned his attention to the road ahead. "Good."

* * * * *

Never in its long life had the streets of Cobaltus been so quiet and empty at midday, as they were now. Its citizens shut themselves in, on the queen's orders but from personal terror in truth; and the reason behind the lockdown—the invading kaglorites—had all been captured or killed, either way taken inside by the city guard.

All but one.

The violet-skinned man ran out from between two of the buildings lining a street near the city's perimeter and onto the road itself. Cornelius, Kiam in hand, appeared from the same place a moment later and chased the kaglorite until the other man was close enough to be knocked unconscious by a blow upside the head from the hilt of the human's sword. Destiny's Catalyst did so in short order and watched the intruder's body carefully after it fell on its face and lay unmoving on the cobblestones.

"Master Arcind!" someone called out behind him, and after another handful of seconds, Cornelius, convinced that the chase was over, looked over one shoulder in the direction of the voice. It was Nadia. She ran to him, halberd in one hand, breathing heavily, sweating profusely under her armor. She slowed to a brisk walk once she was a few paces away from Cornelius before stopping completely at an appropriate distance. "He is defeated?" asked the warlord as she looked around him at the collapsed kaglorite.

"Yes," Cornelius confirmed, turning to face her with the rest of his body.

Nadia nodded once. "Good."

"Any sign of Zage?" inquired Destiny's Catalyst hopefully.

Nadia shook her head, her face a tableau of deep regret. "No, it appears that he and one other kaglorite managed to escape."

"Malun!" Cornelius exclaimed off to one side, though far more composed than any other would be in his position. "And the map and key?"

Nadia grimaced. "There is still a large part of the city that has not yet been searched, but as of right now, we have not found them. It seems likely that one of the kaglorites who escaped has it." Cornelius looked off into the distance when he heard this, consumed by thought. The warlord gave him some time before saying, "What is it?"

Cornelius pulled himself out of his own head with a grave look on his face. "My wagon was right outside the castle. When I left to chase after the last kaglorite, it was gone. I'm afraid Zage or the other one may have taken it and used it to get out of the city. Matthew was sleeping in the back of it when the attack happened."

"Do you not think that he probably awoke and drove the wagon out of the city himself?"

"It's possible, but Matthew's a heavy sleeper," replied Cornelius. "I think it's equally likely that he slept through the attack, and someone else drove it out of the city, not knowing he was inside it."

The warlord nodded. "I see."

"And if that person was one of the kaglorites"—Cornelius began soberly before trailing off as if speaking of the result could bring it to pass—"they'd take him hostage once they found out he was there."

The two of them stood in silence for a moment, looking through each other, before he, with a self-serious expression on his face, instructed, "Assemble as many troops as we can spare. We need to find Zage Batur as quickly as possible."

Nadia brought her feet together and saluted, a similar look on hers. "Yes, sir."

* * * * *

When night fell, Dekkin veered off the path and brought the wagon to a halt in the midst of a vast open field. He was pleased to find all the necessary supplies for overnight travel in the back of his stolen vehicle, including food, bedding, and the materials needed to make a fire. Dekkin coaxed flames into being a short distance behind the wagon so he could sit in the very back of it and still be warmed by them; the loud cacophony that hung over the plains by night was produced by its native swarms of wild insects, and the oracle wanted to avoid having to brush stray bugs off his pants every few seconds. Matthew, conversely, set himself down atop the grass across the fire from the immortal man and stared intently at the multitudinous insects that hopped onto his lower half as if he'd never even heard of such creatures.

The two of them ate stew wordlessly for a good while until Matthew, taking a sip and looking up from his bowl at Dekkin, said, "Oracle?"

The immortal man's face darkened. "Don't call me that." He spoke without looking up from his meal.

Matthew frowned in confusion. "What?"

"I said don't call me that," reiterated Dekkin as his spoon scraped along the bottom of his bowl. "Call me Dekkin."

Matthew's expression turned inquisitive, but one look at the oracle's face dissuaded him from further questioning. "Oh, uh, all right. Dekkin, you've taken the map and key so you can have a wish of *yours* granted, right?"

"I don't need to answer that."

Matthew shriveled slightly. "R-right. Sorry, but whatever your wish is, it must be something bad for you to have to steal them like—"

"That's enough," Dekkin snapped with a scowl, whipping his head up to face the boy.

"A-all right," conceded Matthew meekly, "I'm sorry."

Dekkin, having finished his dinner, stared into the flames before him broodingly as the lorm took another sip of his. The man opened his mouth a crack, closed it, and after a moment, parted his lips once again. "It's not bad."

Matthew looked up at him, his brow raised.

"What I want," the man continued, "is just—no one would understand. That's all."

"Oh." The oracle's answer had only birthed additional questions in the lorm's head, but the boy knew now it would be better and safer not to voice them.

Dekkin set aside his bowl. "At any rate, when you've finished eating, I'll need to restrain you, make sure you can't run off while I'm sleeping."

"There's a couple of pedibi in cages in the wagon," replied Matthew readily.

Dekkin stayed seated for a moment, staring at the boy's forehead as if he could see his thoughts were he to hold his gaze there long enough. Never in the history of Samu had there been a more willing captive. Why was he cooperating so unreservedly? Was it all a ruse designed to catch his kidnapper off balance? The oracle recognized after a few seconds that he hadn't been around the boy nearly enough to form a hypothesis and, accepting this, stood. "Oh, I…I see." Dekkin checked in the back of the wagon, and sure enough, there were a couple of the little beasts imprisoned there.

Fortunately for the immortal, there was a tall, thin tree right by their campsite. He had Matthew sit down and wrap his arms and legs around the bottom of its trunk before taking out two pedibi. Dekkin opened one of the lime-green amphibians' toothless jaws, putting the lorm's hands in between them. Then the oracle grabbed onto its tail and pulled. It snapped clean off, a chunk of the creature's gray matter stuck on the far end of it, and its owner's lips immediately clamped down on the contents of its mouth, its body turning rigid as ice. Releasing the second one, Dekkin did the same for Matthew's feet.

Dekkin turned away and walked back to the fire, storing the dismembered tails in his tunic. Squatting beside it, he laid down on one side with his back to the boy. Matthew scooched back the few inches his constraints allotted him and brought his head to rest on the coarse wood before him. He was a long time falling asleep due to his morning nap.

The surrounding light was still dim when Dekkin shook Matthew awake. As the boy blinked the sleep from his eyes and stretched his painfully stiff back with a grimace, he reasoned to himself silently that if men in their seventies needed less sleep, those whose lives had spanned centuries must require less still.

"Good morning," he mumbled to the oracle as the man took out the pedibus' tails and slotted them back into the creatures' bodies, freeing them from their frozen trance.

"Get up," replied Dekkin shortly as he locked the small beasts back into their cages. "It's time to go."

Much to the immortal's surprise and pleasure, several hours of uneventful travel passed before the boy finally looked over at him and asked, "Where are we going?"

The lorm's timing couldn't have been more perfect. Dekkin pointed at a wide outcropping of towering, directly adjacent stone spires in the distance ahead of them. "Like I said…Mester."

Despite initial appearances, the aforementioned city was actually the second-largest city in Humania. The reason for the discrepancy between its inward and outward impressions was thus—it was a mining settlement over a small stretch of land with, nonetheless, seemingly infinite stores of precious metals and stone beneath it so long as one was willing to burrow much deeper than what had been previously dug. All these treasures were dug up by the employees of the country's biggest conglomerate, the Goti Mining Group. Those workers of low status made their homes underground, but their superiors wanted a home close enough to facilitate close supervision but also clearly geographically distinct from the peasants' abodes. And so the stone skyscrapers, the only indication of the city's existence on the surface, were built to accommodate them.

Upon reaching Mester's perimeter, Dekkin maneuvered his wagon into a long line of such vehicles slowly making their way down a long, wide ramp to its downtown area. It bottomed out into an even more spacious tunnel, with a two-way dirt path down the center and businesses, arranged as claustrophobically as the buildings above ground, and walking areas on either side of it. It was poorly lit for its entire length; the miners couldn't have afforded to purchase lanterns enough to sparingly illuminate half the space with all their coin, and strangely enough, the bountiful fortunes of Goti's wealthy didn't seem to deter them in the slightest from pinching every penny.

Dekkin brought the wagon to a halt just outside a small inn a good ways down the tunnel. Disembarking, he walked around to the back of the vehicle to check on Matthew, who was locked to the pole at the center of its back once again by twin pedibi. "I have to go inside for a moment," the immortal said to the boy.

"Oracle!" called out someone to Dekkin as he made for the entrance to the inn. He looked over in the direction of the voice and found its owner to be none other than Queen Coria. Her long hair unmarred by grime, which would have been incredibly conspicuous in the caverns of Mester, was obscured from view by the hood of a long brown cloak she was wearing. She wore pants in place of her usual regal dresses and had a long metal weapon, one-half of it a hammer and the other a spear, on her back.

"Y-Your Highness!" Dekkin responded, his eyes wide, as she walked briskly toward him and waved. Despite his words, no one within earshot seemed to have any sort of reaction; they were either miners eternally weary from their toils in the tunnels or visiting merchants deafened by their singular, burning desire to take care of their business in the city and be on their way as swiftly as possible.

"Yes!" confirmed the queen, as bright as she had been on that stage back in the castle. She came to a halt and flashed him an inviting smile. "I've a favor to ask of you!"

Dekkin returned his gaze to the inn's front door and continued on his way to it before she'd even finished speaking. "I cannot help you," he said dismissively. "I am in the midst of something at the moment."

Coria caught up to one side of the oracle and matched pace with him. "Please? I've got to get to the eastern border, and given what's just happened, I don't want to have to go there with a bunch of soldiers guarding me. It'd attract too much attention, you know? That's why I came here after the attack, to find somebody to take me there. I don't have any coin on me at the moment, but I'll see that you're handsomely rewarded eventually!"

Dekkin, a sour look on his face, turned his head a 180 degrees away from hers in an attempt to brush her off. "No."

It didn't work; Coria's only response to it was to lean toward him as they kept moving in tandem. "B-but you have to! I'm the queen!"

"I'm an oracle," countered Dekkin.

"That's no more important!"

"Yes, it is." Dekkin arrived at the front of the inn and went to open its door, but Coria placed one hand flat against it to keep him from doing so.

"W-well, you're traveling, aren't you?" The queen was beginning to sound desperate. "That's why you're here? Then"—she scrunched her brow before lighting up at the inception of an idea—"then I could be your bodyguard! It's not safe to travel alone, you know."

Derision was etched into Dekkin's features as he finally returned her gaze. "Ah, yes, perfect—a pampered royal for a bodyguard, that's *just* what I need, thank you."

"That's not—"

"I SAID THAT I CAN'T, DID I NOT?" Dekkin thundered, or least as close to it as could be gotten with a voice as thin as his. "GOOD DAY!" Gripping the wrist attached to the hand blocking his way tightly, he flung it off the wood and went inside.

The inn's foyer was an eatery with several circular wooden tables, many heavily chipped or stained, scattered around the room and a bar at the back. The middle-aged human man sitting behind it looked up at Dekkin as he walked in and flashed him a wide, friendly smile once he saw who it was. "Master Eterden!"

"Hello, Charles." Dekkin had known the other man's family going back a dozen or so generations. "Can I have a room?"

Charles knelt to reach under the bar for a room key. "May I ask what brings you to these parts?"

"There was an attack during the ceremony in Cobaltus yesterday. Kaglorites. I managed to get out of the city, came here to lay low while things settle down."

Charles, his eyes wide with shock, stood and handed Dekkin his key. "An attack? Are you serious?"

The oracle nodded.

"*Tantus mirus*, I swear, it gets more treacherous in these parts by the *day.*"

Dekkin returned to the wagon and freed Matthew from his restraints long enough to bring him and the stout little beasts, the former clutched in one of the oracle's hands and the latter held by the boy in cages concealed under a drape, up to his room. Once there, he used the pedibi to shackle Matthew loosely to one of the metal bedposts nailed into the floor and then went straight to bed. The boy puzzled over this for a bit as he sat uncomfortably on the wooden floor, concluding after some thought that the oracle must have required more sleep than it had initially seemed or else the dim median level lighting in the surrounding tunnel had been such so as to successfully encourage him—even though he'd just awoken from slumber not long ago and despite the fact that one of the area's few lanterns hung just outside their room's window—to lie down. If Matthew could've peered down at the oracle from above, he would've seen that the immortal's eyes were wide-open as he, perfectly still save for his steady breath, blankly stared up at the ceiling.

As the sun set (or so Matthew guessed), Dekkin rose and turned to look at him. "I'm going down to eat."

"What'll *I* eat?" inquired Matthew, hunger beginning to grow in his gut.

Dekkin started making for the door to their room before the boy finished speaking. "I'll bring you something."

The oracle went downstairs and took a seat at an empty table resting there. His order was taken shortly thereafter, and he received it after a short wait. As Dekkin raised a chunk of meat he speared with the fork provided to him, he heard the sound of footfalls and creaking wood approaching him from behind, much to his dismay. His mood did not improve when he looked over one shoulder and saw Coria walking to him.

"Horb it all," he muttered in exasperation to the plate before him.

The welcoming grin Coria flashed him as she moved went unnoticed by its intended recipient because he kept his head bowed, hoping that would ward her off. It didn't. Coria came to a halt beside one of the empty chairs at his table and, after a moment, loudly cleared her throat.

Dekkin looked up at her with a scowl. "Yes?"

"Can I sit here?" she asked.

The oracle looked back down at his plate. "No."

"Oh, you jest!" replied the queen cheerily as she pulled out the nearest chair. "So where are you traveling to?" she asked after taking a seat.

"That is not your concern."

"Must be heading east, if you've come here," Coria hypothesized. "Same as me." She and Dekkin sat in a silence, broken only by the sound of the latter's eating for several seconds, and in that time, her grin became a tad strained. "So you're sure you won't take me to the eastern border?"

"Yes," confirmed the oracle with his mouth full.

The queen didn't respond for a bit, and Dekkin allowed himself to hope the situation was resolved only to be disappointed immediately thereafter. "Because I could have you imprisoned, you know, for refusing one of my commands."

"What?" Dekkin responded as he met her gaze once again, more weary than anything.

"Or put to death. As I said, I'm the queen." Coria wondered to herself if her tone was as cool as she hoped, if it masked the hammering of her heart sufficiently. "So either you take me to the eastern border, *or* I find a soldier in the city and tell him you've disobeyed your queen. Then neither of us are happy. So how about we do things in a way that'll make us both happy?"

Dekkin stopped chewing his dinner at this but said nothing long enough for Coria to have doubts as to his response. But finally he frowned down in resignation at his plate and grumbled, "Fine."

The queen perked back up instantly. "Truly? Oh, thank you! Oh, I'm sorry, that was so *mean*, what I just did. It's just that I have to get to the eastern border, and you're the only one in this city I trust."

"You trust me?" asked the oracle incredulously.

Coria frowned slightly in puzzlement. "Of course, I trust you! You're an oracle."

"Don't call me that," Dekkin ordered with a scowl.

"Call you what?" The queen was even more confused at that.

"An oracle."

"Well…that's what you *are*, isn't it?"

"Just don't do it," insisted the oracle. "Call me Dekkin."

Coria nodded, though unsated curiosity was plain on her face. "All right. Dekkin then."

The immortal set aside his empty bowl. "In the early morning, I'm going to buy supplies. After that, we'll leave."

"That sounds good!" the queen exclaimed brightly, her unvoiced inquiries already forgotten. "Thank you again!"

Dekkin pinched the bridge of his nose between thumb and forefinger. "Please stop talking."

* * * * *

The oracle tossed and turned most of the night; the undying light shining through his window certainly couldn't have helped. An hour before dawn, he decided it would be all right to rise a little earlier than planned; after all, he hadn't asked the queen when she would be up, and it would be wise to secure the provisions needed for the remainder of his journey prematurely enough to ensure his shopping wouldn't hold her up too much given that she'd threatened him with execution the previous evening. Dekkin purchased all that he needed with an infinitesimal sliver of his staggeringly sizable means before returning to the inn. He looked around, both inside and out, for Coria and found nothing, so he sat by his carriage and waited.

He needn't have worried about timing, at least not in the way that he did; it was almost midday by the time Coria finally appeared, still rubbing sleep from her eyes no less. Dekkin furrowed his brow as deeply as he could and opened his mouth wide to tell her off as she got close to him, but he balked upon envisioning himself sitting on hard stone in one of the royal castle's dungeons.

"Good morning!" greeted Coria with a yawn as she waved to Dekkin. "Are you ready to go?"

Dekkin pressed his lips together tightly. "Yes, but I...I have to tell you something before we go."

The queen stopped a pace away from him, her gaze turning curious and expectant.

"In the wagon, there's a boy in pedibi—Cornelius's apprentice, Matthew."

Coria's eyes, drowsy slits beforehand, flew open at this, and she unconsciously leaned toward him a little. "*What?*"

"Yes," the oracle confirmed solemnly. "I have reason to believe that he has been conspiring with the kaglorites, that he's why they were able to get into the city two days ago. I'm taking him to the Lormish Isles to be tried for his crimes. You asked me where I'm traveling to. That's where. I'll need you to help me keep an eye on him, as he's undoubtedly planning his escape as we speak. And it's important that you don't believe anything he says. He'll say or do anything to try to get you to free him from his restraints. Do you understand?"

The queen nodded readily. "Yes, I understand."

"Good." Dekkin clambered up to the driver's seat of his wagon before looking back at Coria to find her returning his gaze in uncertainty. He realized she was wondering whether to sit on the coach box beside him or within the vehicle's main body. And as risky as it was to put her together with his hostage, Dekkin couldn't imagine being beside her as they crossed almost half an entire country; he motioned for her to climb in back. "With your hood up, the odds are overwhelmingly against the possibility someone will spot you on the road even if you sit with me, but I don't believe we should take that chance, don't you agree?"

The queen didn't seem to respond to his natural prickly demeanor, so the oracle decided to temporarily feign some good manners, at least as much as he was able.

That night, as they sat around the fire they'd started a good distance from the path (at Coria's insistence and to Dekkin's irritation), the queen closed her eyes, leaned back her head, and grinned as a warm breeze ruffled her hair. "Feels nice out here."

"Are you jesting?" replied the oracle venomously. "It's far too hot."

Coria opened her eyes and looked over at him. "You think so?"

"Yes."

"Hmm." The queen shifted her gaze to the boy, who looked down at his feet bashfully in response. "What do *you* think, Matthew?"

"What do *I* think?" the boy reiterated the question as if he wasn't fluent in the language it'd been spoken in. "Uh, I…I don't know."

"You…don't know if you like the weather?" Coria reiterated back in puzzlement.

Matthew's nod was a stiff jerk. "R-right."

"Hmm." The queen turned her eyes to the oracle. "You must always know what the weather's going to be like, right?"

Dekkin let out a deep sigh as he stared into the fire. "What do you mean?"

"Well, you're an oracle! You can see the future, can't you?"

The immortal refused to meet her gaze. "It's not that simple."

"Well, then, how does it work?"

"I don't want to talk right now," asserted Dekkin in a display of reluctance.

Coria leaned toward him as if her crown was still securely fastened around the top of her head, and he was a man made of magnets. "Please? I'm bored! Tell me how it works."

"No."

"Come on!"

"*No.*"

"Tell me how it works, and I won't talk for the rest of the night." Coria looked like a little girl who'd just delivered her closing argument in favor of a later bedtime to her parents. "How about that?"

Dekkin's interest was visibly piqued. After examining the fire before him a little further, he replied begrudgingly, "All right."

A thrill shot through the queen's body. "*Yes!* Thank you!"

Dekkin winced though Coria's voice was still less than a shout and snapped, "Don't make me regret this."

The queen caught herself and deflated with some effort. "I'm sorry. I'm done talking."

"Good." Dekkin repositioned his body such that it was facing Coria. "Now what gives me my precognitive powers is the turins on my back."

The queen's expression became one of confusion. "Wait, the what?"

"What did I *just* say?" the oracle barked.

Coria immediately raised her hands, palms facing Dekkin, slightly in a placating gesture. "*I'm sorry!* I'm sorry. It's merely… there's something on your back?"

"Yes," confirmed the immortal incredulously. "*Tantus mirus*, did none of your doubtlessly innumerable tutors teach you anything of oracles?"

The queen chuckled sheepishly. "Well, they might've. I don't tend to…pay a lot of *attention* during my lessons, to tell you the truth."

"Well, I suppose I should've guessed that," Dekkin retorted after a huff.

Coria prided herself for the incredible restraint she displayed by asking the following without a hint of the eagerness she was now realizing to be bait for the oracle's seemingly endless supply of sharp ire. "Can I see it?"

"No."

"What?" The queen couldn't keep herself from pouting a little at this. "Why not?"

"Because you want to," replied Dekkin with not a trace of humor.

She could only keep her enthusiasm bound for a handful of seconds at a time. "That's not funny! *Please* show it to me?"

"*Fine.*" Dekkin was coming to recognize some of Coria's attributes as well, one of them being a persistent spirit that would lead her to pester him unendingly were he to deny her something she wanted. "But only if you promise to stop talking."

"I promise," the queen responded, swift and sincere.

"All right." Dekkin rose from the ground and turned his back to Coria before raising his tunic up to his shoulders. Neither of them noticed, but Matthew was for the first time since his forceful inclusion into the group showing signs of engagement at this. When the cloth surrounding the oracle's upper body passed the large hump at the top of his back, it revealed not a bodily deformity but an insect, bigger than any Coria or Matthew had ever seen, latched firmly onto his skin. Its skin was yellow and its segmented body curved outward as it extended down. The others couldn't see it from their points of view, but the creature's large black eyes were at the top of its head.

Coria swiftly raised a hand to her mouth as soon as she saw it, shocked at the sight of the gargantuan bug. "Oh my!"

Dekkin put his shirt down and walked back to where he was sitting before lying down, back to the others. The queen waited for him to continue, turn around, or both, and when he didn't for some time, she asked, "Wait, what are you doing?"

"You know what I said," answered the oracle over his top shoulder. "You refuse to stop talking."

Coria realized for the first time that he was right; her vocalization had been reflexive. She reached out to the immortal with one hand in a gesture he had no way of seeing. "No, wait! I'm sorry. I won't talk anymore. I promise I won't."

Dekkin was unmoving long enough for her to conclude that she'd blown it, but right when she'd given up hope, he sat up and turned around. "All right." He reached into his tunic. "The turins allow me to have visions of the future"—the oracle pulled out what appeared to be a small flask of water—"when I drink this."

Coria opened her mouth, and Dekkin hurriedly cut her off. "Now I know what you're wondering. Isn't this just water? No, it's not. This is water from a special, rare kind of spring called a Destiny Spring. It's called Destiny Water. When I drink some of it, it induces a vision about whatever it is I'm looking at at the moment. So I can control what my visions are about somewhat by looking at certain things, but I can't really influence exactly what my vision will be like. Unfortunately, after having a vision, I lose all control of my body except for my lungs and gain it back slowly over the course of a day, from top to bottom. And during that day, I can't induce another vision."

Coria looked about to speak once again, and Dekkin jabbed a finger at her. "You promised!" She closed her mouth and nodded. What neither of them recognized was that Matthew had just as many questions as her, more even, burning inside his mouth as if he was submerged, and he could quench the flames by parting his lips. And how could they? There was no outward nonverbal indication of this, and the boy wasn't going to ask. He figured that, if he voiced the newly formed inquiries, they would either go unanswered or be met with disappointing answers, as such things always did.

5

THE ATTACK HAPPENED IN the middle of the following day. Coria insisted on sitting beside Dekkin on the coach box as they prepared to set out that morning, saying it would be a colossal waste to spend a day's journey through such beautiful scenery inside the wagon. The oracle, of course, disliked this idea very much, but as had often occurred since the queen joined his party, the looming threat of discovery she carried with her wherever she went led him to relent. Much to his delight, however, she said nothing in the hours of travel preceding the assault, though she clearly became bored shortly after the beginning of the day's journey and twisted her head this way and that even when they were surrounded by nothing save for an unbroken expanse of tall grass. It was good for all involved that she'd done this, though, as Dekkin, single-mindedly boring a hole into the road before them with his gaze, might not have seen the dust being kicked up in the distance like she did had he been alone at the front.

"What's that?" Coria inquired as she pointed at the approaching cloud.

Dekkin looked in the indicated direction with great reluctance but then started and swore when he saw the churning earth.

The queen shifted her eyes back and forth between him and it in concern. "What? What is it?"

"It's an uvis!" answered the oracle.

Coria's brow jumped as high as it could and stayed there, like an earthbound bird taking flight. "*What?* But…but there aren't supposed to be any here, at this time of year!"

"I know!" Dekkin barked, though dread softened the edges of his outburst. He began pulling over to the near side of the path. "There's no point in trying to outrun it. We've got to face it." The immortal began climbing down from the driver's seat as soon as the wagon came to a complete stop. "Well, you said you'd be my bodyguard. Now is your chance to do so." He drew his dagger from its sheath and began heading for where the creature would be in a moment, a short distance southeast of the carriage. By the time he brought himself to a halt, the uvis was close enough for its details to be discerned—its long, bloated dark-green body, the massive protruding nose where its eyes should've been, and its toothless maw, open wide.

Almost as soon as Coria came to stand beside Dekkin, gripping in one hand the hammer on her back, the beast burst out of the ground and let out a screech so piercing it startled them, though they had known it would be coming. The queen withdrew her weapon and held it at the ready in both hands.

"I won't be able to do much with this dagger, so I'll distract him, and you'll do the fighting, understood?" instructed Dekkin, raising his voice to be heard over the sound of the creature's passage.

"Yes!" Coria confirmed readily as the uvis drew nearer still.

Just as the dust cloud it was creating blotted out all else before them, Matthew kicked open the back of the wagon and called out, "What's going on?"

The queen whirled around, her eyes wide. "Matthew, stay back!" She was too late however; the uvis heard the boy's voice and leaped up once again over Dekkin and Coria, landing with a violent rumble just behind the wagon. The beast stuck its head inside and began rooting around, shrieking all the while. The queen ran to it, and the oracle followed shortly thereafter purely so she wouldn't begrudge and rag on him for the rest of the trip over a failure to do so in the event of their survival. Just as they were about to reach the uvis, however, it pulled its head out of the wagon and, turning to one side, burrowed back into the ground, beginning to carve a path of retreat.

Dekkin and Coria watched the creature retreat until it was a considerable distance away and then peered inside the wagon, the latter leading the former. Matthew had a prominent bruise on one side of his forehead and was understandably rattled by what just occurred but otherwise unharmed. The pole he'd been shackled to had been broken by the uvis's rampage.

"Are you all right, Matthew?" asked Coria, her eyes wide.

"Y-yes," the boy answered. "It hit me with its head a few times, but I'm fine."

The queen nodded. "Good."

"Horb it all!" shouted Dekkin in fury, for his focus was on the food stores surrounding the lorm or rather what was left of them; almost all of it was gone. "It ate everything, didn't it? Everything that wasn't meat?"

Matthew bowed his head as if he had been the one to devour the goods. "Yes."

"Malun!" The oracle turned around and began making his way back to the coach box. "We've only got enough food left for a few days. We'll have to stop at a village somewhere to get more."

"Well, that's not so bad, is it?" replied Coria as she watched him go. "It's more annoying than anything." When the immortal said nothing to this, she looked up at Matthew and inquired, "What is it that makes him so…disagreeable?"

Matthew shrugged. "I don't know. I just met him, like you."

"No, no!" Dekkin said, turning around and holding up one hand in a halting motion when Coria began to follow him. "I need you to be inside the carriage with Matthew. The uvis snapped the pole, so there's nothing stopping him from jumping out now."

The queen nodded with great reluctance after a handful of seconds. "All right."

A few hours later, the path split in two, with the leftward branch extending to one of the many small and quaint yet dull villages on the plains. Dekkin steered the wagon thataway and brought it to a halt before the first store he came across before disembarking and walking to its front door. He opened it and stepped inside to find Cornelius Arcind, in full armor, standing at the counter. As Dekkin took this in, it felt like his heart had been thrown off a tall cliff and was now racing toward the ground below.

Cornelius looked over one shoulder at the creak of the door and started. "Oracle!" He flashed the other man a radiant smile. "Greetings!" Destiny's Catalyst turned around to face the oracle and frowned at the stiffness of the immortal's stance and the rictus of terror stuck to his face. "What's wrong? You look terrified! Surely I'm not looking *that* poorly!"

Dekkin managed to recover somewhat as the other man walked up to him. "N-no. I'm…simply surprised to see you here, that's all."

"I see," responded Cornelius with a nod. "I could say the same to you! What brings you to these parts?"

"Just trying to get far away from Cobaltus, after what happened."

"Ah." The other man pointed out a nearby window at the vehicle the oracle had driven there. "And I see you've taken my wagon!"

Dekkin used his admittedly limited acting skills to work crafting an apologetic expression. "Yes, I'm sorry about that. When the attack happened, I took the first vehicle I saw."

Cornelius shook his head immediately. "No need to apologize. That's perfectly understandable. You can keep it, in fact. I've gotten a new one." The look on his face turned sober. "Can I ask you though? Was my apprentice Matthew inside it when you took it? Is he with you now?"

"No, I can't say that he is." This time, Dekkin's facade was flimsy at best, but the other man bought it regardless.

Cornelius considered these words gravely. "I see. He's gone missing since the attack. I figured that Zage Batur must've taken my wagon…and my apprentice while he was at it. It's good that he didn't make off with the former, I suppose, but it seems as likely as ever he or one of his cohorts *did* do so with the latter."

Recognizing then the gullible nature of Destiny's Catalyst, the oracle dropped all pretense. "That's awful. I'm sorry to hear that."

Cornelius's grin reappeared. "Thank you. At any rate, he won't be missing for long now!"

"What do you mean?" Dekkin asked in confusion.

"Why, that's why my men and I have come to this village! After the attack, I assembled an army in order to hunt down Zage Batur. The map and key that I was to be given during the ceremony in Cobaltus has gone missing as well, and I believe that Zage or one of his coconspirators are almost certainly to blame. We cannot allow them to take the Orb of Desire for themselves, of course, so my men and I traveled through the night following Zage's trail, and it led us here. And then we discovered, to our immense joy, that the townspeople here found Zage trying to steal some food and imprisoned him. Now we're in the middle of interrogating him as to the whereabouts of the map and key and Matthew. He's refused to tell us anything so far, feigning ignorance, but I believe we're close to a breakthrough."

Dekkin turned around so that the other man couldn't see the mixture of relief and dismay on his face. Cornelius thought Zage had done it, but the former was within a dozen paces of the apprentice he was searching so voraciously for, and if the two met, the oracle's entire plan would be for naught. "I see. Well, I wish you luck."

"You'll stay for dinner, won't you?" said Cornelius, stepping forward and reaching out to grab one of Dekkin's forearms as the immortal began to leave.

The other man's light grasp felt like an iron death grip. "I'd like to, but I really should put a little bit more distance between myself and Cobaltus."

"Oh, come now! Please don't make me ask for that wagon back!" Cornelius laughed heartily as his offhand comment made sweat run down Dekkin's forehead.

"All right," Dekkin conceded in resignation, "I will."

Cornelius laughed again. "Excellent! Thank you!"

Now that a hasty retreat was off the table, Dekkin didn't mind sticking around in the store while the other man was there to procure the needed supplies for the rest of his journey. His purchase amounted to several large, heavy wooden boxes of goods that he hefted to the back of his wagon, refusing to accept help from Cornelius. Once the last container was aboard, Dekkin took a seat beside Matthew, who he had covertly covered in a drape before bringing the first one, and across from Coria.

"Cornelius Arcind is here," revealed the oracle grimly, his gaze on his feet.

Coria's eyes bugged out, and her mouth fell open slightly. "*What?*"

"And a small army of soldiers." Dekkin lifted and rotated his head to face the queen's. "He's making me dine here tonight." His gaze turned firm. "You two must stay in this wagon for the entire time that we're here. Understood?"

"Understood," Matthew said readily before the queen could. Both her and Dekkin looked to him in surprise before she shifted her focus back to the oracle and replied, "Yes."

Dekkin ran a hand over his face. "Good."

That night, Dekkin sat at a long table with benches on each side of it, but no chairs at its head or foot in the center of the local tavern's main room along with Cornelius and his entourage, which included the warlord Nadia Torum as well as a fresh-faced and clumsy young man with curly black hair the oracle thought he'd never seen before. The immortal would've liked nothing more than to wash his worries away with drink like the others, as he had done on so many occasions, but as you can imagine, he refrained, making spring water his beverage of choice. He wasn't alone, as both Cornelius and Nadia did the same. Dekkin deliberately chose a chair on one end of the table and directly across from that of the latter when he walked in; he knew that the former would try to bring him into one of the multitudinous discussions happening around the table out of misplaced courtesy unless he already had a main conversation partner, and Nadia, infamously reserved and equally resolved to maintain that reputation, was the ideal choice for his purposes.

Just outside the front of the tavern stood Dekkin's wagon. Coria and Matthew sat in still silence as they had for the last several hours, the former holding the tails of the pedibi binding the hands of the latter in one of her own. Or rather, the lorm was still and silent. The queen sighed to herself loudly and fidgeted constantly as she had the entire time before leaning forward to unlock the pedibi. "All right, I can't take this anymore. Come, we'll go for a walk."

"What?" replied Matthew in confusion. "But Dekkin told us to stay here."

Coria stood up straight as she could given the wagon's height. "Yes, but I'm bored, and no one will see us, anyway. Everyone'll be inside at this time of day. And I can't leave you here by yourself, so you're coming with me. All right?"

Matthew acquiesced immediately, and the two of them clambered out into the open air before beginning to make their way through the village streets.

Some time after this, both their gazes were drawn down and to their right, wherefrom a voice called out to them, "Hello!"

Coria and Matthew, having failed to encounter a single soul since they set out from the wagon as the former had predicted, froze, startled. Recovering soon after, they turned rightward to find a prison and the Dark Lord Zage Batur standing in one of the outside cells with his face pressed against the bars over its window. "Hello."

At first, Coria didn't recognize the man before her and assumed him to be a common kaglorite delinquent, but a feeling of familiarity scratched at a corner of her mind, light yet insistent until she remembered seeing an artist's rendition of the man's face during one of the few royal council meetings she'd bothered to attend. Her brow furrowed out of incredulity as she rotated her body to face him and stepped toward him.

"*Zage Batur?*"

The kaglorite nodded quickly. "Yes."

"You've been imprisoned?"

"Yes, please could you help me get out? The guard is asleep at the moment."

Coria started before responding vehemently, "*What? No!* You're the *Dark Lord*. You've killed *so many people*, innocent people!"

"*Please*," Zage begged, "I have had a change of heart. I just want to get back to my people."

The queen's eyes narrowed suspiciously. "You're lying."

"No, I am not!" insisted the prisoner. "I do not want to fight the humans anymore. I want to go back to Kagloris and never return here. Please I beg of you. You are my only hope."

Coria considered this seriously for a moment before replying, "How do I know you're telling the truth?"

"I promise! I promise you that I am. That is the most that I can do, is it not?"

Coria stared at him in silence for a moment before saying hesitantly, "You swear you'll not harm any more people?"

"Yes," Zage confirmed readily, "yes, I do."

"Wait," said Matthew, his eyes wide in surprise, as he looked up at the queen, "you're not truly going to do it, are you?"

Coria returned his gaze. "He seems sincere, and everyone deserves a second chance." She began leading the boy around to the prison's front entrance. "Come, let us go."

As they went down the stairs separating the building's cell block from its foyer very shortly thereafter, they spotted the guard, who was sleeping slouched in a wooden chair against the far wall with a ring of keys on his belt. Coria, with Matthew in tow, stepped lightly across the room before kneeling beside the guard. The queen unlatched the ring from the belt it was attached to and gingerly removed the former from the latter before standing and walking to Zage's cell, the only one occupied in the building. The kaglorite, who she could now see, had his hands cuffed in a pedibus, stepped to the bars eagerly as he gazed at her.

"I'm only going to unlock your cell," she whispered as she did so, "not your pedibus."

"That is fine," assured Zage in equally muted tones.

Coria opened the door, and the kaglorite walked out into the adjoining hallway. "Thank you. Thank you so very much."

* * * * *

Back in the tavern, Dekkin stared off into space with a dour expression, his cup and plate empty, as his tablemates talked and laughed loudly among themselves. The oracle rose and walked to Cornelius.

"I'm going to retire for the evening!" the former said to the latter once they were a pace away from each other, raising his voice out of necessity.

Cornelius turned his head to meet the oracle's gaze. "What? No! Don't! Stay with us a while longer, won't you?"

Dekkin began making his way to the tavern's front door. "I'm very tired! Good night!"

"Oh, all right!" conceded the other man with no small disappointment. "Good night, Oracle! I'll see you tomorrow!" As soon as he finished calling out to the immortal, he was beset by several of the people surrounding him for conversation and forgot about Dekkin immediately.

The oracle turned to his right as soon as he was out of the tavern to head for his wagon. As he walked, there was a flicker of movement that started at the top of his point of view and raced down to the bottom, and suddenly, he was choking. Dekkin let out a strangled gurgle as he felt the well-muscled chest of another man on the back of his neck and the slimy skin of a pedibus pressed up against the front.

"Goodbye, Oracle," a voice muttered in the oracle's ear. "I made a promise to someone not to kill any more humans, and I am *so* eager to break it."

Dekkin grabbed at the arms of his attacker desperately as he struggled against the other man's grip and saw the violet skin upon them in his periphery as he did so. At this, a harried idea came to the oracle's mind. "W-wait!" He gagged as the kaglorite tightened his hold in response. "Wait!" grated the immortal, barely and with much effort, after choking once again. "I'm going east! I'm going east!" The pressure was unceasing, and if Dekkin could've seen the way his face was changing color, he would have been horrified. Just as his vision was beginning to black out however, his attacker relaxed his arms and shifted them forward slightly, enough for his victim to gasp for air.

"What?" whispered Zage as Dekkin let out a string of emphatic coughs.

"I'm going east!" the oracle repeated breathlessly. "That's where you're headed, yes? East, to Kagloris? I can take you in that direction. I can be useful to you. Don't kill me."

"Why would I not simply kill you and take your wagon?" pointed out the kaglorite.

Inside the tavern, a soldier who was directly across from one of its front windows looked out to see Dekkin's lower body standing on its heels and leaned backward. Frowning, he stood from his seat at the table and started walking to the door.

The repetitive sound of clanging metal as the soldier moved to them was unmistakable even from Dekkin's position. "S-someone's coming! You have to make a decision *now*!"

The soldier stepped around the table and out the door to find the oracle standing by his wagon with his back to the other man.

"Is everything all right, Oracle?" Cornelius's man asked with a squint.

Dekkin turned to face the soldier with a look on his face as if he'd been unaware of the other man's approach until just then. "Oh yes, I'm quite fine, thank you."

"Are you certain?" pressed the warrior. "I saw you standing on your heels out here."

A corner of the oracle's lips twitched slightly before they spread to form a cordial smile. "Oh, that! I was just stretching my legs. I'd been seated for so long, you know."

"Oh." The soldier nodded and turned around to head back inside; if an oracle was undeserving of one's faith, who wasn't? "I see. Well, you have a good night, Oracle."

With his back to Dekkin, the warrior couldn't see the disdainful scowl on the other man's face, so incongruous with the warmth of his words. "Thank you, and you as well."

As the soldier walked back into the tavern, the oracle closed his eyes and let out a heavy breath. He turned around and went to the back of his wagon before opening one of its doors a crack and looking in at Zage as he sat within.

"We are safe?" the kaglorite asked solemnly.

"Yes." When Dekkin didn't hear from Matthew or Coria, he widened the gap between the doors and poked his head inside to find them missing.

"What is it?" inquired Zage upon seeing the other man's face.

"There are some other people who should be in here."

"Hello!" the queen called out from behind the oracle, who, startled by the sudden and unforeseen intrusion, jumped slightly and cried out.

Dekkin whirled around and glared at Coria accusingly. "What are you doing?" As he still wished to avoid drawing the attention of those in the tavern, his inquiry came out as a pointed whisper.

"We decided to go for a walk!" answered the queen, either not picking up on or merely ignoring the oracle's harsh tones.

"*She* decided," Matthew corrected her as he peeked out from behind her back, "that we should go for a walk."

"A *walk*?" repeated Dekkin incredulously. "Are you jesting?" He stepped away from one of his vehicle's doors and opened it wide for his fellows outside it. "Get back in the wagon *now*."

"All right, all right, Master Cantankerous," Coria conceded playfully as she clambered inside. "No need for anger."

"I tried to stop her," muttered Matthew defensively as he began to follow suit.

"Be quiet and get in," Dekkin snapped.

The next morning, the oracle walked to the wagon from the inn and peeked inside at Matthew, Coria, and the newest member of their group. "Is all well in here?" Everyone answered in the affirmative. "All right then." Dekkin climbed up to the coach box and resumed course.

At the outskirts of town, however, the path was blocked from a distance by Cornelius astride a kresh. The oracle swore under his breath and brought his vehicle to a halt just behind Destiny's Catalyst.

Cornelius rode up to Dekkin. "Good morning! Couldn't let you go without saying goodbye."

The immortal flashed the other man a tight smile. "I see."

"Oracle, let me ask you something before you go. You didn't happen to hear or see anything unusual last night, did you?" Cornelius leaned toward Dekkin expectantly as he said this.

Master Arcind's expression was perfectly neutral, but it bored a hole through the oracle's gut nonetheless. Cornelius's face was always a picture of easygoing amiability, regardless of whatever emotion he was actually feeling at any given moment; the look upon it now was what you would see when he was discussing the weather, but also when he was impaling a kaglorite terrorist through the stomach.

"No, I don't believe so. Why do you ask?"

"It seems that the Dark Lord escaped captivity last night. We're searching the village now, but so far, there's no sign of him."

Coria noted no change in Zage's countenance as she sat across from him in the back of the wagon, though the conversation outside could be heard clearly by all within. "If we don't find him, we may meet again in the near future!"

Dekkin despaired in secret. "And why is that?"

"If we can't find him in the village, we're going to head down the Peacepath," explained Cornelius. "He almost certainly went that way if he managed to get out of the village."

The two men sat in silence for a moment. The oracle was visibly deep in thought, but Destiny's Catalyst mistook this as concern over the status of the fugitive at large. "I see. Well, good luck with your search."

Cornelius lit up as if that statement was anything more than a nicety. "Oh, thank you! I appreciate that. Goodbye for now, at least!" He chuckled and turned his mount to one side before riding off. Dekkin stared down at the ground before him contemplatively for a handful of seconds, after which he whipped his kreshes and led them out of town.

"Malun!" Dekkin muttered sharply to himself behind gritted teeth. "Malun!"

That night, as the four of them sat around a campfire, Coria noted that the look on the oracle's face was even more dour than was typical and asked him, "What's wrong?"

Dekkin shut his eyes tightly and grimaced. "The remainder of our journey's just become a great deal more difficult."

"Why's that?" inquired the queen further in concern.

The immortal raised his lids with great reluctance. "Cornelius Arcind and his men are going to be searching the Peacepath for Zage."

"The what?" Coria said with a frown.

The oracle looked at her with incredulity. "You don't know what the Peacepath is?"

Coria shook her head.

"You're the queen of Humania!"

"Well, I apologize, I've never heard of it," replied the royal defensively. "What is it?"

Dekkin sighed in exasperation. "Up ahead, the land narrows, and there are two paths through the thin area. One is the Peacepath, so called because it's very safe to travel on. The other…well, it's the exact opposite. People try to avoid having to take that path at all costs. Unfortunately, we now have no choice but to avoid the Peacepath, as we can't risk another run-in with Cornelius and his men." He threw up his hands. "Such is our dilemma."

Coria's face fell in dismay, and she shifted her gaze to the ground, her expression thoughtful. "I see."

A hush fell over the group for a short while until Zage turned to Dekkin and raised his bound hands up slightly, saying, "Oracle, release me from this pedibus."

The immortal nodded and stood. "I will, though only to put you in one I have the key to."

The kaglorite's mouth twisted. "I should have expected as much from a filthy *human*."

"Well, that's certainly going to bring me around to your way of thinking," Dekkin retorted as he unsheathed his dagger to bisect the pedibus around Zage's hands. "Stupid animal."

The Dark Lord's eyes flared at this, but even he managed to rein in his anger, recognizing as he did that his hands were cuffed and the other man had a blade in hand.

Coria's brow flew up, and she looked over at Zage. "I thought you said you'd had a change of heart!'

"Do you jest?" snarled the kaglorite. "I was lying! I would have killed the both of you if it wouldn't have drawn the attention of your stinking kinsmen."

The queen slumped a little. "Well, that's very disappointing."

"I do not care about what the *leader of the humans* thinks of me!" He shifted his gaze to Dekkin. "I would have killed you as well, if you had not proven that you could be of use to me. And I or another kaglorite will, eventually. Every human and lorm will one day be slaughtered by my people and me."

"Enough!" the oracle roared.

Coria and Matthew both started; they'd never heard him speak anywhere near as passionately in the short time they'd known him. Dekkin saw this and, suddenly self-conscious, forced himself to deflate. "That's enough. No one here wants to hear it. We may need you for the time being but don't push it."

Zage cracked a fiendish smile and chuckled, making the immortal shake his head.

"Should we kill him?" whispered Coria soon after, as she and Dekkin watched the kaglorite lying on one side with his back to them, seemingly asleep.

"I'm surprised to hear you say that," the oracle replied quietly.

"Well, he said he hasn't had a change of heart. That means he's still the Dark Lord, slaughterer of men and lorms. So I think it might be best to kill him, for the greater good. I don't mean a long-drawn-out execution, just a death that's as quick and painless as it can be."

"We can't." Dekkin's voice was full of regret. "We need him."

"You said that before," responded Coria quizzically. "What do you mean?"

"Now that we can't use the Peacepath, the road ahead has become extremely treacherous. With him, we have a powerful, if untrustworthy, magic user on our side. Without him, we're nothing but a boy, a man who can't fight, and a queen without guards."

Coria crossed her arms over her chest and pouted. "You know, I *am* your bodyguard."

"Ah, yes, how could I forget?" Dekkin's tone was mocking. "Excuse me if I have little faith in the combat prowess of a noblewoman. For now, we keep him alive."

"All right," the queen conceded with great reluctance.

Unbeknownst to them, Zage was awake during their entire exchange. But he cared about their words roughly as much as they cared whether or not he heard them.

6

AS THE FOLLOWING MORNING progressed, Dekkin's passengers could see for themselves the truth of his words the previous night as the ocean appeared on their right, at first from a great distance and then slowly advancing toward the path until a foot in the wrong direction would've sent them plunging to a watery grave. The oracle found himself physically drawn to the crashing surf below, as if the sound of its breaking waves was history's greatest love ballad. When he caught himself doing this, he hastily straightened, though there was no one around to see any of it. The road forked at midday, and Dekkin grudgingly turned right at the intersection. A half hour of travel later, a cave so massive it looked like the empty eye socket of a mountain came into view.

Coria pushed open the slat behind the immortal and peered out it at him as they approached. "Dekkin?"

"Yes," said the oracle.

Inevitably, the queen's gaze was soon drawn to the gaping granite maw before them. "*Tantus mirus*, what is *that?*"

"It's the Cave of a Thousand Thieves," Dekkin explained. "As the name implies, it's home to many outlaws. It's places like this where Zage will come in handy. Get ready to fight them off, if you're serious about this bodyguard business."

"I am!" replied Coria ebulliently. "I'll protect you with my life."

The oracle rolled his eyes as he grabbed the keys to Matthew and Zage's pedibi and handed them to her through the opening behind him. "I'm simply *oozing* with confidence in you. Here, take the keys. Don't unlock the restraints, just have the keys in your hand. I'll bring the wagon to a halt in a bit. I want you to be up here with me when we enter the cave. Understand?"

"Yes."

Dekkin returned his gaze to the cave's opening. "Good."

When the wagon was at last swallowed by the dark within, Coria sat in the coach box along with the oracle, and twin lanterns hung on either side of the vehicle's front lit the way.

"Doesn't look like there's anyone here," the queen remarked as she looked this way and that, her weapon clutched tightly in both hands.

Dekkin shushed her sharply. "Keep your voice down," ordered the immortal in a harsh yet fearful whisper. "There's never any trouble at the entrance since it'd be quite easy for their prospective victims to escape. We'll find them further in."

Once they'd gone far enough for the rays of the sun to disappear behind them, the path took on an amorphous quality; the light of the lanterns wasn't enough to illuminate the walls even dimly, and so all Dekkin and the others could see was the unbroken stone beneath and immediately surrounding them.

There suddenly came a knock in the distance ahead and to the right of the wagon, and both of the coach box's occupants whirled their heads around to face its direction, their eyes wide with alarm. It wasn't a loud noise, but in the seemingly deserted, enclosed cavern, it seemed to them like that of an explosion.

"Did you hear that?" Dekkin asked Coria an instant later, mentally berating himself for asking the question; did he think there was a chance she hadn't?

"Yes," confirmed the queen, and the oracle knocked her as well for responding. He gradually brought the wagon to a halt, and the second she saw what he was doing, she turned to him and hissed quietly, "What are you doing?"

"If they're coming for us, there'll be no escaping them," Dekkin stated. "We'll have to stand our ground and fight. Get Matthew and Zage. Unlock Matthew's pedibus. *Don't* unlock Zage's, just be ready to do so." He stepped down from the driver's seat and advanced in the direction of the knock, a hand on the dagger at his hip, as she went around to the back of the wagon and opened its doors before freeing Matthew and bringing a bound Zage along with them to meet the oracle.

"See anything?" inquired Coria at a low volume once she was standing beside the immortal.

Dekkin said nothing for a moment as he desperately, painstakingly strained his eyes to peer ahead of him for any signs of danger. Failing to spot anything, he answered in the negative, his expression grave. "It must've been a rock falling or some such. Let's get back to the wagon."

As the four of them retreated to their vehicle, there came another knock, just like the first one except for its increased volume, in the same direction as its predecessor. All of them whirled around at this, and Matthew unsheathed his sword with his right hand. It began to fall once free, and the boy gripped its hilt with both hands, straining to keep it aloft, to no avail; the blade hit the ground hard, and a resounding clang rang out, bouncing back and forth against the walls with the speed and intensity of Samu's finest carnival workers.

"Malun," Dekkin swore, frozen in abject terror.

Coria frantically grabbed his shoulder. "Let's get back in the wagon! We can still—"

"I told you," interrupted the oracle shortly. "There's no point. We have to face whatever's coming head-on." He swiveled his head to return the queen's gaze. "Unlock Zage's pedibus."

"Are you sure?" Her voice ached with faint hope.

"Yes."

Nodding, Coria reached into one pocket for the key to Zage's restraints and inserted it into the pedibus, unshackling him. Under different circumstances, she might've been reprehensive, worried that the kaglorite would strike at her and the others as soon as he was able, but the surrounding, stifling mask of near-complete darkness sapped the possibility of that thought from her mind and the notion to act on his newfound freedom from his.

It started as a twin set of soft clunks in the distance, like the sound of someone chopping firewood on the other side of a vast forest. Then it began to gradually grow louder and louder, and others like it started to join in until they formed together a cacophony. After what seemed like hours, Dekkin and the others spotted the foot of a kresh at the far edge of their lanterns' light, and from there, a small army, some of its members mounted and others not, advanced into view. They'd armed themselves with all manner of weapons—swords, scimitars, morning stars; one near the back of the vanguard even seemed to be holding in his arms a bag of small crudely produced bombs.

* * * * *

Beams of sunlight snuck between the tops of a forest's trees to dot its grassy floor. A human man rounded one of their many trunks and scanned the area ahead of him intently. He was in his fifties, with a lean yet muscular build and shaven head. A woman of the same age with long brown hair appeared right from where the man had and did the same. Both of them wore ratty tunics, each stitched together from many different kinds of furs and large leaves. The man came to a halt, allowing his companion to catch up to him before halting herself.

"See anything?" she asked him, as if they weren't standing directly beside each other and looking in the exact same direction.

The man shook his head, seeming not to notice the redundancy of his partner's question. "No."

"Hmm, for how long do we keep moving?"

"Not long," responded the man as he relaxed his gaze and shifted it to return hers. "It's been days. If we don't find something soon, we'll know there's nothing beyond the forest."

The woman nodded. "I see. You should tell that to your son, the one who's sent us on this wild avid chase." Her tone was playful but with a hint of genuine frustration.

The man smiled despite that. "Oh, *my* son, is he mine alone? I don't recall *birthing* him, as did a certain someone."

The two of them turned around to face the rest of their group, which numbered a few dozen and was following them from a short distance, its members conducting surveys of their own in every direction. The older couple's son, a thin man of twenty-five with short brown hair, had positioned himself at the front of the crowd, as a leader was wont to do, with his wife holding their infant child in her hands directly beside him. His father raised one hand and waved, catching his son's eye.

"Dekkin!"

The sword at the hip of the outlaw sitting astride his kresh ahead of the others, as a leader was wont to do, drew the oracle's gaze.

"Hello," the former greeted the latter without looking at him while he ponderously dismounted.

"Hello," parroted back Dekkin.

The head thief looked up at the immortal as soon as both his feet were planted firmly on the cave floor. "I'll make this quick. Give us everything in that wagon, and we'll make sure you pass through here unharmed."

The oracle shook his head, deeply regretting his need to do so. "I can't do that."

The leader of the outlaws placed a hand on the hilt of the sword at his side. "Well, then we have a problem."

Dekkin followed suit with his own weapon. "Yes." The other mounted ruffians began clambering down from their kreshes. "Zage, are you prepared?"

"Yes," the kaglorite answered, and when the oracle looked back at the other man as the former unsheathed his dagger, the latter's hands were already glowing red. Even before he returned his gaze to the enemy forces before him, Dekkin could hear them readying their weapons for combat. Immediately following this, the one holding in his arms a bag of bombs lobbed one toward the four new arrivals. Each of the would-be blast victims leaped in a different direction from the projectile and managed to do so swiftly enough to emerge from the subsequent explosion unharmed.

However, when Dekkin raised his head to shout, "ZAGE, DO IT NOW!" nothing came of it. After a few seconds, the immortal whirled to face the kaglorite only to find him curled into a ball, trembling violently with both hands over his head. The oracle furrowed his brow in confusion. "Zage?"

The kaglorite made no move to engage the enemy.

"Zage!" His plea went unanswered yet again, and soon after, he realized it would remain so indefinitely.

Dekkin heard the sound of approaching footsteps at his front and turned to face the noise just in time to see the leader of the thieves standing directly before and above him, raising his sword high in the air as he prepared to strike the newcomer down. Dekkin swore under his breath and hesitated just long enough to ensure his doom. He closed his eyes but hadn't the time to put his hands over his ears and so shortly heard quite clearly the sound of metal hitting…metal. Dekkin frowned and opened his eyes to find that Coria had rushed to his aid, blocking his adversary's blow with the handle of her weapon. In that harried moment, he didn't have the luxury of time in which to marvel at her speed, but later on, he would do so upon thinking back to it. The head thief recovered quickly (he was surprised as well but had no qualms about slaying women) and swung for Coria's neck in a downward, diagonal motion. She was able to dodge the blow by a measure of inches with a swift step to her left and, pulling back her own weapon, smashed him over the head with its hammer, the force of the blow making him crumple instantly and knocking him onto his back.

The three ruffians now at the front of their group, who stayed back to permit what they had thought would be a landslide victory by their leader, made for Coria before her opponent even hit the floor, weapons at the ready. They moved single file, with a man wielding a scimitar at the front, a morning star user in the middle, and a bomb thrower at the back. The one nearest to Coria stopped a pace away from her and stabbed at her stomach with the tip of his weapon. She dodged away from it and swung herself and her own weapon about until the latter's pointed tip was facing his own midriff before using the momentum to impale him completely there. The fatally wounded outlaw cried out in agony as he was pierced.

The attacker next in line smiled to himself at his good fortune as he approached the queen from her right; he was close enough that she wouldn't have time to remove her weapon from his predecessor's gut before his morning star punctured her skull or so he thought. Coria pushed her weapon, and the body connected to it rightward, turning the latter into a shield of meat that caught the morning star in its back. The spike's unintended victim screamed in anguish as they sunk into his flesh. When the man with the morning star began working to remove his weapon from his comrade, it gave the queen enough time to plant one foot on the latter's crotch and pull the lance she ran him through with out his gut. Blood spurted from the open wounds, and chunks of gore clung insistently to the blade of her weapon.

Hearing a metallic rolling sound at her feet, Coria looked to the floor to find one of the miniature explosives held by her third attacker at her feet. She paused to kick it lightly to the man with the morning star before setting course for the man with the bombs and beginning to run to him. The queen heard the chain on the second man's weapon rattle as its owner finally managed to pull it free from the flesh it was lodged in, and a second later, the deafening boom of the bomb at his feet going off was heard. The blood of her enemies was thrown far, some of it splattering on the back of her head. Once the man with the bombs realized Coria was coming for him, his face expanded in panic, and he began to turn around with intent to retreat behind the backs of his fellows. The queen found herself within a pace of him when he was halfway through his rotation and, raising the hammer high, kneecapped him on his right side. The affected leg bent at an unnatural angle with a crunch, and he fell to his knees as a strangled cry left his lips. Flipping her weapon around, Coria slit the man's throat in one swift motion.

There were two more men, wielding swords, running at her from her front now. Side by side, they each swung down at her head but were stopped short when she shifted her grip on her weapon to its middle and raised it up horizontally, blocking both blades. Seeing this, the two men next tried slashing at her hands, but she moved them to either end of the pole they were gripping, and they missed their target once again. Coria attempted to stab the one on her left, but he batted away the lance she thrust at him, and his partner began circling her clockwise, clearly wanting to get behind her for an unexpected attack. The queen was about to whirl around to answer this, but at that moment, the one in front of her slashed at her neck, an assault she was only just barely able to prevent with the very tip of her lance.

Coria didn't need eyes in the back of her head to see the outlaw was now behind her and about to deal a killing blow. Without looking back, she pulled her weapon in sharply, bludgeoning him in the stomach with the hammer. As he clutched at his bruised midriff, the queen returned her gaze to the front, sidestepping another stab from her opponent standing there. Another downward arc of the front one's sword was halted by the middle of her weapon, and when the man behind her did the same with the hand not at his gut, the movement pulled in enough to hit home should all elements of the situation remain as they were, she ducked and slid it down the other man's blade to block both of them simultaneously. Pushing the swords to her left, Coria executed an overhead strike of her own upon the blade of the front man's sword right as he was holding it over his right shoulder in preparation for another assault, driving his own weapon deep into it. No one who heard the cry that erupted from the freshly injured man's mouth then could have taken pleasure in it, not even Coria.

When she turned around to find the thief behind her readying yet another swing of his sword, she leaped forward and to one side, dodging the blade before stabbing him in the chest with the pointed end of her weapon. His subsequent pained exclamation was muted from the blood now coursing through his throat and foaming at the corners of his mouth. Coria removed the lance from its target and returned her attentions to his comrade, whose expressions of agony had begun to die down as his mind was numbed by the unimaginably torturous sensation in his shoulder. Lifting the hammer over her head, the queen brought it down on the near protruding end of the sword embedded within him, driving it into the top of the corresponding pectoral like a stake into dirt. This time, all within earshot, it felt as though they'd been the ones mutilated as soon as they heard his voice.

Coria, her breath a little louder than normal but with not a drop of sweat on her skin, turned to face the rest of the enemy force. They stared at her grisly display in awe for a moment before whirling around and running for dear life. One of the outlaws dropped both the daggers he held in each hand as he retreated, and she went over to them soon after they clattered to the floor before picking up and stashing them in one of her pockets.

"Are we ready to go?" asked the queen of her companions with nonchalance as she looked back at them. They themselves were watching the small army fleeing from the single woman before them in utter disbelief.

That night, as the four of them sat around a campfire just within the far end of the cave, Coria held the daggers she'd recently acquired out and level with her chest, the flames backlighting them as she gazed at the twin weapons intently.

"Where did you learn to fight like that?" Zage inquired with great curiosity, vocalizing the only thing he, Dekkin, and Matthew were thinking of since the queen's grand, brutal demonstration of power.

Coria looked up from the daggers in her hand at him. "Combat training at the royal castle."

The kaglorite raised his brow. "Truly?"

"Yes," confirmed the queen. "I train with the captain of the guard every day…rather, I used to."

"When you said you'd be my bodyguard, I thought you were merely desperate," Dekkin said, in spite of himself leaning toward her with eyes bright from more than firelight. "But you're actually… quite capable in a fight."

Coria chuckled. "Thank you."

"I'm surprised the queen of Humania would enjoy such a thing," continued the oracle.

"Well, I do." The queen's eyes went wide, and her mouth fell open a little. It was as if the flesh before her heart had fallen away in chunks, exposing it to the outside. "It's…when you're fighting against someone—just you and another person—you only have to worry about yourself. You don't have to concern yourself with the needs of others. It's just you. There's something very…freeing…about that."

"Hmm." Dekkin considered this.

"Why do you use that sword, Matthew?" Coria asked the boy as she shifted her gaze to him. "It's clearly much too large for you."

"Why?" repeated the lorm, saying it to himself but almost seeming to be directing it at her. "Um, well, my master gave it to me. It's the same kind of sword he has. He wants me to use it."

The queen held up the knives in her grasp, higher still. "Well, it's too big for you. Something like these would work far better for you."

Matthew blinked. "You think so?"

Coria flashed him a roguish grin. "I *know* so. Come, I'll show you how to use them."

The boy stood dutifully. "Yes, my lady."

"What?" Dekkin, incredulous, said as he swiveled his head to face the queen's. "No! You're not giving him weapons!"

Coria waved his concerns away without returning his gaze. "*Calm* down. There's three of us and one of him, and he's never used these before besides. He's not going to turn them on us."

"I said *no!*" barked the oracle with even further heightened intensity as he leaned toward her.

"Here you are," the queen said to the lorm, now standing directly before her, with a warm smile as she offered him the daggers in her hand.

The boy took them. "Thank you."

Coria stood up, turned around, and began walking away from the fire and further into the cave as Matthew followed close behind. "Now then, those daggers aren't made for throwing, so you'll be using them exclusively for close combat. It'll be far more difficult than fighting with a sword, but if you can master it, you'll be a better fighter than you ever could with a sword." She came to a halt several paces from Dekkin and Zage and turned to face the lorm as she took her weapon from its sheath on her back. "I'll teach you a basic technique that'll serve you well."

The boy stopped a few paces from his teacher. "All right."

The queen was now holding her weapon out in front of her with both hands. "Blocking an opponent's swing with a dagger is naturally much more difficult than doing so with a sword, but it is possible. And as you block your opponent's swing with one dagger, you can use the other to stab him or her at the same time. Let's try it. Are you ready?"

Matthew balked, albeit meekly. "W-wait, you want me to stab you?"

"No, no," assured Coria with a shake of her head. "We're just pretending here. I'm not really going to swing my hammer at you either."

The lorm exhaled in visible relief. "Oh, all right."

Coria stepped toward Matthew and raised her hammer over her head. He watched it as it moved and assumed a defensive stance, gripping the twin daggers in his hands tightly. She slowly and without much force began bringing down her weapon such that the end of it would—were it allowed to continue moving untouched and with its course unaltered—deliberately overshoot his head, leaving him to contend with its long handle. The boy brought one of his knives up to successfully block the practice swing. However, after that, he stood unmoving, his mind clearly hazed over by an imagined pressure.

After pausing for a moment expectantly, the queen said to Matthew lightly, "See, as you block the swing, you need to stab me."

The boy lowered his gaze, sheepish and apologetic. "I...I know. Sorry."

"That's all right," Coria assured him as she assumed an offensive pose. "Let's try it again."

The lorm got into position himself. "Yes, my lady."

"Not my lady," chided the queen very lightly. "Call me Coria, all right?"

"Yes, m—" Matthew stopped himself and blushed a little. "Coria, my apologies."

"No need to apologize either!" Coria added, her voice tinged with a bit of exasperation. "*Tantus mirus*, you're very proper, aren't you? Are you ready to try again?"

The boy nodded solemnly. "Yes."

"All right." She carried out her part of the exercise again in a manner identical to the first, but this time, the lorm did his part too, jabbing the air directly before her stomach with one of his knives. The two of them held their poses for a moment before the queen smiled in commendation. "Good!" She lowered her weapon, pulling it in as she did so. "*Very* good. You learn quickly."

Matthew looked down at his feet bashfully. "Oh, well, thank you. It was nothing, truly."

Coria sheathed her weapon and walked around him on her way back to her spot by the fire. "Hardly nothing. Don't belittle yourself. You've got skill, that's for certain."

"Th-thank you," said the boy as he lowered the blades in his grasp, turned around, and returned to his own place. A short while after the two of them had taken their seats, he turned his head toward Zage's quizzically and asked, "Why did you freeze up back there? After that man threw that bomb?"

"You dare to mock me, little lorm?" bellowed the kaglorite, making Matthew start while half rising from the cave floor.

The boy, completely thrown, raised up slightly both hands, facing Zage. "Wh-what? No! I—what do you mean?"

The man with the violet skin regarded the youth with the green incredulously. "You have never heard of the Kaglorite Massacre?"

"The Kaglorite Massacre?" Matthew repeated before shaking his head. "No."

Zage scoffed pointedly. "It makes sense that you would not have heard of it, now that I think of it. The filthy humans and cowardly lorms would not want their young to know of their greatest atrocity. Listen well, boy. The kaglorites' war against its eastern neighbors began long before I was born. And when I was but a boy, the bastard human king's cripple of an adviser uncovered the means of producing a substance, a liquid that turned the soil it wetted into a powerful explosive. They made plans to use it to burn Kagloris, which was then a land of dense jungles, to ash, but the border between our two nations was too strongly defended on our side to be crossed. And so they made for the land to our west, the Lormish Isles. The people there, *your* people, boy, allied themselves with the kaglorites long before then, though they had never fought by our side against the humans, but the simpering *mostella* betrayed us the first chance they got, and so our mortal enemies were able to covertly infiltrate our great motherland. They built towering metal drills in secret that burrowed deep into the earth, and innumerable jugs of the explosive liquid were poured into the holes in the ground they made, over time permeating almost every speck of the soil beneath us. And then it was ignited…and in a matter of minutes, Kagloris became a wasteland, and its people brought to the brink of extinction." The storyteller grinned nastily. "Our only consolation was that even those of a nation as wicked as Humania were not immune from guilt. A few days after the massacre, a human assassin slew the king by whose hand the destruction had been wrought." Coria had no visible reaction to this final part of the tale.

The boy stared back at the kaglorite as if stricken. "*Tantus mirus.*"

"That bomb the man threw at us was made of the same thing that destroyed my home," explained Zage further. His gaze's focus shifted from Matthew as if he was seeing through him to something in the distance behind him, and he clutched at the spot on his chest where, unbeknownst to the others, severe burns discolored his flesh. "When it exploded, memories of that day…came back to me."

"How did you survive?"

"My family and I were in one of the few areas that wasn't affected by the explosive soil, though we were still burned by the flames."

The corners of the lorm's mouth fell in sympathy. "That's terrible. I'm sorry that that happened to you."

"Do not *dare* pity me, boy!" thundered Zage, his mouth open wide. "It is because of *your people* that it happened at all. You disgust me."

"What he isn't telling you is that the kaglorites started the war to begin with *and* were given the opportunity to surrender before the soil was ignited," Dekkin cut in bitterly.

"Silence, human *scum!*" barked the kaglorite in fury as he whipped his head around to face the oracle's. "It is *not the fault of my people* that we have been tasked with carrying out a righteous crusade against the inferior beings of this land, who long ago *murdered* the great warlock Zeli *without provocation*!"

"There's no evidence that ever happened!" the immortal snapped. "And even if it did, what does that have to do with any of the humans or lorms living today?"

This gave Zage pause, but after a moment, he recovered, saying with a snarl, "*Curse* you, you filthy caneo."

An uncomfortable silence fell over the group that hadn't lifted by the time its members turned in, save for Coria, who agreed to take the first watch.

As he lay asleep on his back, Dekkin dreamed he was standing atop a large dune in the middle of a vast desert, the sun beating down harshly upon him. After a while, he realized there was a patch of green along the very edge of his right eye's periphery and looked over at it to find a single grassy hill topped with a massive pine tree among the ocean of sand. As the oracle stared at it, someone close behind him called out his name, and the immortal turned around to see the speaker. It was an elderly man of a species Dekkin had never seen before; the former was about as tall as an adult human male but with yellow-brown skin and a heavily disfigured face with several scars upon it. The two of them stood and stared at each other for a handful of seconds.

"Dekkin." The old man's mouth wasn't moving. And the voice the oracle had just heard sounded like that of a woman and a very familiar one at that. "*Dekkin.*"

The immortal awoke to find Coria kneeling beside him as she shook one of his shoulders in a slight yet insistent motion.

"Hmm," replied Dekkin blearily as he looked up and over at her through half-open eyes. "Yes?"

"It's your turn to keep watch," the queen responded.

"All right." The oracle sat up as readily as if he'd been lying on a bed of red-hot coals.

7

"**D**EKKIN?" CORIA PEERED OUT the slat behind the oracle at him as he drove the wagon the following morning.

"Yes?" replied the immortal, his tone chilly.

"Are we going to be passing through any other places like the cave? Places that are dangerous, I mean."

Dekkin chuckled humorlessly. "*Oh* yes. There're many more to come. We're approaching one now."

The queen's eyes widened, and she looked off into the distance ahead of them only to frown in confusion when she saw nothing. "Really? What is it?"

"The Lake of Monsters," the oracle revealed, "which is…exactly what it sounds like. We'll need to charter a boat to get across it, and even then, it shall be no easy task." Coria took this in. Her fear was strong enough to shut even a person such as her up, and after a moment, she shut the slat and sat in the back stewing in her own fright.

Even with such an arresting landmark on the horizon, Dekkin kept his eyes glued to the dirt directly before him. So it wasn't until the kreshes came to a halt at the Lake's borders that he spotted something amiss. It was completely dry, a deep, wide hole in the ground.

"Well, that takes care of *that* problem," remarked Coria after she disembarked from the back of the wagon with Matthew and Zage and walked up to stand beside Dekkin.

The oracle nodded nigh imperceptibly. "Yes."

The queen turned her head to look at him. "When was the last time you were here?"

"Four hundred years, give or take," Dekkin answered with nonchalance. "I suppose I should have anticipated a change of some kind." He clambered back up onto the coach box and gestured for the others to return to the back of the wagon. "Well, let's get to it."

"Matthew, there was something you wanted to ask Dekkin, wasn't there?" said Coria as the boy began making his way back to his seat.

The lorm stopped and turned around, shaking his head vehemently. "Um, no. No, I didn't."

"Oh, yes you did!" the queen pressed insistently. "Come now, say it." When the boy refused to speak, she said to the oracle, "Matthew wanted to ask you if he could sit beside you for a little while."

The immortal nodded surprisingly soon and without reservation. "He isn't much for talk, so yes, he may."

One corner of the lorm's mouth twitched upward a little as he went to Dekkin's side, and the others got back to their seats. The kreshes took some convincing to start making their way down the steep slope before them, but the oracle wasn't shy about coaxing them to do so quite aggressively, and they were soon moving. It seemed as the group advanced along the lake bed that the waters there had been deliberately and swiftly drained at some point, based on the presence of gargantuan aquatic skeletons, imposing even in their immobility, dotting the surface. They were the only decorations along the bottom of the chasm, which was otherwise as flat and featureless as the plains surrounding it.

When Dekkin, after some time, scoffed, Matthew started at the sound. "Look at this. Once the largest lake in Humania, now a giant dirt *pit*."

The boy considered this. "But—" began the lorm before cutting himself off.

The oracle frowned and looked over at him. "What?"

Matthew shook his head.

"What, what is it?" the immortal continued in irritation.

The boy tensed up, paused, opened his mouth to say something, closed it without doing so, and then finally said, "But...it's a good thing it's dried up, isn't it? If it hadn't, it would've been really dangerous for us to cross it."

"Well...um, yes, I suppose," Dekkin, visibly taken aback by the challenge, replied. "But"—and there he recovered—"it certainly is ugly to look at."

"Wh-what does it matter what it looks like though?" pointed out the lorm. "Isn't its function more important?"

"No," the oracle responded shortly, returning his gaze to the wide trail before them.

Matthew thought on it for a moment before looking back at the immortal. "Maybe someday somebody'll fill it with water again. Then it'll look as good as it did before *and* without the monsters."

Dekkin scoffed. "Yes, that would be nice. And that's exactly why it'll never happen."

Behind them, Coria tried making conversation with the prisoner sitting across from her a few times to no effect. She was completely befuddled by this but realized after some thought he may be intentionally ignoring her. However, when she followed Zage's gaze, she recognized that he was utterly entranced by the sight of the dirt behind and beneath them.

The queen leaned toward him, her brow furrowed in confusion. "What are you staring at so intently, Zage?"

This time, the kaglorite was shaken from his reverie, though his eyes didn't move, and answered with a surprising lack of hostility, "The soil in this country is so rich. Dark brown, creatures burrowing their way through it. I love the sight of it, the smell too."

Coria's puzzlement was not assuaged in the slightest by this response, if anything increasing from the violet-skinned man's light tone. "You think *this* is beautiful? It's a hole in the ground. Most people here would call it ugly, actually."

Zage fixed her with an indignant scowl. "The *people* here are not used to black earth, *barren* earth, charred air, aching hunger, burning thirst sated only when it rains."

The queen looked stricken and, after a few seconds, nodded in grim concession. An awkward silence fell over the back of the wagon. Coria's demeanor brightened upon thinking up a conversation prompt. "What do you think of the ocean?"

The kaglorite frowned at her. "What do you mean?"

"You came to Humania from the east, right?" explained Coria. "You couldn't have breached the western border. It's too well defended. I still don't know how you got past the guards on the *east* coast, but that must've been what you did. So you passed through the Lormish Isles. You sailed over the ocean, and you would've had to do that, albeit on a much smaller scale, for your raids in the tropics too. What was it like to see such a vast body of water, for a man from Kagloris?"

Zage shook his head sullenly. "For all our journeys out of Kagloris, we have hidden below decks on a merchant's ship docked on the bank of a deep river in the motherland and have not come out until we were at our destination. I suppose we could have looked at it from there, and before we boarded the vessel again, but I never have, and neither I think, have any of my fellows. So no, we have not seen the ocean."

"You couldn't have risked it, just once, while you were in the isles?"

The kaglorite sneered. "Oh, we could've certainly. The craven lorms patrolling their lands posed little threat. It just…never occurred to us. What would be the point?"

The queen looked at him as if that was a trick question. "To see something amazing? A sight you've never beheld before?"

Zage shrugged.

Coria smiled wistfully, watching the lake bed without seeing it. "You missed out. I visited the Lormish Isles many times after… once I was queen. It's paradise next to *this*. It's the air. In Humania, it's so…heavy."

The kaglorite frowned uncomprehendingly. "Heavy? It is far warmer there, far more humid, isn't it?"

The queen nodded but took on a similar expression as if her sentiments were as much a mystery to herself as to him. "Yes, yes.

It—I'm not sure. It simply…feels heavy when I'm here. That's all."

* * * * *

A journey across the Lake of Monsters would've taken far longer than a single day back when it had lived up to its name; not only did a boat in water move at a slower pace than a kresh-driven wagon like Dekkin's over land, but the presence of the multitudinous, ravening creatures' larger and, as a result, more aggressive packs lurking beneath the surface of the water would have necessitated the adoption of an extremely roundabout route to have a chance of missing them and therefore reaching the other side. As it was, however, the oracle and his companions, willing and otherwise, were past the perimeter of the chasm by the time they made camp for the night.

Each of them selected and prepared their own food from the stores within the back of the wagon. As they sat and ate, Coria proffered one of the pastel mushrooms on her plate to Dekkin, asking, "Would you like to try one?" She'd noticed a complete lack of vegetables in the oracle's diet since joining his party, and the observation had led her to try and change that. He refused instantly.

"Come now!" Coria insisted, bringing the fungus in her hand closer to Dekkin's face in an effort to change his mind. "Try it."

"No," replied the immortal flatly. "I don't eat vegetables."

"So I noticed." The queen's tone was chiding. "That's not healthy, you know. If you keep eating the way you have since I've been with you, you won't be able to maintain your slender frame for long. I'm surprised your diet hasn't caught up to you already, in fact."

The oracle scoffed. "You truly know nothing, Coria Roneage."

She tilted her head to one side. "What do you mean?"

"When a turins attaches itself to someone, it freezes the host's bodily functions," Dekkin explained with a sigh, "in *every* way. You see what I'm saying? I'll look how I do right now no matter what or how often or how little I eat, so why would I bother with a balanced diet?"

Coria brought the mushroom in her hand back down to her plate, a look of realization upon her face. "Hmm, some people get all the luck, I suppose." The oracle shot daggers at her that went unnoticed by their target.

After a moment of thought, the queen put one of her fungi in the palm of one hand and rotated it to face the immortal. "Well, it's not only healthy. It tastes good. How about you try it because of *that*?"

Dekkin shook his head adamantly. "*No.* I don't like mushrooms, even for their flavor."

"When's the last time you *had* one though?" countered the queen in mild exasperation.

"One, two—" muttered the oracle with a shrug.

"One, two what? Months?" Coria raised her brow. "*Years?*"

"One or two…hundred…years," the immortal admitted under his breath.

"Well, if it's been over a *century* since you've eaten one—" began the queen.

"I don't need to confirm it!" Dekkin snapped. "I decided I wouldn't eat them, and that's that!"

"But you decided that *so long ago*. You might feel differently now. People change."

The oracle looked away and grumbled, "No, they don't."

Coria thought on this for a handful of seconds before an idea came to her and incredibly pleased with herself, she said, "All right, then how about this? We've done a bargain for silence before. If you eat one of these mushrooms, I shall refrain from making a sound for the rest of the night."

The immortal glanced at her, keen on the proposal but distrustful of the woman offering it up. "That would be…acceptable. You must stick to your word however, not like last time." When Coria raised one hand up in a gesture of promise with a sincere look on her face, Dekkin considered the situation briefly before reaching out to grab one of the mushrooms off her plate, holding it up to gaze at it with trepidation and then hesitantly popping it into his mouth. He chewed quickly at first, trying to get it down and out of his mouth as fast as he could, but as the taste hit his tongue, he caught himself and began to savor it. After keeping it from his throat for as long as possible, grinding it into the finest mush possible in the process, he swallowed, and a neutral expression (his version of a smile) overtook his face.

His unusual look evaporated as soon as the queen leaned toward him and elbowed his near side. "Well?" said Coria in triumph. "Good, is it not?"

"No," Dekkin grumbled. "My opinion is unchanged, as I knew it would be."

"You liar!" pouted the queen. "You—"

"I've kept my end of the bargain," the oracle pointed out. "Now you must do the same."

Coria opened her mouth to reply but caught herself in time and nodded. She stared into the fire for a few seconds before beginning to fidget, her movements growing more and more pronounced with each moment. She looked around in every direction but found nothing to hold her attention, seeing only the flat, featureless stretch of grass immediately about them and, a little further off and to one side of them, gray, craggy rock obscured mostly by darkness black as pitch. She briefly considered sharpening the pointed end of her weapon but soon realized it would be loud enough to violate the terms of her agreement with Dekkin. When she unwittingly brushed the prominent oblong bulge in one of her pants pockets with one hand however, she finally saw a way out of her current predicament.

"Are you—" began the queen as she turned to face the oracle again.

"CORIA RONEAGE!" he roared back.

"A drinker?" finished Coria. When the immortal raised his brow in response, she reached into her pocket and pulled out a bottle of wine. "I took this from the castle. Been holding onto it ever since I left. It's from *Humania*. What do you say I give this to you instead of keeping quiet?"

"You have yourself a deal," Dekkin replied instantly, swiping the bottle immediately afterward. His fervor was quite understandable. Humania's vineyards were located in its western reaches and so were ravaged by the kaglorites' invasion at the start of their war against their eastern neighbors. The damage was so severe as to be irreparable in most of the affected areas even now decades after the massacre; only a few wineries remained. The effect of the war on the Lormish Isles was negligible, and wine from that region was far superior to that of Humania's, but when the tropical country had become a dominion of the human monarchy soon after the destruction of Kagloris, one of the many edicts handed down by the newly minted Queen Maescha was a prohibition on alcohol within the lorms' territory. The rumors of the human vineyard owners persuading her adviser, Samuel, to convince his liege of the necessity of the law in order to establish a monopoly on the market within Humania's borders was denied publicly but true nonetheless.

After a few glasses, downed in very quick succession, the oracle became cordial, soft-spoken even. The queen picked up on this a little late, but when she did, she took full advantage of the situation, asking and being allowed to touch the turins on his back. The chuckles she received from him in response to her good-natured jokes made her feel like her heart was a flower, blooming at the sound of his voice, as opposed to wilting as it had done previously. Watching the immortal drink made Coria lick her lips, but the idea of a well-fed, rested, and sober Zage pouncing on the two of them while they were intoxicated was enough to give even her pause, and she did not partake. When Dekkin began pouring a fourth glass, the queen had reservations about this; wine from Humania was always nigh unbearably strong, one of the ways its producers justified its exorbitant price. When she voiced them however, the oracle briefly shifted back to his usual persona, growling at her to mind her own business. To her amazement, he showed no signs of illness during the fourth and fifth glasses, but finally halfway through the sixth, he vomited violently on his feet before lying on his back where he sat, unable to move any more and falling into a drunken sleep.

Though Coria was meant to keep watch first, she began to nod off shortly after Dekkin did and was asleep in minutes. Fortunately, she'd had the forethought to shackle Zage's hands in a pedibus beforehand.

As the oracle and the queen slept, the kaglorite nudged Matthew with one of his feet. "Boy," whispered Zage (a quiet voice coming from his mouth was like a bird's call leaving a duracut's maw), "get that bottle and pour me some drink."

The lorm nodded; he knew Dekkin and Coria wouldn't approve and was of course a faithful follower of rules by nature but shrank under the kaglorite's intense gaze. Matthew tiptoed up to the oracle's side and grabbed the bottle of wine next to him as well as his cup. After emptying out the latter, he brought both of them back to Zage and filled it from the former before lifting the drink to the kaglorite's lips.

"You should have some as well," Zage muttered after swallowing the last of it, "while you can."

"Oh. Uh, I don't think so," replied the lorm immediately.

"Come now!" The kaglorite forgot himself for a moment and spoke loudly. He whipped his head around to check on Dekkin and Coria. When they didn't stir, he continued, at a low volume, "Drinking is one of the things that separates men from boys. Do you want to be a child forever?"

"Well, no. But…I'm twelve," the lorm pointed out.

Zage scoffed. "Kaglorite boys become men at eight. *Drink.*"

Matthew hesitated but then looked down at the ground, despaired at how short the distance was between it and his head and, without any further thought, threw back the latter to quaff the wine as if it was a magic potion that would instantly lengthen his torso by several inches. If Zage hadn't been beside him, watching him closely as he drank, the boy would've spit it out as soon as it touched his tongue. It tasted like poison, quite literally as if consuming it would kill you. The lorm gagged as he forced it down and regretted his decision utterly as he sat there with the taste stuck in his mouth, but for some reason, when he looked back at the kaglorite, the man's eager expression led him to lie, saying it was delicious and put away even more, albeit slowly.

"How do you feel, boy?" asked Zage once the lorm finished.

"Like I could beat you," Matthew slurred with a genial smile, "like the next time you yelled at me, I could turn your violet skin black."

The boy's brow leaped as soon as the words were out his mouth, as if he, like Zage, hadn't been the one to think them up, and a needle of worry pierced through the drunken mist around his brain, but the kaglorite laughed heartily at the response.

A thought popped into the lorm's mind then, and he asked Zage, "If I was your child, wouldn't you scold me for talking back to an adult?"

"Well, you're *not* my child now, are you?" countered the kaglorite.

A rebuttal formed within Matthew's subconscious but was swept away by a torrent of alcohol as it tried to reach the front of his brain. The boy's stomach grumbled loudly at that moment, and he frowned. When everyone were selecting the contents of their dinners, he didn't know how to pick for himself, so he simply copied Dekkin's choices. But the oracle's meal—the lorm discovered too late—consisted of the blandest food imaginable, and so Matthew had little motivation to finish what he chose and stopped when his plate was barely a quarter clean. The boy attempted to stand and fell flat on his face, much to Zage's amusement. It took the former a few more tries, the failures of which ended for him in dull pain, but eventually the lorm learned how to correct his muffled senses and rose before beginning to walk to the back of the wagon.

"What are you doing?" the kaglorite called after him.

"I'm getting a snack," answered Matthew.

"Ah! What will you eat? Some fish?"

The boy froze and looked back at Zage, affronted. "Why did you say that? Because I'm a lorm?"

The kaglorite furrowed his brow in confusion at the lorm's uncharacteristic indignance. "Well, yes! Lorms like fish, do they not?"

Matthew flashed him a scowl that would've made Dekkin proud. "Not *all* of them." Turning around, he went back to the fire and laid down. "I'm not hungry anymore. Good night."

"What—" Zage said, baffled and defensive. "It's true! Why are you angry with me?"

When the boy didn't reply, the kaglorite scoffed and looked away. Why were lorms so horbing *sensitive*?

* * * * *

Dekkin woke some time later in the night with a start. As his breathing began to slow down, he realized he was the only one not sleeping, and its pace sped up once again, but upon investigation, he found nothing had been touched, and Matthew and Zage were still there, the latter sitting up with his head bowed. The oracle could've gotten Coria up to keep watch but didn't even think of it; instead, he began to scan their surroundings immediately. The still silence about him soon lulled the immortal into a calm trance that after a while was violently shattered by Zage bursting back into waking life with a bloodcurdling scream as he clutched at the burns on his chest. The kaglorite threw his head this way and that as if he could sense some source of danger in his immediate surroundings.

"Stop!" ordered Dekkin, unsettled himself from the abrupt and forceful interruption of the quiet night and cross about it. "It was just a dream. You're safe."

Zage returned his gaze and saw the oracle spoke the truth. The kaglorite slowly relaxed before scowling bitterly and saying in response to the immortal's final statement, "No. I *never* am."

Dekkin's face was a mixture of distaste and pity, and Zage, unsure which of the two he despised the most, looked away. As the two of them sat there around the fire, the kaglorite began to nod off and, much to the other man's surprise, reached into the flames to touch some of the burning wood. He instantly cried out and recoiled from the searing agony this brought about in the hand he'd done it with, and for a while, he was wide awake. After some time, though, drowsiness began to overtake him once more, and he did it again. The oracle realized then what was happening, and when Zage's eyelids next began to flutter, he went over to the kaglorite and shook him awake. The violet-skinned man's expression as he gazed at his savior from dreams immediately thereafter was almost thankful.

"You do the same for me, all right?" the immortal muttered with averted eyes after seeing this. Zage said nothing, but for the rest of the night, each of the two of them kept the other up whenever slumber seemed imminent. And at one point in the night, Dekkin walked over to the back of the wagon to grab a handful of the mushrooms Coria had been eating earlier.

8

WHEN DEKKIN SAW THE clean, lavish village on the horizon several days later, he swore emphatically.

Matthew, who was sitting next to the oracle and had been admiring the approaching settlement, started and looked around, thinking without seeing the immortal that the man must be looking at something else. "What? What is it?"

Dekkin gestured toward the town in the distance grimly. "That's Fetemsip, the diamond in the rough."

"So?" asked the boy uncomprehendingly. "What's the matter?"

"Fetemsip was founded by a handful of noble families from Cobaltus who sought to enrich the lives of those unfortunate enough to live hereabouts by building the only village this side of the mountains with some semblance of safety for all its occupants and thus bringing in much-needed commerce. So they *said*. In reality, they wanted to take advantage of the area's natural resources, which could be done without much oversight from the crown on account of its distance from the capital and reputation for peril, and lord over larger territory, even if it was but a wasteland. And that's exactly what they did. Not all the thieves in the cave are ordinary folk who were disrupted by the construction of Fetemsip or their descendants, but many are."

The lorm raised his brow slightly. "Oh, but…what does that have to do with us?"

The oracle grinned nastily in his head at the apparent callousness of Matthew's words, though in truth, the latter did feel something—in this case, great sympathy for the plight of the locals—and merely didn't show it, as usual. "The nobles of Fetemsip's greed wasn't sated even when they'd conquered what they'd set out to. They demand a heavy toll from all those who wish to pass through the town." Dekkin pointed first at the steep mountains to their left and then the sheer cliffs shooting down to the sea in jagged lines like bolts of lightning. "And as you can see, that means anyone who needs to get to the other side and can't take the Peacepath."

The lorm nodded in realization. "I see." He looked over at Dekkin anxiously. "So what are we going to do?"

"The only thing we can," the oracle answered with a world-weary sigh. "Pay up. Money's no object to me, but that doesn't mean it feels any better handing over some of it to those pampered frauds."

Fetemsip was surrounded on all sides by a tall wall of timber several feet thick in spite of the settlement's meager size, and on the walkway atop said wall, there was an imposing armed soldier stationed every few paces along the path. The upper sections of most of the town's buildings were still visible from outside even in spite of the barrier's considerable height, as they took the form of towering spires. There were intricate designs inlaid into the rare, expensive varieties of stone and gems the structures were composed of, so vast even their tiniest details could still be discerned from well beyond the wall.

No soldier rode out to meet the immortal and his passengers even as he brought his wagon to a halt before one of the wall's proportionately titanic gates. Instead, one of the men standing on top of it leaned forward and called down to them, "FIVE HUNDRED PACS TO CROSS!" The guard looked to be about forty-five, his frame stocky, and the skin beneath his copiously begrimed armor tanned and worn, and yet his booming voice was carefully measured and clipped.

Dekkin nudged Matthew. "Tell him we'll pay. Straining one's voice is a game for the young, no matter how it may seem looking at that fellow above us."

The boy suppressed a chuckle at this and turned his head to face the soldier's, doing as he was instructed. The guard nodded immediately thereafter and motioned to another the newcomers couldn't see to go down and collect the payment.

The oracle heard the metallic scrape of the covering over the slat behind him being pushed open.

"Why have we stopped?" asked Coria with a slight anxious quiver in her voice, looking around as much as the squat aperture before her allowed. When the lorm explained the situation after the immortal refused to, she said, "Oh. Well, don't pay, Dekkin!"

"What other options do we have?" he pointed out dismissively.

"We can go through it without giving up the toll."

Dekkin scoffed. "Oh, yes? And how do you propose we do that?"

The queen paused. "Uh, well…we can figure something out! I'm a good fighter. And you can see into the future, right? You could induce a vision, and we could use that to find a way through!"

The oracle shook his head. "Destiny Water is rare, and I don't have much on me. I'm not wasting a swig just to get out of a fee that I can comfortably pay. Besides, it'd be too much work, putting together some elaborate plan, trying to execute it."

"But wouldn't it be worth it?" continued Coria. "To pull one over on those crooked snobs, to see the looks on their faces as we ride off on the other side, with them none the richer?"

The immortal opened his mouth before she was even finished speaking but stopped short of interrupting her as she kept going and began to mull the issue over when she'd completed her statement. After a brief pause, he said with great reluctance, "All right, I'll take a drink. It won't help, but I'll do it." Unscrewing the cap of his flask, Dekkin downed a mouthful of Destiny Water as he gazed at the village before him. His body went limp and came to rest against the front of the wagon's back while in his mind a vision of the town at sunset, from the exact same angle, played. He thought at first, seeing nothing of note, that he'd been right, but as the premonition continued, he spied something in his periphery—a waste pipe jutting out the side of the cliffs on its right. Though the vision-induced paralysis of the oracle's body was still complete when the soldier sent to collect the payment arrived at the wagon, Coria turned him away, so sure was she that the immortal would reveal another way through once he could speak again.

"All right," Dekkin began when, a few hours later, he could move his mouth. "Coria, I want you to examine the cliff face next to the village. There's a waste pipe sticking out of it there. Check to see if there are handholds and footholds in the rock, enough to allow someone to climb over to it from this side of the wall. Be discreet, however; don't let the guards see what you're doing."

"All right!" replied the queen with gusto before walking to the cliffs and turning toward and looking directly at the pipe with one hand jutting out from her brow.

"*Stop!*" the oracle barked at her. "*Stop. What are you doing?*"

Coria returned his gaze in bewilderment and brought her raised hand down to her side before retreating back to the wagon. "What do you mean? I'm doing what you said."

"How is that *discreet?*" hissed the immortal.

"I'm hiding my eyes with my hand," the queen explained, speaking slowly and with a patronizing tone. "That way, they can't see where I'm looking."

"They can see where *your head* is—forget it. Matthew, *you* do it."

The boy nodded dutifully. "Yes, sir." Stepping to the right of the wagon and up to the coast, he looked out in that direction as if admiring the sea beyond it before turning his head to his left and down as he pretended to cough. When the lorm doubled back immediately thereafter, Dekkin thought Matthew lost his nerve before his task was complete, but then the lorm said after coming up to the oracle, "Yes, there're enough crevices for someone to climb to it from up here."

The immortal blinked. "You saw that in the *second* you were looking at it?"

"Yes." The boy took a step back, self-doubt suddenly playing across his face.

Dekkin could tell however that this was true and said before the lorm could retract his report, "Hmm, observant. Well, I hope for your sake that you're right because *you're* climbing down there."

"Wʜᴀᴛ?" exclaimed Coria incredulously even as Matthew nodded readily. "You're going to make him *do that* and then *crawl through a waste pipe?*"

"He's the only one of us small enough to do it!" the oracle countered with a dismissive scowl. "And that was the only other way in I saw in my vision. Here's the plan. We drive the wagon over to the top of the cliffs to hide Matthew from the view of the guards as he begins to descend. He sneaks into town and opens the gate from the inside. We race through Fetemsip with Coria fending off any attackers. Zage blows the far gate open with red magic, and we make our escape."

"But Matthew is—stop nodding!" said the queen, whipping her head around to face the boy after she spied him doing so. "Matthew is *twelve*, and you want him trying to infiltrate a *stronghold?*"

"Do you have a better idea?" the immortal asked, his voice dripping with contempt.

"Yes! We break down the gates ourselves and fight our way through."

"Oh, because *that's* never been tried before," snarked Dekkin. "Thank you, why didn't I think of that?"

"I agree with Coria," Zage interjected.

"And there's another point against it," said the oracle. "Look, I know I'm an invalid right now, but I'm the leader of this group," he continued, addressing Coria.

"I'm the *queen!*" she pointed out indignantly.

"Oracles outrank queens."

"Nᴏ, ᴛʜᴇʏ ᴅᴏɴ'ᴛ!"

"Look, Coria, we can do it your way if you insist, but if we try it and it goes south, it's on *your* head," declared the immortal.

The queen deflated instantly, looking as if she'd been stricken. "All right, let's use your plan," she conceded in an uncharacteristic murmur.

* * * * *

Matthew hated heights. And as he edged along the face of the cliffs leading to the waste pipe, its surface with as many craters upon it as a field in Kagloris but as steep as one of Itrasia's mountains, the sound and smell of the sea below, the mist it produced bringing moisture to rest on his face like kisses called to him, adding a longing for other things to his fear. Nevertheless, he had his orders, and after ten minutes that felt like as many hours, he reached his destination and curled into a ball, beginning to slink down the pipe. As he moved, the light behind him shrank to the size of a coin, then a pinprick, and finally, he was in complete darkness silent as a grave. Strangely enough, he found he enjoyed this new environment, though the surrounding smell was so strong and vile he gagged several times; in this area of near-complete sensory deprivation, he could pretend for a few fleeting minutes that there were no directives to be followed, expectations to be lived up to.

But his reverie was rudely interrupted by the sound of a sloshing torrent carrying many passengers approaching from his front. Before he even had enough time for the appropriate horror to set in at what was to come, the boy was slammed head-on by a wave of urine and feces. Fortunately for him, he had the forethought to dig deep furrows into the bottom of the pipe's inside with his long white nails right as it happened, and he was able to hold fast in that way. As soon as the current ceased, the lorm leaned forward and vomited profusely. When he begun to recover, he picked off the many pieces of wastes now hanging off or sticking to him, including one thin strand that ran from the top of his head almost all the way down to his lips. The lorm fretted to himself as he resumed his pungent journey about the reactions the others would have to his smell once they were in proximity to him again.

Matthew emerged from the depths on the ground floor of what looked to be servants' quarters within one of the buildings short enough to be completely obscured from an outsider's view by the surrounding wall. The boy only encountered one other person as he made his way to the front door, but he was asleep. He was a grizzled man with a much-protruding gut, snoring loudly as he sat in an armchair with empty, dirty mugs dotting the rest of the room's span. When the lorm smelled beer and heard the pitter-patter of a single infant on the second floor, he hurried out into the open as fast as he could. All the while as he made his way to his target, Matthew never received anything more than a passing glance from the many adults whose paths crossed his. This was perfectly understandable as it was not at all uncommon to see a lorm among humans here, somewhat close to the border, and not only that, but of course, his goal was to carry out his mission undetected; though for reasons he himself couldn't put into words, he actually *wanted* someone to see him. He wanted anyone to see them.

But there was one thing he himself *didn't* want to see. As he cautiously inched up inside the gate, looking this way and that for potential witnesses, and eased it open a mere few inches, gazing through the crack, he beheld it—the wagon and its other occupants were all gone.

* * * * *

Several minutes after sending away the man who came to take the toll empty-handed, Dekkin felt a thrill of triumph upon seeing the gate before him begin to swing open once again. *The boy is fast!* he thought to himself. But the feeling curdled when he saw not Matthew but a platoon of soldiers on kreshback led by the man who'd shouted down at the oracle and his fellows from atop the wall, coming through.

"Travelers!" the head guard called out after bringing his steed to a halt; though when he did so, he was ahead of the newcomers' own tamed beasts by but a few inches. "You must leave sight of this village at once." He grinned nastily at this display of callous power.

Coria frowned. "Why? We're doing nothing wrong."

"You are loitering," responded the soldiers' leader. "And it has been decreed that you must cease this at once lest you be *forced* to do so."

"We are not within Fetemsip's borders!" the queen countered, insistent and defensive. "You have no jurisdiction here."

"That is where you are mistaken, *my lady*." The guard tinged those last two words with ironic contempt. "All that we can see from our posts belongs to the nobles of Fetemsip."

"You brought this before the queen, and she agreed to this?" asked Coria incredulously.

"The details of the matter were indeed sent to the crown. We received no response, and after a period of several months passed, we had permission to enact the edict without her approval, as per Humanian law."

This shut Coria up, with great reluctance, and she took the reins to turn the wagon around. As she did so however, there suddenly came a murderous roar from off to her right, and Zage, his hands still bound and who'd disembarked from the back of the wagon before creeping up beside her unbeknownst to either of its coach box's current occupants, sprinted at the guard's leader from that direction before swinging them both at the other man's head, knocking him off his kresh. The queen called out to the Dark Lord, telling him to stop, but it was as if he'd lost his hearing; he crossed the short distance between himself and the soldier he'd just struck once again, crouched after taking up a position directly above the other man and began beating the armored human about the head and chest with long, brutal swings of his shackled appendages. When the kaglorite looked up from what he hoped would be the first of many victims however, he spotted the other man's comrades taking out and arming small crossbows they'd kept hidden behind their backs.

After turning around, Zage lifted up one foot just in time for an arrow to sink into the spot on the ground it had been resting a second before. He made it to the backs of the kreshes leashed to the wagon before a bolt buried itself in one of his thighs. The kaglorite fell forward, though only with a kind of pointed growl and crawled the rest of the way to the coach box, rolling and diving a few times to avoid the flurry of projectiles now aimed right at him.

"Come now, Zage!" Coria chided as if he'd merely committed a social faux pas instead of nearly cracking a man's head open. "Why would you do that?"

Zage's expression was part gleeful grin, part pained grimace as he reached for the arrow embedded in his thigh. "It felt *amazing*!"

"Oh yes?" interjected Dekkin. "How does the bolt in your leg feel? Good?"

The kaglorite was too preoccupied with ripping the projectile from his flesh to provide a retort.

"What do we do?" the queen fretted aloud as she brought the wagon about and began driving it to safety. "Matthew is still back there, and there's no other way to head east from here."

"Either we'll have to hatch a new plan to collect him, or he'll have to save himself, and we'll need to find a new way to clear Fetemsip regardless of what happens," replied the oracle grimly. "The odds aren't with us in both cases."

Coria didn't reply, as there were soldiers in pursuit and arrows flying over her head or into the wagon. She had become focused entirely on the path before her and made it race by as fast as possible. She was like the immortal when he drove however, seeing only the ground immediately ahead, and so when he called out, "Rock. *Rock. Coria, Rock!*" she didn't pick up on it until it was too late.

The wagon's front right wheel hit the tall outcropping Dekkin had been referencing, and its whole back compartment bounced up high enough to turn the stomach and shake the oracle, who was still mostly immobile, off the coach box to hit the ground behind it.

"Keep going!" the immortal shouted after the queen, reading her mind even without seeing her begin to come about again. "Try to find another way in! Matthew and I shall try to break free and do the same!"

Coria at first rejected the notion with all her heart but then realized she'd never stand a chance against numbers like those massed against them behind the wagon without the help of an unbound Zage…something even someone as trusting as she was unprepared to allow. Instead, the queen righted course and disappeared from the guards' view as they stopped to surround Dekkin, load him onto one of their horses, and ride back to town, the gargantuan gate thicker than any two of them put together slamming shut behind them.

* * * * *

Matthew had tears in his eyes as he milled aimlessly about Fetemsip, his stomach grumbling and his feet aching, unbeknownst to him, with every step. After an hour of this, he was ready to give up and begin making plans to head west when he walked by a thin alleyway where two other children were gathered and speaking to each other in hushed tones.

"They're going to *execute him* tomorrow," said one to the other giddily.

"My brother said he's an oracle, the human oracle," the second responded in awe.

"Your brother lies!" The first child waved away the suggestion dismissively. "He hasn't been to these parts in centuries."

The lorm came to a halt as these words reached his ears and doubled back to approach the two speakers. "This man you're talking about, where is he now? Do you know?"

The other children started at the sound of his voice and even after taking in a view of him gazed upon the lorm as if he were a growling ghost. Matthew was beginning to think it was due to his race until one of them asked quietly, "If I tell you, will you promise not to tell our parents we were discussing it?"

The lorm nodded, taking on the others' air of solemnity. "I promise."

He was directed to a large square in the middle of town, where Dekkin had been tied to the top of a stake much taller than himself. The boy looked around anxiously and, finding no one in view, climbed up to cut the oracle down. The immortal was still unable to move his legs, and Matthew hadn't the strength to carry him, so the latter had no choice but to drag the former along the cobblestones beneath them to the closest alleyway. Once there, each of them brought the other up to speed.

"Left together, Coria and that moronic kaglorite will decide on a frontal assault in short order," predicted Dekkin with disdain. "Go to the gate and open it when you hear them approaching." The oracle who made note of his surroundings when he was being transported to the square then directed the boy to drag him into another alleyway directly adjacent to the village's main street, where he could hide until the wagon came by on its way out of town and then be swiftly retrieved.

SEEDS IN THE SAND

The lorm found his way back to the appropriate gate with some difficulty and hid from view behind one side of a squat hovel until he heard the soldiers atop the wall calling out to each other in alarm and loosing arrows at something beyond the village's borders. Matthew then walked inside the gate and, with great effort, pushed it open completely. Sure enough, there Coria and an unshackled Zage were sitting on the wagon's coach box and racing it toward the village. Both of them were surprised, but while the queen lit up, the kaglorite, one hand surrounded by red magic, looked disappointed. Instead of extinguishing the crimson glow, he lobbed it at a section of the wall off to one side. The boy smiled affectionately at Coria and Zage as he watched the former turn to say something to the latter, knowing the Dark Lord was being chastised, albeit lightly.

The lorm caught the queen up after leaping into her lap as the wagon was passing him and clambering over her to sit between her and the kaglorite. Only a few seconds after the intruders entered Fetemsip, the clanging call of a warning bell sounded from atop the wall, and within a minute, soldiers began appearing ahead of them on foot in an attempt to cut the invaders off. Zage startled most of them with a volley of red magic long enough for the wagon to pass and put enough distance between them as to make pursuit impossible, and once a select few on kreshback of the necessary disposition and location started sidling up to the vehicle, Coria handed Matthew the reins and went to work beating them back with her weapon.

When the alleyway within which the immortal was sitting like a beggar came into view, the queen was clashing with a mounted soldier to her left, careful not to strike or slice the boy by accident as they battled over and beside him, but no one in the street was riding on the right and therefore cutting Dekkin off from the others.

"Take the reins in your left hand and hold onto me with your right!" Matthew said to Zage.

The bulk of the wagon's back compartment prevented them from being able to grab Dekkin on the fly unless they did as the boy said. The kaglorite obeyed, and the lorm's heart pounded even faster than it already had been, something he would've thought impossible a moment ago, as he hung off the side of the speeding vehicle, arms outstretched, face inches from the street racing by below him, kept from the harsh scrape of its embrace only by the grip of an unrepentant murderer's single hand. The oracle inched forward with his hands as the wagon drew closer, and fortunately, at the moment of truth, he and Matthew were able to link each of their sets to the other. Unfortunately, the boy still didn't have enough strength to lift the immortal up (something he, in the heat of the moment and with very limited time, failed to take into account), and Dekkin winced as his unmoving legs dragged against the street behind him.

"Pull me up!" yelled Matthew at Zage.

The kaglorite answered gruffly in the affirmative and lifted his right arm with complete confidence only for it to stop after moving only a few inches, though it was supplied with all his might. Thanking the gods that no one around him was able to see him blush in embarrassment, Zage hastily evaluated his options. If he took his left hand off the reins to pull Dekkin and Matthew up, he'd need to retake them in time to keep the kreshes pulling the wagon from having to screech to a halt before the front of one of the houses lining the street they were racing down if the twin beasts began listing to one side of the avenue once the guidance of a higher intelligence had gone. Seeing no alternative and remaining assured of his unwavering competence in spite of recent evidence to the contrary, the kaglorite did just that. The kreshes pulling the wagon were inches away from stone when Zage finished hoisting the lorm and the oracle up and snatched the reins before yanking them leftward to get the creatures back on course.

Matthew squirmed as he sat crammed on the coach box with the others. When next he looked to their right, another guard astride a kresh materialized, and Zage was in the midst of fending him off. Coria was likewise occupied on her side. The boy got to savor the simplicity of merely minding the road for a total of four seconds before his reverie, the eye of a storm, was abruptly interrupted by a loud thump behind him. He started and looked over one shoulder to find an enterprising young soldier that had laid in wait for the wagon atop the roof of a building directly beside the main street and leaped upon the top of the speeding vehicle at just the right moment as it passed. The lorm instinctively offered no response other than to return his gaze to the road, thinking someone else would step in to take care of the problem, as was typical. But then reality hit him like a high-speed collision with one of the houses lining the street they found themselves on—no one was stepping in. Coria and Zage were otherwise engaged, and Dekkin still couldn't move his lower body, not to mention the fact that he couldn't fight off a newborn caneo on his best day. No. It was up to Matthew.

As the boy clambered up onto the top of the wagon to face the intruding guard, he felt like his own personal world was a greased marble he'd never seen before in the palm of his hand as he stood; it seemed nigh impossible to keep it from slipping out his grip and shattering on the floor, taking all of existence with it, especially given that it was entirely new to him. And if that happened, the blame would rest solely on his shoulders. His hands shook as he unsheathed the twin daggers at his hips, and when the soldier before the lorm raised his own weapon, a standard sword, over his head in preparation for a downward strike, Matthew froze long enough to nearly spell his doom; in the last handful of seconds, he managed to raise one knife up to block the swing.

The boy stabbed at his opponent's groin after the latter withdrew from his initial assault, but the lorm's movements were ponderous and therefore easily evaded. And when the soldier swiped down at him once again, and Matthew tried dodging to one side, he came up short, and the blade caught the edge of one of his arms, slicing off a layer of green skin there. The boy cried out in agony as blood of cobalt streamed down the wounded appendage, and as he looked at the guard before him, fear for his life melded with the responsibility-induced anxiety that already had him in its grip, paralyzing him completely. As the guard raised his sword once more, the lorm's mind raced; he knew he should have thought of something profound or come to some depthful realization in what it would seem were to be his final moments, but everything was happening much too quickly for that. Just before his opponent swung his sword though, Matthew heard Zage barking out insults and expletives at the man he was dueling, and the sound of the kaglorite's voice took the boy back to the previous night...

* * * * *

The lorm had been practicing his knife fighting with Coria at a short distance from the crackling fire they and the others had eaten their dinner around. Just like the battle with the soldier Matthew now found himself in, when he fought against the queen that night, he came up short in every department; his attacks were either too slow or with force insufficient enough to be easily batted away, and his defense was tepid and brittle. Zage watched the fight closely, and Dekkin glanced over at it when no one else would notice though infrequently.

"Stop!" the kaglorite called out after Coria knocked both daggers out of the lorm's hands. "Stop. I would advise the boy." Zage walked over to Matthew and, placing one hand on the scruff of the latter's neck (a movement that sent a chill down the lorm's spine), steered him a short distance away from his teacher. "Listen well," murmured the kaglorite once he brought them both to a halt.

"There's no need for"—the boy began before he was pointedly shushed by Zage—"there's no need for secrecy," continued Matthew at a whisper. "It's just practice."

The kaglorite threw up his hands. "And *that* is the issue. That is why you cannot perform in combat. You're impassive, detached. A great warrior uses *emotion* when he fights."

The lorm considered this. "But...does passion not cloud the mind? *Hinder* a warrior?"

Zage gave a reluctant nod. "Yes, there are many fighters whose central flaw is an overabundance of heart, who must therefore work to rein in their emotions. But you are not one of them. You must work to *feel* deeply on the battlefield."

"Even rage?" Matthew inquired further dubiously.

"Yes," exclaimed the kaglorite, "rage *especially*. It is the most powerful, the most *important* emotion. The next time you take on an opponent, you must *enrage* yourself. Understood?"

The boy nodded and put forth much effort to follow Zage's instruction but continued to be trounced by his sparring partner throughout the rest of the night.

* * * * *

All this flashed back into Matthew's mind in a fraction of a second, and in the next, he thought about what would happen if the soldier before him had his way. He imagined himself being killed at only twelve years old, and he imagined the painful deaths of the other three members of his party—Coria, who made him feel strangely warm every time she spoke to or even just looked at him; Dekkin, who was so cold and prickly and yet hadn't killed him when the oracle had had the chance, choosing instead to bring him along on an extended journey as a prisoner, expending no small amount of time and energy in the process; and Zage, who spat hatred often directed at him or the Lormish people or both every other minute but still attempted to connect with him, teach him things.

The boy felt nothing at the thought of his own demise, but picturing his newfound companions having their lives brutally ripped from their breasts, in spite of the nature of his association with them, incited pure fury within him. Every part of his body tensed, and unbridled energy rushed through it like he'd just eaten several large sugar cubes at once. The lorm lifted one of his knives to block the swing that would've cleaved his head in two while with the other he stabbed out at the opening in his opponent's defenses. The soldier released his naked left hand's grip on the hilt of his sword and grabbed the advancing blade. Though said hand was soon slippery with blood as the dual sides of the dagger dug into its flesh, for a moment, the guard halted its motion completely. However, Matthew merely stoked the fire inside him and, with a battle cry that managed to intimidate in its volume in spite of his voice's light, thin quality, shoved the tip of the knife deep into the soldier's gut. His victim dropped his sword, which clattered to the wood beneath him before sliding off it, and clutched at the dagger in his stomach, his eyes wide and his mouth hanging slightly agape, and before he could do anything more, his attacker sprinted across the distance between them and shoved the man backward and off the wagon's top to slam into the road below it, long strips of his skin tearing off as he tumbled along it.

The lorm turned around to find, to his great dismay, that none of the others saw the fight and, to his immense relief, that the crowds of riders on either side of the wagon's front were gone after being thinned by Coria and Zage over the course of the last several minutes.

"A head-on assault worked fine after all, no problem!" the queen said brightly.

At that moment, the far gate came into view, and the small army massed before it on foot too.

"So *that's* no problem, eh?" replied Dekkin as he pointed at the living barricade in the distance.

Coria shook his retort away, a little sheepish. "Yes, yes. Does anyone have any ideas?"

Without responding, Zage stood and, summoning a ball of red magic in one hand, lobbed it. The projectile connected perfectly with and consumed completely the top hinge on the right door. Conjuring a second, he threw this time toward the bottom one, once again with flawless accuracy even in spite of the considerable range between himself (who was also, after all, in swift motion) and his target. His gamble paid off; the door fell backward with a guttural groan, and the soldiers before it were either forced to scatter or failed to do so in time and were crushed like honeycomb beneath a pestle. As the kreshes pulling the wagon stepped over the bridge of a door, the survivors of its descent attempted to rally in one last attempt at capturing the intruders but to no avail; Dekkin and the others had too much of a head start by the time they were able to marshal their forces.

"Well, now!" the queen said to her fellows once their pursuers faded into the distance behind them. "If we hadn't done that, we would've had to pay that ridiculous toll." The other three—Dekkin with his lame legs, Zage sporting a hole in one thigh, and even Matthew cradling the scrape along one of his arms—stared daggers at her.

9

"DEKKIN, DO YOU THINK it might be time to give up on this ill-advised quest?"

The brown-haired man rolled his eyes at his father's question, several dozen iterations after the original, and shook his head. "*No*, Father, not just yet. If there's something beyond the forest, the forest itself must be vast. Otherwise, someone else would've discovered another part of the world before us."

Dekkin's father raised his brow. "Oh! '*If* there's something beyond the forest'? You're not certain any longer?"

His son couldn't lie to himself and deny it, after weeks of travel through miles of homogeneous greenery, but he could to the older man. Just as he was preparing to however, his mother piped up, "Biu, leave the boy alone. The others give him enough grief over his theories without his father chipping in." She smiled at Dekkin sweetly. "*I* think you're right, son."

The young man grinned back. "Thank you, Mother."

"That's it," said his father, playfully gruff. "It's happening at last. Dekkin, I'm leaving your mother hopefully for a much younger woman. In fact, how've things been between you and your wife lately?"

"I can hear you!" Seren, her hair red as blood but with light-brown skin called out with good nature a short distance away, quickening her pace to catch up to her husband and his parents.

"Well, what do you think?" asked Dekkin mock-solemnly. "Is our union in peril?"

His wife shook her head and giggled. "No, my father was much older than my mother, and I swore to myself when he died, so long before her, that I would never be with an aged man, for the sake of our children." She burst out laughing when her husband pantomimed great relief.

"Father, what will you do if there *isn't* anything outside the forest?" their son, his tone a little pouty from having to walk for so long, inquired as he walked beside Seren hand in hand.

Dekkin shrugged as he smiled down at Anter. "Well, I'll simply…go back to doing what I used to."

"You won't be sad because it turned out you were wrong?"

A look of concession crossed his father's face. "Yes, I'll be a little sad, I suppose." A smile made his cheeks shoot up like well-watered saplings. "But I don't *need* my theory to be true. Here, under the trees, there's plenty to eat. The gods bless us with fair weather most of the time, and we have shelters to protect us when it's not. There's hardly any strife between the members of our tribe. Our lives are long, *decades* long."

Anter's face screwed up in confusion. "Then why did you want to go to all this effort to search for somewhere new?"

Dekkin thought on this for a moment. "Because if there *is* more to the world than trees and grass, then it might be even better."

"But it could be worse too," pointed out his son.

Dekkin nodded. "Yes, I suppose. But I have lived for twenty-five years, and in that time, I've reached out for the unknown every chance I've gotten. And you know what, Anter? I've never regretted it."

The boy's expression became incredulous. "*Never?* You lie, Father."

"No, never!" Dekkin insisted. "When our tribe was but a dozen strong and we first encountered another, when I was a boy, I was the one who convinced both sides to unite their forces. I began pursuing your mother when I'd only known her for a few days. And I sired *you*, though I'd never had children."

A gust so hot it burned as it blew against his head from the front made him look up from his son to find a sight neither he nor any of his tribemates had ever beheld. It was so far off into the distance that Dekkin wondered if his eyes were playing tricks on him, and he began running to it, motioning for the others to follow suit while several of them offered exclamations of confused wonder as they registered the contents of the horizon. The forest's moderate temperature increased steadily as they drew closer to the otherland, their lips growing chapped as they moved. With each step toward the place beyond the green, it remained and blossomed (figuratively, that is), and after a certain point, Dekkin came to see that it was without doubt real.

There were no trees to shield the lower reaches of the otherland from the sun's rays, and the result was an area so bright he was forced to squint until only a sliver of vision remained to him, and after doing so for some time, his head began to ache. The terrain's height was much more varied than that of the forest; there were more hills large and small across it than patches of level footing. The heat within it was such that even after but a few minutes of exposure, Dekkin grew light-headed and ravenously thirsty. But the most immediately noticeable facet of the otherland was what seemed to serve as dirt there; it was yellow as honey and had a sort of loose quality to it, flowing like water when the wind, as unabated due to the lack of natural obstacles as the sun, whipped across it.

Dekkin turned around with an exultant grin, waving the others forward. "Come! Let us explore this new land!" Many of his tribemates cast dubious gazes at the otherland before them as they fanned themselves furiously with one or both their hands, but he didn't notice the heat. All Dekkin was thinking of as he led the others out of the forest was the soft feel of the ground beneath his feet.

* * * * *

Dekkin's brow raised as he heard Matthew humming while the boy mended the tear in his shirt that night.

"*You're* in good spirits," observed the oracle to the lorm sitting to his left of him around the fire.

They entered Humania's wetlands, and though none of the wagon's current occupants cared a whit about the sticky dark-brown mud there coating soon its wheels and the bottom of its back compartment, it did force them to search for much longer than usual in pursuit of a place to start a fire and make camp. In the end, they'd settled on the first hill tall enough to reach well and truly over the standing water surrounding them now.

Guilt rushed across Matthew's face faster than he could conceal it, as if he'd been caught in an indecent act, and he stopped midtune. "Ah…n—yes. My dinner was…most delectable."

The immortal knew at once this was a lie, and not just from the nonverbal cues he was picking up from the boy. When it was time for dinner and Dekkin saw the lorm standing before and looking back and forth indecisively at the culinary options in the back of the wagon once again, the oracle offered to select a meal for Matthew. The boy lit up and gratefully accepted, and the immortal with a hidden, malicious grin put together a grouping of the most poor-tasting, albeit nutritional, foodstuffs available before watching with nasty glee as the lorm visibly struggled to get it down. Strangely enough, after observing Matthew's pained grimace for a while, Dekkin developed a feeling in his gut, one that was as if his innards had been hurled off a tall cliff. Deciding that something in his own dinner must disagree with him, the oracle pitched the remainder of it into the damp grass around them. "Why, are you truly?"

The boy's mouth fell open very slightly in disbelief at the failure of his flimsy facade and, after a moment's hesitation, answered, "I enjoy mending clothes."

The oracle nodded. "Ah, why do you look like I've just caught you holding someone up in a dark alley?"

"Well, it's not very fitting for a warrior's apprentice," the lorm pointed out.

"Yes," conceded the immortal, "what of it? You like what you like. I cannot abide those who would deny themselves pleasure for no good reason."

Matthew wilted a bit. "You dislike me, don't you?"

SEEDS IN THE SAND

Dekkin shrugged and averted his eyes. "No more than I do anyone else." This brought a smile to the boy's face, and when the oracle spotted this after returning his gaze to it, he began to examine the stars. "So a boy enjoys tailoring but ends up volunteering to apprentice with a traveling swordsman? A strange choice to be sure."

Beyond the immortal's field of view, the lorm's features took on a glum quality. "I didn't volunteer. I was chosen."

Dekkin's eyes were wide as he looked back down at Matthew. "You became Cornelius Arcind's apprentice against your will?"

"Well, I wouldn't say that," the boy said with a vehement shake of his head. "It's simply not something I would've agreed to of my own volition."

The oracle furrowed his brow in exasperation. "How is that any different?" The lorm was at a loss for words at this. "So you were picked, based on your abilities."

"Not...exactly, no." Strangely enough, his reticence didn't seem to be for his own sake.

The immortal waited for Matthew to elaborate before, when the boy didn't, snapping, "How were you chosen then?"

"My father"—the corners of the lorm's mouth dropped as he said those words—"is the prime minister of the Lormish Isles. He thought it would bring our family honor for me to travel with Master Arcind, so he...arranged for it six years ago."

Dekkin started. "Did you say *six* years ago?" Matthew answered in the affirmative. "How old are you now?"

"Twelve."

"So you were six when you were sent away from your parents."

The boy winced when he heard the end of this statement for reasons the oracle couldn't deduce.

"That...that's *wrong*."

"I...I can understand why he did it," replied the lorm meekly.

"Just because you can understand it doesn't mean it's right," the immortal countered. "I didn't know how to *feed myself* when I was six. And the path of your future was forced on you besides." Dekkin closed his mouth, opened it, shut it once more, and then finally said with his eyes to the ground, "I'm sorry that happened to you."

Matthew was visibly taken aback by this but was after a moment glowing, something the oracle spied at his periphery.

* * * * *

Shortly before the beginning of this conversation, Zage announced his need to relieve himself and was escorted out of sight of the others by Coria, his hands bound. When the kaglorite reached a point at which anyone else who was searching for a place of discretion would, satisfied, halt, he kept going, but the queen, glad at the chance for some exercise after a day entirely spent sitting, allowed this, continuing to follow him closely. Several minutes passed before she recognized that the kaglorite could be luring her away from camp in order to face a diminished level of resistance while attacking her, but just as her body began to tense and one of her hands began drifting to the hilt of the weapon on her back, he came to a halt and looked back at her.

"Pick this up for me, woman," instructed Zage brusquely, pointing to a sapling at his feet with his shackled appendages.

Coria stepped to the side and angled her body and head in order to get a better look at it, seeing after she did so that it was a burgeoning kumakala. The kumakala tree was originally native to the seabed beneath the Lormish Isles, and the large circular fruit it produced remained a popular breakfast item among its indigenous people. Humans were first made aware of the kumakala fruit's existence during the first-ever meeting between them and the island dwellers, and it became an instant sensation among the people of the plains. However, in an uncharacteristically assertive move, the Lormish government denied their new allies permission to transport kumakala seeds back to Humania, as they recognized the value of maintaining a monopoly on such an in-demand product. The humans agreed to their terms, only consuming the fruit within Lormish territory and abiding by the prohibition on exportation…for a time. When the isles became a dominion of Humania in the aftermath of the Kaglorite Massacre, the chief royal adviser, Samuel Roneage, quietly broke with the recently established convention and had literal tons of kumakala fruit and seeds shipped to Cobaltus, where a team of the country's best botanists got to work breeding a variety of the tree that could flourish outside Lormish salt water. They managed to produce a strain of kumakala capable of growing in the freshwater abounding in Humania but were unable to make it such that it could grow entirely in the open air; the soil immediately surrounding the roots needed to be completely submerged, the base of the trunk too, and so Humania's eastern wetlands became the kumakala capital of Samu. In response to the outcry of his citizens, Prime Minister Ben of the Lormish Isles publicly objected to this violation of their agreement with the humans as his country's economy floundered without its exclusive rights to the prized fruit, but when it came time to track down the formal documents which sealed the deal between the two peoples long ago, they were all found to be mysteriously missing, and the matter was dropped without any further action from the plaintiffs in question.

Coria walked over to the sapling and thought she was obeying Zage's command as she grabbed the kumakala by its spindly trunk, but then the kaglorite barked, "STOP! STOP!" She froze and gazed up at him quizzically. "Not just the plant," Zage continued by way of clarification, "pull it out with the mound of soil just around the roots."

The queen raised one eyebrow but acquiesced, and soon mud stained the insides of her fingernails as she held up the growth and the earth encompassing its feet.

The kaglorite gestured to the pot he'd had her bring with them; she guessed for the purpose of storing waste though there was no reason she could see to do so out on the open road. "Good. Now put it inside that."

Coria did so, but it wasn't until he had her fill the bottom of the receptacle with some water that she understood what was happening.

"You want to grow fruit?" asked the queen in surprise.

"Yes," Zage confirmed as nonchalantly as if the answer to that question was self-evident.

"Huh." She followed him as he led her back to camp.

"What?" said the kaglorite irritably at this, looking over one shoulder at her.

Coria waved her free hand sheepishly. "It's nothing! I simply… wouldn't have guessed you had an interest in agriculture."

Zage turned his head back around. "Of course, I do. That's true of all kaglorites."

"Really?" the queen replied with incredulity.

"Yes." The kaglorite seemed confused by her response. "Farming is the most important task of all. Only the most skilled and intelligent workers are allowed to do it, and they are regarded as society's highest class. Is that not true of human culture as well?"

Coria shook her head. "No. Quite the opposite, actually."

"Hmm"—Zage considered this—"I suppose that makes sense, now that I think of it. You spoiled humans have more farmland than you would know what to do with."

The queen's eyes narrowed as questions came to her mind. "I didn't know there was any farmland at all in Kagloris. Did not the massacre render its earth infertile?"

"Not all, remember? And besides, a—" Since the kaglorite wasn't facing Coria, she couldn't see the pain that flitted across his violet face. "There is a breed of vegetable that we're able to grow even in our desiccated soil, though even then, only a few out of several hundred survive long enough to be harvested."

"Ah," said the queen, "so back in Kagloris, you're a farmer?"

Zage shook his head. "No, I could have been one, but I am the strongest magic user among my people, so I had to be a warrior." He turned around as he kept moving and gazed intently at the potted plant in Coria's grasp.

"What is it?" she asked after a moment.

The kaglorite pressed his lips together. "It is not growing."

The queen frowned. "Well…yes, of course. It takes weeks for a sapling like this to get to full size."

Zage took this in and, after a beat, said, "Forget about it. Leave it behind."

"What?" replied Coria. "It'll grow into a tree if you take care of it. You just need to give it time."

The kaglorite scowled stubbornly. "No, I do not want it anymore."

The queen opened her mouth to say something but balked at his forbidding expression and, after a handful of seconds, knelt to remove the sapling from the pot and replant it among its brethren.

* * * * *

Back at camp, Matthew had been staring into the fire for some time before his ears picked up the telltale scritching of a pencil on paper by his side. Looking over in the direction of the noise, he saw the oracle writing in a thick pocketbook.

"Dekkin?" the boy said then.

The immortal's brow furrowed at the interruption. "Yes?"

"What are you writing?"

The tip of Dekkin's pencil paused without leaving the paper beneath it. "It's a sort of journal, I suppose. A long time ago, I began a chronicle of my entire life, a way to pass the time while I'm here, and...a record of what I did when I'm not."

"So you're a writer," concluded the lorm.

The oracle shook his head in an ephemeral gesture. "I wouldn't go that far, no."

Matthew frowned. "But...you're writing, a lot. What else would you call someone who does that?"

"It's not as though I'm inventing a story, speaking as a character separate from myself," the immortal countered. "I'm simply dictating my thoughts, my experiences, talking to myself essentially, and talking isn't writing."

The boy shied away from further objection initially, but then something he'd never before felt and couldn't have identified moved his tongue for him like it was a tentative child being pushed into a pond from behind by one of his friends. "Sure, it is. You're talking to your audience."

Dekkin grunted and went back to writing. The lorm looked off into the inky darkness around them to mask the oracle's surly expression from his view and, after a moment of this, got up the nerve to reopen the conversation, asking, "How many other people have read what you've written?"

The immortal held up one hand, forming with it a zero.

Matthew started in surprise. "Truly, none?"

"I'm five hundred thirteen years old," replied Dekkin. "My memoir is so long it's had to be divided into multiple volumes, each running about a thousand pages, and there're enough of them to fill an entire bookcase. I've never met someone willing to sift through all of that, if you can believe it."

"Have you ever *asked* somebody to read to them?" the boy challenged.

At this, the oracle said nothing. "*I'll* read them."

The immortal scoffed. "An empty promise."

The lorm leaned toward him. "No, I'm serious. I'll read them, all of them. Five hundred thirteen years…I'm sure you've led an interesting life."

Dekkin nodded. "Samu is a much different place than it was when I was a boy like you." The sound of graphite curving and looping atop paper began to slow until, after half a minute, it ceased completely. The oracle glanced over at Matthew hesitantly. "You truly want to read them?"

"Yes," insisted the boy, "please let me, sometime."

The immortal cracked the slightest of smiles. "I haven't spoken to children in centuries. I had forgotten what they were like."

"What they're like?" the lorm reiterated quizzically. "And what *are* they like?"

"They're naive enough to think it's worth it, devoting energy to kindness."

"Or maybe children possess more wisdom than adults," pointed out Matthew.

"So people's wisdom decreases as they get older. That's your theory," Dekkin surmised. "Well, what does that make me then?" He fixed the boy with a harsh glare, then chuckled at the latter's mortified expression. "I jest. Or rather, there's no need for anguish. Relax. I'm not your master."

Matthew motioned toward his pedibus as it sat sleeping in its cage in the grass. "But you've got me in handcuffs." He'd meant it as a joke, but it came out flat. The oracle's face fell, and with a glower, he was back to his writing. The boy wanted to apologize, explain himself, get back to talking with this ill-tempered yet intermittently good man, but this time, when he went to do so, he got in his own way like he usually did, and what they'd shared for a few fleeting minutes vanished as if it had never existed in the first place, like a dream did upon the awakening of the dreamer.

After a while, the fire Dekkin and Matthew were sitting around came back into view for Coria and Zage, a point of light in the distance and above them like a firefly. However, the queen ended up stopping well short of it, to stroke the feathers of the kreshes carrying them across Humania. Seeing what she was doing out of the corner of his eye, the kaglorite went to her side, asking her, "You like kreshes?"

"I like all varieties of animal," replied Coria as the kresh she was petting purred loudly at her touch.

"You like the subservience they possess, like your subjects," Zage presumed, a storm passing over his face.

The queen shook her head immediately and with confidence. "No. I've never thought about why I like them, but I'm certain it's not that." Her gaze dropped out of focus, and the hand she was running through the kresh's feathers fell still, causing the creature to nudge the woman in a demand for the return of her attention. "I suppose...I like animals, domesticated and otherwise, for a trait of each group, one being entirely separate from the other. The notion of a domesticated animal has always seemed to me tragic. They may be safe from most harm unlike their wild cousins, but they're also kept in cages, told everything they can and can't do and when. For some reason, I'm drawn to that. And *un*domesticated animals, they go where they want, do what they like. I appreciate that about them. So I like them both, for completely opposite reasons, and I haven't the foggiest why in either case."

"Hmm." The kaglorite reached up to caress the spot right along the bottom of the kresh's jaw, and it nuzzled the hand he did it with.

Coria raised her brow in surprise. "You know about the kreshes' sweet spot?"

"Of course, I do," replied Zage, shooting her a gruff glare. "They're the most popular mount in all of Samu. You thought just because I am a kaglorite I wouldn't know how to handle animals gently?"

"No!" the queen responded defensively. "I just wouldn't have guessed that you, specifically, would have a rapport with animals. Why do you always jump to the worst conclusion?" She paused and, after some introspection, admitted reluctantly, "Actually, I suppose on some level I did, yes. …I'm sorry."

The kaglorite said nothing, and his jaw remained tight.

Coria returned to her spot around the fire like a caneo with its tail between its legs, hoping to find a lighter atmosphere, but no sooner had she sat down than Dekkin started grumbling to himself and violently crossing out entire lines in his notebook.

"What's wrong?" asked the queen.

"It's *shit*!" the oracle cried, moving to throw the entire book into the fire but thinking better of it at the last moment. "It's shit," repeated the immortal sullenly, his eyes on the grass. "Everything I try to write turns out like shit."

Coria nodded. "Yes, yes, it's all shit."

Dekkin started and, eyeing her dubiously, responded, "What was that?"

"You're correct," the queen confirmed, seemingly sincere. "No matter what you do, it never turns out right. The whole thing's a terrible pursuit."

The oracle's eyes narrowed. "What are you doing?"

"Trying something out," answered Coria. "My natural personality seems to turn you off, and I'm nothing if not a people pleaser, so from now on, I'll don a different persona for you, one that aligns with your own. How's that sound?"

The immortal considered this before replying, "That sounds great. Thank you." He genuinely meant that, but as with everything he said, it came out sounding sardonic. For the rest of the night, every time Dekkin complained about something, the queen would egg him on. And then rather than his frustration and anger being exacerbated by resistance to it from others, he was able to let out the steam inside him.

10

SEVERAL DAYS LATER, AS Dekkin drove the wagon and chatted with Matthew, he had no idea—as is the case with everyone whose fortunes are about to take a turn for the worse—that in a few minutes, he'd be lying paralyzed in the mud beneath him. The oracle was describing the plot of his favorite novel, which was several hundred years old and of which he possessed the only remaining copy, when they hit a sizable bump in the road he didn't notice beforehand since his gaze was focused on the boy at his side. The wagon and all its occupants jumped a good ways, and the immortal fell to his left after they came down hard immediately thereafter. His flask of Destiny Water was thrown from the pocket it called home, and as Dekkin fastened the cap very loosely when last he'd closed it, some of its contents spilled into his open mouth. He swallowed on instinct before he could think better of it, and suddenly, he was a man out of time and space.

    The lorm said the oracle's name to him quizzically after the man didn't stir for a short while. Receiving no response, Matthew repeated it with urgency and then once more in anguish, grabbing the immortal by the shoulders and shaking him a little. Panic began to take over the boy's face when still he got no response, but then his gaze fell to the open flask lying atop the man's neck, sprinkling it with drops of Destiny as he was waggled. His nerves as easily frazzled as they were, the lorm started as he screwed the cap back on the minuscule container when Coria pushed aside the slat at the front of the wagon's back compartment with a metallic scrape.

"What was *that*?" the queen asked, her eyes wide.

Matthew explained what happened.

She nodded. "I'll have to take the reins then." Coria stepped off the wagon and walked around to the coach box before clambering up onto it and moving the immobile Dekkin out of the way, took the driver's seat, whipping the kreshes to get them going once again.

Beside her, the oracle screamed in silence. He strained himself trying to grab her right arm with his left hand because he'd just come out of the vision that the water had brought him. In it, the wagon stood in the middle of a swamp, its wheels almost completely submerged in murky green water. Its current occupants were scattered around outside it, but only Zage was on his feet; the others were floating face up, motionless, as blood gushed from their many open wounds, tainting further the surrounding scummy pond's other contents immediately around them. And the kaglorite was flashing a grin of vicious triumph as he looked down at them.

The queen struck up a conversation with the boy sitting beside her, as you would expect, and with his eyes on her as they talked, he hadn't looked at the road ahead of them for some time when the wagon suddenly came to a complete halt. Casting his quizzical gaze forward, the lorm saw a fork in the path straight ahead of and directly before them. To the left, the ground rose to a narrow ledge in the ever-present mountains, and to the right, it fell into a dense swamp.

"Wh-which way do you think should we go?" inquired Coria, her eyes flicking back and forth between the two options in an uncharacteristically anxious motion.

"I don't know," Matthew answered. As the apprentice of Humania's foremost adventurer, he should've by all rights known a thing or two about the country's geography, but Cornelius had never bothered to school him in it or insist that he receive such instruction from elsewhere; after all, what was the point of that when his master was never incapacitated and already knew every inch of the map by heart?

"W-well, I don't know what to do," said the queen insistently, turning her body toward the boy as much as she could and looking over at him.

"You'll have to pick a path," the lorm replied lightly.

Coria thought on this for a moment. "C-could you do it?"

"What?" responded Matthew with a confused frown. "No, I'm sorry. I'm but a child, after all."

The queen grimaced but nodded at this. There was a moment of still silence between the two of them for a handful of seconds. Then she looked over one shoulder at the slat in the front of the wagon's back compartment and slid it open, saying into the thin opening this created, "Zage! You traveled this way when you were coming to Cobaltus with the other kaglorites, yes?"

"Yes," Zage confirmed, rising to a crouch and shuffling up to the slit.

Coria explained the situation, describing where they now found themselves, and immediately after she finished, the kaglorite declared, "We must go through the swamp."

"The swamp?" repeated the queen with furrowed brow as she looked back around at the invitingly plain leftward path beside the disquieting pool of sludge on the right.

Zage nodded. "Oh yes, we have no choice. That ledge leads to a dead end. The only way across this stretch in either direction is through the swamp."

Coria's eyes widened in realization. "Oh, all right. Thank you, Zage." As the kaglorite grunted in response and shut the slat between them for her, she turned the wagon to the right and began riding down the hill leading to the swamp. Just beside her, Dekkin was furiously blinking, hoping that this would attract either her or Matthew's attention and give them pause long enough for his mouth to unfreeze. But neither of them glanced his way as the wagon's wheels descended into watery sludge.

The swamp was so humid it felt like a lukewarm sauna to those few unfortunate enough to find themselves there. Flying insects buzzed around Coria and Matthew's faces, sometimes in swarms; every other second, one of them was swiping the bugs away in irritation that increased incrementally with each frustrated movement. There are no words to describe the smell, which made even Zage, sitting in the comfort of the wagon's mostly enclosed back compartment, cover his nose beneath the top of his shirt (no one thought to do this for the paralyzed Dekkin, which dismayed him nearly as much as their impending doom when he caught his first whiff of the air in the swamp). The two areas in which our beleaguered heroes could count themselves lucky was that no creature larger or more hostile than a small fish was awake during the day, and provided one traveled at a steady pace, they could pitch camp at day's end relatively far from the natural borders of the swamp.

As you could imagine, Coria was already quite on edge as she directed the kreshes, visibly repulsed and refusing to move unless under insistent and pointed prodding, pulling the wagon, and it certainly didn't help matters when she spotted smoke rising off the surface of the water up in the distance.

"Uh, Zage?" the queen quavered through the slat behind her after sliding it open as she pointed at the unsettling sight before them. "What is *that*?"

"That," answered the kaglorite as he peered in the indicated direction, "is Deathsdrink. It is only ever been found in a few small areas of the swamp here. It is a liquid that melts flesh on contact, though only that and nothing else. It repels water, so there is no danger of it spreading from where it already is, but as you have probably surmised by now, we should give it a wide berth."

Coria nodded and turned the wagon to one side of the Deathsdrink. Matthew's and her entire body was as taut as keethar strings when they began to pass the smoking water, but the kreshes moved without issue, and both of the passengers at its front exhaled loudly upon seeing this. As soon as Zage could see the smoke through the thin opening below the closed doors in the back of the wagon, he crept up to the edge of the latter and slowly lowered himself into the water. He looked over one shoulder, checking if the others picked up on either of these movements, but Coria and Matthew were utterly unawares. With a malicious smirk, the kaglorite waded to the Deathsdrink and, without hesitation, plunged his shackled hands inside it. The pained screams of his pedibus as it melted went unheard by the wagon's remaining occupants, literally drowned out by the layer of water as well as the distance between them. Zage waited until he felt his hands start to burn before removing them. Now unchained, he turned to face the receding wagon and began to advance to it, no longer making any effort to mask the sound of his movements.

Dekkin waggled his tongue all around the inside of his mouth fervently as he waited to regain feeling in his lower jaw. He could've cried out as soon as his upper had unfrozen, of course, but it would do no good to say something if Coria and Matthew couldn't understand him. The two of them went back to conversing, this time clearly for the purpose of distracting themselves from their foreboding surroundings, and so were listening only for each other and not the swirling sound Zage made as he worked his way through the water back to them. The oracle, however, was drowning out their conversation (and had been ever since it had first been struck up), and because of that, picked up only too well the swish of the reaper's cloak in the distance.

The immortal felt as though the noise of flesh cutting through water was right inside his eardrums when the numbness in his lower jaw finally gave way to feeling. "Zage!" he cried out, as loud and urgent as he could. "Zage's escaped! He's going to kill us all!"

The kaglorite popped up directly beside Matthew right on cue, grabbing the boy by the shoulders and lifting him off the coach box. As Zage began to shift his grip in order to snap the boy's neck, however, the lorm bit deep into one of the kaglorite's forearms with his long white fangs. Roaring in agony and outrage, Zage instinctively dropped Matthew and cursed in reflex. As soon as the boy was underwater, he sped out of reach with the mastery of a lorm. Coria stood and whipped around to face the kaglorite, her eyes as wide as they could be, as he boarded the coach box. He grabbed for Dekkin but shied away under a barrage of blows from her balled-up fists. The queen, even in spite of her frankly unwise levels of optimism, given that she was facing a kaglorite in a one-on-one battle, resigned herself to swift defeat. She waited for a blast of red magic to tear the wagon to pieces or for blue magic to spawn a sword Zage would run her through with. She waited, and it didn't come.

The frown that'd already sprouted on Coria's face from the heat of battle deepened in confusion as she chopped the kaglorite's hands away from grabbing for a lock of her long, flowing hair. He was free. Why wasn't he using a kaglorite's greatest asset? Then it dawned on her. He didn't want to risk damaging the wagon, his only way out of the swamp before the certain death that arose there after nightfall and the fastest mode of transportation available to him for many miles around besides. This was true for the queen as well, of course, and so atop the coach box, the only type of combat each of them was willing to try in their effort to defeat the other was, for those reasons, hand to hand, and in that department, Coria felt very confident of her success indeed.

What she failed to account for, however, was that Zage was much bigger than her and even more seasoned on the battlefield, the *true* battlefield. She quickly lost control of the fight, and after taking a few heavy blows, her head was too fuzzy from the force of the impact for her to keep him from pushing her off the wagon and into the foul drink below. Spitting out a mouthful of brackish water as she surfaced, the queen spotted through the cognitive haze over her vision the kaglorite reaching for helpless Dekkin's throat. Coria screamed at her body in silence to come to the oracle's rescue, but she stumbled woozily as she rose and, with a sinking feeling in her gut, realized she couldn't save the immortal.

Zage's bellow of agony was so loud and emphatic the sound of it cut right through the fog over the queen's brain like a strong wind would to the genuine article. When he whirled around, releasing Dekkin as he did so, she spotted the source of his pain—there were several steaming burns across his back. She started to wonder what happened but brought her train of thought to a screeching halt soon after it got going, recognizing that she needed to focus entirely on clearing her head if she was to reenter the fray with her wits sufficiently about her and in time.

As Matthew was swimming away from Zage after escaping the kaglorite's clutches, his every instinct screamed at him to keep going until he hadn't the strength to move, to never look back. But then he thought of Dekkin and Coria being left alone to fight Zage themselves, and something compelled him to turn around, his limbs moving against his will as if he was a puppet whose master was moving the strings. As he sliced his way through the surrounding grotty water, he racked his brain for some way in which a boy two feet tall could turn the tide in a fight against the Dark Lord, and after a short while, something came to mind—Zage said that the Deathsdrink melted flesh…but only flesh.

The boy resurfaced at the back of the wagon, the sound of Coria and the kaglorite fighting each other at the front sending a thrill shooting through his body, and grabbed from inside it a large pan. Then the lorm sliced through the stagnant, brackish water around him to the Deathsdrink and filled it up about halfway. Just as he'd hoped, the pan was unaffected by its latest acidic contents. Wading to Zage as quickly as he could without making too much noise, Matthew approached the kaglorite from behind and placed both hands on the handle of the pan, planning to douse the kaglorite's head. But as his target came into full view, the boy saw Dekkin lying motionless as Zage began choking the life out of him. Feeling at once as though a hive of ants was crawling around under his skin and the itch they produced could only be quelled by movement, Matthew flung the Deathsdrink thoughtlessly, and it had splashed across the kaglorite's back.

The intensity of fury on Zage's face as he turned around to face his attacker, reaching for his back in a futile gesture with one hand and strangely enough clutching at one pectoral with the other, was inordinate even given what the boy had done to him. The sight of the kaglorite leaping off the coach box felt to the lorm like a splash of cold water to the face interrupting a dream; the boy furrowed his brow, mystified at how he'd come to stand where he was, what he was doing with a pan in both hands, and why Zage was after him with such zeal, his face clouded with unbridled rage. Matthew stood there frozen in thought for a split second, but at the sound of the kaglorite's feet plunging into water, the boy remembered himself and whipped around before beginning to run away as fast as the liquid chains around the bottom half of his body would allow.

In the heat of the moment, the lorm forgot about the pan in his grasp until he was several seconds into his retreat. Pitching it to one side freed up his arms, and his pace quickened, but every time he looked over one shoulder at the Dark Lord pursuing him, he saw that it wouldn't be enough. Matthew decided then to stop looking back, that he didn't want to see his doom as it approached and consumed him. No, the only indication of his short life's end in his final moments would be the set of sloshing footfalls behind him—the twin sets.

The boy furrowed his brow and broke his own, still freshly established rule, turning around. Right then, Coria, who caught up to Zage while the lorm wasn't looking, smacked the kaglorite in the back of the head with her hammer. Strangely enough, it seemed as though Zage himself didn't hear her coming. Matthew quickly recognized that now was not the time to muse over such things and scampered off the way he was heading before the queen intervened.

The queen swung at the kaglorite again as he turned to face her and cursed herself for it a second later when she saw his head and both his hands radiating red; she hadn't considered, in all the commotion, that this far from the wagon there was nothing stopping him from wielding magic. She managed to bring her weapon to a halt in time for it to narrowly avoid touching down on Zage's forehead and losing one of its ends instantly, but she couldn't retreat fast enough to keep him from reaching out with one hand and grasping the middle of its shaft, snapping it in two. Despair started drowning her stomach in the instant immediately thereafter as she stood with a hammer in one hand and a short spear in the other; she had no idea how to defend herself this way.

Her only chance was to try talking him down, the prospect of which even she recognized as incredibly dubious at best. "Why are you doing this?"

"For the same reason I killed all the humans and lorms who came before you," replied Zage with a sneer, though he did pause to deliver this declaration and give Coria time to back away a little and begin to collect herself.

"But…you need us!" the queen pointed out, confusion muddying the white waters of panic in her soul a bit. "You won't make it to the border by yourself. You need us to conceal you, take you there, and you've got a bum leg. How are you going to get all the way back to Kagloris alone?"

"You lot are replaceable," replied the kaglorite. "I will simply find another wagon heading east, threaten them into helping me."

Coria's eyes narrowed as far as they could without closing. "But why would you go to all that trouble? We've gotten you this far without turning on you. That should tell you that we can be trusted. So why wouldn't you go all the way with us? Kill us at the border, if you truly feel you have to."

"The fire in my blood defies reason, and I obey its whims above all else." As that last word left his lips, the queen suddenly rushed him, and he raised both hands up slightly, palms facing each other, his eyes wide. Blue magic started to form a sword for him in between them, but Coria got to him before it was complete and slashed the ethereal light down the middle, disrupting and therefore ending the spell. Next, she stabbed out at his stomach. Zage, seeming not to have expected this, paused for a split second before protecting the skin it would've normally pierced via a thick stretch of solid metal created with blue magic at the last possible second, but he wasn't watching her other hand as he did this. Having pulled it back behind her head, the queen sent it crashing into his side.

Much to Coria's dismay, the blow didn't even move Zage's head all the way to one side. And as she began stepping back in retreat, he saw what she was doing and, using blue magic, conjured up a bump in the ground right where her back foot would land, just large enough to throw her completely off balance and onto her back, which it did. As soon as the queen finished her fall, the kaglorite rushed up to stand over her, placing both feet firmly on each of her splayed forearms. Kneeling, he wrapped his violet hands around her neck.

"I thought we were becoming friends," she said, the disappointment in her heart more prominent than the panic in her head.

The kaglorite burst out laughing venomously. "Then you are an even bigger fool than I took you for. I could never be friends with *oppressors*." Coria began to choke as his grip on her throat tightened. Her hands floundered uselessly at her sides, and after a while, the edges of her vision went black, and the curtains of darkness began to move inward, covering more and more of it with every second. Just as only twin pinpricks of light remained for her to see through however, the pressure around her neck abruptly ceased. The queen gasped for air and coughed violently as the curtains retreated into nothingness. She looked to one side of her to find Zage lying unconscious and Matthew standing over the Dark Lord with one of his daggers clutched in his scaly right hand.

The boy regained his composure after the kaglorite had stopped pursuing him, and a plan came to the former's mind. The lorm crept up to a gargantuan tree with long, overhanging limbs just beside where Coria and Zage were duking it out and climbed up to the nearest of its wooden appendages, his long white claws digging deep furrows into the bark as he did so. Walking along the leafy tightrope upon reaching it, Matthew looked down once the sounds of the nearby struggle were directly below him and found that the queen was moments from death. His eyes wide, the boy unsheathed one of his knives and dive-bombed Zage right then, smashing the hard metal hilt onto the violet-skinned man's scalp.

The kaglorite expected to awaken in a dense, vibrant jungle, with his father there to show him the way, but instead, he found himself sitting around a fire in the early evening with Dekkin, Coria, and Matthew, propped up against a tall outcropping. Zage tried to bring his hands to his face to rub at his bleary eyes but was met with the feel of flesh not his own; he retracted them to find they were bound in another pedibus.

"I am alive?" the kaglorite asked, his voice hoarse from slumber.

The oracle held out one hand to the boy, palm up, and the lorm put the hilt of one of his daggers onto it. "Yes." The immortal rose and started walking to Zage. "I wanted you to see your death coming before it happened."

The kaglorite bared his teeth, readying himself to lash out at Dekkin, futile as the effort may be. But before the two men met, the queen stepped in between them, her arms raised slightly and spread out to each side.

"No!" said Coria to the oracle. "Don't kill him."

The immortal came to a halt with great incredulity. "What? Why not?"

The queen crossed her arms over her chest. "We're not killing anyone we don't have to."

"What…he tried to *murder all of us!*" Dekkin pointed out. "If he ever gets another chance to try it again, which he probably will, no matter how closely we watch him, he'll take it. I'd say that's reason enough for an execution."

Coria frowned, and her eyes darted back and forth as she strained her brain for further arguments. "Well, we…we might need him somewhere down the line. He's the strongest magic user in all of Samu. There's a good chance that'll come in handy sometime soon."

"That possibility is not worth *serious risk of death* for *all of us*." The oracle took a step toward the queen.

Coria didn't budge. "If you do this, I'll never forgive you. *Matthew* will never forgive you. Isn't that right, Matthew?" She looked over at the boy pleadingly.

The lorm shrunk at this, averting his eyes from hers; but after a moment, he donned a determined expression and, turning to face the immortal before standing, confirmed, "Y-yes, yes, I…I won't forgive you, Dekkin."

"I don't care about your forgiveness!" snapped the oracle. But when he saw the crestfallen look on Matthew's face, it gave him pause; and after standing there for a long moment, Dekkin, visibly deflated, lowered the knife in his hand to one side of himself. "*Fine*," he conceded through gritted teeth, turning his head to face the queen's. "But *you* need to do your job better. I want him watched *constantly*, understand?"

Coria nodded eagerly despite his biting tone. "Yes, it will be done. Thank you."

"And *certainly* don't *look to him for advice*, even if I'm indisposed," continued the immortal. "What were you thinking taking him at his word? Did you honestly believe he was telling the truth?"

"Uh…yes," the queen answered half-heartedly.

Dekkin shook his head firmly. "No, you didn't. Even *you* aren't so naive. Why did you do it? Why did you go along with what he said?"

"I"—Coria paused and frowned; she didn't know the answer any more than he did. After some introspection, she continued—"I didn't want to be responsible for something going wrong if I made the wrong decision, so I left it in Zage's hands."

The oracle scoffed. This line of logic didn't, of course, hold up very well at all; asking the kaglorite his opinion and acting on what he said was in and of itself a choice, and she was partially responsible for the damage it caused as a result. He thought this but chose not to speak it, finding he was already tired of talking. Instead, he turned around and walked to his spot along the fire's perimeter, laying down on one side with his back to the others.

Zage looked to the queen from across the fire. "Thank you for saving my life." When she ignored this, he said sharply, "What? What is it? It is beneath Your Highness to address me now?"

"No," replied Coria as she stared into the flames before her. "We're not friends, remember?"

11

FLAT, UNBROKEN PLAINS OF grass had never inspired more excitement than it did in Matthew when he first spotted them in the distance as the wagon rounded a corner, skirting the edge of the mountains' base.

"We made it!" the boy exclaimed in giddy relief as he turned to face Dekkin, both of them sitting atop the coach box.

Dekkin pressed his lips together tightly. "Not quite."

The lorm peered back at what lay before them quizzically. "What do you mean? What else is there?"

"Wait for it."

Matthew watched with great apprehension for something to appear on the horizon some distance ahead of them, picturing an imposing black castle or another towering wall. Minutes passed by, and the wagon along with it, and he spotted nothing. Eventually, he lowered his gaze on his way to face the immortal once again and inquire of him when they would come into view of whatever he'd alluded to, and it was then that he saw it—a tiny shack of well-worn wood, its single door in view closed, stood directly between the mountains and the coast, at a point where both tapered to a single-file path. The boy guessed as he gazed intently at it from a distance that no more than four adults could stand inside it at the same time.

"That's it?" asked the lorm, still uncomprehending. "What's so frightening about a little shack?"

"It's not just a little shack," the oracle replied gravely. "It's enchanted."

Matthew was getting tired of failing to understand the immortal's words. "Enchanted? What does that mean?"

Dekkin sighed almost imperceptibly. "Long ago, kaglorites could use magic not only to create or destroy matter but to cast spells on inanimate objects, giving them supernatural qualities. That shack was enchanted during that time."

"You said kaglorites could use magic on *objects*"—reiterated the boy incredulously—"cast *spells* on things, why can't they do that anymore?"

The oracle shook his head. "No one knows, not even me. A little over a century ago, they simply…stopped doing it. And eventually, when someone thought to ask why this was, none of the kaglorites had any memory of how it was done." He pushed aside the slat behind them. "I'm sure Zage's been listening ever since we started talking about his people, and I'm sure he's got a conspiracy theory of some sort as to the cause of the phenomenon. Zage?"

The kaglorite was indeed standing crouched right by the front of the wagon's back compartment. "Even I do not know the answer to that mystery, but I have no doubt humans or lorms or some combination of the two were responsible."

"And there you are," the immortal said with a smirk as he shut the opening the violet-skinned man had spoken through. The lorm barely managed to keep his laughter to a soft chuckle Zage wouldn't hear.

A moment of silence passed. Dekkin never took his eyes off the enchanted shack, while Matthew looked all around him, his lips moving very slightly as he processed this new information. Naturally, questions formed. "So…what is the shack enchanted to do? Why are you so afraid of it?"

"Because I don't know the nature of its enchantment," answered the oracle. "And the reason I don't is that only a handful of people have ever traveled into it and managed to escape."

The boy swallowed loudly before furrowing his brow. "So…what did the people who *did* escape say about it?"

"No one knows," the immortal responded, frowning as if he was looking at one of his children, all grown up, and ruminating on his disappointment in his offspring. "The only ones who ever made it were kaglorites, and as you could guess, they aren't eager to share their findings with my people or yours."

The lorm turned his attention to the front, looking without seeing. "Do you think it was their race that did it? That, say, the enchantment lets kaglorites go since it was their people that created the spell?"

Dekkin nodded. "Possibly, and that's what I'm betting on—that if Zage's with us, we might be allowed to pass."

A tense silence between the two of them followed. Matthew searched for something to distract them both until the wagon's driver brought it to a halt so abrupt the boy almost pitched forward to the ground below. The lorm glanced at the oracle for answers but, seeing that the immortal wasn't looking at him and didn't register his gaze, shifted his attention to the spot immediately ahead of them and found a family of small quadruped creatures scurrying across the middle of that area as they crossed the path.

The animals had long bodies that bulged considerably on just one side. Their heads and faces were at about the halfway point between rodent and feline, including whiskers, and mottled green-and-blue fur covered them. However, there were also gills on each of their cheeks, and where a furry tail might've been on a more traditional land dweller, there was that of a fish, proportional to the rest of their bodies. Matthew pointed at them as they went on their way. "What are those?"

Those, Dekkin told him, were called emmits. They were native, originally, to the area within which Humania's vineyards had once stood. Their bodies had adapted to living purely off the fermented grapes and wine (only needing to eat about every four months to survive) they stole from the beleaguered owners of the wineries. This is why they had that long, wide lump on one side of their bodies; a diet like theirs required a massively enlarged liver to properly process the alcohol constantly coursing through their system. Their aquatic features formed in response to their environment as well; they would've been hunted to extinction by their human victims were they to live in the grass or up in the trees, and so they chose instead to make their nests deep beneath the surfaces of the area's many lakes. However, after the destruction reeked by the kaglorites in the west, there wasn't enough food or drink to go around for the little creatures, and they'd been forced to move east. After decades, they came all the way to the other side of the country, never managing to carve out a steady new habitat for themselves. They soon ran out of unexplored space to move too; despite their gills, they couldn't survive in salt water.

The years may have been visible in the grain of the wood making up the small shack, but it was still perfectly sturdy after all this time, due to the enchantment, no doubt. There were no windows nor space beneath the front door to provide a preview of what might lie within, which certainly didn't help the general mood within and immediately without the wagon. When they found themselves at said door, it seemed to Matthew like it had come too soon, though in reality, it had been dozens of minutes since the shack first came into view.

"Coria!" called out Dekkin through the slit he'd just opened behind him. "Get out and open the door for us, would you?"

"Me?" the queen squeaked uncharacteristically. "Why me?"

"You *are* my bodyguard, are you not?" pointed out the oracle with no small degree of satisfaction. He wasn't looking at her but knew what she was doing, darting her eyes back and forth, searching for a way out. After a few seconds of this, she swallowed loud enough for him to hear and assented with great reluctance. Coria got off the wagon and walked around it to the front of the shack. She unsheathed her weapon, which she'd had Zage repair, and prodded the door open a crack with one end of it, standing as far away from the foreboding wooden structure as she could. The queen was met with silence, and nothing leaped at her out of the pure black void within, though she noted much to her disquiet that it was entirely unpierced by the daylight which should've by all rights come streaming into it through the long vertical slit in the doorway. A little emboldened by this, she took a deep breath and, leaning forward, pushed the door all the way open. Again, nothing came of this, except for an expansion of the dark abyss before her.

Coria breathed a heavy sigh of relief, keeping her mind off the fact that she'd still have to go inside with the others, when Dekkin called out to her, "All right, now get in there a little bit. Tell us what you see."

The queen whirled around in panic. "*What?* Dekkin, please!"

"What does it matter?" the oracle countered. "You'll have to do it no matter what at some point. *And,*" interrupted the latter when the former opened her mouth, "you'd most likely be no safer with us by your side, given our lack of knowledge about the enchantment. This way is less risky, for the group as a whole anyway."

Coria knew he was right. She waited as long as she knew he would let her and then in several small steps went inside the shack, vanishing from Dekkin and Matthew's view as she did so.

The immortal waited for her to report back to him from within, but a minute passed, and there was no sign of her, visual or auditory. "Coria?" said Dekkin, annoyed at the delay but also genuinely concerned for his fellow. Nothing moved in the following silent moment. After holding fast for another handful of seconds, the oracle took the reins and coaxed the kreshes pulling the wagon forward.

"Wh-what are you doing?" asked Matthew frantically as he whipped his head around to face the immortal.

"We have to go through it," Dekkin insisted. He gestured toward the sheer rock face to their left. "We can't climb up that way, and we'd have to leave the wagon behind even if we could besides." The oracle indicated their right with the corresponding arm. "And on the other side, we've got the ocean, and no boat for us to travel across it with."

The boy looked to each side and recognized that the immortal was right. The lorm clenched both hands as the wagon passed through the open doorway. A few seconds after the darkness consumed them, Matthew grew concerned the kreshes before them would crash unseeingly right into the far door, but some time passed, and they never even broke stride. Looking back, the boy saw the rectangle of daylight behind them receding into the distance while they continued through the void. The lorm wondered in bewilderment how it could be possible that this was happening in a space so seemingly confined from the outside, but his ruminations were soon interrupted by a change in the surrounding atmosphere; the air became so humid it was hard to breathe, and as the wagon went along, the temperature dropped steadily to the point that Dekkin and Matthew were both soon shivering.

When the doorway they'd come through completely vanished from view, the boy was on the verge of crying out in terror; but just before he did, another patch of illumination, far enough away to appear to him a mere pinprick, popped up on the horizon. The lorm lit up at this and felt as a human coming up for air after two minutes underwater while he watched the light up ahead grow larger and larger. A patch of shadow appeared to him in the middle of the approaching radiance, and he was heartened further when over time, it expanded into Coria's silhouette. The air cleared and heated up gradually as the wagon got closer to the light, which was in such stark contrast to the inky emptiness around it that its occupants couldn't look at the coming luminescence directly for any length of time or make out most of its contents until they were practically within it.

They came out in the middle of—they saw after their eyes adjusted—what looked to be one of western Humania's famed vineyards. The simultaneously sweet and bitter smell of fermented grapes wafted through the air on a gentle spring breeze across fields of the fruit seeming to extend forever in each direction. The sound of conversation between many of the workers tending the vines mixed with noise from emmits squeaking hungrily as they scampered across the wet, fertile earth, and in some cases, the two melded, as one or more of the roguish little creatures were caught in the act of theft by one of the winery's employees. Coria stood before it all, taking it in with a broad smile. An older woman some distance away from the queen called out her name then, and the young royal looked in the voice's direction.

The speaker was one of the workers, an elderly human woman with a few streaks of blond left in her silver hair and the wrinkles at each corner of her mouth far more pronounced than their cousins in the other areas of her face. Dekkin had the uncanny sense that he'd seen this person before, and after racking his brains for a few moments, he realized it was the late queen Maescha. The deceased matriarch flashed her daughter a warm grin.

"What are you doing, daughter of mine, just standing there? We've work to do, you know! Your brother could use your help at just this moment, in fact." Maescha turned around and pointed toward an older man everyone recognized as a mobile Samuel, who at this waved invitingly to his adoptive sister.

Dekkin stepped further forward, asking with furrowed brow to no one in particular, "What is this?" Soon thereafter, a shadow fell over him and his immediate surroundings, and he heard the sounds of woodland creatures coming from his left. He turned to face them and found much to his surprise that there was now a vast forest of towering trees a short distance away in that direction, which hadn't been just a moment prior. A number of humans, primitive hunter-gatherers from the looks of them, stood gathered at its near edge directly ahead of him, a tan woman in her seventies at the group's head.

The oracle's eyes bugged out. Could it be? "*Seren?*" breathed the immortal in desperately hopeful disbelief.

The woman came up to him ponderously before reaching out a hand toward him. "Come, my love. Let us go home. After all, we haven't much time left, you and I."

Dekkin frowned. "And I?" At that moment, Matthew came around to his front and gasped at the sight of the oracle's face. "Dekkin!"

The immortal looked back at the boy. "What?"

"Y-your face…"

Dekkin's brow dropped even further. Looking around, he saw a nearby puddle and walked to it before bending over its surface. He was greeted with a most unexpected sight—he had aged, decades, just like Seren. As he turned to one side to look at his profile, he saw too that the turins on his back had disappeared.

At that moment, someone said the lorm's name from back where he and the others came. Matthew looked over there, clutching at his face and body in search of physical alterations but finding none. The passageway from which they'd arrived in this unearthly place and the fields behind and on either side of it were gone, replaced by an ocean that covered the entire area, and yet did not spill over into other sections of the space at its borders. A Lormish couple floated suspended in the middle of the seawater; the boy recognized the man as his father but couldn't place the woman. And then it hit him.

"Are you my mother?" Matthew asked with a quaver in his voice, and the woman before him nodded, an affectionate smile on her face.

When Zage saw this through the opening in the back of the wagon as he sat inside it, he got up and stepped off it, looking about at his new surroundings. The kaglorite came to a halt upon facing Matthew's left, for there was a scene taken straight out of one of his childhood memories—Kagloris, a dense jungle as it had been before the massacre, and standing within a farm amidst the foliage were his parents and brother.

Though turning away from the sight of his parents felt like ripping skin off his arm with his bare hands, Matthew did so, saying as he looked over at Dekkin, "This isn't real. This is an illusion, part of the enchantment. We need to find a way out of here." When the boy heard the *plip plip plip* of falling droplets coming from the oracle's direction but saw no rain coming down on the immortal, the lorm frowned and walked around to face Dekkin's side, finding the man in euphoric tears.

"I had no idea," said the oracle. "If I had known sooner…a few centuries ago…"

Matthew went to the immortal and grabbed one of his hands, shaking it. "Dekkin, we should leave. This is fake. It isn't worth our time."

The immortal burst into ecstatic, incredulous laughter. "*Leave?* I'm not going anywhere. I'm staying *forever.* You can leave if you want." He advanced to Seren and took her outstretched hand. An overjoyed sob shook his entire body. "I can feel her, just as if she were really here."

The boy looked this way and that for the exit, finding nothing. Despair began to fill his gut as he surveyed the vast illusory world he and the others found themselves in; would they have to search this entire area for a way out? Panic set in as he wondered then if there was a way out at all.

When pure black swallowed the fantasy realm surrounding them, Matthew thought at first that he'd passed out, possibly as a result of the magic that brought it to life. But then he heard the startled exclamations of the others just about him. The boy walked carefully forward with his arms outstretched as far as he could, which was but two short steps, and felt smooth wood on his fingers. It appeared they'd returned to reality and now stood inside the small shack they'd entered when last they were there.

The lorm started as Dekkin pounded on another of the hovel's squat walls. "Take me back! Take me back to my people, horb it!"

"I cannot" came a soft voice, sounding as if it were just above them.

The oracle looked up. "What do you mean? Who's this?"

"The first people to ever meet me here asked the same," the disembodied speaker replied. "It took me some time to give myself a name. Such a thing had never occurred to me before. You can call me Utopio. I am a living spell, that which resides in this shack and created the unreal world all of you just found yourselves in."

Matthew needed a moment to process this; he was still adjusting to the knowledge of the existence of enchantments, not to mention those with minds of their own. "Can you show us the way out, on the other side from where we came? May we leave here?"

"No!" the immortal shouted, as loud and emphatic as he could. "Put us back, back where we were!"

"I'm afraid I can't fulfill either of those requests," replied Utopio, his tone perfectly measured. "The only thing keeping me alive is the presence of living hosts, those who pass within the range of my power. I can last for some time without them, but eventually, I'll go hungry, so I must stockpile as much sustenance as I can when I get it. And I can't take you back to the realm of your fantasies. I was designed to provide the illusions that make it up as much as was needed, but alas, my creator was a warlock of questionable talent. As it is, I can only produce the dream world for my hosts for five minutes every three months."

"Five minutes every *three months?*" Coria repeated in dismay. "And the rest of the time we're stuck in this tiny pitch-black room?"

"Correct," confirmed the living spell.

"But if we can't leave and you can't create anything for us for three months, we'll starve to death in here!" the queen pointed out.

"Yes," said Utopio evenly, "I'm truly very sorry."

"You *traitor!*" Zage bellowed, stomping on the floor of the shack with one foot for emphasis.

"How's that?" asked the spell.

"A kaglorite made you, and now you're sentencing another of his kind to *death?*" the kaglorite growled up at the ceiling.

"Oh, you who just spoke, you are a kaglorite? I can only sense the desires of my hosts. I cannot see them. If you are truly a kaglorite, conjure up some magic. If you can, I'll be able to detect that as well, and I'll let you go, as I do for all my kaglorite hosts."

Zage covered one of his hands, slightly raised, with red magic, illuminating his violet visage.

"Ah, so you are," Utopio said. "Right, then you're free to go."

Though Zage's face didn't change when it was still visible to the others, Dekkin could see the kaglorite's malicious leer as if the room they were in was fully lit while the other man walked across the floor of the shack after extinguishing the crimson flare.

"Zage, don't leave," implored Coria. "You need us to get to the border, remember?"

"Better to take my chances out here than stay with you people and die slowly," Zage observed.

"We're not going to die," assured the queen. "We're going to find a way out of this, somehow." She whipped her head around to face the direction of the immortal's voice as he snorted loudly. "What, Dekkin?"

"We're going to find a way out of this, somehow," the oracle repeated mockingly. "You sound like Cornelius Arcind."

"That *is* something he says a lot," added Matthew.

"Oh, quiet, both of you," Coria chided. She paced up to a wall and felt across all four of them for a door only to find none at all. Turning around, she rushed to the one opposite from where she was standing with one shoulder extended forward. The queen made impact with a thump, but the wood didn't even shake. Unsheathing her weapon, Coria swung it at the wall before her. Its tip bounced off with a metallic ping. She tried again with a flurry of wild slashes, and not a chip broke off the wooden barrier before her. Damn enchantments.

The queen, breathing hard from the exertion, paced around the shack a few times, apologizing whenever she accidentally bumped into one of its other unwilling inhabitants, when an idea came to her mind. Raising her brow, she looked up at the ceiling and said, "Utopio! You said you're a living spell. So you have a heart. You can't condemn people to death even if it's to save your own life. That's *evil*! You don't want to be evil, do you?"

"I'm sorry, my lady, but I am not a complete person," replied Utopio. "Even in the heyday of kaglorite wizardry, when I was created, it was impossible for complete life to spawn from magic. I am missing several aspects of what you would call a soul. One of my shortcomings is that I am incapable of being selfless, of practicing altruism."

Coria swore silently.

"There is one way you can escape from here."

The queen lit up to such a degree it was a wonder it didn't bring to light the entire interior of the shack. "*Truly?* Well, what is it?"

"I will let you go, and you will bring me replacements, for you and your companions."

Coria's heart sank along with her face. "Well, we can't do that, Utopio."

"We may have to," the oracle interjected. "You heard him. It's the only way we're getting out of here. The only way we don't *starve to death*."

The queen was appalled. "Dekkin, *no*! That's *barbaric*!"

"It *doesn't matter*," the immortal forced past gritted teeth.

"Of course, it *matters*. It's four people's *lives!*" In the darkness, Coria, of course, saw nothing and so assumed Dekkin simply pouted in silence at this when he in fact opened his mouth to say something in response before stopping himself.

Hours passed. Or was it minutes? Days? It was impossible to tell inside the shack, and after a while, it was difficult for the prisoners within to differentiate between waking and sleeping as well. They talked to try to keep their minds off their impending demises (unsuccessfully, it should be noted), except for Dekkin, who as you might've expected sat in one corner of the room running his fingers through his hair, quiet as a graveyard at midnight. Fortunately, when they got hungry, they had access to the food in the wagon, though it could only be gotten by blindly groping around in its back compartment, and none of the four of them remembered enough about its layout to be capable of picking exactly what they'd be having. Utopio allowed this; after all, their dining increased the volume of his own feast.

Dekkin started when all of a sudden, Coria cried out in delight and triumph. He shot to his feet. "*What?* What is it? Did you get an idea?"

The oracle could tell the queen had been rummaging around in their stores from the noise and, by that same token, recognized it when she carefully stepped off it. "No, but I found the wine!" The immortal asked after a pause if she was joking, and Coria answered merrily that no, her proclamation was entirely genuine. The surrounding void was filled up with words of rage for a while then as Dekkin screamed bloody murder at the queen for getting his hopes up over nothing, unintentional though it had been. Coria, meanwhile, was too busy downing drink to reply or even truly listen to what was being said to her.

When the oracle's tirade was forcibly brought to a halt by a need for the intake of air, he picked up for the first time on the sound of the wine as it sloshed in its bottle while the queen quaffed from it.

"Can I have some of that?" asked the immortal with an unseen blush of embarrassment, speaking in such an uncharacteristically polite way because of the knowledge that she could keep the wine from him rather easily under this ocean of pitch were she to take offense at something he said. There was no response. "Coria," Dekkin reiterated, a little louder, "can I have some of that?" The only thing this was met with was the sound of the queen noisily swallowing more wine, and at that point, he gave up.

Shortly thereafter, the oracle heard the boy begin to sob from across the room. "Matthew," said the immortal, "what's wrong?"

"He's twelve years old, and he's looking a slow, painful death in the face," Coria pointed out lightly.

"Hmm, true." Dekkin shifted his weight. "He's fortunate though compared to myself, all of you are."

The queen frowned in puzzlement. "What do you mean?"

"I don't need to eat or drink," the oracle explained. "I still do so every once in a while, for the taste, but I can go without them indefinitely, thanks to my turins. And if we can't find a way out of here, I'm going to have to—"

"Excuse me," interjected Utopio, so sudden and unexpected after such a prolonged silence from him that his prisoners jumped a little. "One of you is an oracle?"

"Yes, that's right," the immortal confirmed. "I am."

"So you're immortal? I could live forever with certainty if I keep you here?"

Dekkin grunted in assent.

"I sensed a fifth set of desires when your group came in. Still do. That's from your turins then. Well, since that's the case, the rest of you can go. I no longer have any need of you."

Zage crowed in triumph as he rose to his feet, but Coria said before he'd even finished, "Zage, no! We're not leaving Dekkin behind."

"So what, we will stay here and starve to death for the sake of nicety?" countered the kaglorite.

There was a brief pause as the queen, recognizing the absurdity of that despite her trademark sense of personal honor, thought the situation over. "Give us three meals to think of something, then if we haven't…"

Time went by—one meal, two. Everyone ran out of things to say. Without his sight or sound for his ears, Dekkin started to feel disembodied; he lost track first of his own body, then his mind. And with no sun or moon to hint at the passage of time, the very idea of the construct began to fade as well, and of course, without time, there could be no change; there was no hope of salvation from the torturous void he currently found himself trapped in the midst of. Holding back a scream of terror, the oracle started relying on recent memories to keep him grounded. He remembered being frozen in place while Zage tried to murder him and the others in the swamp. He remembered talking to Matthew as they'd first approached the shack, explaining its history. He remembered jerking the wagon to a halt when just in front of them that family of emmits had passed by.

The emmits! Dekkin bolted right up, crying out in pain as his limbs, more sore than he'd known, groaned loudly in protest at the sudden motion. "Utopio!" exclaimed the oracle. "I have an idea for replacing us."

"Oh?" the living spell replied. "Do tell."

"Dekkin, *no*!" interjected Coria insistently. "We're not *sacrificing four other people*!"

"Calm yourself!" the immortal, his tone crabby, responded. "I have no intention of doing so. My plan involves *saving* lives in fact, saving an entire species even." He looked up. "Utopio, there're several nests a short walk from here where creatures called emmits make their homes. They're not native to this area. They've been displaced by change over time and are no closer to finding themselves a permanent home than they were at the start of their journey. They only need to eat and drink once every four months. With them in the shack, you truly could live forever, guaranteed. What do you say?"

There ensued a pause that was brief and yet agonizing for the oracle nonetheless. "I can only sense desires within these walls," said Utopio finally. "I have no way of knowing whether or not you're telling the truth. My apologies. We haven't a deal."

"Send Zage to bring them back here," Dekkin suggested. "You're willing to let him go anyway, correct?"

"All right," conceded the living spell after another short bout of silence, excruciating on the immortal's part. "I will allow it."

When Zage walked out the way they'd come after having his targets' appearance described to him by the others, a blast of light shot through the open doorway and seared his and everyone else's eyes to such a degree that they thought for a second that they'd gone blind. Dekkin, Coria, and Matthew all worried that Zage would abandon them, dooming both his unwanted fellows and potentially himself out of pure spite, but after several minutes, the door opened again from the outside, and the kaglorite walked in with an armful of emmits.

"Ah," Utopio said a short while after Zage closed the door behind him, "I can see from their desires that what you said of them is true. Yes, this will work splendidly. Thank you. You're all free to go."

Both of the shack's entrances swung open of their own accord, and after pausing for several minutes to allow their eyes to readjust to the illumination outside (it was midday), Dekkin and the others continued on their way. As the oracle drove the wagon, the mountains they'd grown accustomed to on their left sloped down to their end just above the ground, and the party saw before them a massive expanse of green fields bisected by a wide, well-worn path. Even the immortal couldn't resist bursting into giddy laughter at the sight of it all.

12

SEREN'S LOVE FOR HER husband was such that she waited until she was drenched head to toe in her own sweat to snap him out of the awed trance that'd fallen over him as he walked through and surveyed intently the strange land of loose yellow earth they found themselves in. "Dekkin!" she called out to him as she followed a short distance behind. "I think it's time to head back. It's been hours since we left the forest, and we haven't found one spring or river or even game."

"Do you jest?" cried back her husband, showing the wonderment in his eyes as he looked over one shoulder at his wife. "How could I possibly go back now, knowing that my theory was true, without crossing every inch of this incredible new place? Get used to this, Seren! This is our new home!"

His wife blanched. "My love, we'll all drop dead long before you get to see even a fraction of this world beyond the forest!" Dekkin said nothing at this, and she decided then to change tack. "We're ill-equipped for an extended journey at the moment. We didn't expect the rest of the world to be so vast, and there's too many of us. Let's return to the forest, stockpile supplies. After that, you can come back here, with as much of those stores in hand as possible. That's the only way you'll get to fully explore this area."

This got to her husband, and a short while after swallowing dryly, Dekkin nodded. "You speak true. We'll return to the forest then."

Seren, her face flushed as much with relief as from heat, whipped around immediately and began heading back the way they came when she spotted something in the distance that made in an instant her heart feel like a strongman was throttling it. It had the proportions of a person and seemed to be roughly the size of an average adult, though it was nigh impossible to tell at this distance, but the details of its features couldn't be discerned as only its eyes and the skin immediately surrounding them were unclothed. "Dekkin!" she yelled, more shrill than she'd wanted, as she pointed to the faraway figure.

Her face fell as her husband gazed in the given direction with a wide smile of fascination and curiosity. "Ah, one of the locals. Perfect." He passed his wife on his way to the distant onlooker. "I'll go speak with him."

Seren started and rushed to her husband, catching up with him shortly and clutching desperately one of his shoulders. "Dekkin, *no*! We have no idea what that is."

"Precisely," her husband countered as he delicately extracted her hands with his own. "We haven't a clue what it is, and so it's as possible as anything else that it's a person, a kind and benevolent one who can direct us to the nearest watering hole and hunting ground." He looked back to the watcher on the horizon and resumed course.

His wife began speeding after him again. "At least let the rest of us come with you, for security!"

"Absolutely not!" refused Dekkin with a disapproving frown. "How do you think even the best of people would react to an unfamiliar pack advancing on them? You and the others would scare him off!"

"Do you remember when you thought you could tame that *surveset* we caught a few years ago?" Seren reminded him gravely. "And how it broke your arm when you tried to feed it? Or what about the time you traded, against my many protestations, a week's worth of meat in exchange for a 'rain charm' right before the drought?"

Her husband pressed his lips together in embarrassment. "And your point, simply to drudge up shameful incidents from my past?"

His wife shook her head. "No, I merely wish to remind you that many times previously your opinion of others has been higher than it should've been, and it's gotten you into a fair bit of trouble." She softened. "I just want to make sure you're safe, for you are my love, the father of my child."

She brought Dekkin around with this. "All right," conceded the brown-haired man. "We'll all approach him, as one." And so they did; the stranger they walked to remained unmoving the entire time. When the whole group came to a halt and Dekkin stood a pace away from the shrouded spectator, the latter removed its headdress to reveal quite a curious sight—it was a man, but though his face was young, his long hair had already turned completely silver.

"Hello," Dekkin greeted him with a warm smile.

"Hello," repeated the other man. "Tell me, did you come here in search of me?"

Dekkin furrowed his brow in perplexity. "Not...specifically, no. We're explorers from a forest initially, a place so vast it was believed by my people for centuries that it was all there was to the world. I thought otherwise and led the others on a journey to cross its borders." His expression turned quizzical. "Do you know of any shelters or sources of water or food around here? Do you live here? Have you lived here long?"

The man with the young face and the old hair chuckled for reasons Dekkin couldn't place. "Yes, I've lived here for a good while. The only places fit for resting, eating, or drinking in the desert are found below ground. I can take you to my home. It functions as all three."

Dekkin lit up. "Oh, thank you, good sir! You are most generous. Please lead the way."

Seren started to protest but recognized before she could that even if this desert dweller was some kind of supernatural entity, he could surely be felled, in the worst-case scenario, by the sheer numbers of their tribe.

"I am called Cula, by the way," the native said to Dekkin as the brown-haired man walked beside him.

"Ah," said Dekkin to Cula, "well met. I'm Dekkin." He paused, opening and closing his mouth a few times as he gazed at the other man, before finally steeling himself and gesturing at Cula's hair, asking, "I mean no offense. I'm merely curious. Were you born with hair the color it is now?"

Cula shook his head. "No, I wasn't. I'm an oracle."

"An…oracle?" Dekkin repeated in confusion. "And what is that?"

"Someone who can see into the future."

Dekkin began to chuckle but cut it short upon seeing the other man's solemn expression. "You're serious? It can't be. Such a thing isn't possible."

"I can assure you it is," insisted Cula. "I don't blame you for your distrust, of course. You've never met an oracle before, have you?"

Dekkin shook his head.

"That's unsurprising. There're only three of us in the whole world, after all, and I'm the only one on this continent."

Dekkin felt as if these unfamiliar words were water, and his mind was a boy who couldn't swim, drowning in them. He had the concept of a continent explained to him before inquiring. "So there are three oracles, you said? And you are the only one on this continent? Why is that? Why are there only three? How do you *become* an oracle? Are you born as one?" He saw himself then. "I'm sorry. I'm assaulting you with inquiries."

Cula flashed him a light smile. "Oh, it's quite all right. I welcome it. I'm the only permanent inhabitant of the desert as far as I know, and so I have not many opportunities for conversation. Even I don't have all the answers however. I will tell you what I know though." He explained the concept of turins. "I have no idea where turins came from or why there were only five so long ago, but that is how things were, and so a council of oracles was formed—one for each race and a master oracle to rule over it all."

Dekkin inquired about these "races" and was stunned when Cula informed him of the existence of the other three peoples of Samu.

"So there were five. But long before my time, two went missing at the same time—the Lormish representative and the master herself.

To this day, no one knows what happened to them. And so now there remain three—myself, the itrasian oracle, and the kaglorite oracle."

Dekkin nodded in an unsuccessful attempt at a matter-of-fact motion. "So you're immortal. You'll live forever except in the event of an unnatural death?"

"No. Only the itrasian representative and the master oracle are supposed to live indefinitely or were in the case of the latter. The others are to serve a thousand-year term before passing along their turins to another."

"Can the turins be passed along to anyone?" Dekkin asked.

"No," answered Cula, "only a select few are capable of becoming a host to one. There are two signs that someone can become an oracle: the first, a tendency to get painful headaches for no apparent reason; and second, an ability to, at times, predict or foresee things in the immediate future, without any other possible explanation as to how they can do this."

Dekkin came to a halt, and after a few steps, Cula stopped himself and looked back to see an incredulous look on the other man's face. "Is this some sort of jest?" asked the man with the brown hair.

Cula squinted from puzzlement. "What do you mean?"

"I experience both of those," Dekkin replied.

Cula's brow shot up. After a brief pause, he said, "Now *I* suspect *you* are the one playing a prank."

Dekkin shook his head so vehemently and with an expression sincere enough to make the older man believe him.

"Well now, that's incredible. However, I'm afraid you cannot be my replacement. My term won't be up until your grandchildren are long dead."

"That's quite all right," responded Dekkin with a smile. He stepped forward, and both men resumed their journey. "I wouldn't change a thing about my life as it is now…and over the course of a thousand years, quite a few things, very probably *all* of them, would be bound to change."

* * * * *

Another night beside the open road was a most welcome reprieve from the constant peril and harsh conditions of the previous several days.

Dekkin scratched at one foot with a grimace as they all sat around the fire eating dinner. "Matthew, you said you like to mend clothing. What about *creating* such items?"

The boy looked up from his plate, pausing for a handful of seconds to swallow the food in his mouth. "Well, I've never done it, but I suppose I could try."

"Good," the oracle said, clawing within his shoe once again. "I've had these socks for several years, and they make each foot itch horribly all over."

"You said you've had them for *years*?" interjected Coria.

The immortal looked at her and nodded.

"And you never just…threw them away, got new ones you liked?"

Dekkin stared at her with such confusion that she felt like she'd just spoken a language he'd never heard before.

"So you want me to make you some socks?" Matthew inquired.

"Yes," answered the oracle, "please. You did a right proper job on the tear in my shirt the other night."

The corners of the lorm's mouth lifted up ever so slightly. "All right."

The immortal smiled back at him before detecting movement in the bottom-left corner of his periphery and looking there to find one of the queen's hands creeping toward the bottle of wine at his feet. "Coria!" Dekkin exclaimed as he grabbed the bottle and moved it to his other side. "No alcohol while we're traveling. You're supposed to be the muscle of this excursion. How do you expect to fend off assailants with a hangover?"

"I'll just have a little!" whined Coria, leaning toward him to reach for the bottle again.

The oracle moved it even further away from her with one hand. "Oh, as you did back in the shack?"

"I only drank so much then because we weren't on the move!" the queen pouted. "And because I hadn't had a drop since, I joined up with this group, thanks to you, just let me have a bit every night, and I'll be satisfied."

"I've heard stories of your alcohol-related exploits," countered the immortal. "And I saw how you were in the shack. I don't think you're capable of having just a bit." Dekkin softened a little from the look on Coria's face, which was as if he'd physically stricken her. "It's not good for you, to drink as you do, you know," the oracle murmured with averted eyes. At that, the queen gave a small smile and relented, leaning back to her previous position. "I want to rant about our time in the shack," said the immortal next, gazing over at her. "I need you to activate your...yes-woman persona, all right?"

Coria lit up and brought her forearms to rest on the tops of her thighs. "Deal."

Dekkin sighed deeply, gazing into the flames before him. "Being trapped there was awful, of course, but it was also strangely...relaxing. I couldn't see *anything*, so I didn't spot anything that enraged me, disappointed me. I could hear some, of course, but it was the rest of you, so it didn't bother me too much. I was losing my mind in there, and yet I almost wish I had been left there for the rest of time."

"Life is horrible," the queen affirmed, "so much so that you have to be insane or shut out of the world or both in order to be truly happy."

The oracle leaned toward her and clenched one fist in excitement. "Yes! Yes, exactly!" Catching himself, the immortal, self-conscious, returned to a neutral position and shifted his expression to one of his usual cynical looks. "And we've doomed those emmits and their descendants to life in there. They'll survive, sure, and they don't have the range of emotions we do, but nevertheless, that shack is no place for any living thing, even an animal such as that. It just illustrates that happy endings don't exist except at the expense of someone or something else's life."

"Happiness can only be found at the tip of a knife drenched in the blood of another, and even then, it is an incredibly fleeting thing," supplied Coria.

Dekkin nodded. "I can't stop thinking about all those people that went in there and died of starvation, such a prolonged and agonizing process. If more than one got stuck inside, they probably resorted to cannibalism after a certain point, killed someone they supposedly loved, and tore the flesh from their cold bones. Things as horrible as or even more so than that happen every day, in all three continents, on each of the Lormish Isles. How can a person claiming to be a moral individual bear to willingly bring children into a world such as that? Parents are responsible for every tragedy there's ever been in Samu. They're the worst breed of villain I can imagine."

"No parent has ever truly loved their chi—" A smile had already begun sneaking onto the queen's face when she started speaking, and near the end of the statement, she couldn't hold in the raucous laughter that followed.

The oracle scowled. "No!" He slapped Coria on one shoulder harder than he'd intended and felt poorly about it for a split second before recognizing that the strike of his frail hand had simply bounced off her body's highly developed musculature. "You were doing so well."

"I'm sorry, I'm sorry!" the queen forced out in between mirthful giggles. "It's just hard for me to lie that much. Because those were lies, everything I said, you know. Truthfully—"

The immortal raised up one hand. "No, no! This arrangement won't work if you tell me what you truly think after each session. Let's just call it there."

"All right," responded Coria with a chuckle. She looked over at Matthew to find the boy, who'd begun nervously fidgeting once voices were raised, had stood, and walked a pace away from the others to practice some of the combat training maneuvers she'd taught him. "Good work, Matthew!" she called out to the lorm. "Your form's gotten quite good."

Matthew shocked the queen by returning her gaze and full-on beaming at her. "Thanks." A cloud passed over his face, and he averted his eyes. "I worry that I'll never be a *great* fighter though."

Coria turned her body to face the boy with a quizzical frown. "What makes you say that? If you keep working at it the way you have been, you'll be better than me in a *year*!"

The lorm stopped practicing, his gaze on his feet. "Without a teacher, I won't. And when I'm back beside my master, he won't have the time to continue my training."

"Well, if that's so, you'll just have to come visit me every so often for a checkup," replied the queen matter-of-factly.

Matthew's brow jumped, and he whipped his head around to face hers. "Truly? We can meet? After this is all over?"

"Of course!" Coria confirmed.

The boy shifted his weight from one foot to the other. "Like… once a year? Or is that too much? That's too much, isn't it? I'm sorry-"

The queen raised a hand to stop him, a little exasperation on her face. "Matthew, Matthew! I'm sure as apprentice to Cornelius Arcind you'll be on the road most of the time, but whenever you're free, you can come to me. Stay for as long as you're able."

The lorm's eyes were wide again. "*Truly?* Oh, thank you, thank you!" He looked off into the distance wistfully. "I've never stayed at the royal castle. Could I have my own room? Close to yours though?"

Fortunately Matthew couldn't see Coria's face fall when he said this. "Ah…yes," responded the queen; it was a testament to the intensity of the boy's elation that he didn't pick up on the quality of her tone, utterly unconvincing as it was. "We'll…stay together…in the castle." She turned toward the oracle readily. "What about you, Dekkin? Can Matthew and I come see you when this is all over, wherever it is you call home?"

The immortal returned her gaze with an expression as if she'd asked him what breed of sea creature he'd want to be if he had the choice to reincarnate as one. "Can you…uh…no. No, I don't think so." His tone wasn't cold in the slightest; if Coria hadn't known any better, she'd have thought it sounded almost regretful.

The queen's face fell. "What? Why not? That's terribly rude, you know!"

"It's not for the reason you're thinking," assured Dekkin, his mouth tight.

There was then a silence, expectant on Coria's part, that she cut short after a handful of seconds, asking, "Well, then, what *is* the reason? Speak up!"

"Um…uh, it's much too remote, where I live," the oracle answered unconvincingly. "Part of the tradition with oracles, you know. The way there is quite hazardous as well. That's another of my position's conventions."

The queen got up at this and went to the wagon's back compartment, rummaging around in it for a while before popping back out and returning to the campfire's perimeter. She held out the object of her search, a detailed map of Samu, to the immortal. "Mark where you live."

"*Coria*—" began Dekkin insistently.

"Is it that you don't want to see us?" Coria, suddenly in anguish, questioned. "Is that another reason?"

The oracle sighed in exasperation. "I told you it isn't."

"So you'd like it if we visited," concluded the queen, the distress vanishing from her face as quickly as it had come and being replaced by a triumphant, exultant grin.

The immortal scowled back at her immediately. "I didn't say that."

"Well, if you *don't mind* us coming to see you, the rest doesn't matter." She proffered the map again. "Mark it."

Dekkin turned his head away from it and held it there for several seconds, but soon, he reluctantly capitulated, marking a tiny island off the northern coast of Humania with a stubby pencil he kept in one pocket of his tunic. Coria beamed at the oracle as he handed the map back to her with averted eyes.

Zage frowned at Matthew as the boy ate his dinner; ever since the incident in the swamp, the kaglorite hadn't been freed of his organic shackles even for meals; instead, he was being hand-fed by the queen after everyone else finished theirs. "Why is the lorm released from his pedibus so often, and I never am? It is not fair!"

"Because Matthew has been a model prisoner and hasn't attempted to *murder us* besides," the oracle pointed out with a glare directed right at the other man. To this, the kaglorite had nothing to say, and he moodily turned his attention back to the flames before him as his stomach loudly grumbled.

All of them fell silent for a bit, and the boy, whose attention had been devoted to either his dinner, his training exercises, or the preceding conversation, surveyed their immediate surroundings for the first time in half an hour, and what he saw to his right chilled every drop of blue blood in his body. Hundreds of mounted soldiers, illuminated by the torches they carried, were making their way directly to them, though they were still a good ways from what seemed to be their destination. "*Dekkin!*" cried the lorm as he pointed at the approaching intruders.

The immortal's gaze followed Matthew's direction, and the former swore emphatically when he saw the army in the distance. "That can't be...please don't tell me that's what I think it is." But it was; at the front of the group, Cornelius Arcind's gaudy armor was visible by the light of the torch in one of his hands.

"Everyone get in the back of the wagon, *quick*!" Dekkin ordered as he shot to his feet.

The others did as they were told, and then the oracle was left to wait several excruciatingly long minutes for Cornelius's arrival, alone.

"Dekkin!" Cornelius got off his kresh and walked toward the other man with a welcoming smile, seeming not to recognize that hundreds of armed men now surrounded the oracle on one side and were as a result understandably setting him on edge. "We meet again."

The immortal swallowed heavily and fretted over whether Master Arcind had noticed it (he hadn't). "So we do."

"My, my, when you said you were heading east, you meant it!" pointed out Destiny's Catalyst as he came to a halt a pace away from Dekkin. "We're not far from the border!"

The oracle tried to smile, and while he succeeded in keeping the corners of his mouth from falling, he also failed to lift them up any. "Yes, and...I'll be crossing it too. I've been tasked with investigating how Zage Batur and his forces made it past our security there."

Cornelius's brow dropped a little. "Truly? You didn't strike me as the type to accept such an assignment." When the immortal didn't respond at this, the other man continued, "Hold on, *who* tasked you with this? The queen's missing, again, you know."

"Ah, yes, um," Dekkin replied, his eyes darting to and fro, "it was the adviser who gave me the task, Samuel Roneage."

Destiny's Catalyst brought a hand to rest on one of his hips, his face scrunched up in curiosity and puzzlement. "Truly? I would think he would've mentioned that to me when we spoke last, right before I set out in search of the Dark Lord." A frown sprouted on his face like a tenacious weed as another thought visibly formed in his head. "And…when would you have *received* the details of this mission? You left Cobaltus during the attack, yes? And you didn't mention it to me when last we met, but a letter about the job wouldn't have gotten to you this quickly, and he wouldn't have known where to send it besides."

The oracle only had enough time to form half of a lie. "All right, you've caught me. I gave myself the task, but I've been telling all who've asked that Samuel did. The authority of my position has shrunk considerably since the old days. To get where I need to go quickly, I needed something more to give to people, and I simply *must* reach the border with all haste. This is a matter of national security, after all."

The debate on the two sides that Cornelius was having over whether or not they bought this story visibly played out on his face, but in the end, trust won out, much to the immortal's relief. "Ah, well, yes, you shouldn't have done that. I will have to report this to the crown sadly. Why didn't you simply ride with my people and me, use the authority of *my* position? It's never been stronger, thanks to these kaglorite terrorists. After all, we're old friends, are we not?"

Just because you know someone for a couple decades doesn't make you old friends, thought Dekkin with gritted teeth, *especially when one of you is over five hundred years old.* He sucked up his pride and was about to grovel a little, anything to get this walking storehouse of potential destruction out of his face, when Destiny's Catalyst spoke again.

He asked, "Which way did you come to get here, Dekkin? It would've had to have been the Peacepath, yes? But you couldn't have gone that way. *I* traveled that path, with my people, scanning every blade of grass along it, and none of us spotted you or that sizable wagon at any point. You didn't—"

Again the oracle decided to throw a little spice of truth into his pot of deceit; wasn't it said that was the best way to tell lies? "No, I did. I took the other route. I hadn't been along the other side of the mountains in centuries, and part of an oracle's job is to keep up to date in regard to his home country, wouldn't you agree?" He could see he'd hit the other man's breaking point; Cornelius was obviously unconvinced. "All right, that's not it," the immortal admitted. "You said you were going the other way, and I didn't want to run into you, understand?" He put on a good show of this, using a tone of great reluctance when he spoke as if he'd exposed the very center of his soul to the other man.

It must've been done with a sufficient level of skill, for Cornelius anyway, as the adventurer winced and replied, "Well, that hurts, Oracle. I know you're not much for company, but nevertheless—"

"I'm sorry." Acting on this level, given Dekkin's blunt nature, took all he had, and he didn't know how much longer he could keep it up. "How goes the search for the Dark Lord?" he asked this quickly, and with a bit of a strain in his voice, like he was itching to change the topic of conversation from his forced admission.

Destiny's Catalyst sighed deeply in frustration. "Not well, as I'm sure you can see, given that we're still heading due east." He clenched one hand into a fist. "It doesn't make any sense! There're only two ways to the border. There's not a *chance* he slipped by us along the route we took, and I'm sure no one would've gone along the other path"—he stopped himself and, after a brief pause, frowned at the oracle—"except you, of course."

The immortal blinked. "Strange." The two men stood locked in each other's gazes for thirty days (or rather seconds). Cornelius broke the visual contact to glance over at Dekkin's wagon. A bead of sweat flowed down the oracle's forehead. Destiny's Catalyst shifted his eyes back to the immortal's and opened his mouth.

"Well, we'll just keep going east, I suppose, into the isles," said he. "I'm certain there're things about kaglorite magic we don't know.

Perhaps one of them gave the Dark Lord some means of outpacing us."

Dekkin's heart pounded like it was about to burst from his chest as he forced himself to exhale in a slow, measured manner. "Whoever knows with those vicious caneos?"

Cornelius's face froze in objection to that comment, but he didn't reply to it; instead, he turned about and called out to his fellows, "All right, everyone! Onw—"

Boom! Clack clack clack! Both men whipped around to face the direction of the sound, which came from the wagon. Adam Hefull stood before the doors to its back compartment, one arm up to the shoulder in the hole it had punched through it. The oracle looked at the young man's feet. He seemed to have tripped over a small pebble on the ground; how could someone fall so heavily from *that*?

"Oh!" Adam exclaimed sheepishly as he withdrew the offending arm from the wood. "I-I'm terribly sorry. I—"

"It's ALL RIGHT!" cried out the immortal before stopping himself as he felt the eyes of everyone around fixing themselves on him; he hadn't meant to speak that emphatically. He deflated slightly with some effort. "Th-that's quite all right, young man. I'll have it mended myself. I wouldn't want to keep you and your party from your duties on my account alone."

"Ah, as you say then. I'm truly very sorry, Oracle." The young man held the torch in his grasp up to the left half of the hole he'd made and peered through the right. "Heh, I did quite a number on this, didn't I?"

Dekkin froze in terror.

Adam furrowed his brow. Then turning to look at Cornelius, the young man said, "Master Arcind, your apprentice is back here and the *queen* a-and *the Dark Lord*!"

13

CULA'S APPEARANCE SNAPPED DEKKIN out of his awe-induced trance, and a good thing too; by the time they reached the oracle's home, a short walk from where they had been, the brown-haired man felt about ready to collapse from thirst. The entrance to the underground abode was protected from the elements by a cloth tarp held in place by metal stakes buried into the ground at each of its four corners. Cula removed one of them from the earth and lifted up the newly freed corner of fabric to allow himself and the others to descend into a massive subterranean tunnel. It was lit by hanging lanterns on both its walls every few feet, and there were several rooms right along its left and right walls, their size in keeping with the hallway they rested directly adjacent to.

"How did you make this?" Seren asked the oracle, looking from side to side as she went down the corridor.

Cula looked over one shoulder and flashed a slight smile at her as he led the group. "I didn't. This was made by a duracut." The others stared back at him uncomprehendingly. "Oh, ah, duracuts are a type of burrowing animal. The only way to survive out here is to go underground, and that's what they do, to make their nests."

Dekkin's wife ran one hand along the partition to her right while reaching out with her left, failing, of course, to make contact with the corresponding wall. "These duracuts must be quite large, if just *one* of them can make all this."

The oracle nodded. "Oh yes and vicious too. It was no small task to kill this nest's inhabitants so I could take it for myself."

The hallway split into multiple different routes, and when they reached the intersection, Seren looked down all of them to find several adjoining rooms along each. "So much space, so many rooms. Who else lives here with you, Oracle?"

"No one," answered Cula, "not on a permanent basis, anyway. Every part of this place was made by the duracuts who used to live in it. But I could've chosen my room and let the rest go to pot, of course. I didn't because on the rare occasion I receive visitors, people wanting for shelter or a look into the future or both, I want them to be able to stay here, as long as they like, no matter how many of them there are."

Dekkin's wife beamed at the oracle. "You've a generous soul, Cula."

"I'm simply doing my job," the old man replied. "Generosity is one of the qualities a person of my position ought to have."

"What do you do for food and water, Oracle?" interjected Dekkin.

Cula gestured to a door up ahead and to one side of them. "Several of these rooms are living spaces for small animals. I let that happen so I can pinch a few of them at a time to keep myself fed. As for water, there's an oasis nearby." When questioned on what an oasis is, the oracle answered.

"And you said we can stay here, for as long as we want?" the brown-haired man asked.

Cula nodded. "Absolutely, I'd very much appreciate the company, after so long without any. You said you came from the forest, didn't you? Unless living conditions outside the desert have improved a lot more than I'd guess, staying in these tunnels should be a great deal less dangerous than what you're used to. Once a duracut nest has been dug, the others stay away from it; the creatures are so aggressive and powerful they scare even the other members of their own species."

Dekkin put one arm around his wife's shoulders, looking over at her and saying with a grin, "New life starts here."

* * * * *

The oracle whipped around to face his wagon's coach box and started sprinting to it, though he knew this was a futile gesture with Cornelius so close and sure to be pursuing the other man after a few seconds. However, his luck changed after two paces when Zage, in a moment of hurried ingenuity, fired off a ball of red magic at the doors to the vehicle's back compartment, which seared a hole right through them before shooting out at Adam and evaporating upon making contact with the skin under his armor. Master Hefull, despite, of course, coming away from this untouched, save for a circular gap in the front of his chestplate, didn't recognize this in the moment and let out a piercing shriek that drew the attention of his fellows. Destiny's Catalyst did what he always would when a cry for help reached his ears; he turned away from the immortal and ran toward its source. This bought Dekkin enough time to get up onto the driver's seat and whip the kreshes lashed to it into a swift gallop. Before there came the inevitable sound of hooves clopping as the mounted soldiers began chasing after him, the oracle dug into the back alleys of his brain for a moment in search of some sort of plan and, miraculously, found one.

"Zage," called out the oracle over one shoulder after he pushed open the slat behind him, "Get up here *now*!"

The kaglorite yelled back in affirmation and walked with an unsteady gait to the wagon's back doors. As he reached them, an arrow shot through the hole he'd just made in them, nicking one of his thighs. Zage immediately stepped to one side, out of range. How in Samu was he going to get up front without becoming a living pincushion? He couldn't produce any good ideas in the five seconds allotted him, so he seized the best bad one and decided to run with it.

Rushing the nearest of the two doors, the kaglorite shoved it, grabbing onto and coming to hang off its top edge as it swung open. Another arrow landed just below his armpit as he moved, but before anyone else could get another shot off, the door moved all the way out, giving Zage cover enough when he stepped to and hugged the side of the wagon, for the moment at least. The kaglorite had just about shimmied up to the coach box when a rider beside him planted an arrow right into the back of one of the hands he was using to climb. Zage cried out in pain and almost fell to the ground racing by beneath him once he instinctively released its grip. Imagining his flesh being torn apart by the impact, the kaglorite managed through sheer force of will to, with gritted teeth, grab hold once more with his punctured hand and get up to Dekkin's side.

"About time!" the oracle shouted over the sound of massed battle cries from Cornelius's retinue, pointing at the group of soldiers gathering on their right. "Shoot some red magic at the ground, just ahead of where they are! Trip their kreshes up!"

Zage considered this for a moment and nodded. He turned ninety degrees; after which, his feet hung freely, and summoning a ball of crimson in both hands, anticipating where two of the riders would be in a few seconds before lobbing the mystical orbs there, he successfully upended the beasts they were riding.

"Coria, Matthew!" said the immortal back. "They're going to try to board us from the back! Hold them off, push them out if they get inside!"

"All right!" the queen replied with a metallic *shing* as she unsheathed her weapon. The boy said nothing, but Dekkin knew even without looking that he was doing the same. Ten seconds later, the oracle began hearing the clashing of metal on metal, midbattle grunts from both sides, and the panicked yells of soldiers being pushed off the wagon to land heavily on the ground behind it.

Zage swiveled his head swiftly around upon hearing the sound of steel cutting into wood with a chunky thud beneath and behind him. Sure enough, one of their pursuers, clever man, was trying to chop one of the wagon's back wheels apart. But how to stop him? The kaglorite wasn't risking another climb along the side of the wagon. A second possibility came to mind then, but it would require complete mastery of the mystical arts and pinpoint accuracy. Zage smirked to himself; if anyone had both, it was him.

He conjured up a needle of red magic and, grasping it in one hand, pulled back the corresponding arm before flinging it end over end to slice off the blade of the soldier's sword at the top of the hilt right as the other man brought it into the proper position with another slash at the wagon wheel. Immediately thereafter, the kaglorite heard Dekkin cry out in alarm, and their vehicle lurched heavily to the left. Zage whirled about to find one of the riders with the oracle's left shoulder in his grasp, attempting to snatch him right off the coach box. The immortal was struggling but, with only his feeble twig of a body at his disposal, was quickly giving ground.

"Dekkin!" called out the kaglorite as he summoned a whip into one of his hands with blue magic.

The oracle looked over at him, and Zage tossed the weapon to the other man, who caught it and lashed across the face the soldier currently assailing him. The soldier recoiled and released the immortal from his grip. Zage swiftly brought into existence a chain shot and hurled it at the legs of the enemy's kresh, entangling them and bringing both mount and rider crashing to the ground.

In the back, Coria and Matthew were each wrestling with one of the two soldiers just behind the wagon, trying to throw them off their kreshes and keep from being boarded. Each of their respective opponents was putting up a great fight, and so when a third rode up to one end of the vehicle's rear, they couldn't keep him from leaping into it from his mount. Matthew looked over at the invader just in time to see the man rise to his feet, turn to face the boy, and deliver a mighty kick to the lorm's head, knocking him unconscious instantly.

"*Matthew!*" the queen cried out in dismay. The interloper was but a pace away from her; she had one second to rid herself of the other two before she'd have to face the third. Coria thought of being seized, of her journey with Dekkin and the others being cut abruptly short, and suddenly a wave of power rushed through her body. She slammed the rider she had her hands on into the one directly beside him, shoving them both off their kreshes and then backpedaled as fast as she could at a crouch to evade the grasp of the third. Standing, she unsheathed her weapon again and charged.

Her newest foe had a sword in one hand and a shield in the other. The queen held her hammer-spear right in the middle of its shaft, slashing with one end and pounding with the other. Her pace was swift but measured; she didn't want to exhaust herself right off the bat, especially given that there were many more opponents to go, and she didn't imagine this nameless fighter would require anything more besides. She was wrong. Cornelius's man blocked the blows with ease and then suddenly began pressing the offensive, slashing and stabbing at her with his blade. It was all she could do to dodge these attacks, and in an instant, she found herself pushed up against the front wall of the wagon's back compartment.

Coria was seconds from defeat. She thought again of the consequences of that outcome, and the adrenaline that once again coursed through her veins then allowed her to do five minutes of thinking in two seconds. She went on the attack again, her movements wild and quick as lightning. The soldier steadily gave up ground but gazed at her with a bemused expression; she couldn't keep this up long enough to force him off the wagon. The look on his face was unchanging even when his heels were on the threshold behind him; they both knew she only had one good swing left in her, and it wouldn't be sufficient. The queen raised her weapon, pointed end down and over her head in preparation for a downward strike, and her opponent readied his shield to repel the blow. However, when she brought her lance down and at a forward angle, it was aimed not at her enemy but rather the section of wooden floor directly ahead of his feet. The soldier frowned down at the weapon as it sank into the planks beneath them with a splintering noise; how could she have missed so badly from that close? He got his answer as the chunk of floor directly below him collapsed from the fracture, and he lost his footing, falling backward off the moving vehicle.

Up on the coach box, Dekkin was looking from side to side frantically as the parties on either side of the wagon's front grew, becoming swarms, and their increased numbers led them to more boldly move in on him and his fellows. The oracle gazed straight ahead as he thought to himself that he was out of ideas when suddenly he spotted salvation in the distance there. A short ways ahead, the path forked, and its rightward offspring happened to be the sole path through a nearby thicket of trees, standing alone in the middle of the surrounding grassy field like a leafy island in a viridescent sea. The immortal lit up, and when they reached the intersection, he jerked the reins in his grasp to the right. The kreshes attached to them loudly protested at the sudden change of course but obeyed his directions, and as they turned, a few of the riders, who had sidled up to the right of the wagon, were either knocked from their mounts or forced to dart away before they could be.

Dekkin and the rest of his party reached the edge of the trees a minute later, and none too soon either; they were being assailed on all sides. The oracle looked back as they came under the cover of the hanging branches overhead and, just as he'd hoped, the mass of soldiers had no choice but to squeeze their formation into a single-file line behind the wagon. "THEY'LL HAVE TO COME AT US ONE AT A TIME NOW!" called back the immortal to Coria, as much gloating to himself as addressing her. "IT'LL BE AN ENDURANCE MATCH, BUT BETWEEN YOU AND MATTHEW, I THINK WE JUST MIGHT BE ABLE TO BEAT THEM!"

"I DON'T THINK THAT'S GOING TO WORK, DEKKIN!" the queen yelled through the open slat in response. "MATTHEW'S OUT COLD, AND I DON'T THINK EVEN I CAN GO A FEW HUNDRED ROUNDS BY MYSELF!"

The oracle blanched at this, and dread had started eating away at his fleshy heart when the horizon came to his rescue yet again; there was a wide, violently raging river cutting straight through the road up ahead, and unless one crossed the sturdy stone bridge built over it, they'd have to go all the way around on either of the two footpaths bordering each side of it to cross.

"Zage!" cried the immortal without looking away from the road before them. "U—"

"Yes, yes, I have got it!" the kaglorite replied, standing and turning about. When he heard the *clickety-clack, clickety-clack* of their kreshes' hooves striking the rock, Zage summoned a saucer of red magic and launched it straight up. It soared in ascent for a moment and then came plummeting down, collapsing the bridge in that one motion and leaving the soldiers without an easy path to their targets. Dekkin risked a glance back when he heard this and burst out laughing in great relief, clapping the kaglorite beside him on the shoulder in congratulation, a gesture that was met with a triumphant grin.

Several minutes passed as they made their way across the path; they were completely unfettered, and yet never relaxed, as the sounds of yelling men and the footfalls of their kreshes were always playing in the background behind them. Even this uneasy respite was better than gazing at the edge of a knife from two inches off though, and when the trees finally thinned to reveal the continuation of Humania's trademark plains, it seemed to the oracle that the time passed so quickly he hadn't even had the chance to blink.

The immortal brought the kreshes to a halt just outside the woods. "What are you doing?" asked Coria from the back. "Why have we stopped?"

"Cornelius and the others will be around in a short while," Dekkin answered in resignation. "We won't be able to outrun them. I don't see a way forward."

"Well, we can still *try*, can't we?" insisted the queen. "You never know."

The oracle sighed deeply. "Oh, I know all too well." He soon frowned to himself as he sat up on the coach box. "Coria, why are *you* still eager to evade the soldiers? You don't want to attract attention with a large escort, but we're but a few days from the border. Does it truly make a difference at this point?"

The immortal didn't see her eyes drop to the floor, but he heard her unconvincing tone as she replied, "These are dangerous times. You can't relax, even for a very short while, can you?"

Dekkin was about to press the issue when another line of inquiry he'd been too preoccupied to think of during the chase popped up in his head. "For that matter, Matthew, why were you *helping* us back there? You're a *captive*, and unlike our kaglorite friend, you *want* to be taken in by Cornleius, don't you?"

A total silence ensued, broken only by the appearance of a single light a great distance directly ahead of them. The oracle started and squinted out at it. "What is that light? What's it coming from?"

"Perhaps there's someone up there," Coria pointed out.

The immortal nodded. "Hmm, yes."

"Well, what are you doing?" questioned the queen after he then sat unmoving and without speaking for a short while. "Let's go investigate it!"

"Why?" Dekkin responded over one shoulder. "What good is a single light to us? What will we do—use it to give the soldiers a good view as they lock my hands in a pedibus?"

"A light could mean a *town*," countered Coria with a little exasperation. "At this time of night, it's entirely possible there's only one of its residents left awake. And in that town, there could be a map of some kind, to show us a way out of here."

The oracle shrugged. "The chances of *that* are quite slim, I believe."

"Possibly," the queen admitted, "but it might work out if we try. If we don't, there's no chance of escape at all."

The immortal thought on this for a moment before reluctantly conceding. Taking the reins in both hands, he ushered the kreshes toward the earthward star in the distance, hoping with the others that its light would show them a path to salvation.

14

"ARE YOU IN THE mood for a hunt?" Dekkin looked up from his breakfast as he sat beside Seren one morning. The grubs nesting in the tunnels were quite succulent once cooked. They were also, even unseasoned, several times spicier than anything he or anyone else in his tribe had ever tasted in their lives, and many of his fellows had complained during their first meal below the desert, but Dekkin, despite his discomfort while and immediately after eating the sizable bugs, relished the challenge of becoming accustomed to it. The speaker was Cula, standing beside him, the back end of the spear in his grasp resting on the floor.

"I could be convinced to take part," replied Dekkin with a slight smile; he didn't relish in such things, but his hunter-gatherer lifestyle had, of course, molded his body into perfect form for it, just like the other forest-dwellers, and as the head of his tribe, he was used to being called on to lead when the time came to seek out edible prey. He frowned then. "I thought you said the creatures nesting here would be enough to sustain us."

"That was before I knew you and all your people would be staying here indefinitely," Cula responded. As Dekkin began to open his mouth with an apologetic look on his face, the oracle held up one hand to stop him. "I am not complaining. I said I was happy to let you stay as long as you like and I meant it. I and the rest of you will simply have to hunt and only from time to time; one duracut is enough to feed an entire village for quite some time."

"Ah"—Dekkin dabbed at his mouth and stood—"well, all right then. Could you take point this time though? I've never faced one of these burrowing beasts before."

"Oh yes, yes," affirmed Cula. "The kill won't be yours."

* * * * *

For the sake of increasing their speed and decreasing their visibility, Dekkin and the others agreed to abandon the wagon at the thicket's perimeter, loading as many supplies as they could onto the two kreshes before mounting them, two to one beast, and beginning the ride to the pinprick of light on the horizon. They did their best to stay on the path without being able to truly see it; for obvious reasons, they opted not to light any torches. Luck was on their side once again that night; they made it a good distance without incident, after which Dekkin, steering the frontmost kresh, pulled back on the reins in his grasp, leading the primary rider of the one behind him to do the same.

The light that had led them there was indeed coming from a town, a small but respectable and roughly square farming settlement with its fields facing and running perpendicular to them. The tightness in the oracle's chest had loosened a little when he'd gotten close enough to see there was no wall surrounding the near side of the village, but upon closer inspection now, he saw that there were guards stationed all around its borders, or at least the section of them he could make out at that time. Dekkin's kresh took a step forward of its own accord, and he had to reel it in to prevent further movement, stroking its neck to quash any audible protest before it started. How in Samu could they get past that guard? The oracle frowned in irritation as he was forced to rein in his mount once again…and at that moment had an idea.

He and the others downsized their personal stores for a second time, holding onto only as much as could reasonably be kept on their persons. Then the oracle led his kresh and the one behind him off the beaten path until they were directly across from one end of the crop fields before them. He and the others got off their mounts once they were there, letting the beasts trot over to the titillating foodstuffs growing in the distance straight ahead as planned. The nearest guard, standing, from his point of view, perfectly centered in the frame of the crop fields, cried out in dismay when he spotted the mounts nibbling on a few of the stalks behind him and ran over to ward them off. Alas, this took some doing. "Never get between a kresh and its dinner" as the saying went. And while he tangled with the bleating beasts, Dekkin and his fellows snuck into town.

Once the guard sent the kreshes packing and returned to his post, all four of them ducked behind the cover of the nearest row of crops. Then each of them poked their respective heads out in search of the right moment to pop out and advance a few paces before hiding among the stalks once again. They repeated this a few times before Dekkin, walking backward so as to keep an eye on the man standing watch, stepped into a massive footprint in the earth and, not expecting the sudden drop, tripped, falling flat on his back with a clear, very much audible sound of impact. The oracle scooched out of view in time, but the damage was done; the guard, his brow furrowed, turned around and began making his way toward the noise's general location.

Zage, thinking fast, conjured a pebble out of thin air with blue magic and pulled back his arm to throw it a good distance away from the immortal and the others. He stopped before completing the motion however as a savage notion entered his mind. The kaglorite turned about and pitched the small stone directly forward. It landed just outside the field of crops he was standing crouched in, and at that, the guard's attention shifted there. The watchman began cutting between two rows of stalks to get to it; they grew so thick and had been positioned so close together that Zage wasn't spotted even from just a few feet away, fortunately enough for him. The kaglorite trailed just behind him in his own column quietly and without rising, materializing a curved dagger in one hand as a wicked grin cut across his face like the tip of a sharp blade.

As Zage advanced on the guard, the other man looked left and right, up and down, every which way except where he needed to, just like every other one of the innumerable humans that had fallen by his hand. The kaglorite came to a halt just far enough away from his prey that the latter couldn't feel the breath of the former on the back of the neck and lifted the dagger high above his head. Right as the blade stopped its ascent, Zage heard a woman grunt with effort ahead and to one side of him, and Coria came out of nowhere, knocking the guard unconscious with a blow to the head with her hammer.

The queen stepped between the kaglorite and his would-be victim, now lying limply on one side in the dirt. "Come now, Zage!" she chided at a whisper. "No killing any innocents, all right?" Coria heard the sound of the pebble striking the ground and remembered then what she'd forgotten once the chase had begun; she was traveling with a serial killer. She'd resolved then to save the guard's life, and not a moment too soon.

The kaglorite threw up his hands but made no move to finish what he'd started, turning to one side and continuing on his way instead. "Gods forbid, I try to enjoy myself every once in a while."

The four of them were able to move more freely with the watchman out of commission but still maintained a tense, careful quietude. When houses began to come into view after a few minutes of picking their way through the crops, Dekkin held up one hand to bring the others to a halt and slunk up to the nearest domicile for inspection. There were no lights on in the house. The next step was to check the windows, an endeavor that involved thanks to the existence of a second floor a climb up the sides. Fortunately, the slapdash arrangement of the stone blocks they were made up of allowed for a relatively easy journey to and along their higher reaches, and after only a short while, Dekkin had checked every room in the building and seen them all empty. Turning to the others after this, he beckoned them to him.

"Well?" asked Coria softly.

"I didn't see anyone at all," Dekkin replied. "Nevertheless, let's not risk discovery even in the slightest." He turned to face the kaglorite. "Zage?"

The kaglorite nodded and went up to the near wall, placing both hands flat against it. If red magic was thrown into something, it would make a sound as it dissolved, the kind of noise it would produce if it were broken by another physical object. However, if the mystical energy was applied directly to it, it would disintegrate silently, as was needed in the present situation. Both of Zage's hands had just begun to glow red when there came the sound of a thundering cavalcade back the way they'd come. It was their pursuers.

Dekkin, Matthew, and Coria moved to hide behind the left wall, but Zage stopped them before they got far; he had a better, less strenuous idea. The kaglorite spread his hands out to each side of himself as far as he could, like a bird in flight, while keeping them a bit ahead of the rest of his body. Blue magic radiated between them, and a tarp materialized there. He made another and then draped them over himself and the others as they sat crouched side by side up against the side of the adjacent house. Even under cover of the cloth, everyone held their breath as the sound of kreshes' hooves pounding on dirt raced by them shortly thereafter, but they were not discovered.

Breathing heavy sighs of relief as the *clomp, clomp, clomp* faded into the distance ahead of them, Dekkin and the others unveiled themselves, and Zage got back to work continuing to cut a hole in the near wall large enough for each of them to crawl through. Once he carved an appropriately sized circle in the stone directly above the ground, he carefully grabbed the now-disconnected chunk of rock and pulled it out from where it was, setting it down on one side behind him. Then one by one, they crawled into the house. They came out in the dining area, which shared a room with and was off to one side of the foyer. There was a mat by the inside of the door, as you would expect, but it extended out from it about a dozen feet, which you might not have. A thick layer of dust covered every inch of the place.

"All right," whispered Dekkin to the others as he started making his way around the room. "Let's search the whole house, try to find a map of some kind." And so they did but were met with no success. The oracle swore as he began walking back to the foyer beside Coria. "Nothing. We'll have to try another. I hate to say it, but we should probably pick one that's occupied next time. It looks as if this house is abandoned, has been for some time."

"Ye—" the queen began before crying out as she stepped on the carpet before the door and dropped into a hole hidden by the fabric above it.

The immortal's pulse raced as this happened, but fortunately, it was over as soon as it had begun; she only fell for a split second. Dekkin recalled then where they were and under what circumstances and looked up from her fearfully for signs of approach from curious townspeople or soldiers attracted by the noise. When he saw none, his concern faded into frustration.

"Would you *keep it down*?" hissed the oracle quietly as he gazed down at Coria flat on her back. "The goal here is *stealth*, remember?"

The queen got to her feet. "Well, I'm sorry I couldn't keep my composure while I was *suddenly and unexpectedly falling into a hole in the ground*." She looked around her. "What *is* this, anyway? Why is it here?"

"Climb back up here," the immortal said. "Let's remove the mat and take a look." They did so, finding a set of stairs leading down to a short stretch of dirt, where Coria had landed, at the mouth of an underground tunnel. Dekkin walked down it a few paces and, taking a torch he'd cinched to his belt, lit it, seeing by its illumination a passageway far longer than its reach with several doorways on either side of it.

The oracle froze.

Coria waited for him to move or say something and, when he didn't for some time, called out to him, "What? What is it? We're a tad low on time, you know."

The immortal muttered something under his breath. The queen squinted at him and raised a hand to one of her ears. "What was that?"

"I said I've been here before," Dekkin replied without turning his head, "a long time ago."

Coria raised her brow. "Truly? You've been *in here*, in this tunnel?"

The oracle nodded. "Yes, this all used to be desert, back then."

"Do you think it leads out of town, somewhere far off from here?" asked the queen hopefully.

"No," the immortal responded as he broke from his trance and came about. "Not this one, but there are others nearby, many others, and if it's still standing, there's one that goes out for miles, toward the border."

Coria lit up. "Truly? Oh, that's wonderful! Do you remember where it is exactly?"

Dekkin shook his head as he walked toward her. "No, but give me some time, and I can figure it out. Let's go."

The two of them, along with Matthew and Zage, snuck out of the house through the same hole they used to enter it and followed the oracle as he made his way to the center of town, creeping through alleyways and darting between the sparse spots of cover when forced to step outside them. When he came to a halt just beside the edge of one of the houses, the others followed suit behind him.

"It's up ahead, I think," said the oracle. He peeked around the corner for a split second before retracting his head, swearing softly. "I think the building, its mouth, is directly below is the mayor's house, and it looks like *everybody* who's after us is gathered there at the moment."

"So what do we do?" Coria inquired anxiously. "Try to draw them away somehow?"

"Too risky," answered the immortal with a vehement shake of his head. "What we should do is far simpler than that. We wait here, watching for them to disperse and then sneak inside as soon as everyone or at least all but a few are gone."

The queen considered this for a moment before nodding. "All right." She leaned up against the wall they were hiding behind. "When were you last there, that underground tunnel? What were you doing there?"

Dekkin pressed his lips together tightly and looked away. "I don't want to talk about it."

"Come now!" Coria insisted. "Tell us please! It must be a most interesting tale if that's your response."

"Is now truly the time for a story?" countered the oracle bitingly as he gestured toward the soldiers gathered around the corner with his head.

"Now is the *perfect* time for a story!" the queen pointed out. "Who knows how long we'll need to wait here?"

The immortal glanced over at Coria and something about the look of longing on her pretty face unlatched his heart. He sighed deeply. "All right. I'll tell you, *all* of it." And so he related the parts of his past we've been made privy to…and more.

* * * * *

When Dekkin spotted the first duracut, no one had ever been more happy to find a savage, imposing brute of a creature such as that; he didn't know how to conserve his water like Cula did and had almost entirely drained his personal flask after only about ten minutes of travel. He had a moment of clarity after taking a swig however and went up to the oracle's side with some reluctance. "So… ah…how dangerous is it, hunting these creatures?" asked the brown-haired man.

"Quite," Cula answered matter-of-factly without looking away from their target. "We don't stand a chance of returning to camp unless this is all done to the absolute letter."

Dekkin gulped loudly. "I see." He shifted his weight from one side to another. "So what is it that must be done to bag such a beast?"

"Like I told you before, these are burrowing animals," the oracle explained. "They spend most of the time traveling underground. But when they're doing that, a small patch of skin on the top of its head remains above ground. In the middle of that patch is the opening of a sort of small mouth. By keeping it out of the sand, the duracut can breathe indefinitely even with the rest of its head completely submerged. What we need to do is spot that patch as the creature moves or, better yet, while it's sleeping beneath the ground, and block it off."

"And then its head will come up, and we can shove a spear through it?" assumed the other man with a hopeful light in his eyes.

Cula shook his head, and that light was immediately extinguished. "No, a duracut's skin is harder than anything else I've ever seen in six-hundred-odd years of living here. No, the only way to attack it is in its eyes. Luckily for us, it has quite a few of those. You'll step on it, and I'll wait just ahead of it for the head to emerge, and then I'll throw my spear into one of its eyes or try to, anyway." Dekkin started at this; he couldn't think of anything worse than dying before his time, leaving behind a devoted wife and infant child.

The two of them lay in wait for their target to dig in and start moving. Dekkin measured the time by the number of sweat droplets that ran down his face. He'd counted up to a high two figures when the beast finally began burrowing itself into the sand. Dekkin found then that, because of a duracut's massive size and the fact that they traveled mostly by carving through many pounds of earth, when it moved in that way it did so very slowly. He and Cula easily caught up to it within a few minutes even though it was headed in the same direction.

"Now" the oracle yelled over the thundering sound of churning sand before them, "JUMP ON IT!"

Dekkin looked at him with eyes as wide as they could be. "*What?*"

"It'll be more dangerous for me!" Cula pointed out. "As long as you stay on top of its head, it can't possibly get to you!"

The brown-haired man considered this and realized the other man spoke truth. Nodding to the oracle, he increased his pace until the tips of his toes were almost touching the duracut's exposed flap of skin before leaping forward and onto it, covering the mouth there with his feet. The creature immediately surfaced, rearing up with a mighty roar at the same time, and Dekkin had to get down on his stomach and cling to the creature with both arms to keep from sliding off, and then only just. After fully emerging from the sand, the beast violently shook its entire body from side to side in an attempt to dislodge the intruder from the top of its head, and once again, the man himself barely managed to stay put.

While this was happening, Cula circled around to the front of the duracut and pulled back one arm, readying the spear in his grasp. When the beast let its head drop a little after trying to snap up at Dekkin in a series of futile gestures, the oracle pitched his weapon right into one of its multitudinous eyes and immediately following this began advancing on the creature as he pulled out a knife to gut the corpse. However, the duracut didn't fall, instead bellowing even louder than it already had been; the spear hadn't gone in far enough.

The oracle stood frozen in uncertainty; he'd only brought the one weapon. Dekkin saw this, and the old man's empty hands and the spear protruding from the beast's face and the creature's hearty movements and put it all together even as he hung on for dear life. A plan popped into the brown-haired man's mind, one which was wildly ill-advised but gave him a better chance at survival than doing nothing at all as he was currently. Reaching forward, Dekkin began inching his way up to the duracut's face, holding fast against its fervid gyrations all the while. After several minutes, during which he lost ground numerous times, he was atop the frontmost section of the top of the beast's head.

When Dekkin went to reach down for the shaft of the spear in the creature's eye, it bucked, and with only one arm grasping its head, he couldn't weather the motion and pitched forward. Fortunately for him, as he fell, one of his hands shot out faster than thought and gripped the spear's protruding shaft. Dekkin, coming to hang off the wooden pole, instinctively flinched as the beast snapped its jaws at him, though he knew they couldn't reach him. What now? If he were to drop down from his present location, the fall would break his legs at the very least, and if he was lucky enough for that to be all, then the duracut would be free to have its way with him. But what else could be done?

Another perilous plan sprang to mind for him then. He decided to attempt carrying it out after only a split second of thought, in part, because he saw no alternative and also because of that, he was prepared to do anything other than stay where he was. Dekkin inched closer to the duracut along the shaft of the spear as much as possible without being in danger of losing his legs to its gnashing fangs. Then he grasped as best he could a natural handhold on the creature's face with one hand for leverage and, using the other, pushed the weapon deeper into the beast's eye, far enough for the motion to be fatal.

The creature cried out in agony and anguish, lifting its front feet high off the ground. Dekkin gripped the shaft of the spear tightly with both hands as the world tilted violently around him, hoping it would hold but suspecting it wouldn't, imagining the wood without breaking apart from that within and sending him plunging to his death. It did crack in several places as it cut through the air but remained intact, and as the duracut began to slump forward, the brown-haired man waited until its head was a safe distance away from the ground and started preparing to let go; this was the idea he'd just had. But right before he released his grip, the beast dipped its head inward, and as Dekkin plummeted, he looked up and saw the creature's considerable bulk rushing down at him from directly above.

The brown-haired man landed on his feet hard and watched his doom as it advanced toward him. There wasn't enough time for any sort of profound final thoughts. But suddenly, a second before his grisly demise, Dekkin's body was thrown to one side. He soared through the air to safety, landing on a pillow of fine sand. The brown-haired man looked back at where he'd been an instant ago and saw Cula, who'd come up and shoved him out of the carcass' path, placing himself in harm's way as he did so. The oracle leaped then toward Dekkin as quickly and forcefully as he could, but only his top half got out from under the creature's shadow before its corpse slammed into the ground, crushing the rest of him.

"Cula!" screamed Dekkin as he stood and sprinted over to his mortally wounded friend.

"The turins," the oracle replied through gritted teeth and a tortured grimace.

The younger man frowned. "What? What's that?"

"You must take my turins," croaked Cula. "I'm going to die any second now, and you're…capable of becoming an oracle."

Dekkin's face fell as he recognized the truth in the old man's words. His eyes darted back and forth for a few seconds as he searched for a way out before finding one and replying, "Do you think the world truly…*needs* an oracle, a human oracle? I hadn't even *heard* of you before we met a few days ago, you know, and there are other oracles of different races out there—"

"Dekkin," the old man interrupted sternly. "There are only three turins left alive. We cannot pass up an opportunity to preserve one when it presents itself to us." The brown-haired man considered this and, after a moment, nodded with great reluctance. Cula's features softened when he saw the copious amount of water the younger man had drunk so many minutes ago leave him as tears. "I'm truly sorry, Dekkin." The oracle closed his eyes, concentrating on the backs of his eyelids, and shortly thereafter, his turins removed its teeth from his flesh and began crawling about on the sand beneath him. Cula scooped up the large bug and placed it right-side up on Dekkin's upper back, and the insect latched onto this new host. "Take heart" rasped the former oracle to his successor seconds before the former's death. "You need only live another one thousand years."

* * * * *

Coria's cheeks were wet with tears by the time Dekkin finished whispering his story to her and the others in the middle of that narrow alleyway. "You never wanted to be an oracle," she barely managed to choke out. "But you're living out your term?"

The oracle nodded. "I'm not a hero, but I'm not so much a villain that I would do something so dishonorable."

"Your wife and child?" squeaked the queen.

"Died long ago," the immortal confirmed. "What else?"

Coria thought on this for a while. "Could you…at least meet with the other oracles, form friendships with them? Relationships that…could last your whole life or at least more of it than your average person?"

Dekkin shook his head. "No. The itrasian oracle keeps to herself, as you can imagine, and the one in Kagloris…he's been missing ever since the massacre, and I don't think it's any mystery why."

"So everyone you've ever known is dead," summarized the queen with a haunted look in her eyes. "Or they most likely will be before you." The oracle confirmed this, his lips pressed tightly together. She reached out to squeeze one of his shoulders. "I'm so sorry, Dekkin."

The immortal paused for a moment before simply nodding once.

"Ho!" Zage called out softly as he looked around the wall they were all standing beside. "If you two are quite finished, the crowd around and inside the mayor's house seems to have dissipated completely. Let's go."

Coria opened her mouth to chide the kaglorite for his insensitivity, but before she could say anything, Dekkin put a hand atop one of her shoulders and shook his head when she looked over at him. "No time," said the oracle. "As he said, let's go."

He, Matthew, and Coria all peeked out of the alleyway to find what Zage had; there was no longer anyone milling about just outside the mayor's house, and no candles burned within its first floor. The oracle motioned for the queen to quietly open the front door once they were all standing just before it.

"Help!" the kaglorite suddenly cried into the still night. "The intruders, they're here!"

15

Before Zage's voice had even finished reverberating off the surrounding houses he shoved the others aside, quick as lightning, and opened the door before shutting it behind himself. Dekkin heard a click on the other side of it; even still he tried to turn the knob, to no avail.

"What do we do?" quavered Coria beside him. The oracle asked himself the same question, sent it bouncing against every corner of his mind in a matter of seconds. He raised his brow when an idea presented itself to him. Would it work? Well, it already had once before, hadn't it?

The immortal started jogging to the nearest house with candlelight behind its windows. "Follow me." He opened the front door and burst inside, loping to a bedroom on the first floor, where an elderly human woman lying under the covers on the bed gazed back at him through slitted eyes once he'd arrived there. "Get up," he said to the old woman. She didn't move, and he crossed the room to her side before gently helping her to her feet. Then Dekkin steered her to just behind the front door. Looking out a nearby window, the oracle saw Cornelius's troops massing at the front of the house, though he didn't spot Destiny's Catalyst during his cursory glance. "Don't any of you dare come in!" yelled the immortal to the soldiers outside. "I've got a knife to an old woman's throat, and if you don't let me pass unmolested, I swear I'll slice it open!" Dekkin's hands were resting at his sides as he said this, but when he saw one of the enemy peeking through the same window he'd used to catch a glimpse of the outside just then, trying to determine the veracity of his statements, the oracle unsheathed the dagger at one of his hips and brought its point to within a few inches of his hostage's jugular.

"*Dekkin!*" Coria cried out as she took a step toward him from behind, one hand raised and extended slightly in that direction.

"You *know* I won't actually hurt her," muttered the immortal to her once she was within earshot. At this, she backed off. She, Dekkin, and Matthew waited, expecting any second to hear a declaration of acquiescence from outside, when one of the soldiers kicked the door down and rushed into the house along with several of his fellows.

* * * * *

Five minutes prior, Allard Adelis, one of the soldiers accompanying Cornelius Arcind, had been torturing a newborn caneo. He found its mother and her six suckling pups just outside someone's front door as he patrolled in search of the fugitive Dekkin Eterden and decided to have some fun. Most likely, he reasoned, the owner of the expecting caneo and therefore its spawn left it out in the open air, alone, to give birth and first meet its offspring, as was the custom, and so he or she wouldn't yet know how many popped out of their pregnant pet. Ergo, he could take one, kill it, and get away with the deed, scot-free.

Allard turned the young caneo onto its back and, taking out a knife, stabbed it several times in the stomach, pushing the blade into its flesh slowly so as to savor the moment and its resulting cries of agony. The pup was just about dead, blood seeping out of its open mouth, when one of the psychopath's comrades in arms appeared from around the nearest corner.

"Allard!" the other man called out. He looked down and saw the mortally wounded infant at his fellow's feet but did nothing; he knew Allard turned his attentions to other people whenever any of them tried to interfere with his sick games. "We found them holed up in one of these houses. They've taken a hostage. Master Arcind hasn't arrived yet. That leaves you to take point."

Allard looked up from his maimed plaything and grinned maliciously.

* * * * *

Dekkin released the old woman and turned around. As he made for the stairs to the second floor, the frontmost of his pursuers slashed out at him with a sword. The oracle winced as the blade nicked the back of his waist.

"Dekkin!" the immortal heard Matthew call out behind him as he bounded up the steps three at a time. Looking around to face the boy, Dekkin saw that he and Coria were surrounded on all sides by soldiers, distress plain on their faces as they gazed up at him pleadingly. The oracle turned his head away from them with great reluctance; what in Samu could *he* do for them at this point? His heart was unaffected as he, cresting the top of the stairs, felt the pounding of his pursuers' boots on the bottom few steps; it already seemed like it would give out from the strain of its hammering any second.

Though he never risked a glance behind him as he crossed the floor on the second level to the master bedroom, he could tell the leader of the soldiers chasing him was but a pace away when he shut and locked the door behind him. After trying the knob to no avail, the other man went to work hacking through the wood with his sword. There was no time to lose. The immortal went to a window directly across from the mayor's house and opened it before walking back from it as far as he could. Dekkin looked over at the locked door; the gash down the middle of it was a stroke away from being big enough to accommodate the soldiers chasing him. Shifting his gaze back to the open window, the oracle ran to it, getting up as much speed as he could in such an enclosed space and dove out of it.

The cool night air blew through the immortal's hair as he soared out of the building. Strangely enough, the nameless domicile he'd just come from was taller than the residence of the town's most important man, but he didn't question miracles; it was because of this that, if all went well, he could leap from the second floor of the former to grip a windowsill on that of the latter. *If* all went well, which it didn't. The front of his feet clipped the bottom of the opening he went through as he did so, and suddenly his gaze, which had been fixed on his destination, was flipping end over end wildly along with the rest of him. Your average person would've tried in this situation to land flat on their back, distributing the force of the impact over the largest surface area possible, but Dekkin's instincts told him different; after all, were he to do that, his turins would be summarily crushed between his back and the street. Instead, he turned to land on his feet. And so he did, although they buckled from the impact immediately, and he winced as his knees slammed into the hard stone beneath him. Soldiers piled on him from every direction as soon as he touched down, rendering him entirely immobile.

"Allard!" called out one of the four men dragging the oracle along, one to grip in both hands each of his limbs as they brought him before a man with raven-black hair and a cruel twist to his mouth. "Here he is."

Allard nodded. "Good." He gestured toward the house the immortal had just come from. "Bring him back in there. I'll handle him until Master Arcind arrives."

His subordinate answered in the affirmative with a sympathetic grimace. Dekkin was brought back into the foyer of the old woman's house, where he was left alone with Allard, Matthew, and Coria. "You can go," Allard said to the latter two. "You aren't needed for this."

"Let me stay, please," replied the boy.

Allard frowned over at the lorm. "Why?"

"I want to see what you're going to do to him," Matthew answered. "He kidnapped me, held me for weeks."

Coria looked over at him as if stricken, but the boy didn't return her gaze.

Allard paused before flashing the lorm a savage grin. "Ah, well, all right then." He turned his head to face the queen's. "What about you, Your Highness?" Those last two words sounded derisive coming from his lips.

"Oh no, I don't"—began Coria before Matthew, out of the soldier's sight, nudged her near foot with one of his own; the queen brightened upon realizing the boy's seeming callousness was being manufactured in service of a plan before quickly tamping down her expression so as not to alert Allard to what was happening—"uh, yes, I would like to stay as well."

Allard drew a knife from his hip and began advancing toward Dekkin with depraved glee written large on his face. "Understood. Well, I wouldn't want to keep you two waiting." Four seconds later, a scream erupted from the foyer they all stood in...as Matthew drove one of his daggers into the back of the soldier's right knee. The boy pulled the blade free of its fleshy target, allowing Allard to fall to the ground on his back, before walking over to the man's neck and skewering it as he knelt beside it.

"MATTHEW!" Coria cried in shock and horror as he slid the knife out of Allard's throat, uncorking a geyser of blood. "WHAT ARE YOU DOING?"

"It's Allard Adelis," replied the boy matter-of-factly. "He deserves it."

The queen wanted to argue the point much further but realized as she opened her mouth that starting such a debate would be at the moment ill-timed. "Well, *now* what do we do?" She and the lorm looked to Dekkin.

"He can put on Allard's armor," Matthew said, taking her and the oracle aback. "Pretend he's escorting us. Then we can get away without a fight."

Coria thought about this. "But the armor won't shield his *face*. And a lot of the soldiers know what Dekkin looks like!"

"It won't work if anyone looks too closely. But it might be enough to let us get away if no one does." The boy shrugged. "It was the best I could come up with."

The queen ruminated a little longer before nodding. "Yes, that could work." She put a hand on one of the lorm's shoulders and smiled down at him. "Under the circumstances, it's a great idea. Inspired, even. Nice job, Matthew."

The boy lit up as he returned her gaze. Dekkin pried the armor off Allard's corpse with the others' help, all of them doing their best to wipe the bloodstains off the cool metal, and donned it himself. It hung loosely on him but not enough for it to be a serious wrench in their scheme.

When the oracle walked out of the front door, head ducked as low as it could reasonably go, with his companions trailing behind him, they found to their immense relief that none of the soldiers had stuck around to have to hear the sounds of torture they thought would be ringing out from the old woman's foyer. Unfortunately, that was where their luck ran out, as he saw when he turned to face the front door of the mayor's house; Cornelius had posted himself just outside of it and stood there unmoving. Dekkin swore under his breath at the sight of the other man and walked back into the old woman's house, shepherding Matthew and Coria in that direction as he did so.

"What do we do now?" asked the queen in distress after the situation had been explained to her by the oracle.

"I don't know," the immortal admitted. "How do you like your odds in a fight against Destiny's Catalyst?"

"I don't," confirmed Coria.

"Me and Dekkin could help!" the boy interjected.

The queen smiled down at him, sweet and apologetic. "I appreciate the offer, sweetheart, and I don't mean to be insulting to you two, but I don't believe that would make much of a difference." The lorm frowned. She raised up both hands slightly along with her brow, her mouth slightly agape, saying, "*I'm sorry!* Like I said, I wasn't—"

Matthew shook his head. "Uh, no, that's not it. I just realized something. I've had the feeling that I've been here before ever since we arrived. And I remember now. I have. This village is called Gred. My master and I stopped here on our way to the ceremony."

"All right," responded Dekkin. An expectant pause followed. The oracle furrowed his brow when it wasn't filled after some time. "So what? Can that help us in some way?"

The boy nodded. "Yes, it gives us an opportunity. It's so dangerous it's idiotic, but I think it might be our only chance. And if it works, we won't just evade my master, but we'll beat him."

This piqued Dekkin and Coria's interest, of course, and so the lorm related his idea to them. When he finished his pitch, both of them were staring back at him in utter incredulity.

"*That's* the plan?" the oracle said after a brief pause. Matthew blushed and shrunk at this, averting his eyes from those of the immortal. "Well, you're the king of understatement, calling that merely dangerous. I'm sorry, but I'm not sure I can sign off on it."

"But do any of us have a better idea?" pointed out the queen. "Or even...*another* idea?"

There was a moment of silence as all those gathered there considered the question. Finally, Dekkin signed in resignation and said, "Oh, horb it, we'll use Matthew's plan. It's only the *fourteenth* time we've willingly walked into the *jaws of death*, after all."

The three of them left the old woman's house again, turning their backs to Cornelius, and walked about until they found a pair of riderless kreshes, each accompanied by a soldier standing beside them with reins in hand. Dekkin and Coria each picked one and, going up to them, shoved them to the ground before seizing their mounts and riding off, setting a course for the mayor's house. Matthew climbed up onto the back of the oracle's right before it took off and fastened his little green arms tightly around the immortal's waist as the creature beneath them raced through the streets. When Cornelius came into view, he was already looking in Dekkin's direction due to the cries of protest by the soldiers they'd just stolen from as the two victims of theft pursued them on foot, their heavy metal armor clinking and clanking loudly with each hurried step. The oracle brought his steed to a halt once he could make out the features of Master Arcind's face, and therefore vice versa. Taking off his helmet, the immortal pitched it to the ground and after giving Cornelius enough time to register his identity brought his kresh about and rode off at full speed.

Hearing a few sets of footfalls from behind as he made his way back to the crop fields astride his newly and immorally acquired bolting beast was more than manageable for Dekkin's nerves. That small collection of rhythmic hoofbeats on cobblestone turning into a thunderous cacophony as a small army assembled on the move proved disconcerting, even though this was all according to the boy's plan. After speeding down the center of the crop fields, the oracle and the others turned left toward a huge cavern he hadn't noticed as he'd first passed it. As the immortal and his companions allowed themselves to be swallowed by the darkness within, he marveled in silence as Cornelius called out for the other members of his retinue to stop at the mouth of the cave, just as the lorm had said they would. The vice around Dekkin's heart relaxed its iron grip once there came the sound of but one rider behind him, although this feeling too was totally irrational given that the identity of their lone pursuer was the strongest fighter in the history of the world.

When the three of them reached the massive chamber with the spiral walkway, Dekkin and Matthew began making their way down to its floor while Coria remained at the room's top entrance, disembarking from her mount and unsheathing her weapon. As the oracle eyed the stone floor racing by beneath him while he and the boy began to descend, a nervous thrill shot through his already-taxed system; there was more than enough room for a person of any size to run down the swirling ramp, but someone astride a kresh was a tight squeeze, and he worried that at any moment the beast he was riding would slip off the edge and send the both of them hurtling toward their doom. About halfway through his and the lorm's downward journey, the immortal heard the sound of metal striking metal up where they'd left the queen. Fortunately for Dekkin and Matthew, the former's concerns about the width of the walkway proved to be for naught, as they got to the bottom without incident.

From there, the boy led the oracle down the adjacent corridor to the room with the paralyzed duracut. This particular animal was on the verge of starvation after weeks trapped in the webbing ensnaring it, but even still, the immortal swallowed loudly upon first viewing it, both from his personal history with the species and the knowledge that even a day from death one of its members possessed more than enough destructive potential to massacre not only them but the entire populace of Gred too. When the beast's gaze fell on him and the lorm, Dekkin preemptively clapped his hands over his ears, but all the creatures had the strength to do was snort loudly and let out a weak (for it, at any rate) groan.

"You'll take the right, and I, the left," the oracle instructed Matthew once they reached the captive duracut and dismounted from their kreshes. "That way, if it decides to attack us once it's free"—there was a grave quality in the immortal's eyes as he paused there—"there's a better chance one of us will make it." The boy nodded, and the two of them made their way around each side of the beast, unsheathing their respective weapons.

* * * * *

Coria dreamed for years of getting to face off against Destiny's Catalyst. Potentially wounding the most important man in the history of the world was, however, so imprudent, especially for a woman of her position, that she'd never even dared to inquire as to the possibility. But now? She was no queen. She was a young woman tasked with buying some time for her friends.

It wasn't long before Cornelius caught up to her. "Your Highness!" called out the hero in relief as he reined in his kresh a few paces from her. "Dekkin let you go?"

Coria assumed a combat stance, holding her weapon of choice in both hands. "Not exactly. I can't let you through here, Master Arcind."

Cornelius's face fell. "He's making you defend him? He has a hold over you in some way?"

"Something like that," the queen replied.

Destiny's Catalyst dismounted from his kresh and hesitantly drew Kiam from one hip. "But if I defeat you in fair combat, he won't retaliate against you?"

"Oh, yes, I'm sure," confirmed Coria. One corner of her mouth raised a little to form an expression that could almost be described as haughty. "*That* is a big if, however."

Even an optimist like the queen recognized that, not being a great hero of prophecy, she was at a disadvantage against Cornelius here. However, she had at least one thing working in her favor; there was little chance he could have in the past faced someone with her type of weapon; hers was the only one in all existence as far as she knew, after all. And she planned to capitalize on that fact.

Positioning a hand somewhat close to each of her weapon's dual ends, she swiped at her opponent's chest from his right with the lance. He blocked this easily with his sword, of course, but holding its hilt in both hands left him open on the opposite side of wherever he brought it to whenever he did so. This detail was negligible in a standard bout between two fighters with conventional arms, but that's not what this was now, was it? Bringing back her left hand and moving forward her right while maintaining contact with the tip of Cornelius' sword, Coria hit him upside the head with her hammer. Even a warrior of his considerable caliber could not help but be repelled by such a blow, his or her head swimming.

The queen turned her weapon upside down and swung at him with her hammer. Your average combatant would've been too dazed to counter the hit, but this was Cornelius Arcind we're talking about, and so, of course, he had the wherewithal to meet her steel with his. However, his left side was still fuzzy from the strike on his head, and so he didn't have the presence of mind to prevent Coria from slicing open his thigh on that side with the tip of her lance. Destiny's Catalyst grunted in pain, and the queen winced guiltily, though she only did this for a second; the thrill of battle was too much for her sense of empathy to drag down her mood for very long at all.

Years of constant intensive combat training told Coria that she'd gotten as much mileage as she could out of her opponent's unfamiliarity with her weapon. From here on, she'd have to try getting one over on him through sheer speed and reflex alone. Bringing back the hammer, the queen brought it around, aiming for the right side of his head. She did this so quickly that the wind around it whistled as it sliced through the air, and yet Cornelius jumped back from it in time. Instead of stopping the momentum of her swing, Coria let it spin her around, and as she twirled, she shifted her grip and stabbed down at her opponent's right foot once she came fully about. The targeted appendage darted back a fraction of a second before a tip of hard steel would've been driven clean through it.

The queen was wide-open and expected the tip of Kiam at her neck any second as she reared back to prepare, futile as the motion seemed, for another blow to her opponent's head with the hammer, but Cornelius merely collected himself and held position for longer than he had to, giving her time to complete the movement. But when the hammer approached his head, he, of course, blocked it easily, and then before Coria had time to think up her next step, he overpowered her, pushing the near end of her weapon back and to the side. Then he rushed her left hand and raised his sword over his head. The queen blanched in disbelief; he wasn't truly going to—no, he wasn't. When he brought his weapon down on its target, he moved the blade out much farther than he would've needed to for a dismemberment; instead, slammed its hilt into Coria's left hand. The queen let out a pained cry, which was chased very shortly by another as Cornelius did the same to her right.

Coria's weapon clattered to the cold stone beneath her and Cornelius, who then finally brought the tip of his sword to the top of his opponent's neck. "Well?" he said with a playful smile.

The queen, donning a similar expression, nodded as she tried and failed to clutch each of her bruised hands in the other simultaneously. "I yield."

Destiny's Catalyst sheathed Kiam and stepped around her before starting to sprint further down the corridor. "HEAD OUTSIDE, YOUR HIGHNESS," called out Cornelius over one shoulder as he ran. "MY MEN THERE WILL ATTEND TO YOU."

Coria bit her lip as she watched him go. She hoped with all her heart he was victorious—Dekkin, that is.

* * * * *

It was slow going cutting through the giant, tangled mass of sticky webbing with but a dagger, so much so that Dekkin began to worry they wouldn't get the duracut free in time. But by the time the oracle heard Cornelius's hurried footfalls on the hard stone off in the distance, the immortal was pleasantly surprised to find that he had—

he suspected—only a handful of thick strands left to slice before the beast would be free.

Dekkin was down to three when Cornelius called out to him from behind, "Dekkin Eterden! Whatever in the name of the gods you're doing. *Stop right this instant!*"

The oracle, focused on the task before him and not wanting to strain his voice (especially on that dullard's account), didn't respond, continuing instead to saw away at the wide lengths of white gunk. He started, however, when, as he finished bisecting the penultimate organic thread, Destiny's Catalyst spoke to him again, this time from mere paces away. "What are you—*stop*! You don't know what you're doing!"

The immortal shook his head and gritted his teeth. "If I had a pac—" As the rapid set of footsteps grew closer, he realized he didn't have the time to free the duracut after all; their plan would fail. Dekkin lowered the dagger in his hand to his side and came about while Cornelius pulled back his sword in preparation for a blow to the oracle's head with its hilt. The oracle wouldn't have had the reflexes to dodge out of the way if the distance between him and his pursuer had been twice as long…and yet he did, for as he turned around, his feet slipped out from under him on a puddle of the duracut's spittle laying atop the floor and fell to safety. Not only that, but as Destiny's Catalyst swung the bottom of his famed sword at where his target's head had been a split second earlier, its blade sliced cleanly through the last strand of webbing, unshackling the beast before him completely.

"Matthew!" Dekkin cried out as he scrambled to his feet and into a spirited sprint. "It's free! *Run!*" As he passed the frame of the giant creature, the oracle was relieved to find the boy was heeding his words.

It took the duracut several seconds to recognize through the haze of starvation swirling around its mind that it had been unbound. When it finally did, it lowered its gaze toward the pitter-patter of rushing feet to find the lorm who it had last seen at the start of its adhesive imprisonment. It snorted loudly at this and took a half-step forward with its front feet. However, before he began to chase after the boy, some ineffable animal instinct in a dark corner of its mind compelled the beast to turn its head further downward, and upon doing so, it saw the man who'd shot sharp metal spikes into several of its eyes. And *that* was truly the sort of prey that could not be ignored.

Dekkin jumped at the sound of the duracut's weaker-than-usual yet nonetheless deafening bellow and looked back to find much to his elation that the plan had worked; the creature was after poor Cornelius. As he and Matthew made their way up the ramp in the neighboring chamber, they nearly lost their footing and slipped off it, a motion that would've meant their doom after the first several minutes of upward progress, several times as the force of the beast's pounding footfalls shook the entire cavern. But neither it nor its heroic target made an appearance for the oracle and the lorm as they completed their ascent.

Coria, standing at the top of the walkway, saw Dekkin and Matthew coming as soon as they bolted into the room and let out a joyous giggle at the sight of them.

"Everything went to plan?" asked the queen as the two of them caught up to her, and she came about before matching their pace.

"Unbelievably, yes!" the oracle confirmed without turning his head.

Coria burst into ecstatic laughter at this. There was a smile on her face for a good while after that, but the sight of the cave's mouth, and more specifically the small army gathered in a semicircle completely cutting off the path of their marks from the outside of the opening, wiped it right off. The soldiers at the front of the group drew their weapons and assumed combat stances as the three of them approached, and those further back did the same in response, even those who couldn't see the enemy.

A chill ran down the queen's spine as she and her fellows came to a halt at the perimeter of points. This was the final point of uncertainty in their plan. "Everyone, *run*!" cried Coria to the crowd before her as she pointed back at the cavern. "A *duracut* is loose!" She waited with bated breath for their response...and got dubious looks from all of them. Her heart sank. After all that, things were falling apart at the last possible moment. She couldn't believe it, the injustice of it all. The soldiers began to move in on her and the others, several of them holding in one hand a pedibus…until a faint yet powerful roar echoed forth from the depths of the cave behind her. Every member of Cornelius's retinue froze and gazed fearfully out in its direction. There was a brief pause…and then pandemonium. All the soldiers turned and started to run away, knocking into one another in their haste to reach their kreshes and get as far from Gred as they could.

    Coria shared relieved grins with Dekkin and Matthew, and then the three of them started moving themselves, back to the mayor's house, with all possible speed; after all, it was unlikely anything could hold back Destiny's Catalyst for long, even a fully-grown duracut. Upon arriving at their destination, it was a simple matter to break one of the first-floor windows and climb inside. The mouth of the tunnel beneath the building was hidden beneath a long rug, just like the first one they'd encountered, and after each of them lit a lantern, they ventured into its inky maw.

16

"Seren?"

Dekkin's wife looked over at him. They were both lying in bed one early morning, enjoying a moment of serenity before the day's start proper as they always did. However, this time, instead of being sprawled on soft grass under a thin cloth tent, they were lounging atop what used to be Cula's bed. It was much too big, even for two, and so there was a wide gulf between the couple when each of them first got under the covers on either side of it at the end of the day.

The newly minted oracle held his tongue for a bit tentatively before asking, "Does it bother you being married to an immortal?"

"No," his wife replied after a short pause.

Dekkin's heart sank at the sound of that silence before her answer.

* * * * *

As Dekkin, Matthew, and Coria made camp in the middle of the underground passageway after moving through it for what felt like a few hours, the light of their lanterns illuminated but a short strip of the tunnel, but it was, of course, better than the alternative of total black. The boy found the homogenous nature of the corridor more and more eerie as they progressed; he was known to be a little claustrophobic, and the irrational fear that they would never reach the end of the tunnel no matter how far they walked down it had begun to grow in a corner of his heart as soon as he first looked back to find the light from the mayor's house completely gone from his view. There was also the silence. At this time of night, several feet underground, they heard not a sound save for that of their own movements. For some reason, it made the lorm think something would leap out at them from the shadows ahead of or behind them more so than if they heard something off in the distance, clawed feet kicking up dirt or a snarl from the muzzle of a wild, bloodthirsty beast. Despite the fear blossoming in his breast however, Matthew managed to keep these thoughts under wraps. Being with Dekkin and Coria helped a bit, after all.

The boy yawned as they sat huddled around their lanterns, which they pushed together at the center of the corridor, eating their dinner cold for the first time since they'd first set out. The oracle looked over at him and tutted, "Always yawning, you are, at all hours of the day and night. What gives?"

"I'm sorry." That's what the lorm was about to say when he stopped himself. *Sorry? What for? One of his body's natural processes?* Instead, he answered, "I haven't been getting nearly as much sleep as I usually do ever since I started traveling with you."

The immortal knit his brow in utter puzzlement. "What? You've slept through the night for as long as you've been with me."

Matthew nodded. "Well, yes. But when I was with my master, I slept more."

"Truly?" asked Dekkin incredulously. "How *much* more?"

The boy thought about it. "About sixteen hours a day, I'd say."

The oracle choked on his food. "*Sixteen hours a day?* This must be a jest. How is that possible? That's not a Lormish trait. And how could you serve as apprentice to Destiny's Catalyst if you were only awake for such short periods at a time?"

The lorm shrugged. "My master is perfect in every way, you know? Having me by his side is truly more of a formality than anything else. He requires very little of me, and anything else I *could* do for him, he does himself."

When the immortal took a swig of wine, he spotted Coria eyeing the drink yearningly and passed her the bottle, for which she was visibly most grateful. "Have you done this your entire adult life?" he asked her. "Drank like a fish?"

The queen pressed her lips together tightly. "No. I started... about four years ago."

"Oh, did something happen at that time?"

Coria nodded. "My mother, Queen Maescha, died of illness."

Dekkin raised his brow. "I see," said the oracle with solemnity. "You were close to your mother?"

"Oh, yes," the queen answered. "I never knew my father. He died when I was still a baby."

"So you started drinking to help you grieve for her?" conjected the oracle.

"That's how it started, yes," Coria confirmed with a nod. "It was...difficult, my mother being dead. But then...it became difficult for *me* to *be alive* as well. I was crowned knowing nothing of how to rule over a kingdom. When I was growing up, Mother would try to teach me something about the responsibilities that come with the throne and how to handle them, and I'd say I didn't want to, and she'd reply, 'Well, all right. Some time later then.' My adoptive brother, Samuel, was the one with a passion for that sort of thing. I'm more a figurehead than anything. Samuel's always been the one truly running things. That was another reason I started drinking; I didn't *want* to rule over Humania, but it still didn't feel good, not doing my duty, you know? And everyone in the court...treats me so poorly, have ever since my ascension. I think my brother is to blame for that, though why he'd have it out for me, I have no idea." She fixed the immortal with a slight smile, though there were tears in her eyes. "It's been all right ever since I left though. Started traveling with you. Thank you for that, Dekkin."

The oracle was taken aback by this. "Well, you're welcome, but...you know, I haven't exactly been kind to you."

"You've been *kinder*," countered the queen, "than anyone in my life for the past four years."

The immortal thought on this for a moment before replying soberly. "I'm sorry for how I've acted toward you. I didn't know about all that, and I'm sorry you've gone through what you have."

The corners of Coria's mouth lifted further upward, and she chuckled. "Thank you, Dekkin."

The oracle met her expression with a similar one of his own. Hearing sniffling to one side of himself, he turned in the direction of the noise to find the boy crying. "What's wrong, Matthew?" the immortal asked, his brow furrowed in concern. "Do Coria's words move you so, or…"

The lorm shook his head and, after staring down at the ground for a long moment, looked up and over at Dekkin and said, "You want to die, don't you? That's what your wish is going to be."

When the oracle didn't respond, the queen frowned in puzzlement and interjected, "His wish? What do you mean, Matthew?"

The immortal considered what to do for a handful of seconds before reaching into one of his tunic's pockets and pulling out the black box with the map and key inside. Coria's eyes bugged out. "What…is that?"

Dekkin nodded.

"So…the one who stole it was *you*?" questioned the queen in disbelief. She was met with confirmation once again. "That's why you're heading east," Coria exclaimed after ruminating on this new information for a short while, "to go to the temple, to get the Orb." Her look turned stricken then. "And the thing you're going to wish for…is your *death*?"

"But that doesn't make sense, does it?" said the boy. "Why would you need the Orb to die? You can simply select a replacement, give him or her your turins, and then do the deed yourself. Correct? So that can't be your wish, but it's something like that, isn't it?"

After a long pause, Dekkin answered, "Yes. …I'm going to wish I had never been born."

The air seemed to grow humid for all three of them as the statement hung in it for about a dozen seconds. Then the oracle shrunk in surprise as Coria fixed him with an uncharacteristic scowl.

"You're going to erase yourself from existence," she said. "So if you have your way, none of this will have happened. We will have never met, and you're fine with that."

"I wouldn't say I'm *fine* with that—" began the immortal in protest.

"But you are, enough to still go through with it," the queen countered. "Yes?"

Dekkin huffed. "Look, I didn't plan on you and Matthew being with me for this, all right?"

"But we are. So?"

"You're not enough!" barked the oracle. He deflated immediately upon seeing the wounded look on Coria's face. "Wh-what I mean is, it takes more than a few weeks to turn a five-hundred-year-long life around."

"Hold on," Matthew interjected quizzically. "How do you know for certain that, if you're never born, Cula will be able to pass his turins on to someone else? Aren't you creating the possibility there won't be a human oracle after him?"

"That's not my problem," replied the immortal flatly.

"What…what do you mean it's not your problem?" the queen said with incredulity. "You're the human oracle."

"Not if I get my wish," pointed out Dekkin. "If I get my wish, I was never born. I'm not responsible for anything that happens as a result of that because I don't exist."

Coria pouted. "That's *complete nonsense*."

"Oh?" The oracle raised one eyebrow. "How so?"

"You exist *now*," the queen explained. "You're responsible for your actions. Even if you erase yourself from history, there was once another world where you didn't. Look, if you truly want to make it so that you were never born, I cannot stop you. You are an adult. But do not pretend as if what you're doing isn't selfish and doesn't hurt *a lot* of other people." She softened when Dekkin's face fell, and he averted his eyes to the lanterns they sat around. "Don't do it, Dekkin. Let's just *keep going*. You and Matthew and I—let's find a nice secluded island in the east. Or not, we could just remain nomads, *never* stop moving. You said a few weeks isn't long enough to change your mind. How about a lifetime?"

Matthew lit up at the sound of this and looked over at the oracle eagerly. However, the boy's spirit was crushed in a fraction of a second when the immortal shook his head insistently, his own face completely clouded in despair.

"A lifetime for you is but a drop in the bucket for me."

If the lorm hadn't known any better, he would've sworn he saw tears welling up in the oracle's eyes.

"Other people are the only good reason to keep on living, in spite of everything. I curse the gods for making it so. People are temperamental, deeply flawed, ephemeral. That last point, I certainly know better than almost anyone, and it's the main thing keeping me from letting people into my life. How can I make friends when, as I shake their hands for the first time, I can't help envisioning what will happen decades down the road, how I'll watch them wither and die, and they'll leave me behind in a world of legions with that selfsame affliction?"

Coria opened her mouth to say something but couldn't find the words, and as she finally closed it after some time upon admitting to herself that she had nothing with which to offer him comfort, she hated herself for it.

* * * * *

"So are you prepared for the wedding?"

Seren looked up at Dekkin from the bowl of desert grubs before her as she sat across the table from him in their quarters. She shrugged. "Ponsa's a good girl. It should work out for Anter." She reached up with one hand to wipe a speck of stray food from one corner of her mouth and felt something alien under her fingers as they moved across the skin of her face. Frowning, Seren ran her hand over the same spot again to identical effect. Rising from her seat without a word, she went to the mirror in her and her husband's bathroom and, looking into it, confirmed what she'd dreaded a moment prior; she'd gotten her first wrinkle.

Dekkin stood in the doorway looking at her in concern. "Seren? Is everything all right?"

She returned his gaze wordlessly.

* * * * *

"Do you feel strong, right now?" asked Dekkin of Coria as the young woman laid down for the night.

She looked back at him in puzzlement. "Uh…I suppose. Why?"

The oracle took out his flask of Destiny Water. "We're a short ways from the temple now. I want to induce a vision of the map and key, hopefully get an idea of what I might be facing when I get there."

The queen's brow raised in realization. "So you'll need me to carry you tomorrow while we wait for the paralysis to wear off."

The immortal nodded. "That's right."

Coria did the same. "Sure, I can do that."

"Thank you." Dekkin sprawled out on one side.

The queen sat up. "What're you doing? Do you want me to take first watch?"

"I don't think either of us needs to stay up at this point, do you?" the oracle replied, pointing toward the already-sleeping Matthew with one arm. "The boy doesn't need company, and there isn't any wildlife in this corridor that we've seen or heard after several hours of travel through it either. Besides, when and if Cornelius and his retinue figure out where we've gone, they'll follow us over land, not via this tunnel. There's nothing to watch out for here."

Coria considered this as her gaze followed the immortal's direction and, after a moment, said in response as she laid back down, "Yes, I suppose you're right. Good night, Dekkin."

The oracle screwed off his flask's cap and took out the black box. He looked at it by the light of his lantern, which he'd kept burning unlike the other two for just this purpose. Throwing his head back, the immortal drank before holding the potion of premonition in his mouth as he brought it back down to face the black box, its top off, and swallowing as he gazed at it intently.

In an instant, Dekkin found himself standing in an underground chamber, gazing by torchlight at the Orb of Desire, a solid light-purple sphere small enough to be held in one hand, as it lay atop a weathered altar at the center of the room. As he always did during a vision of the future, he wished he could look for more clues as to his eventual fate but knew, of course, that he couldn't; his point of view was limited to where his future self directed it.

"Did you find it?"

He heard Matthew call out from some distance behind him. The oracle looked over one shoulder to find the boy walking toward him with his own light in hand, looking apprehensive. The immortal was about to reply when there came a gentle, rhythmic quaking in the ground beneath them. The lorm squinted at him quizzically, but Dekkin apparently had no more answers than he did. The slight vibrations gradually became forceful shakes that made the two of them have to work to hold their footing, and those gave way over time to violent, thunderous pounding that finally brought them to their knees. When the duracut came barreling around a corner into view a good ways behind the boy, the oracle's heart convulsed painfully in time with one of the beast's deafening footfalls.

"Matthew!" cried the immortal as he started running to the lorm, one arm outstretched in that direction, but it was too late; the duracut crossed the considerable distance between him and the boy in a few strides…and crushed Matthew beneath one of its front feet in one swift motion.

Dekkin awoke from the vision to find himself breathing heavily and in a cold sweat. He paused to process its contents. He couldn't bring Matthew with him to the temple. He now knew of the duracut's arrival well before it would happen thanks to his vision, but nothing he or even an actually skilled and accomplished fighter could do in preparation would even the odds in that scenario. So he'd drop the boy off before going in for the Orb, not that it mattered. Not that *any of this* mattered. Because none of this would happen once he'd wiped himself from history. Matthew would take part in a quest for the Orb, yes, but at the side of his master as it had originally been intended. They'd go to the temple, with the duracut lurking within.

A tiny thought sprouted in the back of Dekkin's mind then, like a niggling toothache. And like such a thing, it grew over time into a looming, unignorable entity. The thought was this: if the oracle had never been born and Cornelius went into the temple with Matthew, how would he or any of their retinue know about the presence of the beast inside? Wasn't it very possible they wouldn't, and the same events as those in his vision would play out? Wasn't there a terribly real chance that, in this other world, Matthew would *die* the same way he originally would've in this one? And if that were true, wasn't Dekkin the only one who could prevent it by giving up on his wish and warding the boy off from the danger?

But that wasn't his problem now, was it? In the new world, he wouldn't exist, and so wouldn't be accountable for anything that did or didn't happen there. But that conclusion brought the oracle no comfort, and he couldn't help but remember Coria's words on the subject. *You exist now. You're responsible for your actions. Even if you erase yourself from history, there was once another world where you didn't.* That recollection played over and over ad nauseam in the immortal's head as he waited what felt like days for sleep to finally take him.

17

THAT NIGHT, DEKKIN DREAMED again of the desert with a tree in the middle of it and the strange old man with the mutilated face. This time, the oracle turned to face the patch of green in the distance at the beginning of his fantasy and began making his way over to it. After some time, he was standing under and looking up at the branches of the tree. The immortal thought he saw something moving up there as he gazed in that direction and squinted to find that seeds were growing from the bark of its limbs out of nothing and falling to the ground once they'd fully matured after mere seconds. However, with the grass being on top of a steep hill, every time any of the pods touched down, it ended up rolling into the surrounding sand. Dekkin was watching the journey of one of them when he spotted something else moving at his periphery. Shifting his gaze toward it, he saw the old man, who followed him to the tree and was slightly startled by the sudden appearance of the elder's grotesque features.

"It's tragic," the mysterious man croaked as he gestured toward the strip of sand around them littered with stranded germs. "Seeds in the sand can't grow like they're s'posed to."

For some reason, this brought tears to Dekkin's eyes, and he woke up weeping with the others, roused from their own slumber by his sobs, staring over at him in concern.

* * * * *

Zuza was so lost in worry that she almost tripped over the man lying asleep in the street before her as she walked down it. The reason for her preoccupation was Zage, more specifically the fact that she hadn't heard from or seen him in the weeks since their attack on the capital. There was a kaglorite man dozing on hard cobblestones in the human town they'd taken over and made their base of operations in Humania, and in fact, many doing so because her fellow kaglorites were used to sleeping on an open bed of hard dirt and ash, and for some, it was too much of an adjustment to try doing the same atop a cushy mattress within sturdy shelter. When she spotted one of her fellows rushing straight toward her on the horizon, her concern blossomed into panic; this could only mean they were under attack! But as she started sprinting to meet him halfway and got close enough to make out the details of his face, she saw, bizarrely enough, a joyous grin as one of them.

"HE'S HERE!" cried out the man once the two of them were within earshot of each other. His face froze as he recalled the time of day, and he looked about self-consciously for signs of protest but found none.

"*Who's* here?" Zuza asked breathlessly. She could think of only one man whose presence would inspire this sort of response, but she dared not hope for it.

"Zage!" confirmed the messenger.

The Dark Lord's second-in-command could've squealed in elation but held back, knowing she had a certain image to uphold. Instead, she ordered evenly, "Take me to him."

Sure enough, approaching the town within view of its borders was Zage Batur. As he came closer, she could see he looked terrible, grimy, and utterly exhausted, and yet the sight of him filled her with what felt like enough drive to run off for days on end. Zuza tried to rein herself in until her superior was right in front of her, but after a few seconds, she couldn't restrain herself and broke into a run, barely slowing down and therefore almost knocking him over as she wrapped him in her arms.

The Dark Lord was so filled with fatigue it took a few seconds and a great deal of effort to return the gesture. "Hello, Zuza."

Zuza giggled gleefully and gave him a long kiss on the cheek. "Hello! What happened to you, after the attack?" After she pulled back, he told her in detail his incredible tale. Her face fell when he'd finished without saying a word as to the black box. "So you truly didn't get the map and key?"

Zage nodded in confirmation. "No, and I have no idea where it could be. At this point, we will have to retreat and take the loss. It could be anywhere in this accursed country. We have not the manpower to search for it, and after what happened in Cobaltus, the human military will be on high alert as well. I am afraid we will have to simply hope the wrong people do not get their hands on the Orb."

Zuza considered this for a moment before nodding and beginning to lead him back to the town she and the others had taken up residence in. They hadn't gained anything from this entire bold endeavor, but Zage and Zuza were kaglorites; they faced defeat so often that they'd learned for the sake of their sanity to, when met with failure yet again, merely count their blessings they hadn't lost more than they had.

*****

The other side of his bed was empty and cool when Dekkin awoke that morning. Given the blistering temperatures he now had to contend with whenever he needed to venture outside, the oracle welcomed the latter if not the former. However, as the fog of slumber gradually lifted from his mind, he furrowed his brow; Seren had been a late riser ever since they first met, while he always naturally awoke at dawn. Bolting upright as fast as he possibly could while his eyes flew open wide, he scanned his immediate surroundings to find that his wife wasn't occupying any other section of their quarters either. His eyes darted back and forth as he considered what could've possibly led to this; no mundane reason behind her absence made any sort of sense. He bugged out his eyes as panic set in, and adrenaline began to course through his veins. Something must be wrong; someone must've come and woken her because of it. Anter?

Dekkin shot up and clambered out of bed as fast as he could. As he dressed, he wondered at why he, their leader and the oracle of their people, wasn't informed of whatever happened himself. He decided as he left their room that there would be hell to pay for whoever had decided to leave him out of the proceedings they'd instead seen fit to get only his wife mixed up in. The underground corridors the oracle walked through for the first several minutes after he'd exited his and Seren's quarters were deserted. Given the time of day, it wasn't unusual for the tribe's other members to be out of Dekkin's sight in those areas, but on the part of his wife...if she wasn't in their room, and she wasn't in one of the subterranean complex's hallways, then where? The immortal's nerves grew more and more rattled as he came around each corner only to find no one, and he was just about to barge into the nearest room, waking its inhabitants up and questioning them, not recognizing in the slightest how irrational that would be, when he turned right at another intersection and spotted someone walking away from him a good distance up ahead.

It was a man named Nutius. "NUTIUS!" Dekkin cried out as he ran to him, quick as he could in this confined subterranean space. "Nutius," repeated the oracle once he reached the other man. "I can't find Seren. Do you know, did something happen? Do you know where she is?"

Nutius fixed him with a grimace of pity. The immortal waited for him to say something for a few long seconds before snapping, "WHAT? WHAT IS IT? TELL ME, WHAT'S HAPPENED?" Nutius didn't respond, and the truth finally forced the immortal with great effort to face it. His face fell. But no, that couldn't be it. She would never.

Coming about as swiftly as possible, the oracle bolted back to their room and opened their dresser to find his wife's clothes gone. As he lifted his gaze, he caught sight of a small note resting atop the chest. With quivering hands, he picked it up and read its contents:

> A husband should grow old with his wife.
> All I feel when I look at you now is envy.
> I'm sorry.

Dekkin's tears dripped onto the paper, smudging the ink. And as he looked up and around himself, he started; though everything appeared the same as it had when last he'd seen it, it also seemed completely different. He wandered the halls, turning his head this way and that, and all that he saw felt to him like it was a part of a life not his own.

I can't live like this, the oracle thought to himself.

* * * * *

There was, of course, no way to tell the time of day in the middle of the underground tunnel, and so when Dekkin first awoke after falling back asleep following his desert dream, he got the others up, and they continued on their way. As they moved, the oracle kept his gaze off Matthew, and when the boy came to walk beside him, he instantly began increasing his pace until the lorm gave up and resumed lagging behind him. When Matthew tried striking up conversation with the immortal, the latter communicated purely through discouraging grunts.

"Dekkin?" asked the boy cautiously after a few hours of this.

"Hmm?" the oracle replied quizzically.

"Would you," began the lorm before stopping himself and averting his eyes sheepishly; after a few seconds, his gaze returned to the immortal and he blurted out faster than his brain could work to stop him, "would you mind holding my hand?"

Dekkin frowned. "Mm-mm."

"Please?" Matthew pleaded.

The oracle spent a moment trying to find a way to get his point across without words before realizing he couldn't and reluctantly responding, "You're *twelve years old*, boy, well past the age of needing to hold an adult's hand."

The lorm brightened a little, just happy the immortal was talking to him again. "Y-yes, I know. It's just—it's so dark in here, and we've been inside this tunnel for so long. And…I don't like very closed-in areas like this. Please could you let me hold your hand?"

"No," insisted Dekkin vehemently. It was a good thing for his mood that he wasn't looking at Matthew, as he didn't see the crestfallen expression on the boy's face.

"You can hold *my* hand," Coria interjected with an inviting smile as she sped up, coming to one side of the lorm. Matthew lit up and eagerly accepted her offer. "So what did you do when you were traveling with Cornelius and you had to squeeze into some tight space?"

"I'd hate it but go along," answered the boy. "It's hard doing something you don't like that much. But it's even more difficult pretending like you don't mind. But I had to do it. When you apprentice to Destiny's Catalyst, you're expected to present a certain image."

Dekkin watched with a frown as the others talked, one of each person's hands clasped in the other. Then after just a short while, he got on the boy's other side and said, "All right, if having one of your hands held makes you feel better, how would it be if both were clutched in that of another?"

The lorm broke into an elated grin and, putting out his lantern before storing it at his side, took the proffered appendage in his own newly-empty one. And so the three of them moved through the darkness together.

18

WHEN A BRIGHT PINPRICK of light became visible in the distance up ahead several days later, Matthew had never been so happy for his eyes to be burning. As they approached tunnel's end, the boy found himself outpacing the others by a wide margin many times and on each such occasion had to strain himself to slow down. They came out at the front of a rocky valley; they journeyed far enough to cross over into Humania's eastern mountain ranges.

Coria's eyes lit up, and she giggled joyously as she looked all over at the surrounding gray stone. "From what you told me, it looks like we're quite close to the border!" she said to Dekkin without shifting her gaze to him.

"Yes," responded the oracle, sounding strangely enough like his head was a good ways *below* hers despite his far greater height. The queen frowned and followed the direction of his voice with her head to find him reclined on the bedrock beneath them.

"Dekkin, what are you *doing*?" she asked in puzzlement. "It's still midday! We can't afford to take breaks unless it's absolutely necessary if we're to outrun Cornelius and his men!"

"I've changed my mind," replied the immortal, his eyes closed. "I'm done running."

Coria brightened. "Y-you've decided not to use the Orb, to make it so you were never born?"

"That's right," confirmed Dekkin to the clouds.

The queen's face extended out in every direction. "Well, that's *great*! Thank you!" She froze upon thinking the situation through a little more. "But…but you can't *stay here*, let yourself get caught! You've *kidnapped a child*. You've *willingly transported the* <u>Dark Lord</u>. You *stole mankind's only salvation*. You…you didn't *actually* take me prisoner, but *they* won't believe you or me if we tell them that—"

"I've committed all these crimes, so shouldn't I be punished for them?" the oracle interrupted flatly.

"Uh, yes, but…but you're a good person!" said Coria, in distress over the thought of his possible incarceration.

"Oh, and if an evil act is perpetrated by a good person, they should get off scot-free?" the immortal countered.

The queen had nothing to say to this. After a moment of consideration, she began with great reluctance. "Well, all right then, but I can't stay with you. I have to cross the border to—"

"To find some hiding place in the Lormish Isles where you can escape the crown," finished Dekkin.

Coria was dumbstruck by this. "Wh-what?" she responded in unconvincing shock. "What do you mean—"

"Coria, don't insult my intelligence," ordered the oracle; his lip curled in irritation. "I already had my suspicions before Cornelius found us out, and in the moment, I didn't have time to question things as he chased us, but once we were given some semblance of calm, I wondered at why in all that is holy you and Matthew would stay with me, help me make my escape once *Destiny's Catalyst*"— he spat this mockingly—"discovered my secret. No one was holding a knife to either of your throats. As soon as that bumbling boy announced your presence in the back of our wagon, you could've jumped out into the soldiers' arms. But you didn't, and I know why." For the first time since he'd lain down, the immortal brought his gaze to rest on her. "Both of you hated your lives before you joined up with me, and even an existence as a criminal's hostage and accomplice was preferable to the prospect of returning to the status quo."

The queen started. "Wh-what, that's not—"

The immortal raised a hand to silence her partway. "Coria, it's all right. Remember who you're talking to. I don't think there's anything wrong with running from a life chosen for you by others."

Coria thought on this for a moment before nodding in reluctant affirmation. She stood there staring down at Dekkin, unmoving, for several seconds. "You're sure you won't come with me?" she asked the oracle.

"Positive," answered the immortal immediately.

The queen sighed in hesitant acceptance. "All right. But before I go, there's one thing I want you to do for me. This is probably the last chance I have to ask you, seeing as we probably won't ever meet again."

"What is it?" inquired Dekkin, though he frowned at her previous statements.

"You know how you'll ask me to say what you want to hear sometimes, to look at the world as cynically as you do?" Coria began.

"Yes," the oracle confirmed.

"Well, I want you to do the same for me, right now," explained the queen. "Be positive like me for a change. Can you do that?"

The immortal donned a disapproving scowl. "I don't think you know how much that would require of me. How about we agree I won't do it?"

"Dekkin, *please*. I"—tears came to Coria's eyes—"I need to hear something good right now."

The oracle took this in and, after a short pause, said through gritted teeth, "All right, all right, I'll do it, just this once." He stood and walked to within a pace in front of the queen. As he talked, he did so flatly and frequently with averted eyes and a slight blush. "I don't want to die anymore. I'll be arrested, but Samuel will grow a heart and be lenient in my sentencing. I'll be out of jail before you know it, and then Matthew and I will find you wherever you're staying in the Lormish Isles, and we'll live together for the rest of our lives. Zage will be there too. He's truly a kind soul. He's been putting on an act all this time when he was murdering and pillaging—" He cut himself off when Coria raised an eyebrow at the mention of darkness in this supposedly bright description of things. He thought to himself that even when he was trying to look at the world with an optimistic eye, he found ways to focus on pain. "Like I said, Samuel will turn over a new leaf. He'll be a kind and benevolent ruler, and after a while, he'll come to see you as his sister just like you always wanted, and he'll visit all of us in the Lormish Isles frequently." Here, he stared directly into the queen's eyes and softened. "You're an amazing woman, Coria. Being with you reminds me why I didn't always want to die."

By the end of this, the queen was crying happy tears. After a little while, her eyes dried up and, wiping each cheek, she started to walk backward, away from Dekkin.

"None of that is how I truly feel, you know," the oracle called out to her.

Coria's face fell. "*None* of it?"

The immortal was silent for a beat before giving her a slight, warm smile, albeit awkwardly. Even if it had been done perfectly, of course, it still would've looked out of place on his face. "A bit of it, perhaps." Tears flowed anew as the queen grinned back at him. Before turning her back to him and Matthew, Coria seriously considered staying behind with them.

Dekkin turned to his right and started making his way up the side of one of the surrounding mountains. "There's something I must do over there," he said to the boy, pointing straight ahead of and above himself. The oracle smirked. "Don't go anywhere." He clambered up the rock face until for him the lorm receded into a speck among the stone and then looked about for a small boulder. Finding one nearby after a short while, the immortal went over to it and, lifting it up, hid the black box beneath it.

* * * * *

Dekkin's heart sank when he saw the grimace on Ponsa's face as she opened the door to her quarters after he knocked.

He held out hope that she was simply having a bad day, for reasons entirely separate from what he feared, but his concerns were affirmed when she said, "Anter's not doing well today."

The oracle nodded and waited for her to step aside, admitting him in. When she didn't, he raised his brow.

"I don't know if a visit is a good idea right now," she added.

"Ponsa, please," replied the immortal, "he's my son."

She mulled over what to do in silence for a moment before reluctantly letting him in. A strand of her silver hair fell across her face as she moved.

Ponsa and Anter's room was on the lowest level of the tunnel system and so was only mildly warm. Fresh air would've done him good, but of course, the only kind he could get would've come with blazing heat. Dekkin's son was sitting in a rocking chair to one side of his bed's head when his father walked in, and Anter turned his head to face the older man as the latter moved into view. The oracle's offspring had as many wrinkles on his face and indeed along the rest of his body, as an aged, wind-weathered rock, and his hair had not only gone completely gray but, adding insult to injury, thinned considerably the last several years until one could see his entire scalp, though he wasn't balding.

"Hello," Anter said evenly as Dekkin came up to him. The former's voice came out as a rasping croak.

"Hello," parroted back the oracle. "Do you remember me?"

His son squinted hard at him. "N-no, I don't believe we've met."

The immortal grimaced before replying, "Yes, we have, Anter. ...I'm your father."

"My father?" Anter responded incredulously and with a disapproving scowl. "Don't be ridiculous, boy. It's one of the worst possible sins, you know, lying to your elders. The color of your hair is quite queer for a young person, I'll admit, but besides that, you look like you could be my grandson! That's what you are, truly, is it not?"

Dekkin's face fell, and he opened his mouth to protest, but then experience made him think better of it. He pressed his lips together tightly. "Yes, that's right."

"Hmm"—Anter nodded—"well, I suppose I can put up with you for a little while. Doesn't matter *who* you are, actually, so long as it's someone other than that old bitch over there." He pointed over at Ponsa, who was standing by the door, as he muttered this, and in spite of the low volume of his voice, the look on her face made it clear she had a general idea of the content of his words. "Nagging me all the time. 'Do this, do that!' Thank the gods, she should be dropping dead any day now by the looks of her."

The oracle's face fell. "You know, Anter, Ponsa's your *wife*."

His son nodded. "Yes, yes, I know. Doesn't mean she isn't annoying." He scooched forward to the front edge of his chair's seat and pointed at a dresser on the other side of his bed. "Say, could you help me over there, while you're here? It's about time I changed my shirt."

The immortal almost walked out at that, but something held him in place, making him respond, "Certainly." He went to his son's side before proffering his near arm. Anter took it and ponderously rose with several pained grunts and grimaces.

"Oh, malun," swore Dekkin's son grouchily. "Be thankful it's me and not you in this old body, boy."

The oracle said nothing for a moment before replying, "Sometimes it's harder on the people *watching* someone suffer from old age than the man or woman actually suffering, especially when you'll have to watch it happen to *every single person* you know."

Anter frowned at this, not understanding what his father meant, while the immortal wished with great fervor he could return to a time where he didn't either.

* * * * *

It was a short trek back to Matthew and downhill besides, and yet by the time Dekkin was back on the floor of the valley, he felt he could barely stand. It was a familiar feeling that had gone away when he decided to steal the map and key, one in which he was wide awake, and yet with every movement, it seemed as though he had heavy weights attached to each part of his body. Right as he laid down on his back however, the thought occurred to him that the boy hadn't eaten in some time. The oracle furrowed his brow, wanting to keep still but finding after a short while that the niggling thought of the lorm wouldn't let him.

With a deep sigh, the immortal sat up. "Matthew, do you want to eat something?"

"Well, do you…want me to eat something?" the boy asked meekly.

"Are you hungry?" replied Dekkin with a little irritation.

"Uh, I'm not hungry, but I could eat." Right as the lorm finished saying this, his stomach grumbled loud enough for even the oracle, several paces away from him, to hear it.

The immortal chuckled in exasperation and shook his head. "All right, that settles it. It's lunchtime."

"All right." Matthew conceded immediately.

There followed an expectant pause as Dekkin waited for the boy to take out his cuisine of choice from his person or else ask for something from that of his fellow, and the lorm sat silent and unmoving. After several seconds of this, the oracle asked a little sharply, "What? What is it?"

"What do you think I should have?" inquired Matthew.

"Well, it's *your* lunch," the immortal pointed out. "You know what we brought with us from the wagon. You must have preferences of some kind."

The boy considered this before nodding. "Yes, I suppose I do." While he took out some dried fish from one of his pockets, Dekkin reached into his own to supply kindling and several tufts of grass.

After making a fire, the lorm sat with the fish in his grip and stared into the flames, sitting stock-still before them. "Now what?" grumbled the oracle.

Matthew looked up and over at him before admitting, "I've never made this myself before. It was always prepared *for* me. I don't know how to cook it."

The immortal shrugged. "Well, I can't help you there. I don't know either. Never was much of a fan of seafood."

The boy tilted his head to one side after sticking the fish on a kebab and beginning to hold it over the fire. "What *do* you usually eat then?" He hadn't been paying attention to the contents of Dekkin's meals while they had been on the road.

"Nothing," Dekkin answered, "I don't need food to survive, remember?"

The lorm narrowed his eyes. "Yes, but…you eat for the taste, right?"

"Only very rarely," replied the oracle.

"Food just doesn't interest you, huh?"

"Well, there's a lot of food I do enjoy," the immortal said. "And it doesn't take much energy to make a meal. But"—he looked then as if his inner workings were as much a mystery to him as to Matthew—"whenever I think about eating something, I decide I don't want to go to the effort of preparing the food, which is a tad strange, I admit. It doesn't take much to do so, and every time I go through with it anyway, I'm glad I did, and yet the next time the thought occurs to me, I usually pass on it once again."

The boy looked over at Dekkin thoughtfully before the smell of burning meat wafted past his nostrils. His brow shooting up, the lorm whirled his head about to face the fire, finding that, yes, his prospective lunch was half-charred. "Oh no!" cried Matthew as he lifted the fish away from the flames. He examined them thoroughly before tossing the kebab aside, saying in despair, "I can't eat that."

The oracle frowned when the boy made no move to begin the process of cooking anew. "Well, what are you doing? Try again! You're still hungry, aren't you?"

"Yes," the lorm admitted glumly to his feet, "but I don't feel like making another attempt."

The immortal leaned toward the boy. "Well, you're going to. You can't just give up on something you want every time you don't get it the first time around."

"Weren't you just telling me how most of the time *you* give up whenever you think about making something to eat?" pointed out Matthew meekly.

"Yes," Dekkin confirmed with a nod, "but the younger generation is supposed to be better than the previous one. That's what pa—ah, that's how it's supposed to go when a child is told to do things by an adult."

After a pause, the boy took out some more fish from his pockets and got to work roasting them over the fire, paying close attention to the color of the meat this time. A few minutes later, his food was cooked to his satisfaction, and biting into it, it tasted better than anything he'd ever eaten in his twelve years of life.

When Matthew heard the faint *clomp, clomp, clomp* of kreshes' hooves on stone in the distance behind and above him and Dekkin, a meaty hand squeezed tight his small blue heart. Turning to look in the direction of the noise, the boy's worst fear was confirmed—Cornelius was leading his small army of subordinates down into the valley, toward him and the oracle.

The lorm whirled around to face the immortal. "There's still time," Matthew said a tad pleadingly. "We can start running away again."

Dekkin was lying on his back, warmed on one side by the fire. "Matthew, I know there's nothing a twelve-year-old wants to hear less than this, but it must be said nevertheless. It's for your own good." As the soldiers approached, he unsheathed the dagger at his hip. This sent a chill through the boy's blood as he looked down at it, but he needn't have worried; the oracle had done so simply to lay it flat on the ground beside him.

The immortal got to his knees and raised both hands, palms open, halfway, facing Cornelius with every part of himself as the other man dismounted from his kresh and walked over to his target. "I'm not hostile," Dekkin assured Destiny's Catalyst, who responded by walking around to the back of him and shoving his face into the rock beneath them, cuffing his hands behind his back. "Cornelius!" called out the oracle indignantly. "Did you hear me? I said I'm not hostile!"

Master Arcind ground the front of his newfound prisoner's head into the stone further as he checked the latter's pockets.

"I'm not resisting!" the immortal slurred through obstructed lips, unintentionally scooping a handful of pebbles into his mouth in the process. "What are you—"

"Silence!" snapped Cornelius with a scowl.

"Master, he's telling the truth," Matthew insisted, standing and taking a step toward the two of them. "He's not dangerous, and... and you don't need to give him that sort of treatment. He never raised a hand to me while we—"

"It's all right, Matthew," replied Destiny's Catalyst gravely, looking up from his shakedown. "He has no power over you anymore. You don't have to be afraid of what he might do to you if you don't go along with him."

To this, Matthew said nothing, and Dekkin, not for the first time, cursed the boy's timidity.

Cornelius completed his search, finding nothing, and roughly flipped the oracle onto his back. "You're the one who stole the map and key in Cobaltus too, *aren't you?*"

"That's right," the immortal confirmed, his earlier expression unchanged.

"Then *where is it?*" barked Destiny's Catalyst.

"I'd be more than happy to tell you. But first, I need you to make me a promise."

Cornelius got right up in Dekkin's face. The oracle noted with great displeasure that the other man hadn't a trace of bad breath, even after a weekslong journey such as his. "You're in no position to be making demands, Dekkin Eterden."

"Nevertheless, I am doing so," the immortal responded firmly. "You have to promise me that when I give you the map and key and you go to the temple to get the Orb, you won't bring your apprentice with you."

A splash of confusion put out a portion of the fire burning in Cornelius's belly. "What? Why?"

Once the liquid puzzlement quenched a few of the flames, it was simple enough for it to flow across the rest of them, entirely extinguishing the blaze inside Destiny's Catalyst within a few moments. When Dekkin refused to answer the question, Cornelius growled, "Well, that may seem like a benign request, but as it's coming from you, I have no doubt there are devious intentions behind it. I reject your terms. We'll hand you over to the royal guard, and they will *extract* the information."

The oracle chuckled humorlessly. "You think I'm any stranger to torture?"

Destiny's Catalyst looked into the other man's light-blue eyes and saw there that his nonchalance was no bluff. After a moment of consideration, Cornelius nodded with great reluctance. "All right, fine. I promise. Now tell me where the box is."

The immortal scrutinized the hero's face and, after determining the latter's sincerity, easily gave up the location of the prized map and key.

"Where are we going?" asked Dekkin as he sat directly behind Cornelius on the other man's mount, and the latter began steering it and his subordinates further east. "I don't think I need to tell you the border's this way, Cornelius."

"You—" the hero began to bellow before catching himself and managing to deflate at the satisfying thought of what he would say next. "You're much too high priority at this point for us to risk transporting you across Humania back to Cobaltus. The nearest village is up ahead, a town called Yinit. You will be imprisoned there"—he paused and grinned with uncharacteristic sadism—"for the rest of your unnaturally long life."

19

WHEN DEKKIN GOT WORD one morning that his son had passed away in his sleep the previous night, he didn't cry or even despair to himself; for so many reasons, it didn't feel real.

* * * * *

"What happened to the queen?" Cornelius and the oracle had been riding in silence for quite some time before the former posed this question to the latter.

The immortal blinked in surprise. "You're only just now inquiring about this?"

"The royal adviser told us Her Highness' whereabouts were not a priority before we set out from the capital," explained Destiny's Catalyst. "I'm truly only asking out of personal concern."

Dekkin smirked at this. "You wouldn't believe me if I told you what's become of Coria. Suffice it to say, she's alive and safe."

Cornelius paused. "I'm not sure I trust your word."

"Well, that's not my concern now, is it?" the oracle countered. "I've told you the truth. What you do with it is up to you." Destiny's Catalyst had nothing to say to this.

After some time, the uneven terrain they were traversing leveled out into a paved path leading to a beach on the near edge of Humania's eastern border. Off to one side was Yinit, an island of stone, brick, and mortar floating amidst an ocean of sand. Cornelius furrowed his brow upon seeing no guards along its perimeter but held course. When he and the others entered the village proper and found it deserted as far as they could see, they drew their weapons and kept going, eyes darting here and there attentively. Something was most certainly wrong here, but the next closest settlement was far enough away that it was still best to proceed into Yinit regardless of the warning signs.

When the creak of a wooden door being pushed open sounded faintly a few streets over, Cornelius started moving swiftly toward it, with the rest of his retinue following close behind. As the riders made their way toward the source of the noise, heavy footfalls could be heard up ahead. Destiny's Catalyst rounded a corner once the noise was to him quite pronounced…and found a kaglorite man shouldering a large stuffed pack as he walked down the road. The violet-skinned intruder's eyes bugged out as he stared out at the small army before him, and then…

"Invaders!" he screamed as he raised one hand slightly and summoned an oblong rectangle of blue magic just above it. A throwing knife was birthed from that cobalt sheen, and before any of the interlopers had the time to do anything, it was buried in the throat of one of their own, fatally wounding him. As they heard the strangled exclamations of their dying fellow, many of the soldiers let loose bloodcurdling battle cries and charged the lone kaglorite.

"No!" exclaimed Cornelius emphatically. "We must retreat! We must—"

Out of some of the alleyways and houses directly beside the street, he and those closest to him were on came pouring several more kaglorites, snarls on their faces as they leaped into battle. Destiny's Catalyst paused to think for the few seconds allotted him, deciding at their end that he couldn't stomach leaving some of his men behind to die. Raising Kiam high over his head, he led those still behind him forward.

Dekkin was having none of these courageous heroics. With Cornelius otherwise occupied, he was able to hop off the kresh they were both straddling. Looking about, the oracle spotted Matthew sitting behind one of the riders himself and, running toward him, grabbed onto one of his sleeves with both shackled hands as the beast the boy was astride passed, pulling him off his mount.

"Dekkin, shouldn't we stay with the soldiers?" Matthew pointed out as the immortal ran from the action with the boy in his arms. "Help them fight?"

"Like *hell* we're going back there," replied Dekkin quickly. "It's too dangerous. Besides, no offense intended, but neither of us are terribly useful in a fight. There'd be no point to us trying."

The lorm didn't take to running away himself but also didn't try to wriggle out of the oracle's arms. After a few minutes of travel toward one of Yinit's borders, they seemed to be in the clear, having encountered no resistance, but just as the beach was coming into view for them, a single unarmed kaglorite appeared directly ahead of them on the horizon. In the heat of the moment, the immortal hurriedly concluded that between himself and Matthew, they could take down a lone, weaponless assailant. The adrenaline rush blinded him to a simple fact that the man in their way swiftly reminded him of by creating a broadsword out of thin air; however, one kaglorite is worth a dozen of any other species.

All right, so full-on attack was out. Dekkin eyed each side of the street the three of them were on and spotted the entrance to the nearest alleyway, coming up fast. Escape then. They'd flee and try to get out some other way, avoiding this kaglorite and as many of his fellows as the situation called for while they did so. But when the oracle turned his attention away from his violet-skinned adversary to head for the thin space between buildings, he heard a few seconds later the sound of wood and metal whipping through the air before and at him and shifted his gaze in its direction just in time to keep from losing a foot to a spear that was hurled mightily at it, yet another weapon conjured up by the enemy's magic.

Dekkin looked over at the kaglorite in the distance to find him already materializing another projectile. It would seem continuing their escape attempt would mean near-certain death. So would surrender, but the odds for survival there appeared to him to be a smidge wider. As he waited for the kaglorite to reach him and Matthew, Dekkin stared back at the malicious grin on the magician's face, picturing all that which might soon happen to him and the boy and marveling at the fact that just a few minutes prior, he'd thought spending eternity in a human prison was the worst thing that could possibly happen to him.

* * * * *

Cornelius crowed in triumph as he knocked unconscious the last of the kaglorites who came crawling out of the woodwork right before his prisoner had flown the coop. However, his face froze when a second later, he heard the sounds of battle behind him. Coming about, he peered between the heads of his fellows to find that what he had just finished dealing with was but the first wave.

"STAY IN FORMATION!" he called out when he saw several members of his retinue begin moving to flank these new challengers. "IF WE REMAIN TOGETHER, WE'LL OVERPOWER THEM THROUGH SHEER NUMBERS!"

"CORNELIUS ARCIND!" He heard the Dark Lord bellow from the front of the newcomers' group. "COME FORTH AND FACE ME, FOR THE LAST TIME, IF YOU ARE TRULY DESTINY'S CATALYST!"

The hero's face darkened. It was not natural for his heart to hate, but his extended history with Zage Batur had brought it the closest to that feeling out of anything he'd ever seen or heard throughout his twenty-six years alive. Ordering his men to clear a path through their ranks for him, Cornelius approached, swift yet measured, his nemesis, Kiam at the ready.

Incredibly enough, never during any of their dozens of confrontations had the legendary longsword of Destiny's Catalyst been broken by Zage's red magic. This was due to a combination of skill on the part of its wielder and the ancient mystic energy the kaglorites who'd forged the sword had imbued it with at the time of its creation.

An amazingly high level of craftsmanship had gone into the making of the blade, and yet it was ultimately somewhat of a liability for its vaunted owner during his battles with the Dark Lord; it was so valuable that Cornelius, albeit unconsciously, ended up pulling his punches in combat to protect his weapon. Zage noticed this after a while and now capitalized on it as much as he could with each new encounter, as he did here; the Dark Lord kept one hand constantly covered in crimson light, discouraging Destiny's Catalyst from making any moves he couldn't cancel out of in time. Cornelius had, of course, noticed this weakness of his himself long ago but was still struggling to find a solution. He possessed the greatest sword of legend in all time; how could he not go into battle with its hilt in his hands?

But experience taught him by now that perhaps this line of logic was flawed, and he had the black box, with the map and key to the shrine within which rested the Orb of Desire, in one of his inside pockets. If he lost and Zage got ahold of it… Spurred on by this thought, Destiny's Catalyst took a step back from his opponent and sheathed Kiam at his side. He took great pleasure in the dumbfounded expression that crossed the Dark Lord's face then. Balling both his hands into fists, Cornelius advanced on Zage once more. Perhaps the key to victory was to use the one type of weapon that couldn't be destroyed with red magic.

When the kaglorite saw what his adversary was going to attempt however, he laughed nastily—the fool coming at him with naught but his bare fists! The Dark Lord used blue magic then to create a whip, its tip sharply barbed. When Zage struck out at his foe however, Cornelius dodged to one side, almost as quick as thought, and got one of his hands around the middle of the whip. Pulling it toward him in one violent motion, Destiny's Catalyst wound his other arm back and slammed it into one of the Dark Lord's cheeks. Even the muscled, battle-hardened flesh of a kaglorite couldn't bounce back from a blow of that magnitude; Zage was thrown to one side. Releasing the whip from his grip, Cornelius clutched next with that hand one side of his opponent's neck and, holding the kaglorite in place, started pummeling him in the stomach furiously with the other.

Zage's hand, the one still clutching the whip, flailed in vain behind the two of them; at this range, the kaglorite's weapon was all but useless. With the other, the Dark Lord began trying to return the favor but found that his blows were stymied by Cornelius's forearm on that side; Destiny's Catalyst was wailing on his opponent with the fist directly attached to it so fast that the portion of limb formed a near-constant barricade there. As his vision began to dim, Zage got a burst of adrenaline and moved to rip the hero's throat out with his teeth, but Cornelius, having anticipated this, headbutted the kaglorite's jaw out of the way before it could do the job. After one more strike to the gut, the hero felt his victim go limp and, releasing the other man, watched, hardly believing it, as the Dark Lord, after all this time, finally collapsed to the ground by the hand of Destiny's Catalyst.

This is it! thought Cornelius excitedly as he gazed down at his defeated opponent. *I've beaten the Dark Lord! And with our numbers, we'll subdue the rest of them too. The kaglorite terrorists' would-be conquest ends <u>today</u>!* But just as he said this to himself, Destiny's Catalyst heard behind him the sound of stone crunching through flesh and bone and cries of agony and looked back to find that one of his subordinates had been crushed underneath a large boulder. His brow jumped in bewilderment. Where could that giant chunk of rock come from, except…

Cornelius looked up and over to the second-story windows on either side of him and his retinue, and his worst fears were confirmed; while he and his fellows busied themselves fighting back against some of the kaglorites on the ground, several more of the violet-skinned criminals had gotten into the houses directly adjacent to the street and now surrounded them on the left and right from above. One of these assailants locked eyes with Destiny's Catalyst, and each of them kept one of their hands raised slightly in a threatening gesture.

Cornelius's stomach dropped. There was only one course of action now. "LOWER YOUR WEAPONS, MEN!" he called out to the soldiers under his command. "WE'RE SURRENDERING."

* * * * *

As Coria sat in the sand, she finished off the last of her lunch. Although it had been made up of some of the same items she'd eaten while she was with Dekkin and the others, for some reason, it didn't taste the same, as good, to be more specific. Placing her plate to one side of herself, the queen looked out at the ocean stretching to the horizon before her. Her journey came to an unexpected halt here because there was no boat in view that she could charter to take her into the isles like she'd assumed there'd be. When she started moving again, she'd have to walk along the border in search of such a vessel.

And that time was now. Coria got to her feet, looking to either side of herself. Left or right? She wished there was someone with her she could ask to make the decision. A moment passed, and just when she was beginning to despair as she racked her brain in vain for some sort of criteria with which to make a determination, a warm breeze blew in from her left. Choosing to view this as an omen and satisfied with selecting it as the basis for her choice, the queen turned in that direction and started moving.

About a half hour passed before a small seaside town came into view up ahead in the distance. Coria lit up at the sight of it and quickened her pace a little. As she approached however, she spotted faintly within the unmistakable neon glow of kaglorite magic. The village was under attack! The queen, eyes wide, started sprinting toward the site of the action, keeping it up for as long as she could before slowing to a brisk jog.

Once she'd gotten close, Coria allowed herself to stray off to one side a little so as to conceal herself behind one of the buildings along the perimeter of the village. After reaching its near, stone wall, she crept up to one edge of it to peer down a neighboring street. What she saw, to her shock, was Dekkin and Matthew, being prodded along on a course heading away from her by an armed kaglorite. This must be where Cornelius Arcind had taken those two after catching up to them! The queen brought one hand back to grip the hilt of her weapon without thinking before stopping herself; if she stepped in to save the oracle, the boy, and the soldiers with them, immediately thereafter she'd be forced to return to Cobaltus, the thought of which chilled her very blood.

But, of course, how could she turn away from people in need? She may not have been the best breed of person, but she was quite far from a villain at least. Unsheathing her weapon with a metallic scrape, Coria leaped out of cover and began dashing toward the man holding her friends prisoner.

* * * * *

"Please let the boy go." Dekkin repeated over one shoulder to the kaglorite holding the tip of a sword to his and the lorm's backs. "He's not a fighter, and he bears your people no grudge."

"And *I said*, the Dark Lord spares *none* born into the twin races of beast-men!" snarled the oracle's captor back to him.

The immortal conceded then with great despair that he wouldn't be able to get Matthew out of the terrorists' clutches. Dekkin began attempting to form a string of comforting words sufficient to put the boy at ease in the minutes before their (hopefully) deaths or (probably) imprisonment and torture, when…

Smack! Dekkin whirled his head to bring his gaze back behind him, finding the kaglorite with the sword falling and hitting the ground face-first, unconscious, and standing a pace and a half behind him…

"*Coria?*" he said with incredulity.

"Hello!" replied the queen cheerily, hefting her combination hammer-spear. "You looked as if you needed some help!"

The oracle nodded. "That we did. Thank you." He pointed down the street in the direction he and Matthew had been walking under threat of violence just a handful of seconds ago. "There's a great deal more people that way who could do with some assistance, as well. Cornelius Arcind and his personal forces. Come on." He started jogging in the indicated direction, with Coria close behind.

The boy stood unmoving for a moment, blinking in surprise as he watched their backs retreat from him, before catching up to the immortal and slowing to match the old man's pace. "Do you not want to use this opportunity to get away? Once Coria gets there, it should be a landslide victory for Cornelius and his men. There's nothing keeping us here now." His voice was tinged with pleading.

"You'd have me start another chase?" Dekkin responded as he looked over to return the lorm's gaze. "Sounds exhausting. Like I said, I'm done running except from murderous kaglorites, in the event of my bodyguard's preoccupation."

* * * * *

"So the vaunted *Destiny's Catalyst* and a few *hundred* of his *best men* were no match in the end for a *few dozen* of an *endangered people* living off *stolen goods*, eh?" As Zage gloated and Cornelius stood with weapons pointed toward his neck from every conceivable direction, the hero's thoughts weren't drawn to either aspect of the present situation but rather the fates of his fellows.

"Yes, you've at last overpowered me, Dark Lord," conceded Destiny's Catalyst deferentially. "My life is by rights yours. However, I ask that you spare my men and allow them to take from me my personal possessions prior to my execution."

"Oh, I do not think so," the kaglorite replied with a smirk. "Quite the opposite, in fact. Before you and those under your command lost the war to my people and I, you yourself won the *battle* against me. You, therefore, are free to go. The same cannot be said however, for the rest of my enemies gathered here currently. And so they must *earn* their lives, as you did yours. We will hold one-on-one duels, a single man from your side against a lone fighter from mine, and any soldier under your command who bests his opponent will be granted a reprieve. Anyone who *cannot*, however..." Zage's expression morphed into a sneer.

Cornelius's stomach dropped even further than it already had, as much as it possibly could. "No! No, YOU CAN'T! You know a kaglorite is worth a dozen humans or lorms in battle. Your proposal is essentially a *death sentence* for my men."

"The true warrior prevails regardless of the odds stacked against him, Destiny's Catalyst. This I believe," countered the Dark Lord. "And now we will see which of these beast-men deserve such a title." He raised one hand over his head, waving it from side to side. "Everyone, clear the way! We shall conduct the tests of strength in this very spot."

With the tips of so many weapons hovering but an inch from his scrag, Cornelius obeyed this edict along with everyone else massed in the middle of the street there. As he moved however, he happened to glance up at one of the second-story windows on either side of the road and found it empty. Frowning, he lowered his head so as to not attract his captors' attention to the same place but kept his gaze upward. The next window he passed still had a kaglorite standing ahead of it, but as Destiny's Catalyst passed it, he saw a human hand come up from behind to clamp down over the magician's mouth and the violet-skinned criminal being yanked backward.

Masking an exuberant grin, Cornelius waited until all the second-story windows were unaccompanied and the kaglorites around him had lowered their swords from his neck as the preparations were made for the tourney of death.

Then drawing Kiam from his sheath with a metallic *shing*, he cried out as he lifted it over his head, "The windows are empty, men! *Attack!*" Not even gazing up to confirm the veracity of their leader's statement out of complete trust in the man, his subordinates drew their weapons and, with a roar, lashed out once more at their kaglorite foes.

* * * * *

Coria's blood pumped at the sound of the resuming battle outside as she ran down the stairs of the last house she'd had to infiltrate in order to incapacitate however many magicians laid within. Such an attack as she'd carried out on him and the others was not her style, but during her rigorous combat training back in Cobaltus, she had, of course, been schooled in the art of stealth.

Bursting out onto the street, she scanned the roiling mass before and on either side of her for Zage and, spotting him at one of its far ends, began making for the Dark Lord's present location. As she ran, one of the other kaglorites saw her through the swinging arms and slashing blades of the men and women around him and intercepted her, raising a spear over his head in preparation for a downward thrust into her stomach. Not even breaking pace, the queen turned to face him and, bringing one shoulder forward, slammed it into him, knocking the violet-skinned man to the ground. Only then did she stop and, standing over him, stab both the kaglorite's arms with her spear, rendering him temporarily incapable of hefting his weapon of choice.

As Coria resumed course, another enemy fighter stepped in between her and her target, conjuring up a throwing knife in one hand. After pulling back the corresponding arm, he hurled the dagger right at the queen's neck. Again without slowing one bit, Coria met the attack, raising the middle of her weapon lengthwise to block the blade rushing at her. The kaglorite's brow shot up at this, and he started walking backward as he summoned another knife. This time, he aimed for one of her shoulders, and the queen foiled this attempt by dodging to one side at the last second. Her opponent started moving away once again, planning on reusing his previous tactic, but while he had been intermittently walking, Coria had been running nonstop, and at this point, she caught up to him and slammed one end of her hammer into the side of his head, knocking him out cold.

"Zage!" she called out over the surrounding clamor once she came to stand a pace and a half from the Dark Lord. The leader of the kaglorites turned his head to face hers and then, rotating the rest of his body to match this movement, raised both hands slightly, palms fully open and facing each other, before beginning to conjure a wide rectangle of blue magic between them.

The queen shook her head vehemently. "I don't want to fight you! I want you to surrender. Tell your men to stand down—" Before she could finish speaking, Zage materialized a long metal chain and, grasping one of its ends in his right hand, whipped it toward her face. She instinctively raised her weapon up, positioned horizontally, to protect her head, and the near end of the kaglorite's weapon wrapped around the middle of it as it was lifted.

Coria tightened her grip on the combination spear-hammer, bracing for the inevitable forward yank, but even still, when Zage did pull it toward him, she was only to keep it in her grasp for a few seconds before it flew from her hands and into the Dark Lord's. The queen didn't even have the time to turn around as the kaglorite rushed her, much faster than you would think a man of his considerable bulk could do so and, creating a knife in one of his hands with blue magic, whipped the blade toward her throat…

* * * * *

Cornelius rejoiced as he dueled with yet another kaglorite as Nadia did the same with her own by his side; whenever he risked a glance away from the action directly before him to that taking place elsewhere, the numbers advantage his people possessed since the outset climbed even higher. His stomach lurched however when he spotted Nadia with her halberd lowered and the tip of her opponent's sword pricking her jugular. He frowned; how could a nameless fighter, even a kaglorite, achieve such a swift and easy victory against her? When he next had the occasion to focus on his periphery however, he saw that she was staring with intent despair at something a good distance ahead of the two of them; it was the onset of this trance that allowed the kaglorite fighting her to checkmate her in such a way. Destiny's Catalyst traded a few more swings with his own personal foe before hazarding a look in the direction Nadia was facing… and his heart started pounding so hard he thought it might crack the bones immediately surrounding it when he saw what she had. Zage Batur walked toward them as he held the queen at knifepoint.

"MEN!" he shouted out as he sheathed Kiam. "STAND DOWN!"

"Zage, you don't have to do this," pleaded Coria out of the hero's earshot as she was pushed along by the Dark Lord. "You've given me no reason to think you could change, but that doesn't mean you can't. Surrender. I'll make sure you're treated with leniency. We could be friends. You could cross the ocean with me, truly look upon it for the first time."

"All right," the kaglorite replied.

The queen's brow shot up, and she wanted to look back at his face but couldn't with the blade to her neck. "Let's cross the ocean together." It's just as well she couldn't see his expression, for it was marred by a sneer. "CORNELIUS ARCIND!" cried out the Dark Lord, making his newfound prisoner wince from the volume of his exclamations. "You will provide a ship for me and my people to head east in and allow us to leave unmolested, or I will be proud to <u>open the throat</u> of Her Highness here." He gestured toward Coria with his head.

Destiny's Catalyst nodded at this. "Very well," he called back, "you'll have to give us some time, but it will be done."

Zage voiced his assent and feinted as if he were about to walk away, having finished speaking, before stopping, looking back at Cornelius, and fixing him with a smirk. "Oh, and I'll require one more thing from you—the map and key to the temple of the Orb of Desire, please."

The hero couldn't stop himself from visibly starting. *How did he...* "The relief on your face when I pretended to list all my demands confirmed it, but I began to suspect you'd gotten your hands back on the contents of the black box when you requested your personal belongings be left with your people. I've got no idea how you did it, but it came to me then that you most likely reacquired the map and key. Why else would you have made that request? The only other item of value on your person would be your sword, and as we all know, in the hundreds of years since it was first forged, you are the only one capable of wielding it, so even someone as hopeful as yourself surely recognizes that it's <u>certain</u> there <u>is</u> no other who could. There would be no point in giving it to another or working to keep it out of someone else's hands." The kaglorite paused to look out at Destiny's Catalyst expectantly.

Cornelius realized in that moment, of course, that were the Dark Lord to get his hands on the Orb, all the humans and lorms in Samu, *millions*, would perish. It wasn't worth it to risk that for a single life, even when it was that of a royal, and yet the hero was just that. He couldn't condemn a good woman to death, even to save so many others. And after all, his optimistic mind noted to itself, if he refused Zage, the queen was sure to die. On the other hand, even if he relinquished the map and key to the kaglorite holding her hostage, there was still a chance they and she could be recovered in time, and he'd lived his whole life betting on the slim odds of the best-case scenario.

"Very well," said Cornelius, with a grimace even in spite of the hope burning at the center of his soul, as he reached into one of his pockets and pulled out the black box, "I agree to your terms."

Zage lit up in evil triumph at the side of the small wood container and motioned with his head for one of his men to go and take it from Destiny's Catalyst, which the other kaglorite did.

It took some time to trick a ship into docking at Yinit. When the town was not open to outsiders, a red flag flew at the shore to ward such folk off. The kaglorites had, of course, hoisted such a thing immediately upon conquering the village, and there it had flown for the past few months. Yinit had been off-limits for so long that, even when Cornelius and his fellows replaced the red with the blue of welcoming, it was nighttime before a vessel's crew bold enough to make land there came upon them. When they did, they were surrounded by both soldiers of Humania and terrorists of Kagloris and forced to surrender their ship. Throughout this entire process and right up until Zage and the rest of his people were sailing off toward the isles with Her Highness in tow, Destiny's Catalyst feverishly racked his brain for some sort of idea as to how the queen could be freed and still win the day, but the Dark Lord's grip on the knife at her throat remained steady hour after hour, and the watchful quality of his gaze never wavered for a second. In the end, much as it went against every one of his predilections, Cornelius had to let him and her go.

"What are you going to do about the queen?" Dekkin asked the hero when shortly thereafter the two found themselves facing each other again. The immortal's voice was sick with worry, and this would've raised Cornelius's eyebrows if he hadn't been so consumed with rage at both his failure to prevent Coria's kidnapping and the audacity of this *criminal* to needle him with such a question at times like these that it went entirely unnoticed by him.

"That is no concern of yours," grated Destiny's Catalyst. "Do you know what is? The fact that you are to live out the rest of your many days in a <u>cell below these streets</u>, and your only company will be the <u>guards</u> at the <u>prison</u> and very occasionally one of my people seeking a reading of the future from you." He shifted his gaze to the soldier guarding the oracle and motioned toward the local jail. "Take him away."

In spite of the dark days ahead that had just been foretold to him, Dekkin would've retained some sense of peace if he could've but glimpsed Matthew's face one last time and committed the sight to memory. But alas, fate was even more cruel than he'd previously thought, for the boy was nowhere to be seen as the immortal was escorted into the prison, and its front door closed before him, never to be opened again for the building's newest resident.

20

ANTER'S FUNERAL WAS HELD in the forest where he had been born. He'd never returned there after his parents made a home in the desert unlike the many others who relocated back among the green shortly after that. Even before his mind began to fail him, he scarcely remembered the days before blistering heat and soft sand. Nonetheless, he was buried underneath the trees, as all members of Dekkin's tribe were regardless of which sect they belonged to. The aversion to depositing corpses under sand instead of dirt had no root in any sort of logic; like most conventions, it simply *felt* right.

Dekkin restrained himself from scoffing at the religious rites recited by a priest before the grave. He once believed in the gods just as his fellows did, but ever since Seren left him, his faith had been utterly destroyed. No deity, no matter how malevolent, would create a world as brutal as this where loved ones could abandon you, taking a chunk of you with them as they left, and fathers could outlive their children. *It is curious,* the oracle thought to himself, as the service proceeded, *that these two latest tragedies to befall me seem so much more biting than the dozens of unnatural deaths I've witnessed in my days before and after immortality.* A dark fate closest to your heart, he supposed, hurt far worse than that which was more painful yet existed only on the fringes of your own personal world.

Dekkin came about and started walking away from the procession before the ceremony was completed, drawing the attention of all its members unbeknownst to him. He had a long journey ahead of him back to the subterranean desert settlement he called home for quite some time now, though he'd already stuffed his things into a pack resting atop his bed there.

"Grandfather," whispered a man directly into one of his ears just a moment after the oracle began moving.

The unexpected nature of this vocalization, as well as its extremely proximity to him, made the immortal jump. He came to a halt and turned around to face Neposo. Dekkin hated that it had only taken one generation to remove all traces of his ex-wife's physical traits from his genetic line. "Yes?"

"Don't go," Neposo pleaded quietly.

"I came to pay my respects, as I should, no?" muttered the oracle back with a hint of irritation. "I want to get back home before dark, and there's no good reason I need to stay for the whole affair."

"That's not what I mean."

The immortal sighed deeply, averting his eyes as he wondered how much to say. Deciding he'd divulge it all, he looked back over at his grandson and replied, "There's no one I can stick around for, Neposo."

The other man raised his brow. "What are you *talking about*? You have *me*. You have my *family*, your *descendants*!"

"Oh, yes?" Dekkin responded, scowling bitterly. "Do any of you happen to have another turins on hand? Which one is capable of being its host?"

Neposo blinked with a frown. "What's that?"

The oracle turned his head to face groundward such that he could hide the tears in his eyes, but this was for naught. As when he spoke, he couldn't keep a quaver out of his voice. "Everyone is born with a number, grandson. The number of their loved ones who can die before their heart is broken. I've reached mine now. I cannot take any more."

"What…but…of course, you can!" insisted Neposo. "There are other oracles, you have predecessors. *They* managed, did they not?"

"No, they didn't, actually," the immortal countered. "Why do you think oracles seclude themselves so? To test those who would seek out them and their abilities, correct? Well, that's not so. They live in isolation, not for the sake of others, but for *themselves*. Because if they live almost entirely apart from other people, they'll never be touched by sorrow from death, as *I* would if I stayed with you and the others, over and over and *over* again. I could never live in a forest if I had to watch every tree I passed catch fire and burn down, turn to a pile of ash. Man lives with man. But I'm not a man anymore, am I? I'm an oracle." He pressed his twisted lips tightly together. "Goodbye, grandson."

Dekkin turned around and resumed course, and his last hope shattered loudly in his breast when, after a short while, it became clear that Neposo wasn't pursuing him any further and never would ever again.

* * * * *

"Why are we returning home?" asked Zuza of Zage as the two of them stood near the helm of their recently commandeered vessel, its wood frame creaking gently and the damp ocean air blowing through their violet hair as the bottom of the former cut a path through the waves. "We have the map and key to the temple, *and* the queen as hostage. Shouldn't we have used this opportunity to head right for the Orb, before *Destiny's Catalyst* and his filthy fellows have much time to think up a means to foil our plan? You haven't looked at the map yet. What if the temple's in Humania?"

"It's not," the Dark Lord assured her with an imperious smirk.

His right-hand woman's eyes went wide. "H-how do you know? You haven't opened the black box once since you first acquired it."

"But Cornelius Arcind surely did, after taking it back," explained Zage. "And he was heading toward the eastern border when we crossed paths." The kaglorite gestured straight ahead of them with one arm. "It must be somewhere in these Lormish Isles."

Zuza nodded. "I see." She thought on this for a moment. "Don't you think we should check the map though, just in case?"

The Dark Lord considered this and realized she, always the voice of reason between the two of them despite the hatred of humans and lorms burning as hotly in her blood as it did in his, was right. He reached into his tunic for the black box and, raising its lid after pulling it out, took in one hand and unfurled completely with both a few seconds later, after putting the container back in one of his pockets, the worn, cracked paper of the map. After scrutinizing its surface for a few seconds, Zage spotted a large *X*, unmistakably denoting the location of the temple, directly over an islet on the eastern side of the tropical country. He sighed heavily. Yet another long, potentially fraught journey lay ahead of him in his quest to rid the world of its human and Lormish inhabitants. But then again, he thought to himself, lifting his own spirits, *What in this world is worth doing that doesn't require a great deal of effort?*

* * * * *

Dekkin didn't know if it was day or night and how long it had been since the beginning of his imprisonment; he paid no mind to the light or lack thereof coming from his cell's single barred window, simply boring a hole into the wall opposite the cot with his gaze and certainly didn't want to stand and directly look out into the world beyond the prison, Doing so would only have proved an agonizing reminder of what he was missing and would miss for a little less than five hundred years. So when the oracle glanced over at his personal door in the dungeon and saw Matthew standing there blankly, he had no idea whether the boy came to Yinit after some time away or in fact not yet left at all. Before the immortal concocted his plan to steal the Orb, there had been monthslong stretches of time in his life that passed completely unnoticed by him.

"Hello there," Dekkin said, noting that his voice, which he hadn't used since the start of his imprisonment was a rasp.

"Hello," replied Matthew, "did you ever look at the map before the black box was taken from you?"

The oracle leaned forward, bringing his forearms to rest atop his knees. "Right to it, eh?" When the boy didn't respond to this, he nodded, continuing, "Yes, I know where the temple is."

The lorm brightened a little. "Truly? That's great. My master is willing to offer you amnesty if you'll join us as we set out to rescue the queen and stop Zage from using the Orb. He knows the relic's location can't be beaten out of you, and of course, it would be quite a boon to have a man who can see the future with us during our travels. Will you do it?"

The immortal let out a long internal groan at the thought of another, potentially lengthy trek but, of course, recognized that even he couldn't very well sit back while the possibility of every human and lorm in Samu being massacred hung in the air if he could do something to, perhaps, stop it, and lest he forget, victory would eliminate the remainder of his centuries-long prison sentence. "Yes, I will."

Matthew lit up a bit more. "Oh, good." He turned to face the guard stationed in the cell block and asked the man to unlock the door to Dekkin's room, which was done promptly.

As the oracle and the boy walked side by side out of the jail, the latter looked up at the former, saying, "Dekkin?"

The immortal turned his head to face the lorm's. "Yes?"

"Is it true what Coria said about you?" Matthew asked. "That you don't want to die anymore?"

Dekkin paused, then nodded. "Yes, it's true." Elation overtook the boy's face then, and the oracle smiled back at him. It was a lie, of course, his answer to the lorm's question, but one which had been crafted with the intention of making someone else feel better. Those were the good kind, yes?

21

"SO WHAT'S THE PLAN, Destiny's Catalyst?" asked Dekkin as they sailed into the Lormish Isles. While the oracle had been in his cell, Cornelius and his fellows managed to hail another ship and commission it to take them eastward.

"First, we'll go to Omu," answered the hero, referring to the tropical country's capital. His tone was flat, dismissive, as it had been near-constantly toward the oracle ever since his capture of the other man. "The governor, Ben, resides there. If anyone knows of some secret that might aid us in closing the gap between us and our quarry, he will."

"Will he know of a way to snap one's fingers and spirit a woman away from her captors?" Dekkin inquired with snark. "Even if there is some special method by which we can catch up to the kaglorites, they still have the queen as their hostage. How do you see us getting around that?"

"I'm hoping a route to the temple, quicker than the one the Dark Lord and his forces are taking, exists, and we'll be able to reach it before they do and set up an ambush."

"The prospect of that seems incredibly unlikely," pointed out the oracle disapprovingly.

Cornelius gave a carefree shrug and looked out at the azure field stretching out before them. "I've grown accustomed to hearing that about the success of my plans."

Recognizing that he had nothing left to say, the immortal came about, looking this way and that for Matthew. He frowned upon seeing that the boy was nowhere to be found and, walking up to one of the sailors now on the kingdom of Humania's payroll, asked him if he knew where the little lorm had gone. Dekkin was directed to a rowboat on one side of and by a rope tied to the ship, within which Matthew sat with his head bent over the water below. As the oracle began clambering down to the boy, he forced himself with great effort to begin exuding an air of contentment. He decided that he would live now purely for the lorm's happiness, and part of that would involve, he thought, continuing to trick the youth into thinking he himself was happy.

"Matthew," the immortal said in greeting as he touched down on the bottom of the boat and the boy looked up and over at him in response. Dekkin decided after but a moment to abandon the strained smile he'd donned and initially planned on sporting whenever he was around the lorm; the effort this required of him was too great to maintain it for even a half minute. "What are you up to?"

Matthew gestured toward one of his hands, which he was holding just above the waves, its fingers and thumb forming a circle. "Trying to catch some *ringfish*."

"Ringfish?" repeated the oracle inquisitively. "What are those?" He hadn't been to the isles in centuries, and the last time he had, civilization certainly hadn't advanced nearly as far as it would've needed to for anyone to have a log of each area in Samu's indigenous wildlife.

"They're only native to Lormish territory," the boy explained. "Their scales can be used to make this incredibly soft type of fabric. That's why I'd like to get some."

The immortal nodded. "I see, but why are they called ringfish?"

"Well, this is going to sound ridiculous to someone who has no experience with them. But ringfish have a natural compulsion to shove their bodies into circular openings of any kind." At that moment, such a creature, possessing a squishy small cylindrical body with soft edges and covered in shimmering white scales, came up to the surface of the water and leaped right into the middle of the ring Matthew formed with his hands. The boy raised the floundering fish in his grasp up for Dekkin to view more clearly with a smile. "See?" Digging his white claws underneath one of its scales, eliciting as a result a cry of protest from his catch, the lorm then removed it from its brothers and released the ringfish back into the drink. It was then that Dekkin saw the creature's "scales" were actually tightly wound pockets of very fine thread as Matthew unspooled that which he had just taken.

As the boy reached down to the water's surface to provide the bait for yet another redfish, he grew self-conscious under the oracle's gaze and said to him with a slight blush, "You don't have to stay and watch me the entire time, you know."

"Oh yes, I know," the immortal assured the lorm, making the latter glow faintly. A moment later, however, Matthew's face fell, and he brought his outstretched hand back to rest at his side.

Dekkin furrowed his brow and looked over at the boy. "What is it? What's wrong?"

The boy pointed to a fish of a different species advancing toward the one he'd just caught and released from a short distance away. The newcomer had a gray body, much larger than that of the other in terms of both length and width. "That's an aihu—one of the ringfish's biggest predators." As the two of them watched, the aihu caught up quickly to its prospective prey with a few powerful strokes of its more sizable fins. Then it unhinged both its jaws, and its tongue darted out at the ringfish. This resident of its mouth was tubular and girthy enough to fit the other aquatic creature completely inside it.

As the aihu retreated, retracting its tongue back into its mouth and swallowing its contents, Dekkin searched for something to say, wanting to lift the spirits of the boy now staring forlornly after the gray creature. "So we're headed for the capital, Omu"—he came up with after a moment—"to meet the governor! You'll get to meet the governor. That's exciting, yes?"

Much to the oracle's surprise and confusion, the boy's features drooped even further. *I suppose that makes sense,* the immortal thought to himself as the two of them climbed back up the side of the ship. *After all, what child dreams of meeting a minor politician?*

22

IT ONLY TOOK DEKKIN and the others in his party a few days to reach Omu, capital of the Lormish Isles. The City of Halves, as it was also known, had always been one of its country's more populous settlements and its most prosperous too because of its proximity to the western border. But, of course, being a week's voyage away from the center of the territory it found itself in hadn't been the capital from the outset and for almost the entirety of the ensuing centuries. If you'd asked a lorm about the prospect fifty years ago or later, they would've scoffed at the idea in a heartbeat. But almost thirty years prior to present day, something the islands' indigenous folk could've never conceived of long ago came to pass—the isles became an official dominion of the human crown, ostensibly so that the islanders would be under more direct protection from the murderous kaglorite terrorists in the east, who now had no choice because of Humania's ironclad border patrol along its western shore but to cross Lormish territory in order to carry out their raids and invasions (and it was the kingdom's official statement on the matter that most of the region's material rights passing to it in the process was but a coincidence, albeit, on its part at least, a happy one).

And so, Omu, standing near the halfway point of human and Lormish territories combined, was rechristened the capital of the island nation. Problems arose almost immediately. The city was large but not nearly large enough to house the new facilities that would need to be built there because of its change in status and all the people, human and halfling, who would be flocking to move into the

Lormish burg for the same reason, in addition to its existing inhabitants. But Omu already crossed the entire span of the island it rested on. The solution? To have natate shipped in from Humania and construct a new perimeter for the city atop the water. Ever since then, Omu had never been busier, and its Lormish citizens, on the whole, never more the worse for wear. You see, bureaucrats and noblemen relocating there, most of them human, were prioritized quite highly in this new era of ostensibly equal interspecies alliance and so given prime real estate for both work and personal life near the center of the isle, a phrase which now applied to many places that had previously been considered midtown as a result of the recent expansion. The poor and middle-class lorms who previously inhabited the areas in question meanwhile had been, at times forcibly, evicted from their homes and forced to relocate to the less prosperous outer section of the city.

Most ships passing into Omu had to be heavily guarded to have a hope of reaching their destination with their vessel, goods, and lives completely intact; thieves waited on the floating outskirts of the settlement for new arrivals to rob. Fortunately, Dekkin's party had no issue there as they entered the city limits, given the presence of Destiny's Catalyst himself, a world-famous warlord, and a retinue, several hundred men and women strong, of the human royal guard.

Despite the numerous clusters of leering hoodlums gathered on either side of them, Dekkin noticed Matthew looking about wistfully at the place as the ship made its way through it via canal. "You've been here before, haven't you?" the oracle asked the boy. "Long ago?"

"I was born here," replied the lorm.

The governor's office, formerly that of the Lormish Isles' prime minister, hadn't been large enough to accommodate the newfound duties of the single man who occupied both positions at different but subsequent points in time, and yet the area immediately around it was too cramped as it was, and it was deemed too costly to demolish and completely rebuild it, so the human-led construction crews had simply added several floors to its top, despite this effort making the newly-renovated edifice tall enough relative to its foundation as to be actually dangerous. Dekkin noticed this firsthand as he, Cornelius,

Nadia, and Matthew ascended the seemingly endless cascade of winding steps up to the top floor and, when they passed a certain point, the proximate section of the spire around them teetered precariously in the wind.

The oracle found much to his surprise upon reaching Ben's office on the top floor that it was scarcely larger than a standard bedroom, and the desk up against its far wall had only a few papers scattered atop it. The Lormish politician, who was seated at it, looked up from what appeared suspiciously like daydreaming as Dekkin and the others walked in, his brow leaping in surprise; Cornelius had, of course, not been required to schedule an appointment or have his entering the governor's chambers foretold.

"Cornelius Arcind!" said Ben as he stood and moved to stand two paces ahead of him and the other new arrivals. The oracle noted that after an initial glance in their direction, the lorm had unwaveringly kept his eyes on the spot of floor directly before and beneath the hero's feet. "This is unexpected! How are you, good sir?"

"I am well as always, Governor," responded Destiny's Catalyst briskly. "Now if you'll excuse me, time is of the absolute essence for me, for *all of us*, and the stakes couldn't be higher at the moment, so would you mind if we dispensed with the pleasantries and got right to business?"

Ben nodded violently. "*Of course*, of course, Master Arcind, my *deepest* apologies. I should've *known*—"

The hero frowned at this as he interrupted. "Well, uh…I don't see how. At any rate, let me explain the present situation as quickly as I can." And so he did just that. "So?" he asked after his summary. "Do you know of any way we might be able to beat the kaglorites to their destination? A sort of secret shortcut or some such?"

The governor shook his head. "I'm afraid not."

Cornelius's eyes bugged out. "*Nothing* at all?"

Again the lorm motioned in the negative. "Nothing." He paused. "Although…there *is*"—he stopped himself and shook his head once more so vehemently Dekkin thought it would fly from atop his thin shoulders—"but no, that would be *much* too dangerous. The chances of it working, almost zero."

"Well, if it's the only option, we have to take it, given the circumstances, yes?" Destiny's Catalyst pointed out.

"*Yes*, yes, of course, I'm so sorry," responded Ben immediately before crossing the room back to his desk and taking out a map of the country from one of its drawers, unfurling it across the length of his work station. With one small clawed hand, the governor traced a line through most of the isles, starting almost at Omu and ending a day's trek over water from the location of the temple. "There's a very strong current that passes through most of this country. If you were to take a ship into it, your journey would be cut short to such a degree that you'd easily outpace the Dark Lord and his forces."

"But?" Cornelius asked next.

"But there are so many sharp rocks strewn along its length that no one actually uses it," explained the Lormish man. "Around here, we call it the fast track to the heavens."

"Hmm"—the hero thought on this for a moment before smiling in victory—"yes, this is just what we need. Thank you, governor!"

"W-well, you're very welcome, of course, good sir, but…you aren't truly planning to *go down* the fast track, are you?" inquired Ben, wringing his hands.

"That's precisely what I've got in mind, yes," Cornelius replied flippantly.

The governor's eyes bulged. "B-but…I'm sorry, I mustn't have explained the situation adequately. *No one* in the *history of the world* has ever made it through the current alive!"

Destiny's Catalyst turned his head to face Dekkin's and gripped one of the other man's shoulders lightly, a most unwelcome gesture for the oracle. "Yes, but I'm willing to bet no one who's ever tried has had a *seer* on their side. We'll have Master Eterden here induce a vision of our vessel before we set out and use what he learns from it to fortify our ship in all the places it's going to make contact with the rocks."

The Lormish man considered this. "Y-yes, I suppose that could work, but I must say it still seems much too—"

"Risky, yes, I know," interrupted the hero. "Such undertakings are the bread and butter of my life, are they not? I'm sorry to keep rushing you, but current or no, we truly must move with all haste, given what's on the line."

The governor bowed very low in a single jerky motion. "*Yes, yes, yes,* you're *right*, of course, Master Arcind. I curse myself for contradicting you."

Destiny's Catalyst opened his mouth to object once more to Ben's self-flagellation, but the other man was talking so quickly he couldn't get a word in without stopping the Lormish man short, something the hero was dead set on avoiding from now on. "And you're *absolutely* right. There's no time to dally. Feel free to go and begin preparations whenever you see fit."

"Thank you, Governor," Cornelius said then sincerely. "You may well have just saved all mankind and lormkind."

He turned around to walk out of the room, and his fellows followed suit a split second later, but before the first of them could crest its threshold, Ben called out after them, "Ah, excuse me, excuse me, excuse me, Destiny's Catalyst, I can't *tell* you how mortified I am for this interjection, but"—he hit himself on the side of the head with one of his hands—"right, right, hurry hurry hurry! Ah, even if you begin modifying your vessel as soon as you leave here, the task won't be completed until tomorrow. W-would you like to dine with me in my home this evening, bringing the others gathered here with you? I'd be delighted to be visited by my son."

Dekkin furrowed his brow in confusion, looking about his immediate surroundings as he spoke for the first time since entering the tower, saying, "Your *son?* Your son is with us? Who?" His gaze fell on Matthew. He felt embarrassed at first that he hadn't put things together immediately but then came to the realization that he shouldn't be, considering what he was about to point out. "Matthew is your son?"

Ben nodded at this.

"He's your son, and you haven't said a word to him since he walked in."

"Well, ah, he's apprentice to Destiny's Catalyst first of all. I didn't want to address Matthew without Master Arcind's approval, to be presumptuous in that way." He blanched when the immortal flashed him a furious glare. "I...I apologize if I've offended you in some way by this, Oracle." *Though I don't know how I could have,* he thought to himself in confusion after speaking.

Dekkin gave him a surly grunt at this.

"We would all be delighted, Governor," interjected Cornelius into the naturally and unnaturally thin air.

Ben beamed at the hero. "*Truly?* Oh, *perfect!* My wife and I will see to your *every* need and those of your companions as well, of course."

* * * * *

After a prolonged descent from the top floor of the governor's office, Dekkin and the others returned to their ship. The oracle took out his flask as he stood before and stared directly at the vessel and, throwing his head back, drank a swig of Destiny Water. Sometimes he liked to close his eyes just before a vision came on, making the scene from the future spring forth from complete black, and he did that now.

Suddenly, the immortal was standing by the helm of the ship he'd just been looking at as it raced through roaring rapids in the middle of the ocean. He had no influence over what his body did during the premonition, of course, but if he had, Dekkin would've frowned; the vessel seemed much lower to the water than it should have.

The question that formed in his mind then was answered promptly when one of the sailors popped up from below decks, crying out as he faced a point directly to the oracle's right, "THERE'RE TOO MANY OF THEM! WE CAN'T BAIL FAST ENOUGH TO KEEP UP!"

"KEEP AT IT!" The immortal looked over in the direction in which the sailor was looking and the second voice had come from to find Cornelius standing right beside him. "PERHAPS WE CAN'T SAVE THE SHIP, BUT WE MAY BE ABLE TO RIDE OUT THE CURRENT IN IT AT LEAST, IF WE CAN DELAY ITS WATERY DEMISE LONG ENOUGH."

Dekkin's future self descended then, first to the main deck and then down below it. Viewing things through his eyes, the present one saw what the sailor had been referencing earlier; there were many large breaches in the vessel below the water line. Salt water gushed out of them onto the wooden floor of the ship, and its crew formed of themselves a long single-file row leading back up to one side of the deck directly above, by which they could get bucketfuls of the intruding liquid and hand them off down the line until it could be deposited back in its home. Both immortals inhabiting the older one's body could tell even from just a cursory glance around that the man who'd called out to Cornelius had been right; there was no stopping the ship from going under.

Walk around and look about! cried Dekkin's present self to his future one, though he knew that, of course, his mental exclamation would fall on deaf ears. The former needed to be able to inspect the damage, so he could tell his fellows where to fortify the vessel once he was back in the real world. The oracle could've kissed the other version of himself then, for the latter did indeed start turning his head this way and that, examining the holes in the hull intently. This happened sometimes in the immortal's visions; his future self would, standing on the brink of disaster, keenly observe his surroundings, knowing that in another life, the sensory information may aid a Dekkin Eterden of the past looking in on what was to come. The oracle, out of time, strained his brain to commit to memory the location and size of each perforation, and just as he managed to log the last of them in his mind, and he could feel the ship slow around him as it reached the end of the current, the premonition ended, and he was snapped back into his proper temporal place.

As soon as the oracle returned, he fumbled around in one of his pockets for the pen, sealed inkwell, and paper he'd stuffed there for just this occasion, and once he had them both in hand, he drew a diagram of the vessel before him, indicating where each of the breaches he'd seen had been. He handed this off to Cornelius, and Destiny's Catalyst got to work along with the soldiers at his command, and the sailors temporarily under his employ to sufficiently strengthen the necessary sections of the ship.

As Dekkin, Matthew, Nadia, and Cornelius walked to Ben's house side by side that evening from where their vessel was docked, the oracle recognized something about the boy from the ponderous way in which the latter walked and the ever-so-telltale downward twist at the corners of his mouth.

"You don't want to go, do you?" the immortal asked the lorm.

Matthew started and gazed back up at him with wide eyes. "N-no, I do," assured the boy, utterly unconvincing. "Of course, I do. Our host is my father."

Dekkin stared down at the lorm for a moment longer before saying, "Hmm, all right," and moving his head to face forward again.

A lorm's house tended to be of much more diminutive proportions than that of a human, on account, as you can imagine, of the shorter stature of the former species. As Dekkin walked through the streets in Omu's most affluent residential district with the others on the way to Ben's house, the roofs of each building on either side of him only came up to his chest. That is, until he and his party actually arrived at the governor's house proper. The Lormish politician's living space wouldn't have seemed out of place in the section of Cobaltus wherein those of Humania's various noble houses resided, and the oracle could see through its front windows that the rooms had been built and arranged for someone of the immortal's size too. Dekkin wondered at this for a moment as he and the others ascended the long flight of steps leading up to the house's front door until it opened and his internal question was answered.

"*Hello*, everyone!" the human woman standing by Ben's side called out to her arriving guests despite the shortness of the distance between them and her as she waved at them furiously with one hand. Her blond hair went down to the small of her back, and the red backless evening gown she had on stopped at her knees, a fashion choice in sharp contrast to that of the long, uniform dresses of brown worn by the Lormish women Dekkin and the others had seen on their way to the governor's subdivision.

"This is my wife, Brea," explained Ben, gesturing toward her as he flashed the oracle and the rest of his party an inviting smile. The oracle, as well as Cornelius and Nadia, turned to face her and bowed only for the woman to hold out one hand, expecting a kiss upon it from each of them. Destiny's Catalyst instantly obliged. Nadia followed his lead immediately thereafter, and then the immortal did so too, though with great reluctance; if she hadn't been Matthew's mother and if he hadn't recently begun his effort to put on a facade of contentment for the sake of the boy, he would've stood unmoving, fixing her with a withering glare.

"Can I get anyone something to drink?" Ben asked his guests once they'd all sat down around his dining room table. "Some wine, perhaps?"

"I'll take some," replied Cornelius, raising one index finger up in the air slightly. "Thank you." Nadia, a teetotaler, asked for water, as did Dekkin; the oracle could always use a drink, but if given the choice between Lormish wine, of which there was a good chance, their host possessed exclusively, and nothing at all he'd unhesitantly take the latter every single time. The isles' prohibition of alcohol had only ended with the beginning of their status as a dominion of Humania, and it would seem twenty-nine years was far too short a time for its green-skinned natives to figure out the intricacies of its production.

"All right then!" the governor said in response. He went into the kitchen to get the wine, still in full view of the immortal, only to find it was on a shelf too high for him to reach. "Darling, could you, uh, help me out over here?" he asked sheepishly as he looked back at Brea. Rolling her eyes, his wife got up, walked over to where he was, and obliged him.

"Tell me, did any of you see anyone out and about in this neighborhood as you were coming here?" inquired Ben as they ate a few minutes later. The meal was bulae meatloaf, mashed potatoes, and corn, all three of which were exclusively cultivated in the farms of central Humania and as such rare and quite expensive to purchase once they'd been exported all the way across the eastern border.

"No, I don't think I did," Cornelius answered after swallowing the food in his mouth. The others indicated the same, either verbally or visually. "Why's that?" questioned Destiny's Catalyst after this.

"Oh, I was just wondering if you'd managed to spot a beige lorm," the governor replied.

The hero furrowed his brow in puzzlement. "*Beige lorm?* I've never even *heard* of such a thing."

Ben smiled widely. "Oh, I'm not surprised. It's a recent development. A dyeing process was discovered just a short while ago that allows my people to bleach their skin that color."

"Ah," Cornelius said with a nod, "only beige?"

"Well, no, it can be done with any hue."

The hero's eyes narrowed even further, as far as they could. "So why are people only getting their skin bleached beige specifically?"

The governor shrugged at his light-skinned guest. "I suppose it's simply in fashion." He reached up to rub at his cheek with one hand. "I quite like how it looks. I've been thinking about having it done myself."

"*No!*" His wife dropped the knife in her right hand, which clattered loudly against the table's wood surface after falling to it and clutched at her husband's near shoulder. "Ben, *don't*." She stroked one side of his neck with her right index finger like a jewel enthusiast feeling reverently one of their prized diamonds. "I wouldn't want anything other than a green-skinned partner."

Ben smiled affectionately back at her. "Well, that settles that. It's expensive to have it done, anyway, though, of course, money's never been any object for me."

Some time passed in silence save for the clinking of silverware against pottery. Eventually Dekkin looked over at the Lormish politician's wife. "Is Matthew your only child, Brea?"

She frowned. "Oh, Matthew isn't *my* child."

The oracle raised his brow. "Ah." He shifted his gaze to Ben. "So where *is* his mother?"

The governor's cordial expression remained but became a little strained. "Well, I have no idea. She left me when our son was five."

The immortal nodded, and Destiny's Catalyst stared at the other human man, waiting for an expression of sympathy from him and, when it never came, offered one himself.

Ben acknowledged it, then filled the void of quiet that followed by saying with an empathetic twist to his face, "I was horrified to hear about Her Highness, simply horrified. I've known Coria Roneage personally since the day she was born." He shook his head from side to side. "Terrifying stuff." Then he brightened as he looked across the table at Cornelius. "But, of course, with Destiny's Catalyst on the case, I'm sure everything will turn out all right."

The hero himself responded to this with a humble smile and by lowering his gaze in the same manner to the top of the table they were all seated at.

"So you've been governor for quite some time then," Dekkin interjected.

The Lormish man's eyes went wide with surprise as the immortal spoke to him, for this was something which had proven thus far to be an extremely rare occurrence. "Ah, yes, ever since the isles became a dominion of Humania. And before that, I was the prime minister for many years."

The oracle considered this. "So you were the architect of the alliance between our two nations."

"Well, ah, in *part*, yes, but truly it would've been forged regardless," said Ben. "The human crown wanted it, and given the vast gulf of difference between our two countries' military might, it would've been futile to resist."

"But, of course, you wouldn't have *wanted* to prevent it, even if you could, yes?" Brea asked, looking over at her husband expectantly. "The alliance has been the greatest thing to happen to this country since its inception, right?"

The governor raised both hands, palms open and facing outward slightly, and with his brow raised as high as it could go, assured her, "*Oh, yes, yes, absolutely, yes.*" As he said this, he looked and sounded like there was a small painful sore resting inside his throat. If his wife noticed this, she gave no indication of it.

Ben turned his head to face Cornelius. "And how is my son performing in his duties, Destiny's Catalyst?"

"Well, ah, he's right here, you know, Governor," pointed out the hero, shifting his weight around uncomfortably as he gestured toward his apprentice.

"Oh, I know," the Lormish man replied with a genial smile, and his gaze still never falling on his offspring. "I'd just prefer to hear it from you, that's all. Children can't be trusted very far, especially in the matter of self-reporting their level of competence." Ben glanced in Matthew's direction. "No offense intended, of course." Both the look and the words following it, though they numbered but two, were enough to make the boy light up, since they were the only ones that had been directly addressed to him since he walked into his father's house.

Cornelius tried to mask a reflexive grimace with a disarming smile but couldn't quite manage it, leaving the look on his face the deformed offspring of both expressions. "Hmm, well, very good, he's very good." The hero hesitated for a few seconds. "He's been a little…strange these last few days, but before that, he was excellent, incredibly loyal, dutiful."

Ben nodded knowingly. "Twelve years old. It's a special time. He's almost a man but not quite there. I'm sure he'll shape up in due time though." The governor's smile was tight, and his last words felt more like an edict than a hypothesis. He turned his head to face Matthew for the second time. "My son, I think I might know what's afflicting you. You're becoming a man, you see, and men have responsibilities. And they must carry out those responsibilities, at all costs. But most of the time, almost *all* the time, when you're told to fulfill your duties, a little voice within you cries out against it, right here." He placed a hand over his azure heart. "It'll tell you that it's wrong to do something you feel goes against yourself. But that is *life*, for a man. It feels wrong to do the right thing."

* * * * *

"Where does your mother live?" Dekkin asked Matthew as they made their way from Ben's house to the inn they were staying at that night. "Is she in Omu? Would you like to visit her too while we're here?" The oracle knew the boy would never speak up and say so even if it was his desire, which was the reason behind the former's questioning.

"I don't know where my mother lives," answered the lorm evenly.

The immortal's brow shot up. "Oh, she didn't just leave your father then. She *abandoned* you." He spat out the penultimate word of that final sentence.

Matthew shook his head nigh imperceptibly. "She didn't leave. She was taken."

"Taken?" Dekkin repeated. "What do you mean?"

"When I was five, a human royal visiting Omu from his home country took a liking to my mother and decided he would take her as his concubine," explained the boy, his shoulders slumping a little in a familiar motion as if large stones that were periodically placed upon them had been lowered onto both.

The oracle's mouth dropped open a little. "*What?* And…and she was? Your father didn't stop it, object to it? He's the governor of the Lormish Isles, yes?"

"He handed her over with a smile."

The immortal had nothing to say to this, and the two of them walked on in silence for a while. When Dekkin next looked over at the lorm, the latter was clearly blinking away tears.

"I'm sorry, Matthew," said the oracle with a sympathetic squint. "I didn't mean to reopen old wounds."

"No, no, it's not that," the boy replied, looking up at him with an infinitesimally quivering lip. "We were at my father's place for *hours*. He never told me I was doing a good job. He never asked me a question directly. He barely looked at me."

"Your father doesn't think well of you…or *much about* you either, I suppose," summarized the immortal. "That's the cause of your sorrow?"

The lorm indicated his assent.

"Well, don't worry about that," Dekkin assured him. "When people are asses, you need not concern yourself with their opinions of you. And, Matthew, that man is an ass."

These words didn't stop the tears from eventually flowing down the boy's cheeks; he wasn't sure anything could. He was at the end of a very long day, and yet he never broke stride. He wanted to stay by the oracle's side, a feeling much stronger than his desire to obey his fatigued body and stop to curl up on the roadside.

23

EVEN WITH HER WRISTS in chains, Coria still preferred the outdoors of the Lormish Isles, with its fresh sea breezes, to the stuffy interior of the royal castle in Cobaltus. It was warm here, warm enough that on the first day of her travels with the kaglorites, she had begged and eventually been allowed, with great reluctance, to cut off the sleeves of her shirt. They encountered no resistance to their passage since setting out about seventy-two hours ago as all of them had expected; the lorms weren't known for their military presence. Shortly after their departure, it was decided that the queen would be allowed to stay above decks rather than be imprisoned down below in the hold so that the Dark Lord himself could keep a constant eye on her, and at this, her heart jumped for joy.

"There is dirt all over your face, has been for a long time. Clean it off. You look like one of your peasants."

Coria, who had been gazing out at their tropical surroundings in wonder, raised her brow at this interjection and shifted her gaze in its direction to find Zage standing beside her. The queen burst out laughing in surprise as she wiped at her cheeks with both shackled hands.

The kaglorite at her side bristled at this. "Why do you laugh? Am I a joke to you?"

The queen shook her head in assurance as she brought her expression of mirth to a close with a few chuckles. "No, no. It's just… no one had ever talked down to me before I started traveling with

Dekkin. Even now that it's happening, I lived so long without it that it still catches me off guard."

"What, do you think any criticism toward you is invalid?" the Dark Lord snapped. "Do you think you are above the rest of us?"

Coria motioned in the negative. "No, not at all. It's merely… unexpected. I actually…quite like it, I think."

Zage grunted dismissively at this before returning his attention to the stretch of horizon before them. The smile on the queen's face stayed there for a little bit and would've hung around much longer had she not shortly thereafter spotted an islet ahead and off to one side of the ship, with two neighboring palm trees forming an *X* with their trunks at the center of it.

Seeing this, Coria's brow shot up. "Zage, we must find another way forward!" she cried to the kaglorite beside her. She pointed at the leafy duo in the distance. "I recognize that landmark over there. We're heading into *dangerous territory*!"

The Dark Lord scoffed. "Oh yes? And how would *you* know this—she who does not even know what her own backyard looks like? You forget I spent quite some time with you, unwillingly, when we were with the oracle and the Lormish boy."

"I know this part of the map," insisted the queen with averted eyes. "This was the route I was going to take to…uh, get to my destination, before I was…routed."

"As if I would take your word for anything, *human wench*," Zage huffed. "Besides, if the path ahead truly is treacherous, what of it? We are the *last of the kaglorites*. None can sway us." He raised one hand slightly to silence Coria as she opened her mouth to protest anew. "*Be silent*, or I will find my mind has been changed when it comes to which section of this ship you should be confined to." This shut the queen up, albeit barely.

Now when Coria looked this way and that at their immediate surroundings, she did so with dread. And as she spotted a large outcropping ahead and off to one side of the ship she thought she knew what would happen next, though she said nothing for fear of being proven wrong and relegated to the hold for nothing. Sure enough, right as the stolen vessel passed the rock, the galleon it had been concealing from their view came out of hiding and set a course straight for them.

"Do you *see*?" cried the queen at the Dark Lord. "*I told—*"

"NOT ANOTHER WORD," Zage growled. He turned his head to address his fellows. "BATTLE STATIONS *now*!" The other kaglorites got into formation, some positioning themselves on the side of the ship that the newcomers were headed for and creating close-range weapons using blue magic and still others conjuring up balls of red magic from behind the first group, each letting theirs fly toward the nearest section of wood below the water on the other vessel, hoping to create leaks. However, before the mystical orbs could do so, they were intercepted by others, and the two making up every pair of them canceled each other out in midair, leaving the enemy ship untouched. The Dark Lord looked up at the deck of the other vessel to find several other kaglorites as part of its crew.

"*Filthy traitors!*" snarled Zage in rage and disbelief. He and his fellows continued trying to magically perforate the enemy ship but were thwarted at every turn once again and in the same manner. Once the bow of the second vessel was almost touching the side of the Dark Lord's, the people manning it maneuvered their wooden craft around, bringing it to rest directly beside and running parallel to its target. Grappling hooks were shot into the sky and through the deck of Zage's ship, too many to sever in time, and suddenly, the vessel Coria found herself on had been reached and ensnared without incident.

"*Prepare for battle!*" the Dark Lord bellowed as he assumed a defensive stance and summoned a sword into one hand. As the invaders began to assemble at their side of the threshold between the two ships, the odds seemed to be in Zage's favor. Their numbers were roughly equal, but the other crew consisted of mostly humans. However, just as the Dark Lord flashed his prospective opponents a haughty sneer, the door leading below decks on the other vessel was shoved ajar from the inside, and several dozen lorms came pouring out of the newly opened entranceway.

Despite this, Zage didn't even hesitate. Coria saw this and grabbed one of his shoulders with her shackled hands. "What are you doing?" asked the queen in bewilderment. "Order your men to stand down! You can't win this fight."

"Better to *die* on the field of battle than *live* as a coward!" the kaglorite countered, baring his teeth.

Coria furrowed her brow as she strained her brain trying to come up with a convincing argument against this line of illogic in the half second allotted to her. It rose when she landed on something after a good deal of effort. "A-a true master combatant uses his head, to…to *win* the fight, *without* dying! If…if we were to surrender, we'd still have a chance to turn the tables on them afterward. Is it a warrior's way to perish when he could've survived?"

This gave the Dark Lord pause, and after a few seconds, he cried out for his fellows to stand down. "If we don't end up avenging ourselves against these caneos, there will be hell to pay for you, woman," he growled as he turned his head to face hers. "In this life or the next, whichever one we find ourselves in."

The queen nodded, trying not to think of what he might do in the event of her plan's failure.

When the invaders' leader, a human man, made his way through the ranks of his subordinates and to the front of the group, into view of Coria and Zage, what they saw surprised them. His face was clean-shaven, his shoulder-length blond hair without a speck of grime within or upon its fibers, and he wore a white robe with gold filigree. The queen thought for a moment he and the others with him might not be a coven of ruffians but rather an itinerant nobleman and his retinue; however, she dismissed this notion almost as soon as it sprung into her mind, as, of course, no human of elevated status would be traveling with kaglorites alongside them.

"I greet the future victims of theft by my hand!" he cried imperiously, his voice perfectly clipped and measured. "My name is Lord Ripla. My band of pirates and I will be taking this ship and everything in it, right this minute."

"You're going to leave us to die in the middle of the ocean?" asked Coria in panic.

"Oh no!" Ripla assured her, emphatic and sincere. "We'll tow your ship to the nearest inhabited island and drop you and the rest of your crew off there before leaving. We're thieves, not murderers."

The queen breathed a heavy sigh of relief. "Ah, very good. Thank you."

Zage jabbed one of his elbows into her ribs at the end of that last sentence, making her start and then look back at him sheepishly.

The visibly loot-hungry lord threw up his hands and lifted his brow in elation. "A willing bunch of marks! Most of them kaglorite, no less. I am indeed fortunate this day." He turned to face his subordinates. "Well, hop to it then. You know what to do."

"Can we fight back now?" muttered the Dark Lord out of one side of his mouth at Coria impatiently as the pirates combed every inch of their newly acquired former quarry.

"No, no, not yet," the queen answered in an identical manner, smiling nervously at one of the thieves when he looked their way. "While they're taking us to the spot where they'll drop up off, we can talk to some of the crew, try to sniff out some sort of weakness in them and exploit it before they sail off with all our possessions." *Stolen possessions*, she said to herself silently but thought better of voicing to the kaglorite.

Ripla frowned petulantly as his lieutenants reported on the contents of Zage's vessel before looking over at the latter and calling out, "Only food and medicine, eh? How disappointing. Ah, well. It's good for *something*, at least." The Dark Lord bristled at this, and Coria had to hold him back to keep the man from starting a maritime brawl.

"Shall I conduct the investigation?" inquired Zage of the queen once the twin ships were moving again on their new course.

"*No, no!*" Coria whispered back vehemently before catching herself when the kaglorite flashed her a questioning frown. "Ah, no, you're little too—I think it's better if *I* do it." The Dark Lord grunted in assent, and the queen looked about the duo of ships around her for someone who looked like a good target for questioning. Naturally, of the three races represented among the group of thieves, the lorms were the least intimidating, so she decided to walk over to where a group of them stood talking among themselves in a tight huddle several paces away from where she'd been before moving.

"Hello!" greeted the queen brightly once she reached the lorms and come to a halt directly beside their formation. Only some of its members looked over to return her gaze, and those that did had an uneasy look on their faces. "I just thought I could pass the time quicker if I talked to someone, like you lot are doing," Coria explained with a relaxing smile that worked not a whit on its targets. After a still, uncomfortable pause, she continued, "So thieving—an unusual profession for a lorm to go into—is it not?"

None of them said anything for long enough that the queen was starting to think getting the lorms to open up was an impossible task when one of them finally managed to squeak out, "We're not doing it by choice."

The queen raised one eyebrow. "'Not doing it by choice'? What do you mean?"

The lorm who piped up opened his mouth as if to say something but then closed it without a word. As Coria was about to repeat her question in a more forceful tone, one of his fellows said, "We were abducted by Lord Ripla and the others, forced to be a part of their pirate band, under threat of injury."

"Ah," replied the queen in realization, "so you don't *want* to be doing this then."

The lorm she was speaking with looked around for any onlookers among the rest of the pirate crew and outside the close-knit group he stood within and, seeing none, shifted his gaze back to her and nodded in a nigh imperceptible motion. Coria considered this before continuing. "So if Lord Ripla and the other members of your crew, those who aren't lorms, were incapacitated, you wouldn't resist those who defeated them following that?" None of the green-skinned people gathered there gave a verbal reply, but she could tell from the glimmer in their eyes at the notion of their unsolicited partners' defeat that the answer to her question for all of them was a resounding yes.

Smiling in satisfaction, the queen scanned the rest of the deck she found herself on for her next target. It wasn't long before she determined who it would be; one of the kaglorites on the pirate crew, all three of whom had been stationed on the transport previously belonging to their prisoners, was keeping watch a short distance away from her.

"Hello!" she began in her usual manner.

"Hello," parroted back the kaglorite immediately, turning his head to face hers.

Coria intended on trying to make some small talk before diving into her questioning, but the intensity of the man's gaze made her abandon that idea and plunge right into starting a discussion about what she truly wanted to know. "So you and the others on this crew decided to abstain from the Dark Lord's 'glorious conquest,' huh?"

The violet-skinned man before her nodded at this. "Yes, we did. Like me, the others were born after the massacre. We have no memory of it, and so we don't see a reason to try to avenge our people because of it."

The queen took this in for a moment. "But…you became criminals of a different sort instead. Why not try to live peaceful lives if you feel none of the burning hatred that causes the terrorists to do what makes them such?"

The kaglorite sighed deeply. "We tried to live among humans and lorms as law-abiding citizens. We were rejected, accused of crimes we did not commit on a daily basis. So…we decided that if we were going to be treated as villains no matter what we did, we might as well actually become them."

"Is there anything that would sway you, make you abandon your crew?" Coria asked hopefully.

But the violet-skinned man merely snorted. "Certainly. When the hearts of every man and lorm have changed, I'll gladly give up my life of crime. Until then, I see no good reason to do so."

The queen tried her best to form some kind of counterargument, but coming up with nothing after some time, she abandoned the idea and, nodding to the kaglorite in farewell, and walked off. The last sect to interview were the humans, who stood on the deck of their own ship, guiding it and that which was tethered to it. With the permission of the guards watching over her own vessel, Coria crossed over to that of the pirates and approached Lord Ripla himself.

"If there's a problem, one of my lieutenants can help you," said the nobleman without looking over at her.

"Oh, uh, no, I was just hoping to talk to *you* for a little bit," the queen explained. "Pass the time, you know."

Ripla's face screwed up. "You'll forgive me, but you and your lot aren't the sort I'm interested in conversing with. So if there's nothing else—"

"I actually wanted to ask you, just out of curiosity, a few questions about yourself," inserted Coria into the following expectant pause.

The lord couldn't hide the gleam this brought to his eyes fast enough to keep it from being seen by the queen. "Oh? Well, on second thought, I suppose I can spare a few minutes of my time, purely from the goodness of my heart. Ask away."

Coria lit up herself. "Oh, great! Thanks! So you're lord of a noble house, correct?"

Ripla frowned at this. "Yes, of course. House Ripla is among the most influential in all of Humania. I must say I'm disappointed and frankly a tad insulted that you weren't already aware of this."

The queen winced and chastised herself mentally for this faux pas; she noted then that she found herself yet again in a situation where she would've benefited from remembering a bit of the governmental minutiae she'd been tutored on and willfully forgotten. "My deepest apologies, my lord," she said with a bow. "I suppose some families are of such an elevated status they're actually *less* known by the common folk." Ripla seemed, against all odds, to actually buy this line, and brightened a little. "So why does the head of a noble house take to thievery? Surely you aren't wanting for anything."

"Quite right," confirmed the lord with a haughty grin. "It's *because* I want for nothing that I do this. Without it, my life lacks consequence, *excitement*."

A thought came to Coria's mind then that piqued her interest, as through it, she seemed to have found connective tissue between

SEEDS IN THE SAND

herself and this odious pilferer. "You must be trained in the combative arts then, *extensively*, if you head this crew, yes?"

"Trained in the *combative arts*?" Ripla repeated with a scoff as if he were responding to a suggestion that he crawl through the mud and eat from a trough like a cusrop. "Whatever for? I *head* the crew. Make the important decisions and whatnot. Give out instructions. My men are the ones actually *doing* all the tasks we take on."

The queen's shoulders slumped a little, and so it was fortunate that the lord was still refusing to return her gaze. "I see. So you don't do battle with anyone personally ever?"

"Oh, gods, no," confirmed Ripla with a vehement shake of his head. "I'm absolutely *worthless* in a fight. One of the only things I truly believe in is utility, and like I said, there'd be no point."

Utility *like a man to whom money is no object stealing from the poor?* Coria thought to herself but knew better than to say.

She went back to Zage then and relayed everything she'd learned. Both of them agreed that it wasn't enough, however, and began scouting around every part of the two ships. Hours passed without incident, and the queen had just resigned herself and her original captors to their fate when she spotted something in her periphery right at dusk—all the lorms going below decks on the pirates' vessel. Thinking on it, Coria theorized to herself and later to the Dark Lord that perhaps there was a limit to how much even the craven lorms could be coerced into, and one of the concessions Ripla reluctantly made for his unwilling subordinates was an allowance for them to turn in early.

With this in mind, the queen and her kaglorite coconspirator formed a slapdash plan on the fly; after all, they had almost no idea how much time they had before the twin ships reached the nearest populated island. Fortunately for them, the setup for their scheme was simple and easy, requiring Coria and a handful of Zage's fellows to talk their way onto the deck of Ripla's vessel. After doing this, the kaglorites huddled around the door leading below decks, and the queen sidled up as close as possible to the lord, the manner of her movements markedly nondescript. Looking over at the violet-skinned accessories to her plot, Coria gave the signal, a very slight gesture of one hand performed without lifting it from where it rested at her side, and the terrorist magicians, seeing this, turned their heads to face the section of deck directly before and beneath them, crouching and raising their hands slightly, palms facing it.

As blue magic radiated from the kaglorites' appendages, the resulting glow attracted the attention of the guards within view of it but didn't lead to a timely-enough response, as the mages' bodies blocked most of the gleam, making it a little unclear exactly what was happening. When the first pirate started making for the small formation of prisoners beside the door, those within it had already successfully pooled their mystical resources to create out of thin air a metal crate so heavy the wood beneath it nearly gave out under its considerable weight. The queen grinned in triumphant elation at the sight of this before shifting her gaze back to the lord of thieves and pulling her shackled hands back behind one of her shoulders, slamming them into the side of his head, knocking him out in one fell swoop.

There were two other humans on Ripla's crew, both of them standing just by him when the action started and both of them Coria's responsibility within the framework of the scheme she'd worked out with Zage beforehand. Moving so quickly that neither even had the chance to come about at the sound of their leader's pained grunt, she brought her back to rest against one of theirs and, reaching behind her, hooked the chain binding her hands together underneath the other human's chin. Then she yanked the ensnared pirate up and over, flinging him forward. He flipped end over end through the air a few times before his head slammed against one side of the pirates' ship, and he was rendered instantly unconscious.

The last human outlaw standing had a distinct advantage over his fellows because he was such and so had the luxury of time to face his future attacker, assume a defensive stance, and unsheathe the dagger at his hip before she engaged him. The odds didn't stay in his favor for very long, however, as when he first stabbed out at Coria's throat she wrapped the chains on her wrists around the blade tightly, stopping it well before it could sink into its target and then wrenching it from his grasp, sending the weapon sliding across the deck below them and well out of the thief's reach. To his credit, the pirate immediately changed gears to fisticuffs, but that is where all commendation for the man should end, as he then jabbed at the queen's face with one hand and failed to pull it back in time when she brought her shackled wrists up to block the blow. As a result, he slammed his knuckles into the hard, biting metal of the cuffs. The pirate recoiled, wincing from the pain, and this allowed Coria to lash out at one of his knees with her right foot, striking it hard enough that the hit brought both of them down to the floor. And as the man knelt there, frozen with indecision over which of his agonizing wounds to caress first, she used the momentum of her previous attack to spin around and deliver another kick, this one up the side of his head, which mercifully granted him unconsciousness.

    The sounds of battle of course drew the off-duty lorms below decks to the door leading outside, but as planned, the crate now blocking their way was heavy enough that it would take as many of them as could squeeze together up against the other side of said door some time to clear the obstruction. Coria smiled to herself in satisfaction when she heard the sound of the metal ponderously scraping across the wood of the deck behind her.

    Zage didn't conjure up a weapon in his hand as he ran toward the enemy kaglorites, all of whom had at this point crossed over onto their own ship as a single unit and were remaining as such while they looked here and there seeking unoccupied prospective opponents; he was certain he wouldn't need one, and besides that, he'd never killed one of his people and didn't plan on starting anytime soon. A few seconds later, there were three pairs of magician combatants, each of its members circling the other; Zage and Zuza were both taking on one of the outsiders, and the last was engaged by an ally of theirs neither of them could see. Of course, the Dark Lord and his forces could've easily overwhelmed the kaglorite pirates through sheer numbers, but they adhered to the way of their people instead, meeting each of the enemy fighters with only one of their own, and in the case of those who hadn't been quick enough to find a partner in time, allowing each duel to play out uninterrupted by a third party.

Zage furrowed his brow when his opponent drew a longsword from one hip, both because it was unusual for a kaglorite to not simply create a weapon using magic at the start of battle and the weapon in question was of a kind the Dark Lord had never seen before, the hue and texture of its blade to his knowledge completely unlike that of any other and yet which seemed to him uncannily familiar. His confusion only deepened when his foe swung the sword in an unguarded motion, setting him up perfectly to cover one hand in red magic and snap the blade in two. Zage wouldn't *complain* about it, of course, but he felt embarrassed for the other man; how could a kaglorite not know how to ward off one of his own people?

The Dark Lord's mental question was answered in an emphatic and sudden manner. As the sharp side of the sword passed into the crimson covering around his right hand, it didn't melt. Even with his battle-hardened reflexes, Zage couldn't pull the appendage in question away before it quite deeply felt the bite of the blade. Roaring in agony, the Dark Lord cradled his fresh wound while retreating a step, sizing up his opponent, and the weapon in the other man's grip, anew. Could he have found a way to imbue his weapon with an immunity to the influence of red magic? No, that was impossible. *He* was the strongest magic user in Samu, and he'd never even come close to achieving that, despite his many attempts. Among the many thoughts swirling about within his mind, Zage grabbed hold of the fact that he felt he'd seen the material the blade was made up of somewhere before, wracking his brain for memories of it. After a good while, the Dark Lord realized when he recalled witnessing such a thing previously, and everything clicked into place.

Duracut flesh. That's what the blade was made of. And so because it was composed of organic material, it couldn't be touched by red magic, and to top it all off, it would shatter any other type of weapon raised against it on account of said material's legendary impregnability. Zage gritted his teeth in dismay though he marveled at the ingenuity of his foe; what could he possibly do to fend off an attack from a combatant armed as the other man was? As his gaze ran along the length of the sword, however, he spotted something at one end of it—the tender flesh of the hands holding it, and at this, an idea sprang to his mind, causing him to conjure up a whip for himself. His opponent smirked at this; trying to yank the sword out of his hands was impossible, as no whip could keep from being sliced to pieces by the sharp edge of the blade upon wrapping itself around such a thing. In addition, the only material capable of contending with that of his weapon would be more of the same, and that, being organic, was one thing even the Dark Lord hadn't a prayer of summoning via blue magic.

And yet it, of course, paid to be cautious, and so when Zage brought back the whip in his grasp and lashed out at his foe with it, the other man positioned himself to guard against it. However, as he watched the weapon unfurl toward him, the pirate saw, too late, that its business end was being aimed not at the middle of his sword's blade but at the hands wrapped around its hilt. A split second later, he felt the sharp sting of the whip upon the soft flesh of said appendages and instinctively released the weapon in their grip. Before the sword could even touch down on the deck with a metallic *ping*, Zage was leaping down and forward to grab at it. The other man shot to a crouch, trying to stop this, and managed to take hold of his weapon's hilt again at the same moment as his opponent, but even his toned musculature was no match for the still more battle-hardened physique of the Dark Lord. Zage wrenched the sword from his foe's grasp and, bolting to his feet, pointed its tip at the other man's throat, ending the fight decisively.

As the violet-skinned magicians who hadn't had the luck of landing a spot in one of the bouts of single combat between their people let out a collective roar of victory, the Dark Lord knew even without looking (though he did anyway) that the other two duels had ended in their favor as well. Shortly thereafter, the lorms finally managed to push the door leading below decks open far enough to squeeze out into the open air, but when they found the rest of their crew incapacitated, all of them surrendered without a second thought just as Coria had known they would, wide smiles on their faces.

Zage had his newly acquired prisoners lined up on the deck of the latter's ship, waiting for the humans among them to regain consciousness, before turning to several of his people and ordering them to ready weapons. As the other kaglorites conjured up swords and knives, Coria approached the Dark Lord and asked, "What are those weapons for? What are you going to do to the pirates?"

Zage scoffed. "What do you mean, what am I going to do with them? Are you *dense*? They will be executed, of course." He turned to face those guarding the kaglorite pirates. "Except for those of my own people, that is. Them we will allow to go free."

The queen's brow shot up, and her mouth fell open. "*What?* No! They're just *thieves*. They don't deserve to *die*!"

"Spoken like a true human," replied the Dark Lord.

Coria furrowed her brow as far as she could without closing her eyes as she desperately reached for a rebuttal. When she came up with something after several long seconds, she looked back at Zage, saying, "Y-you can't spare *just* the kaglorites. You're only giving them special treatment because they're of your people."

"Ah, yes, that is exactly right," the Dark Lord confirmed with confused incredulity.

"But…but…when the oracle would insult you just because you were a kaglorite, that was wrong, wouldn't you say?" continued the queen.

Zage nodded. "Yes, of course."

"Then how can you show favoritism here?" Coria pointed out. "You're doing the exact same thing!"

The Dark Lord frowned and shook his head. "No, no, it is not the same at all. Humans are naught but talking beasts, lorms, two-legged rats. It is only natural that they would be dealt with in a different manner than kaglorites."

"And why do you view them as such?" asked the queen insistently.

"Because they nearly *drove my people to extinction*," Zage replied through gritted teeth.

"And yet *you* and *the remaining members of your race* have murdered and pillaged in the aftermath of the massacre, giving humans and lorms reason enough to despise you, the *exact same* reason for your hatred toward them," pointed out Coria.

The kaglorite froze, his mouth falling slightly agape as if she'd just assured him that her blood was brown. "Uh...well..." He lit up then as a justification came to his mind. "But they started it, this whole bloody affair! They killed the legendary wizard Zeli!"

"The humans and lorms living today—they did that?" the queen retorted in exasperation. "Zeli died over a century ago. Only one person from that era in all of Samu still walks the earth"—she gestured toward their prisoners—"and he isn't among them."

The Dark Lord crossed his arms over his chest as he bored a hole through Coria's forehead with his gaze, lost in deep thought. Finally, after an extended pause, he said, "You are wrong about humans and lorms. They are guilty by association, as you might say. And I know that you are playing on my pride by comparing me to Dekkin Eterden, and yet I cannot help but feel irresistibly compelled to avoid developing any similarities to that accursed immortal. So I will treat all the thieves we have captured here today the same." The queen lit up at this and opened her mouth to thank him when he continued with a cruel twist at one corner of his mouth, "*All* of them will be executed."

Coria's face fell as far as it could. "*Zage, no!*" she begged, stepping toward him as she grabbed at his shirt with both her shackled hands. "That's the *opposite* of what I meant! Let them all *go!* Or at least spare their lives and take them to the nearest prison."

No matter how the queen pleaded with him, Zage was steadfast in his refusal to budge even an inch on the issue. He did, however, delay the pirates' deaths by a day once one of his fellows found a jug of poison in the other ship's hold; he decided upon being told of this that he would befoul the thieves' last meal with it and wait a short while after they ate before ordering their deaths, ensuring that their final moments among the living, those immediately before their oh-so-cathartic (for he and his fellows, at any rate) executions at the hands of the latter, would be accompanied by searing stomach pains.

After the harmful substances had been mixed into enough food to fill the bellies of all the defeated outlaws now confined below decks on what was formerly their vessel, Zage added with great cruelty insult to injury for Coria when he decreed that she would be the one to personally bring said assemblage their last meal. When Zuza, holding out a plate heaped with spiked meat, potatoes, and fruit told the queen of this the other woman was, of course, horrified initially…but as she glanced down at one of the female kaglorite's pants pockets immediately afterward, she had an idea. In order to prevent a breakout, the three violet-skinned magicians among the pirate crew had had their hands bound in pedibi they themselves had been keeping in their hold to potentially use on kaglorite victims of theirs, and Zuza was given the keys…keys which now rested within the fold of fabric Coria had caught a glimpse of, and that their possessor hadn't her eye on as she held out the plate for the queen to take. Taking this opportunity, Coria stealthily snuck one of her hands into the pocket to grip the keys within as she took the plate in the other.

As the queen closed the door at the top of the stairs from just inside it and descended to bring the pirates the tainted food in her grasp as well as the salvation on her person, she thanked the gods that none of the guards around her saw her snatch up the keys and hide them inside a cloth receptacle of her own. Everyone below decks looked her way upon her arrival, and though she sported a gleeful grin, they regarded this very warily.

"It's all right!" she assured the condemned, and all of them lit up when she then took out of her pocket and held up for everyone to see the keys to the kaglorites' restraints.

When Zage's fellows headed below decks sometime later to collect those due for execution, they found a large hole had been bored through the bottom of the hull's back, and the prisoners gone, having long since gotten away through it and in the rowboats those with magical abilities had created for just such a purpose.

The Dark Lord was naturally furious. "Who is at fault for this?" barked the kaglorite to all within earshot.

Coria stepped forward at this. "I am. I freed them."

Zage whirled to face her, directing his wrath entirely on her now. "*You did?*" he snarled, advancing on her menacingly. "I ought to *gut you where you stand*—"

"Oh, as if you would!" interrupted the queen, more exasperated at this than anything else. "I'm your ticket to safe passage through enemy territory. You *can't* kill me yet, and you *know* it."

The Dark Lord froze as he considered this and, after a beat, deepened his scowl before coming about and walking away from her. After the pirates' former ship was stripped of all its remaining supplies, the tether connecting it to Zage's was severed, and he and the rest of his party continued on their way.

24

"How's it coming?" Matthew looked to one side of himself as he sat with his feet dangling off the edge of a pier in Omu to find Dekkin standing over him there and hurriedly swallowed the water he'd been drinking in order to provide a timely answer. His master had him hard at work along with the others, fortifying the necessary sections of their ship's hull with thick wood or in a few cases metal planks. The boy was exhausted as he took his midday break; despite his slight stature and virtually nonexistent musculature, Cornelius assigned him loads as heavy as those he and the other fully-grown humans were carrying. The immortal protested at this upon seeing it to, unsurprisingly, no avail.

"I-it's coming," the lorm answered as soon as he could.

"You've got no idea, do you?" asked Dekkin with a suspicious squint. "You haven't been paying the slightest attention to what the others are doing. You're just doing what you're told, not asking questions, not investigating things further on your own, are you?" When Matthew averted his eyes self-consciously, the oracle continued, assuring him, "Don't worry about it. That kind of work, no one could be blamed for escaping from it as much as they can, into their minds."

The immortal was pleased to see the boy brighten at these words. There was a short pause, the only sound between the two of them being that of the lorm gulping down more water greedily. "It looks like we won't be finished modifying our vessel until early tomorrow morning," Dekkin observed as he gazed out at their commandeered ship. Looking back over at Matthew, he asked, "So do you have any plans for tonight? There's going to be an eliena game here then, if you wanted to go to that." He got his answer from the boy's expression. "All right, never mind. It was just a suggestion. You don't like eliena?"

The lorm shrugged. "No, not much. Sports in general, not a fan."

"Hmm." The oracle narrowed his eyes. "Well, I can see you wouldn't like *playing* them, but even *spectating* you don't enjoy?"

Matthew shook his head. "Can't help feeling bad for the losers."

"Ah," the immortal said in realization, "that would rule most of them out, I suppose."

"I"—the boy paused but then continued at an expectant look from Dekkin—"I don't mind coral tag."

"Coral tag—what's that?"

"Lormish sport," answered Matthew, "like tag but within a coral reef. You can dive in and out and through its openings. Little harder that way."

"I see." Dekkin crossed his arms over his chest with an inquisitive frown. "And why is that the exception? Because of your heritage?"

"No...well...sort of." The boy's expression turned wistful as he looked out at the bottom of the vessel before them without truly seeing it. "My mother took me to a game once. When I was little. It's a...good memory." The look on his face made it clear this was a vast understatement, though in a split second, it was replaced with one containing a slight, mischievous, involuntary smile. "She did it against my father's wishes."

"Why did he not want you to attend?" the oracle asked in confusion.

"Well, coral tag is a traditional Lormish sport," explained Matthew matter-of-factly. "It wasn't made *illegal* once we began our alliance with the humans. But...local conventions were heavily discouraged. That's for sure." His face fell a little at the thought of what he was about to say. "My parents fought all the time over things like that before she was taken."

The immortal's expression moved to match the lorm's. "Why?"

The boy sighed quietly. "Mother was very into the original culture of our people. My father…well, I never got to see this. But she told me when I was little that before we became a dominion of Humania, he was a proud lorm. Or he acted like one, anyway. I think he just wants to go along with whatever everybody else is doing. And when the tide shifted in the other direction, he shifted right along with it. Suddenly, there was this great divide between them, and Mother didn't relent in their struggle. She gave birth to me underwater, which was a tradition that was abandoned by most lorms decades before the alliance with the humans had even started. Right at noon that day, she did. And that's how things were between them before…our family was broken up." Matthew flashed Dekkin a smile then, but it was quite obviously incredibly strained. "I guess maybe it was a good thing when she was taken. No more loud fights late at night when I was trying to sleep."

The oracle wanted to comfort the lorm but, knowing young boys as he did (having been and raised one himself all those centuries ago), recognized that it would be best to play along with the lorm's forced facade of optimism. Instead, he racked his brain for another topic of conversation. How did one go about picking them? It had been so long since he cared enough to put any degree of effort into doing so. Finding nothing within, he began searching without and spotting a young Lormish woman walking an *ilo* and came up with "have you ever owned a pet?"

Matthew motioned in the negative. "My father doesn't like animals, and of course, once I became Master Arcind's apprentice, there was no way I could've kept one."

"Would you want one if you were fr—" The immortal caught himself, his eyes swelling self-consciously a little before he realized this was happening, and brought his brow down to make them contract back to a neutral position. "If you weren't?"

"Hmm." The boy paused and sat there perfectly still and visibly deep in thought, for so long that eventually Dekkin felt the need to break the silence.

"Is that a hard question?" he asked, his voice tinged with incredulity.

The lorm shrugged his shoulders while nodding slightly in a strange heaving combination of gestures. "Sort of, I'm not used to people doing…this."

"Asking you personal questions?"

"Right," confirmed Matthew, oblivious to the reason for and therefore puzzled by the sympathetic squint the oracle fixed on him after he said this, "just give me a minute. World's full of different breeds of beast, yes?" Another extended bout of silence followed, mercifully broken when the boy finally decided aloud, "Yes, yes, I'd like a noinoi."

"A noinoi," the immortal repeated, "and what is that? I've never heard of such a thing. A Lormish animal, by the sound of its name? What's it look like?"

"Yes," the boy replied with an eager nod. "What's it look like? Well, it stands on four legs. It's about as long as an adult man, like you, Master Eterden. Its skin is bright yellow. And it's got sharp fangs large enough that its lips don't even come close to covering them even when its mouth is shut."

Dekkin took this in with a bewildered furrow to his brow. "Ah, that…doesn't sound like a very attractive beast."

"Oh, they aren't," confirmed the lorm with an affectionate smile, his eyes vacant as they looked into his head rather than out of it, "even I can't love the looks of a creature with an appearance like that."

"Well, are they very friendly?" the oracle inquired.

"No, not at all." Matthew's expression was unchanging as he said this. "They're quite hostile, especially toward lorms."

The immortal was completely lost now. "So…why in the name of the gods would you want one?"

"*Because* nobody likes them," answered the boy. "No one's ever taken one as a pet—that I know of. They have no choice but to rough it out in the middle of the wilderness just because they're ugly and violent. Because of what they were born as, I find that sad. I'd want to give one of them a safe home for the first time."

"Hmm." Dekkin tilted his head slightly and raised his brow.

"Matthew, wouldn't you say your break's been long enough?" The lorm looked over one shoulder to find his master standing over him and the oracle. The man's face, like his voice had been just then, was light yet firm, his hands resting on his hips.

"*Oh*, uh, yes, yes, you're right," Matthew affirmed abashedly as he shot up onto his feet. "I-I'm sorry. I'll get back to the ship." With marked pep in his step, he did just that.

"He's a child, Cornelius," pointed out the immortal with a scowl as he watched the boy go. "Hold off on the hard labor, why don't you?"

"Oh, my issue isn't truly with my apprentice's work ethic," Destiny's Catalyst revealed in a frigid tone. "It's more about keeping him away from individuals of a certain character, *lack* of character."

Dekkin opened his mouth immediately to respond to this, an indignant look on his face, but the hero raised a hand to cut him off.

"Look, Dekkin, I don't know what all went on between you two while you had him captive—"

"You wouldn't believe me if I told you," interrupted the oracle.

Cornelius scowled as deeply as he could. "But I don't want a *child under my care* consorting with a *known criminal*. You stay away from him, you understand?"

"No," Dekkin said instantly, sticking out his lips, "I refuse."

The smoldering fire within the breast of Destiny's Catalyst flared into a full-on blaze. "You will obey my commands—"

"Or what?" countered the oracle. "You've never killed anyone in your entire life. You don't even *fight* people unless they swing first because you're a *hero*." This last word he spat in disdain. "You won't *touch* me."

The glare Cornelius fixed the immortal with was menacing even upon his fair features, but now it took on an impotent quality as well. "He's *my* apprentice," stated Destiny's Catalyst after a beat, "and whatever connection you've formed with him over the course of the last *month* can't outweigh the *four years* we've been together."

Dekkin stood and, turning to face the hero, stepped toward him, getting right up in the other man's face with his own. "He was *ordered* to apprentice under you," the oracle pointed out through gritted teeth. "He's *my friend, by choice,* even after I held him hostage, which of those relationships would you say means the most?"

To this, Destiny's Catalyst had nothing to say, though he tried to come up with something for about half a minute; after which, he gave up on the conversation and came about, stomping back to the ship. The immortal, meanwhile, had a queer feeling in his gut; there was the flame of rage burning there, fiercely enough to melt steel, and yet such an emotion still made him feel better than the totally numb sensation that dominated so much of his long life before that fateful first meeting with Matthew.

25

B*oom!* With that sound, the ship came screeching to a halt so abruptly everyone aboard was thrown forward quite violently, those who hadn't been standing behind and near an obstruction skidding across the deck directly beneath them.

"Report!" Zage barked out, shooting to his feet as soon as he could.

A look out and down from the fore revealed that they'd hit a tall, unseen sandbar stretching out from a small nearby island. Soon after this was discovered, panicked cries came forth from below decks, and the Dark Lord rushed down there with a scowl. The impact, he learned then, was forceful enough to tear a sizable hole in the front of their vessel's bottom, and the lower level was currently being flooded with seawater through the newly made opening. Pooling their mystical resources, several of his fellows were of course able to plug the gouge in short order, but the intruding liquid was so vast in volume and the ship's recently minted replacement crew so few in number that it would still take some time to bail all of it out, and such a task would require enough of them that their journey had to be entirely halted until the undertaking's completion.

Zage's breathing was quick and shallow as usual when Coria approached him below decks shortly after he and the other kaglorites began emptying the hold.

She said, "Zage, that island over there"—she pointed in the direction of the tiny piece of landmass connected to the offending sandbar as she said this—"there's an orchard atop it, and several packs of wild, meaty animals too. We could stock up on food while we're waiting to get underway again."

The Dark Lord raised an eyebrow at this; it was an attractive prospect, given that he, his fellows, and their prisoner had just about cleaned out the reserves that came with their stolen ship. Despite this, every man or woman not taking part in bailing out the water below decks ensured that the length of time it would take to finish this operation would increase that much more, and this is what the kaglorite noted to the queen in response.

"Then we won't send many people," proposed Coria next. "Let's—you and I—go, just the two of us." She raised her shackled hands up slightly in a defensive gesture when he glared at her suspiciously upon hearing this. "I'm not trying to trick you." The idea of appealing to his inflated ego came to her then. "There's no scenario in which *I* could defeat *you* in single combat, especially with my hands tied, is there?"

The Dark Lord couldn't help giving a slight, smug smile at this. "Yes, this is true." He started making his way up onto the main deck, speaking to the queen trailing behind him over one shoulder as he did so. "All right, we shall do as you say." His voice took on a menacing quality. "But if this proves to be a trick of any kind—"

Coria nodded. "Yes, yes, I know." She wisely chose not to speak her mind then and point out that. As had been established earlier, there was truly nothing drastic he could do to her given her status as his prized prisoner.

The two of them took one of their vessel's rowboats out to the nearby islet. The queen stayed behind the Dark Lord as they disembarked.

"What is this place called?" asked Zage without looking back as he scanned the area directly before him. "Do you know?"

He heard the sound of wood being firmly pushed through water then but thought nothing of it. You couldn't blame him for such a lapse either, given where he now found himself. The island, which Coria informed him in response to his question was called Ehoko, was by all measures a diminutive slice of heaven on earth. The sand beneath his feet was pure white and seemed impossibly fine. The jungle at its center was composed of towering, lush palm trees that nonetheless were each far enough apart from the others as to allow easy passage between them. Most notable of all, however, was the sound of the place, or rather the total lack of any, save for the lapping of waves on its shores and the faint rustling of its leaves and grass because of the cool ocean breeze gently caressing it all.

All of Zage's appreciation for these sensory delights vanished in an instant, however, when he noticed something missing from the picture—there was no fruit hanging from those curved, towering trees.

"Where is the—" he began as he whirled around to face Coria before stopping himself short upon spotting yet another important omission; the rowboat they'd come to Ehoko in wasn't resting on the shore before him. Frowning deeply and shifting his gaze to the horizon, he saw it there, being carried away atop the waves. He broke into a sprint toward the water.

"Wait!" cried out the queen as his feet started kicking up sprays of salty surf. "It's too far out. You'll never reach it." Stubborn as he was, the Dark Lord dove head-first into the ocean as soon as he could and began paddling forward furiously. Even he could see after a little bit of this that Coria was right, however, and upon realizing this, he turned around and returned to the spot of beach where he entered the sea.

"How could you forget to beach the boat?" the kaglorite growled through gritted teeth at the queen standing near him. "How *stupid* can even a *human* be?"

"I didn't forget," replied Coria casually. "I let it go on purpose."

Zage froze, thinking he had somehow misheard the woman standing less than a pace away from him and replaying the last several seconds in his mind. When he accepted that there was no mistake, his eyes first widened in disbelief and then narrowed with rage. "*What?*" he bellowed, stepping forth and roughly grabbing the front of the queen's shirt. "*Why?* So you could *kill me*, isolated from the others, and run off?"

"*No!*" answered Coria with great exasperation. "How exactly would I do *either* of those things? If I fought you now, I'd be a human facing a kaglorite in single combat, *handcuffed*"—she raised her shackled hands up to hang level with his eyes briefly, eliciting a string of metallic *clink*s in quick succession, before bringing them back down to rest directly ahead of and just below the tops of her thighs—"and if by some miracle I managed to prevail, where would I run *to?*" She gestured out at the sea surrounding them on all sides.

The Dark Lord considered this for a moment and, seeing at the end of it that she was right, released her as he deflated, though only a little, as now the mystery sprung anew in his mind. "Well, then, why *did* you do it?"

The queen flashed a serene smile at the jungle a short ways off from the two of them. "I wanted to force you to take a vacation."

She could've said it was because she wanted to starve herself to death and the kaglorite would've been less perplexed. He was so baffled, in fact, that when he next spoke, his voice lost the emphatic quality it possessed ever since Coria revealed what she'd done. "What?"

"For as long as I've known you—which I realize amounts to but a month but bear with me—you've been so *stressed*," the queen explained with a sympathetic tilt to her brow. "It hurts me just to *look* at you. When we hit the sandbar and I saw this place in the distance, that's when I formed my plan to get you to relax."

Zage stared at her with incredulity for a moment. "Are you serious?"

Coria nodded readily. "Yes."

Sincerity was plain enough on her face that, against all odds, there was no doubt she was telling the truth. The Dark Lord paced around in a small circle a few times, his hands on his hips, before stopping and saying with a scowl, "That is the most idiotic thing I have ever heard, which comes as no surprise, considering who it was that said it."

The queen was visibly hurt by that last statement. "You don't think you could use some time to unwind?"

Zage scoffed heavily at this. "*No!* Kaglorites are not like *humans* or *lorms*, their minds breaking at the slightest of trifles. Yes, our lives are *so* much harder than yours, but we are built from stronger stuff." He threw his hands up in exasperation at the dubious look this tirade got him and, walking around Coria, sat down in the sand at the water's edge.

The queen came about and gazed down at him in puzzlement. "What are you doing now?"

She would've burst out laughing if she'd been able to see the petulant pout on the kaglorite's face as he crossed his arms over his chest. "Waiting for the others to come get us," he growled.

"Well, since we're here, and they're going to be a while, don't you think you might as well make the best of it and enjoy yourself?" asked Coria with a light huff.

"*No*," the Dark Lord grated over one shoulder. As he returned his gaze to the horizon, the queen smiled slightly to herself, knowing that a man such as him, whose life had been spent on a battlefield, couldn't have an attention span capable of withstanding more than a minute of inactivity. Sure enough, she hadn't been waiting on him long before he shot up, turned around, and conceded with great reluctance and averted eyes. "All right, show me what there is to see on this island."

Despite her certainty earlier that this would come to pass, Coria lit up as if it came as a complete shock and, motioning for him to follow her, began leading him into the jungle before them.

"How did you know about this place?" he asked her as they moved single file.

The queen slowed down and stepped to her left, bringing herself to one side of the kaglorite. And she told him everything, the real reason she'd set out from Cobaltus after the attack by him and his fellows, adding that Ehoko was the spot she selected as her destination and new home.

"So," said the Dark Lord with a confused frown, "you are the ruler of an entire nation. You live in a *castle*. You have never and will never need to worry for coin or food or water. And…you hated *that* so much that you *ran away from it*?"

"Yes," Coria confirmed immediately.

"Hmm." Perhaps a man of Zage's background and disposition should have by all rights been infuriated at this, but he was puzzled by it so much that it staved off all anger.

They walked on toward the center of the island in silence for some time. The queen began desperately searching for something to fill the auditory void shortly following its inception.

"So what are you going to do if you actually manage to kill all the humans and lorms in Samu?" was what she finally managed to come up with after several long moments. She winced as soon as the words were out of her mouth; that question probably wasn't the best way to get a casual conversation going.

Zage didn't seem to think so though. "I have not the foggiest."

Coria started at this, her brow jumping in shock. "What?"

"I have no idea what I would do if my life mission were ever fulfilled," reiterated the Dark Lord.

"You've never thought about it?" the queen asked with incredulity.

The kaglorite shook his head. "No."

Coria considered this in silence for a handful of seconds. "Why not?"

"I don't think it will ever truly happen," revealed Zage.

The queen's eyes widened again, this time as much as they possibly could. "You *don't*?"

"That's right," the Dark Lord confirmed. "There are only a few dozen of us kaglorites left, after all, and we are going up against a people numbering in the millions. Our magical abilities must be taken into account, of course, but even those are not nearly enough to close the gap. I recognize that, *all* of that."

"But…when you're with the rest of your people, you say you *will* accomplish your goals, you say it with such *confidence*," pointed out Coria insistently.

"Of course," the kaglorite replied with a nod, "Not many would take part in what they thought was a doomed venture. I have to project certainty, to convince them to join my cause, and keep fighting through all of it."

The queen's eyes moved this way and that, and she frowned deeply in confusion. "Why would you try then? Why would you dedicate your life to something you don't think will pan out?"

"It is what should be done," answered Zage casually. "It is a righteous quest. The fact that it is destined for failure does not make it any less so."

Coria pondered whether or not to push back on this point yet again but, remembering the previous attempts of her and others to do so, decided to hold off. She wondered for a moment what to say next and hit upon an idea as she gazed forward at the surrounding foliage. "You know, as you can see, this island is completely uninhabited," she said as she turned to look back at the Dark Lord once again. "Wouldn't it be nice if you and your people moved here, lived here instead of in the eastern wastes or someone else's house, taken by force or threat or violence?"

The kaglorite shook his head, his lips pressed together tightly. "No, I do not think so."

This man was throwing the queen off at every turn! "You *don't*? Explain."

Zage sighed heavily, mostly in his usual anger but also with a twinge of sorrow. "When I was six, my father and I happened upon an oasis, in the middle of Kagloris. We heard rumblings about the existence of such places for a long time, just like everyone else living there but dismissed them without much thought. The whole area was perhaps half a dozen paces across, or it would be for me now, but when I looked upon it back then, it seemed to me like one of those endless fields back in Humania. The pool at the center was lined on all sides by these colossal fruit trees, their branches sagging under the weight of their bounty." The Dark Lord gave a slight smile at the memory of it, a gesture which was returned eagerly by the queen.

"Neither of us bathed in months," he continued. "When I picked one of the fruits hanging over us and bit into it, I spit it out immediately. It was *succulent* so much so that it was more than I could handle. I was used to charred meat and raw, stringy vegetables at that point. I became accustomed to it though, and once I had, it was several *thousand* times better than anything I had ever tasted in my life. My father and I stayed there, for days."

Coria frowned inquisitively. "Only days? Why would you ever leave?"

The kaglorite's face fell as his answer came to mind. "When we woke up there the morning after we arrived, both of us felt lightheaded, frail. But, of course, a couple of kaglorites weren't going to let that stop them living their lives. So we carried on much as we had the previous day…and awoke the following morning barely able to stand. It was then that we realized the oasis was fake. The area was enchanted, like that hut we came upon while we were with the oracle and the lorm and yet even more devious as the food and water created by this one couldn't fill one's belly."

"So ever since then, you haven't trusted things with the appearance of goodness when you've come upon them," concluded Coria with a sympathetic squint.

"It is not just that," Zage corrected her. "If it had just been that one time, it wouldn't have held sway over my mind for long. All lessons are forgotten over time. They must be relearned and relearned—that one I did, for every time something like that happened to me after my father and I realized the secret of the oasis, it's turned out to be a lie." When he started speaking, his voice took on a bitter tinge that supplanted more and more of the entire thing with each word until by the end, it was the only element remaining within his tone.

The queen took this in before replying as she gestured to the isle around them. "Ehoko is real. Not all good things are a fabrication."

"Hmm," said the Dark Lord sullenly, "I am sure the world *does* seem that way when you live in a castle, never wanting for anything."

Coria had nothing to say to this despite a highly concerted effort on her part to form some sort of grand consolation, and so she and the kaglorite walked on in awkward silence until they reached their destination, a small pond in the exact middle of Ehoko.

"This is what you wanted to show me?" Zage asked gruffly as he surveyed the body of water before him.

The queen nodded in affirmation. "Yes, I thought we could go for a swim."

"Very well," responded the Dark Lord stiffly. Stripping to his underwear, he plunged into the pool and began swimming laps around its perimeter as fast as he could, a speed which was quite impressive given his considerable bulk. Coria jumped in without even removing any clothing and came to rest at the center of the pond, treading water as she watched the kaglorite circle her fervently again and again.

"You're sort of—" The queen cut herself off upon realizing Zage couldn't hear her, what with his head only rising above the water to quaff a split second's worth of air before descending below the surface again and the sound of his legs rhythmically beating whatever section of said surface was behind him at any given moment. "You're sort of missing the point of this!" she cried out, timing this second, louder attempt with one of his head's intermittent ascents into the open air.

The Dark Lord brought himself screeching or rather splashing to a halt once he heard this and, turning to face her with a puzzled frown on his face, asked, "Well, what *is* the point of this then?"

"It's not exercise," answered Coria by way of explanation. "The purpose of this excursion is *relaxation*, remember?"

"And how do you propose I do that?" the kaglorite inquired out of exasperation.

"Do what I'm doing," replied the queen with an inviting smile. "Come over here and just…float."

"Does not seem very productive," Zage remarked before holding up a hand to silence her as she opened her mouth to respond. "The goal is stress relief, I know. But surely there must be a way to do that while still accomplishing something or other."

"Just try it," implored Coria gently, "come over here and try it."

The Dark Lord grunted and scowled at this but eventually acquiesced under the queen's steady and insistent gaze. He paddled over to her side and started treading water with her.

After a short while of this, Coria next instructed, "Lean back. Let yourself float." Again, the kaglorite conceded, though he still looked none too happy about it. His eyes were wide-open when he began, but as he hung suspended atop the water there, with the wind lightly ruffling the surrounding foliage and sending infinitesimal waves across the surface of the pond as the only sounds to accompany him, his eyes grew heavy. Soon, he started to doze, and as his head leaned further back, it submerged itself completely. Only for a moment, of course, for as soon as Zage tried to take a breath, he choked on the water encompassing his head and awoke, his upper half darting up and out into the open air as he coughed forcefully.

The queen saw the whole thing and burst out laughing as the Dark Lord gasped for air, but when he shot her a withering glare at this, she shrunk back and apologized sheepishly.

The kaglorite paddled indignantly to one section of the pond's edge and got out of it. "I am too tired to be in the water," he growled at Coria over one shoulder as he did so before taking a seat atop the short, soft grass immediately around it.

She did the same herself, coming to sit beside him with her hands supporting the rest of her from behind. "Lie down here then."

Zage opened his mouth, looking like he was about to protest, but didn't and brought those parts of his body that weren't to rest on one side in the grass. "Do not let me fall asleep," ordered the Dark Lord firmly.

Coria frowned in puzzlement at this but agreed to his terms, not wanting to spoil this tranquil moment in an otherwise tumultuous time.

The kaglorite tossed and turned restlessly a few times before saying, "The ground is too hard," and after some thought, bringing his head to rest against one of the queen's thighs. She smiled warmly down at him, unseen, and considered running her fingers through his hair but thought better of it, deciding such a gesture would be overreaching.

"Is that good?" she whispered to Zage, who couldn't, of course, nod in his current position but answered by way of remaining where he was. "I'm surprised that's comfortable enough for you," continued Coria at a murmur. "My muscles are quite firm."

"Hmm." You could tell from the Dark Lord's voice he was on the brink of slumber. "No, it is good."

"Does it bother you?" asked the queen after a beat, trying hard to hide the anxiety from her voice but not entirely succeeding. "A woman having my physique? And…the fighting, the…independence?"

"Not at all," Zage answered immediately. "A woman like you would not be abnormal at all among my people. You have all the traits of a first-rate kaglorite female."

This brought a radiant grin to Coria's face, but it vanished just as quickly as it appeared when the Dark Lord suddenly and without warning bolted up to a seated position, his breathing turning quick and heavy. "What?" asked the queen, startled. "What is it?"

The kaglorite looked over one shoulder at her, his eyes as wide as they could be. "I think I might be dying."

Coria's expression shifted instantly to match his. "*What?* What do you mean?"

"I can't"—Zage frowned pensively before relaxing slightly—"oh, I am fine now."

"What happened?" the queen inquired in deep concern.

"I couldn't feel my heartbeat in my chest," answered the Dark Lord. "But now I do. Still, that was quite strange."

"Y-you couldn't feel your heartbeat in your chest?" Coria, confused, reiterated. "I mean, you were just lying on the ground there. Why would you"—her brow leaped again as a thought came to her mind—"wait, do you mean to tell me you can feel your heartbeat in your chest *constantly*?"

"Well…yes, of course," confirmed the kaglorite, just as lost as she was now. "Is that not normal?"

"No!" the queen replied with a vehement shake of her head. "*No one else that I know* would say that's normal." Concern returned to her tone. "You would have to be under an *unbelievable* amount of stress for that to happen." A smile broke through the air of anguish about her then as another idea came to her. "I think you were *calm* just now, for the first time you can remember."

Zage raised one eyebrow. "Oh?"

"Yes," affirmed Coria with a nod before leaning toward him eagerly. "How did it feel?"

"It felt"—it was clear on the Dark Lord's face he was looking back in awe at what he'd experienced—"it felt good," he finished, his expression making it clear this was a marked, deliberate understatement.

The queen patted the thigh he'd been resting on earlier with a welcoming smile. "Well, let's get it going again, shall we?"

"If you insist," grunted the kaglorite as he moved to recline as he had been just then quickly enough to unwittingly shatter the facade of indifference he was attempting to put up.

Several minutes after Zage resumed his earlier position, Coria could tell the peace he'd gotten his first-ever taste of shortly beforehand had returned to settle gently over him once again. And following soon this observation, his breathing changed noticeably as he fell asleep. The queen knew he ordered her to prevent this from happening, but he looked so serene as he lay there she couldn't bring herself to shake him awake.

She realized the error of her ways when, after but a few moments, the Dark Lord's eyes opened wide, and he shot up once more with a bloodcurdling scream that violently shattered the still quietude around them.

The kaglorite whirled about to face Coria, breathing as heavily as if he'd been running for the past handful of hours straight. "I TOLD YOU TO KEEP ME AWAKE!" he thundered furiously.

"I...I don't understand," responded the queen, deeply unsettled by these twin outbursts, after a beat.

Zage kept his gaze fixed on her face, nostrils flaring, for a while before exhaling loudly and visibly deflating somewhat as he did so. "DON'T LET ME SLEEP *ever*, understood?"

"Y-yes, yes, understood," Coria confirmed, her tone apologetic, though she had no idea what she had to be sorry for.

The Dark Lord stood with a huff. "Let us return to the beach. Wait for the others there."

"All right, sure," conceded the queen as she followed suit, desiring with all her heart to stay by the pond as long as possible but also wanting in light of the kaglorite's extremely negative shift in disposition to please him in that moment.

The two of them made the trek back to the section of sands on Ehoko where they'd first arrived. An uncomfortable silence ensued as they watched their ship, its hold now sufficiently emptied of standing water, creep steadily toward them on the horizon, long enough that Coria jumped a little when Zage broke it by saying hesitantly, "Thank you."

The queen frowned back at him. "What for?"

"For…bringing me here," the Dark Lord answered with averted eyes as he gestured around the rest of the island with one hand. "It was nice."

Coria raised her brow before beginning to beam at the kaglorite. "Of course, thanks…for not being repelled by me."

When they were both back aboard their vessel, Zage announced to all his subordinates what happened before adding that he'd already meted out punishment to the queen extensively during their time away and so decreed that there needn't be any more of it now or at any time in the future. Coria ate with the crew during mealtimes and had done so ever since she'd become their prisoner, but this was so that her captors could keep a constant eye on her, not because of any sense of camaraderie between the royal and her violet-skinned oppressors; she and they had never spoken during that time up until then. However, the Dark Lord started to from that point on frequently leave his seat at Zuza's side for one directly across from the queen as he and the others dined and engage the human woman in (for him) amiable conversation. Coria always found herself so wrapped up in these talks she didn't notice his second-in-command staring daggers at her from the female kaglorite's own place at the table.

26

THE RAPIDS WERE HEARD by Dekkin and the others long before they could be seen. That sound of surging water was loud and forceful enough to make even the oracle swallow with a loud gulp.

"Dekkin, I-I'm scared," Matthew admitted to the immortal at his side as he looked up at the man.

The oracle, with great effort, put on a reassuring smile as he returned the boy's gaze. "Don't be. We know exactly what's going to happen, don't we?" He forced his mouth to expand even further upward and outward. "Since there isn't the usual element of danger to it, I'd even say a trip along the current might be fun."

"Dekkin…" began the lorm before losing his nerve.

The immortal stared back at him. "What?" He waited for a moment before saying some of his trademark cantankerous nature coming through in his voice, "What is it? Speak up."

At this, Matthew started and, after weighing whether or not it would be better to potentially arouse Dekkin's ire by speaking or certainly anger him through silence, decided the former would be preferable and murmured with his eyes on the wood deck beneath them, "I know it's fake. The cheer you've had since we started chasing after Coria and Zage."

The oracle looked stricken once the boy said this; after all, the former determined as he'd sat locked up inside Yinit's prison with the prospect of amnesty hanging right in front of him that his purpose in life would thenceforth be to put on an upbeat facade for the sake of the latter. He should've known his plan wouldn't work though; he was a terrible liar, completely inept at concealing any of his emotions. It was somewhat of a relief to be allowed after several days to *relax* beside the lorm, let his shoulders slump and the corners of his mouth droop.

Despair clutched at the immortal's heart anew, however, as he realized he could think of no adequate replacement when it came to his reason for existence. His sense of duty as an oracle petered out over time long ago. He met people he'd connected with over the past month, much to his surprise after decades devoid of such things, but those bonds weren't nearly enough to justify the agony of carrying on with life. When he saw things now, as it had been ever since his wife left him, it was as if he was peering through a heavy fog, and when others spoke, to or around him, it seemed to him like the sound of their voices was muffled by wads of cloth shoved deep into both of his ears.

Now when Dekkin shifted his gaze back to the treacherous rapids before him and the sharp rocks jutting out of the water like the fangs of a wild, ravenous animal, he pictured his death from passage through the approaching seascape with deep longing. When the ship finally entered the current, it lurched forward abruptly. Everyone aboard was clutching onto something sturdy in anticipation of this as it happened, and so none were knocked off their feet. The wind whipped through the oracle's long silver hair and into his eyes, making him squint to look out directly ahead of him, where the first of the stone obstructions in their projected path lay in the distance.

Bang! A split second after, the rock vanished behind the front of the vessel; it rammed right into the middle of its bottom, just as the immortal had foreseen. The *crack* of splintering wood sounded, loud in everyone's ears even despite the roar of the churning drink all around them, as the additional material added there as a barrier broke apart on impact.

This happened all over the ship's hull over the course of the next several hours, to the point that the repetition of it all as well as the extended amount of time it occurred over desensitized the crew to the peril all around them. When night fell and the time came for the oracle to turn in, he did so without hesitation and fell quickly asleep, both because of the aforementioned psychological effects of prolonged exposure to the dangers of the rapids without consequence and the familiar sense of unearned fatigue that settled over him after his brief exchange with Matthew.

Imagine his surprise then when a few hours afterward, he was abruptly yanked from his slumber to find himself choking on a mouthful of seawater.

Before he even began to spit out the brine, a flurry of thoughts flew through his mind. How could this be possible? Not only had they fortified the ship to withstand each of the impacts foretold in his vision, but he selected a bunk located far away from any of the areas predicted to be affected, just in case something, against all odds, went wrong. But as the immortal forcibly ejected the liquid from his mouth, he saw what he thought was impossible; an ocean stream gushed in through a gaping hole in the hull above his bed.

"What happened?" Dekkin barked at Cornelius, his brow furrowed in accusation as he ran out onto the main deck, leaving a trail of salty droplets in his wake.

"You stole my line," responded Destiny's Catalyst immediately and in an identical manner. The hero approached the oracle as quickly as he could until their faces were mere inches away from one another. "You did this on purpose, didn't you?" Cornelius continued. "You didn't tell us where all the holes would be!"

"Oh, stop it!" replied the immortal in pointed exasperation. "How would that make _any kind of sense_?"

"Well, how else do you explain this?" Destiny's Catalyst pointed out, gesturing toward the small group of his subordinates walking past them as they headed below decks to bail out the intruding seawater and attempt to patch the hole in the hull.

"I don't—" began Dekkin insistently before freezing as an explanation came to his mind. "Oh no."

"What?" the hero asked, deflating in time with his conversation partner.

"This happens sometimes," explained the oracle, "with visions. They show the future, yes, but then the future is changed by people in the present having knowledge of what's to come. Even the smallest of alterations to the timeline can completely flip the coming chain of events." The immortal paused briefly, overwhelmed with dread. "My vision of the ship's destruction must've changed things enough that we ran into a rock we wouldn't have otherwise."

Cornelius's face dropped as low as possible. "Is it possible it'll happen more than once?"

Dekkin opened his mouth to answer in the affirmative when one of their fellows stationed at the bow yelled back over one shoulder, "BRACE FOR IMPACT!" and a moment later, another outcropping slammed into a spot on the vessel's hull that its occupants hadn't thought would be the site of such an impact, ripping another yawning tear in its wooden frame. The two of them both managed to grab hold of the mast in time to avoid a potentially lethal and definitely damaging fall. After a beat, both let go and began making for the stairs leading below decks. As the oracle, trailing behind Destiny's Catalyst, was about halfway down the vessel took another brutal hit on one side, and he and the man in front of him were both thrown against and over the railing to their right.

Enough water poured into the hold to cushion their fall as they made contact with first it and then the hardwood below. Cornelius recovered first and closed the distance between him and the immortal as fast as he could before helping the other man, who was still lying on the floor of the lower deck, dazed from his collision with it, to his feet.

The two surveyed their new surroundings, and Dekkin said what he and Cornelius were both thinking. "We can't come back from this."

Destiny's Catalyst nodded hesitantly in response. He and the oracle stood in grim silence for a moment as they wondered what would become of them and the rest of the crew. After just about half a minute of this, however, the immortal furrowed his brow when a beam of sunlight streaming into the lower deck through one of the holes in its wooden frame at the edge of his vision was suddenly blotted out. Whipping his head around to face the direction of this mysterious occurrence, he found himself staring right at the head of a massive ringfish.

It all happened so fast it took a moment for Dekkin's brain to catch up with reality. But after a beat, it did, and he recognized what had just occurred; a ringfish, big enough to plug the hole in the bottom of the ship, came along and, drawn as creatures of its ilk were to snugly slotting themselves into circular openings, had done just that with the large perforation in question. The oracle huffed in joyful disbelief at this (for Matthew's sake, not his), and that wasn't even the last of it; just as he did so, shadow completely consumed the hold as the other leaks were stopped up by more of the cylindrical aquatic creatures.

Cornelius's mind was in much the same place as the immortal's and indeed those of everyone immediately around them, but unlike the rest, his heroic instincts snapped him out of the elated reverie that took hold of everyone below decks shortly after it had begun when he registered their scaly saviors beginning to choke on account of the open air now completely surrounding their heads.

"SOMEONE, EMPTY OUT THE LARGEST CONTAINERS WE HAVE AND GET THEM TO ME!" he cried to his subordinates, and his influence was such that despite the fact they were all still euphoric to the point of distraction, it instantly spurred most of them to action. A large metal tub was brought before each of the ringfish and filled with the water still blanketing the bottom of the hold, allowing the colossal fish to dunk their heads inside them in order to breathe and cling to life even with their mouths entirely beyond and incapable of reaching the main body of the sea.

Never again did the ship as it sailed on suffer an unexpected gouge from collision with one of the sharp rocks dotting the length of the ocean rapids. Over the course of the next several hours, all the water flooding the lower deck was bailed out by a long line of crewmen linking the vessel's twin levels. Among the ship's denizens, only one found himself sinking into self-pity at this most recent turn of events, but when Dekkin saw Matthew for the first time since the initial impact against the rocks, the boy's visible joy lifted the oracle's spirits quite a bit.

"Did you see the size of those ringfish down below?" asked the immortal as he and the lorm leaned against the railing on one side of the ship, gazing out at the seemingly endless, unbroken cobalt vista before them. "You could get a lot of thread from just *one* of them."

Matthew raised his brow. "You're right. I hadn't thought of that."

As a smile broke across Dekkin's face, he detected movement in his periphery, below the surface of the water beneath them. Shifting his gaze to it, his heart dropped into his stomach as he beheld the gray, elongated body of a giant aihu.

"Malun!" he swore emphatically as his eyes followed the creature on its inevitable path to one of the ringfish willfully stuck partway into the ship. He made no move to do anything about it, though; after all, what could he have even done, to prevent what was about to happen? If the ringfish were pulled out of the holes and brought into the ship to protect them from the encroaching predator, the vessel would sink. Instead, all the oracle, and the Lormish boy by his side, did was watch in horror as the aihu advanced on one of the seafaring specimens lodged in the sides of their ship's bottom and forcefully took its prey in its jaws, wrenching the white behemoth it nonetheless dwarfed from the wooden aperture it found itself stuck in and swimming off. There was still hope, however; one hole in the hull was manageable with a crew their size.

It was as the immortal thought this that he spotted beneath the surface of the water, moving as a single unit, the large pack of aihus that first one had been the advance guard for.

Panic had dulled his mental faculties before when he caught sight of the frontmost predator and now though that feeling certainly hadn't dimmed in the slightest he realized in a sudden and unexplained burst of clarity that while *he* couldn't do anything to save the ringfish, he was among those who could.

"CORNELIUS!" Dekkin called out as he whirled around to face the hero. "WE NEED ARCHERS IN FORMATION ON THIS SIDE OF THE SHIP *now*!"

The oracle's tone and expression were so uncharacteristically and convincingly intense Destiny's Catalyst couldn't help but believe his request was indeed one sincerely meant to benefit all aboard despite all his reservations about the other man, and Cornelius immediately nodded, ordering a squadron of archers to the section of the vessel indicated. By the time the men were assembled, bows drawn, the second of the ringfish had met a grisly end at the jaws of another aihu, leaving only one remaining.

"Fire!" shouted the hero as another of the mammoth predators took the lead from its now-snacking fellow, slicing through the drink on its way to the back half of its pack's last current target. Dozens of arrows were loosed at the frontmost aihu, and it met its end flopping about impotently in a pool of its own blood, but all of this happened a smidge too late; before the first projectile could bury itself in the predator's coarse flesh it had already bitten into the last ringfish's torso hard enough as to create fatal wounds and torn its prey from its slot in the side of the hull and completely out into the open water, where it would do Dekkin and the others no good whatsoever.

As the pack of doombringers departed, Cornelius had as many of the other crew members as could be spared begin to bail out the seawater now flooding the lower deck once again as fast as possible; it wasn't nearly enough to stem the flow very much but did buy them some valuable time. He desperately scanned their immediate surroundings for signs of any other ringfish as the ship slowly yet steadily dipped further and further in its continuing voyage, to no avail. So when the hold was almost completely submerged and the hero spotted a large island in the middle of the current up ahead of and off to one side of them, he had his helmsman set a course for it. Their vessel just barely stayed afloat long enough to see them most of the way to shore before sinking down into the dark deep below.

The islet Dekkin and the others found themselves on was warm, possessing several bountiful fruit trees, a good variety of local, edible wildlife, and even a spring at the center. All things considered, it would be a lovely place to stay…for the few days they had left.

27

WHEN THE KAGLORITES' HELMSMAN spotted a mound of land off in the distance up ahead, he thought nothing of it, making a minor course correction that would take them around the coming obstruction. However, as the ship continued on its way, and the island got closer, he saw that it extended out to one side more than had been initially evident. Another alteration to the direction of the vessel's passage was made. This happened again and again over the course of the next half hour until it became clear that the landmass stretched across miles and miles of ocean, blocking their way and ensuring their journey would be significantly lengthened were they to go all the way around it.

As Zage and his fellows swore profusely at this cruel twist of fate, they hadn't heard of this newly arrived wrench in their plans, and because of her willful ignorance of the world around her, neither had Coria, but most everyone else living on or around the isles knew of the wall of sand. Bisecting a sizable section of the tropical nation's southern half where it lay, it had long stymied trade to and from those islets unfortunate enough to find themselves immediately neighboring it, been the bane of human and Lormish merchants the world over. It was so inconvenient to cross or go around that dozens of habitable floating landmasses had been outright ignored or abandoned once the isles had unified as a nation simply because of their proximity to the wall.

Everyone aboard save for the queen was so distraught by this most recent turn of events that only the helmsman noticed the enormous transparent eel that surfaced a good distance ahead of them as it swam on a parallel course and then only distractedly. When it went under after only a handful of seconds with part of its gargantuan body above the water, the only man on board the nearby kaglorite-run vessel with even part of his attention on the beast thought nothing of it. However, as the ship continued on its way to the wall since the Dark Lord had no idea what else to do, the helmsman spotted something where the eel submerged that made even his brow, frozen pensively and in despair, jump up as high as it could and hang there.

"Master Baturi," he called out over one shoulder.

"What?" barked the man himself, irritable at this sudden interruption of his musings over their very limited and, in most cases, outlandish options for the continuation of his plan.

"There's a, uh…hole…in the sea, up ahead of us," the helmsman responded sheepishly.

"*What in hell*—" began Zage in rage as he stomped up to the front of his stolen vessel before his words ground to a halt at the sight of what the other man had been talking about. Indeed, directly before them, there appeared to be the opening of a sort of curved tunnel of air beneath the waves. Again, this was something no one aboard the ship in question had even the slightest idea about, but this seemingly artificial maritime construct was actually the natural creation of what the locals called an airmaker, the giant see-through eel that popped up ahead of them a while back. Airmakers had the, for them, unfortunate distinction of being the only species of fish incapable of breathing underwater. The early days of this breed were almost the last, as you can imagine, before its members developed an ability which single-handedly saved it—one which allowed them to change the layer of water immediately surrounding their bodies into oxygen. With this, they could now hunt for food beneath the surface of the sea, and this newfound power had the added, unintended bonus of facilitating for them fast and painless travel from one side of the wall of sand to the other. The underwater tunnel's airmakers crafted as they swam, each of which had an irresistible current running along the length of its bottom in the direction in which it was carved from the drink, stayed in place for a short time following their creation before they caved in, reverting back to entirely nondescript stretches of ocean, and so if a ship was lucky enough to find itself just behind one of the peculiar aquatic creatures when one was made, as the Dark Lord's retinue had, they could indeed pass through it, sailing for a time with the sea on all sides of them. But the situation presented itself so rarely, and to attempt to take advantage of it in that way would be so risky, which none had ever tried it.

Until today.

Not that it was a conscious decision on the part of Zage or his helmsman, mind you. A "hole in the sea" is not something anyone without further knowledge of the bizarre phenomenon would purposefully head toward, no matter who it might be. But by the time the Dark Lord gave the order to change course, it was already too late. The kaglorite's edict actually made things worse too since they were able to begin turning the vessel before it entered the tunnel it did so sideways. The initial decline beneath the underwater corridor was quite severe and had the helmsman not possessed the wherewithal to recognize what was happening and right the ship, albeit with the seafaring vehicle facing backward, under his control in the fraction of a second given him the vessel would've capsized as it went down.

It was, however and, of course, still not an ideal situation for all or truly any aboard. The severe tilt the ship took on as it began its voyage through the tunnel threw passengers on all decks against the back of each. As Coria slid across the vessel's main level, she grabbed fruitlessly at the wood beneath her and subconsciously (for there was no time for any complex thoughts at the front of her mind) cursed herself for always keeping her nails as short as a man's. After a split second of this, the queen turned her attention to the rapidly approaching wall below (behind?) her and, wrapping her arms around her head, oriented her body such that she landed on her feet. As this happened, both legs buckled, and she fell back to slam her posterior into the coarse wood underfoot. Coria cried out in pain at this before opening her eyes and realizing with a twinge of guilt how good she truly had it; she landed just to one side of the door to the lower deck unlike the kaglorite who'd been just a moment ago standing right by her, who smashed through it and then tumbled end-over-end down the stairs immediately following it, every part of his body making forceful impact with them at some point as he plunged into darkness.

Coria shifted her gaze straight ahead just in time to spot with widening eyes the heavy crate careening down right toward her. She saw this early enough to dive out of the way a fraction of a second before the large box slammed into the spot she'd occupied a short moment ago, and even then, she couldn't avoid one of the long, jagged splinters created by the impact stabbing her in her near arm. With a grimace, the queen pulled the wooden fragment, sunk an inch deep into her comparatively soft flesh, from it. To her left and just on her periphery, Coria thought she caught sight of something that made her heart freeze over instantly. She whipped her head around to face it and in so doing confirmed for herself the awful truth—Zage was lying motionless on the other side of where the door to the lower level had once been.

The queen cried out his name, her voice whipped from her mouth the second it left by the roaring wind all around her as the ship continued to shoot down the steep watery decline, while she crawled on all fours over to her captor and friend. At first glance, her worst fears were affirmed. His eyes were unmoving, and his head, bleeding profusely from a spot on its back where it had hit the wall now serving for them as a floor. However, Coria's spirits rose when she checked the Dark Lord's pulse and found it, faint yet insistent. Before she even had the time to thank the gods for such a miracle though, the path beneath them leveled out abruptly, throwing the two of them across most of the main deck anew, albeit this time in the opposite direction.

The current on the tunnel's floor carried their ship along the bottom of its curvature while they began to rise, dust themselves off, and tend to the wounded, both animate and otherwise. However, without Zage's booming shout giving out directions, his subordinates soon became aimless. Many of them who were gathered below deck climbed the steps (those of them who were still attached to the rest and capable of safely supporting a person's weight, that is) to the main level, their eyes falling on their immobile leader before beginning to shoot back and forth across the vessel, desperately in search of guidance.

"Zuza!" Coria called out nervously when several of them came to gaze at her expectantly. "Where is Zuza?"

"She's in the hold," answered the nearest kaglorite gravely, "got knocked unconscious when we entered…whatever this is." He gestured to the sea surrounding them on all sides.

The queen grimaced. "Well…well, who's *third*-in-command?"

"No one," the violet-skinned magician replied with a shake of his head. "We never thought both of them would be incapacitated at the same time, and for decades, we were never proven wrong."

Coria thought on this. She'd seen both in battle and so couldn't exactly blame them and their people's assumption, no matter how much trouble she and the rest of them now found themselves in because of it. The queen scrunched her brow as she turned her mind from the past to the present. "All right, who's the best magician *besides* Zage and Zuza?"

Her kaglorite companion narrowed his own eyes as he considered the answer to this question but visibly froze before his lower lip began to quiver once he spotted something over Coria's shoulder. The queen saw this and stood unmoving in a thoroughly optimistic gesture. "What is it?"

The violet-skinned magician's mouth fell open widely, and he motioned for her to look where he was. "I…I don't know, but…but it's *big*."

Accepting that a refusal to gaze upon impending danger wouldn't cause it to cease its existence, the queen with great reluctance came about to find far off in the distance (yet not nearly far enough) what we would know to be an aihu, the largest yet featured in this story; it could easily fit their entire ship into its gaping maw. And by the expression on its fishy face, as the creature gazed upon the vessel, it was planning on testing that assertion. Coria blanched and whipped her head around to look behind both her shoulders, feverishly searching for some sort of nearby savior. When she found nothing and, locking eyes with the kaglorite she'd been speaking with, saw his gaze hadn't shifted from her, she accepted with a loud gulp that it was up to her to get them out of this mess.

The queen frowned as deeply as she could, breathing hard as she strained her brain trying to come up with a plan of attack. Their location in the underwater tunnel eliminated basically all conventional means of defense or escape; they could only go forward along a linear path, one which was wide from the perspective of a single person but from the viewpoint of a galleon such as theirs claustrophobic. So what did that leave them? What were their strengths? Well, the crew was composed mostly of kaglorites, the only magic users in all of Samu. They could destroy anything with red magic… and *create* anything with its blue cousin.

It was at that moment that Coria recalled when, several days ago, a small number of them pooled their resources to create the heavy crate, which held back enemy reinforcements during their run-in with the pirates.

"I NEED ALL OF YOU WHO CAN HEAR THIS TO ME *now*!" she cried.

Every kaglorite within earshot lit up now that a definitive command had finally been given and rushed to surround her.

"I NEED YOU ALL TO CREATE THE LARGEST, HEAVIEST METAL CRATE YOU CAN AT THE EDGE OF THE TUNNEL"—she gestured toward the side of the underwater corridor nearest the oncoming enemy, specifically the section between them and it—"ON MY SIGNAL!" As soon as she finished speaking, her very newly minted subordinates gathered on the side of the ship closest to the aihu, spreading out such that each of them could concentrate on the creation of the crate without something getting in the way of their line of sight and therefore interfering with the spell.

The massive predator in the distance, after drawing far nearer to its target, ceased the somewhat idle circling movements it'd been engaging in while doing so and darted toward the galleon before it. Though every fiber of her being screamed out to act as soon as possible, Coria forced herself with great effort to exercise restraint and waited until the beast was seconds away from taking her and the others in its jaws before she shouted, "*Now!*" Many dozens of hands reached out toward the oncoming creature then, and right at the water's edge, straight ahead of the violet-skinned magicians said appendages belonged to, there came the luminescent flash of blue magic, forming quickly a solid metal square several feet across. Just as the aihu breached the side of the tunnel, yawning mouth open wide, the crate was completed and dropped like a shot to land atop its bottom jaw.

Just as planned, the mystically made cube weighed down the creature it now touched, making it begin to curve away from its intended target in that direction. The queen prayed at a feverish whisper as the aihu's head vanished from view, blocked by the hull of the ship, that the beast's course would be altered enough for them to escape relatively unscathed. Her heart leaped up into the back of her mouth when the vessel she'd found herself on quaked violently. She opened her mouth to order someone below decks on a mission of inspection, but one of the kaglorites read her mind and did so without prompting.

"IT WAS JUST A SCRATCH!" called up the man joyously from the lower level a short while later. "THE HULL WASN'T BREACHED!"

Coria shrieked in elation, and the kaglorites around her celebrated too in their own way. She froze after a few seconds of this, though, as a needle of recognition pierced through the layer of relief blanketing her brain just then; their trick with the crate wouldn't hold the predator in the sea outside the tunnel for long, she bet. Coming about and running to the far side of the ship, the queen looked down to find the beast continuing to swim forward and down, visibly struggling to lift the box in its mouth, much less summon the force to eject it.

However, as the creature strained its lower jaw, it gradually got up the strength to begin rising again as it moved, and when it came about to head for her vessel again, Coria blanched.

"GET READY!" she shouted over one shoulder at the others, hearing the rustle of fabric as they turned around and especially their exclamations of dismay at the sight of their animal adversary's return. "IT'S COMING BACK!" While the beast kept coming, Coria squinted at it in confusion, completely unsure of what it planned to do with that crate stuck on the bottom of its mouth. When it began to twirl about as it moved, however, she realized what it was planning, and her own mouth fell open as wide as it could, mirroring that of the creature.

"RED MAGIC!" commanded the queen, pointing again to the section of the tunnel's perimeter the aihu was approaching. "AS MUCH AS YOU CAN, IN A SINGLE MASS, AND GET READY TO THROW IT!" The kaglorites acquiesced, albeit with puzzled looks on some of their faces, but when the beast before them completed its rotation, throwing its head off to one side and flinging the magic box out of its mouth and toward the ship in the process, they all got the picture.

"UP AND TO THE LEFT!" Coria instructed loudly, squinting at the crate as it sliced through the drink and out into closed air to ascertain its trajectory as soon as possible. The kaglorites under her command obeyed, and the ball of collective red magic they'd conjured up collided with the soaring metal cube, disintegrating it completely, a split second before it would've come down to bore a hole right down the middle of their ship.

Once again, the moment of victory was short-lived since the aihu began to advance anew immediately after its long-range attack was foiled. A million harried thoughts ricocheted all over the queen's mind as she tried to wrench a fresh offensive or defensive strategy from its recesses like trying to pull a bucket of mud from out of a deep trough. That which she had already done had just about covered the extent of her ingenuity; even in groups of several dozen, kaglorites couldn't summon up enough magic to create or destroy something on the scale that would be needed to slay the beast currently assailing her and the others.

Just as Coria was about to give up on the prospect of triumph and the aihu had almost reached the stretch of the tunnel's border directly between it and the ship, something glinted off in the distance at the very edge of her periphery. Whipping her head about to face the direction of the gleam, the queen saw there a school of fish with long bodies covered in radiant white scales. Some looked to be the size of minnows, and were far enough away that Coria couldn't even definitively tell if they were actually there or her eyes were playing tricks on her. Others, however, were large enough that a handful of them would constitute a meal for the approaching aihu. But did the species of predator a member of which they now found before and rushing toward them like to feast on such specimens?

There was no time to think. "*Pocket of air!*" yelled the queen, pointing at what she didn't know were ringfish. "*That way now, with fire inside!*" Incredibly, the kaglorites responded in what was an almost impossibly timely manner; one of them formed a bubble of air and shot it out past the perimeter of the tunnel and into the middle of the ocean where the ringfish swam, and the other summoned a small flame to fit snugly, hovering, inside.

Please, please... Coria begged silently, to whom she couldn't have said, as she watched the retreating fire. Her brow shot up when the aihu slowed and its gaze followed the projectile of underwater flame. And when it came to a complete halt and turned around to give chase to the submerged red glow, and the pack of its prey along with it, the queen threw her hands up and shrieked in ecstasy, the kaglorites around her following suit with celebrations of their own immediately thereafter.

When the tunnel's incline began to come into view, Coria and the others gazed out at it with concern, but the current at its floor remained unnaturally steady while the ship began to climb (as we knew it would). However, as the sunlight streaming down on them from above grew brighter and brighter, the queen began to notice with an anxious pang in her chest that the tunnel was getting… smaller, each side of it retracting visibly. And as she studied this phenomenon, she realized the corridor would be completely sealed before they reached the surface.

"Get below decks, all of you!" ordered Coria with great urgency, beckoning everyone else toward the door leading to the lower level. "Have as many people as you can fit right behind that door. Hold it closed as best they can!" At this point, some of the kaglorites were starting to realize what she had just prior and led a hurried retreat into the hold, as many of them as was needed picking up and carrying the unconscious there in the process. The queen stayed behind to make sure everyone else got off the main level…and when she finally began making for shelter herself standing, water splashed at her feet. The tunnel was now thinner than the galleon that had once fit cozily within, and its rate of retraction increased exponentially with each second.

Fortunately (a strange word to use now under the circumstances), Coria had the wherewithal to take in a deep breath before the drink completely consumed her and her vessel. The ship's wooden frame started to float up to the surface, and as it had been pointed toward it, when the corridor had collapsed, the strong resulting current slammed the queen against the wall separating the two higher levels of differing elevation. It then began pushing her to one side; it felt as though the water around her had a mind of its own and hands too and with those hands was trying to drag her down to the seabed far below. Coria, her eyes open wide and attentive, managed to grab hold of the wall's near corner right as it seemed the ocean would claim her. Even with her finely toned musculature, she had to grip the wood until splinters dug into her fingers to keep from being shot back from the others as the ship continued to ascend.

How much further? the queen wondered as she looked up at the sun hanging several worlds away, her eyes squinted both from gazing directly into it intently and the forceful current pushing against them; she was becoming hungry for air. The surface seemed close then, but time dragged on with her and the ship still entirely beneath the waves. Coria's lungs started to simmer before the continued lack of oxygen stoked the flames into a full-on blaze. The edges of her vision were just starting to blacken when, miraculously, she and her vessel breached the waves.

The queen greedily sucked in air with much gratitude…for a split second, before the ship heaved forward onto its bottom, hurling her along most of its main deck's length (how many times could that happen to a person in a single day?).

Much labor lay ahead of her and the others at the conclusion of the excitement with the tunnel. A dozen of the kaglorites' strongest men and women hadn't been enough to keep the door to the lower deck from caving in; the hold was mostly underwater by the time the vessel freed itself from the cold blue chains of the sea. All that intruding liquid had to be bailed out and over the course of the next several hours was. Any of the kaglorites with at least a passing knowledge of medicine was assigned to the bedsides of Zage and Zuza, who still hadn't awoken from their violently enforced slumber.

In all the clamor about these proceedings and those that had come directly before them, it took a while for anyone to even check if they'd achieved their goal of crossing the wall of sand, which much to the relief of that first observer and his fellows they had by a thin margin.

That night, the Dark Lord didn't initially make an appearance at dinner, and Coria caught herself wringing her hands when she wasn't eating as she sat at the table with her kaglorite captors. When there came the creak of a wooden door being pushed open behind her, the queen brightened in hopeful anticipation. And sure enough, as she whipped around to face the location of the noise, Zage walked through a door there, with several layers of fresh bandages wrapped around his prominent head wound.

"Zage!" she cried out, standing. She began moving to wrap him in a warm embrace but stopped herself upon remembering that attempting to make such a motion would be quite cumbersome with her hands in cuffs as they were.

At first, the Dark Lord merely grunted gruffly by way of response, but under the queen's expectant gaze, he eventually cracked a very slight smile. "Hello."

"How are you?" asked Coria as the kaglorite took the place of the one who had been sitting across the table from her.

"Fine, perfectly fine." Zage nodded as he said this and gave himself away with a pained wince while doing so. "Zuza hasn't awoken yet, but all signs point to her being so too."

The queen managed to hide her disappointment at this. After a minute or so, she noticed as she continued to eat no plate or bowl rested before the Dark Lord and inquired curiously, "Aren't you going to have dinner?"

The kaglorite shook his head. "I'm not hungry." A second later, his stomach growled loudly, and both of them pretended not to have heard it. Self-conscious from eating before someone who wasn't, Coria wolfed down the rest of her meal before looking up at Zage. They began a conversation, but several such interactions had taken place over the course of the recent past and, given that their journey during that time had been completely uneventful save for the run-in with the airmaker and the Dark Lord, was naturally terse in his prompts and responses to such from others besides, they soon ran out of things to say.

The kaglorite's intense, unwavering gaze didn't help the uncomfortable silence that followed, and Coria began desperately looking for something to break it. When her mind ended up going to the contents of one of her pants pockets, the queen lit up in triumph. "Do you want to play some *luds*?"

Zage squinted back at her quizzically. "Luds?"

Coria pulled a deck of cards out of her pocket with both shackled hands. "Yes. Have you never heard of it? It's a popular game in Humania…ah, I suppose that wouldn't mean much to you, would it?"

"You called it a…game?" said the Dark Lord.

"That's right," the queen confirmed with a nod as she removed the cards from their tiny container.

"What is that?"

Coria smiled at this; he was developing a sense of humor! But when the kaglorite's dead serious expression didn't change for several seconds, she realized his query was entirely genuine. "You…you don't know what a *game is*?" she asked with great incredulity.

Zage shook his head. "I have never heard of such a thing."

The queen paused. She'd been prepared to relate the rules of luds, not explain the very base concept of games in general to one who'd apparently never even heard of the concept. "Well, it's…it's something you do for fun."

"Fun?"

Coria sighed, a little exasperated. "Yes, ah, something you enjoy doing."

"Oh"—the Dark Lord nodded—"I see, and what is the purpose of these games, aside from enjoyment?"

The queen frowned deeply. "In *this* case, there isn't one. The entire point is simply to enjoy oneself."

"*What?*" said the kaglorite in disbelief and disdain. "That seems horribly unproductive."

Coria suspected he'd respond thus. She ruminated for a moment on what she could reply to sell him on the idea of fun for the sake of itself. "A clear mind makes for a superior warrior, wouldn't you say?" was what she came up with, a sly smile on her face as she spoke.

Zage gave a nod of approval. "Of course."

"And when we were at Ehoko and your chest loosened up, that cleared your mind, did it not?" she continued.

"Well, yes, it did," confirmed the Dark Lord with a frown. "I fail to see how that is related to the matter at hand."

"*Fun*, things like this card game, can give you that feeling too," the queen pointed out. "And I'm sure *that* interests you greatly, for the sake of the fight, that is."

It was comically apparent on the kaglorite's face that this wasn't all that influenced his decision when he replied after a beat. "Very well. You speak true. I will take part in this game so as to improve my performance on the battlefield."

When Coria stashed the deck of luds cards in one of her pockets as she packed in secret for her covert escape from the capital the night before the kaglorites' attack, she couldn't have foreseen a fraction of the circumstances that would lead her to first use them. Luckily for Zage, luds was a game of chance with very little room for skill, and so it was simple to pick up and play; this was a large part of its appeal among the lower-class humans who formed the bulk of its users. The Dark Lord won that first round; his roar of victory immediately following his triumph made the queen jump even though she'd seen it coming.

However, Lady Luck only smiles upon one for so long, and in the kaglorite's case, she turned away from him during the third bout. His cry at the end of it was one of rage this time, and he moved to tear the cards in his grip apart.

"Zage, *Zage!*" Coria called out in protest, raising one hand and extending it toward him slightly in a halting gesture. "What are you doing? Don't *tear the deck up*. It's the only one we have!"

"It _wronged me_!" bellowed the Dark Lord by way of justification. "Among kaglorites, when one is wronged, *revenge is exacted*!"

"Well, that *doesn't always make sense*," the queen pointed out, light yet firm, "especially in this instance. They're cards, inanimate objects. Let it go, calm down, or I'm not playing with you *ever again*."

The kaglorite opened his mouth wide in preparation for a fiery retort but stopped himself when he saw the telltale downward twist at the corners of her mouth. He paused to wonder at the reason for this. And as he did so, he also considered what Coria had said, that this game of hers might create a path toward experiencing that calm he encountered back on Ehoko. Much to his shock, Zage was able to deflate by the power of thought alone, slow the rapids raging across his mind to a gentle flow.

The Dark Lord took his seat once more, saying almost sheepishly and with averted eyes, "Very well, let us continue."

And so they did. After about an hour, as the moon hung high in the sky above and unseen by them, the queen stifled a yawn and, realizing how weary her body had grown over the course of the preceding sixty or so minutes, put down the cards in her hand, saying as she stood, "All right, let's call it a night. It's getting late."

To her surprise, the kaglorite sitting across the table from her jerked forward, one of his hands darting out to close around her right wrist. "*No!*" He caught himself, though his muscles remained tense. "Ah, no. Let us keep playing, for just a little while longer, all right?"

The desperation in his voice threw her off. Coria squinted back at him in puzzlement for a little bit before it came to her, the reason for his insistence that they keep going. She began to beam down at him. "You felt it again, didn't you? Peace."

Zage didn't answer, but he didn't have to.

"We'll do it again tomorrow, after dinner," assured the queen, patting the top of the kaglorite's hand wrapped around her wrist with one of her own.

He truly saw himself then for the first time since the beginning of their luds matches and released his hand from Coria, bringing it to rest on the tabletop before him, as quickly as he'd sent it out. He assumed his usual stoic frown as she came about and went to her quarters, but some time after she'd vanished from his view, he allowed himself a very slight smile.

Strangely enough, though the queen slept well, as would be expected given her fatigue, she only did so for a few hours before awakening, fully alert. As she expected, Zage was up as well, standing on one side of the main deck, resting against the railing there on his hands and gazing out at the inky night directly ahead of him. "Hello," she greeted him brightly.

To this, he didn't reply, didn't even turn to face her in fact. After a brief expectant silence, Coria explained what happened to bring her here in spite of how tired she'd been mere hours beforehand. When this didn't elicit a response either, she furrowed her brow in concern.

"Zage, is something wrong?"

The Dark Lord made neither a move nor a sound.

The queen's mind raced in panic. "What, are you mad at me?" She could tell she'd hit the nail on the head even without the luxury of being able to see his face. "It is. Whatever for?" She thought on this for a while before her eyes widened. "Do you think I was lying about being tired earlier, to get out of playing more luds? I swear, Zage, that's not it, I don't know—"

"That is *not* why," growled the kaglorite moodily and still without eye contact.

Coria started a little. "Then what—"

"I heard from the others about what you did, back in the underwater tunnel, while Zuza and I were unconscious."

This statement didn't alleviate any of the queen's confusion, as you can imagine. "All right, so?"

Zage finally came about, fixing her with a glare so pointed she had trouble meeting it with her own gaze, though doing so whenever someone else was looking at her was one of her most deeply ingrained personal habits. "When I learned from you of your plans to abandon the throne, I assumed you were incompetent, that you were doing so because you were unfit for the position."

Coria flashed him a slight, uneasy smile. "Oh, my! Tell me what you *truly* think. Why don't you—"

"BE SERIOUS," the Dark Lord snapped, loud enough to wake some of his subordinates from their slumber below decks, "for once in your life. You formed plans under intense pressure back there, and they *perfectly* utilized the abilities of those at your disposal. You were—you *are*—a born leader."

The queen frowned in bewilderment, averting her eyes briefly before bringing them back to rest where they had been, as she took this in. "Those...sound like *compliments*, Zage."

"They are not," corrected the kaglorite, his scowl deepening the little bit it still could, "because they are things you do well *that you are not doing*, for no other reason than that *you do not want to do them*."

"W-well, *Dekkin* said—" Coria began defensively.

Zage let out a guffaw of biting derision. "Ah, so you are taking life advice from *the oracle* now, are you?"

The queen silently conceded the point with nothing but her eyes. "Just because he's wrong about a lot of things doesn't mean he is about this though. Why *can't* I give up the throne? Samuel's—"

"Your adoptive brother, Samuel Roneage, the *warmonger*?" interrupted the Dark Lord with a harsh hiss. "The *mass murderer*, the *torturer*, the man who would not pursue peace with my people even if it were offered to him?" He jabbed one of his index fingers right into Coria's face, his lips pressed tightly together. "You may be too young by far to have stopped the massacre, but you could have at the very least tried to work out an agreement with the survivors left behind when the crown was placed on your head. All the kaglorites—*women*, *children*—who died because of Samuel Roneage's *absurdly* aggressive policies in the last four years, their deaths are on *your head*, including Zuza's husband. Did you know Zuza was married? She is a widow now because of *you*."

Zage turned on his heel and stormed off to the helm without another word or look in the queen's direction, leaving her to stand there completely gobsmacked. She'd never thought of things in the way he just laid out for her, not once in her life had she been asked to think of how her actions would affect others. In fact, the focus had always been on *her* needs, *her* desires. Luckily for herself and those who found themselves in her path, she was a naturally kind person, which offset her unbelievably spoiled upbringing for the most part but couldn't keep her from remaining blind to certain perspectives without outside assistance like that which had been so scathingly given to her just then.

Coria cursed the tears now flowing down her cheeks, the sobs undoubtedly drawing the attention of all those awake and near enough to hear them. What the Dark Lord had said *did* make a lot of sense, but he had still been too harsh by far. People widowed, *dead*, because of *her*, a woman who prided herself on her sense of altruism, and had only ever wanted to find happiness for herself? No. No, it couldn't be, yes?

Yes?

28

"THERE YOU ARE."

The thin, quiet voice with which these words were spoken nonetheless hurt Dekkin's ears as it made contact with them. And, of course, they would; the oracle spent the last several days completely alone in the furthest reaches of a dark, deserted cave in the middle of the island he and the others in his party were forced to make land on when their ship had taken too much damage to sail on. The immortal opened his eyes a fraction of a centimeter before the bright (to him) light before him seared them shut. Swearing emphatically as he rubbed at them, Dekkin forced his lids open, adjusting to the illumination gradually until they could be unshielded as much as possible without difficulty.

Rising to a sitting position and coming about, the oracle found Matthew standing before him, a lit torch in one hand and a plate of food in the other. "How did you find me?" asked the immortal, the question coming out as a croak after the dozens of hours its speaker spent in unbroken silence. Dekkin winced at the sound.

"When you disappeared, I started a survey of the island to find you," the boy replied matter-of-factly.

The oracle raised his brow. "The *entire* island?"

"Yes, of course," confirmed the lorm with a nod. He raised the plate of food in his grip up a little. "I brought you lunch." He squinted down at the immortal in concern. "Have you eaten anything since the last time I saw you?"

Dekkin shook his head. "No, nothing."

This statement was as much a reveal to him as it was to the lorm before him; he hadn't thought about it at all since their plans first fell apart. And even immediately after the lorm spoke of it to him, this changed not a whit. Why would it when he never got hungry? But when he then spotted Matthew's gaze darting back and forth between him and the plate of food anxiously, he took the proffered dish, cleaning it ponderously.

"Why did you come here?" the boy inquired while the oracle was midmeal.

"I'd rather see nothing than something I don't want to," answered the immortal readily as he chewed. A twisted smile formed on Dekkin's face. "It's great in here. Can't see, can't hear. If I could just find a way to float in midair, get rid of my touch as well. It'd be perfect."

"I eat darkness like meatloaf, and my arms will fall off if I'm around too much noise." The oracle could've said that, and it would've made just as much sense as what he actually had in the lorm's eyes (that is to say, none at all).

"Do you think you'll come back sometime soon?" Matthew questioned next after a short pause borne of, on his part, bewilderment. "We could use your help in trying to come up with a plan to get out of here."

The immortal let out a bitter chuckle, some of the food in his mouth falling out of it in half-chewed chunks and coming to rest atop the fabric of his pant legs. "If *five* oracles were with us on this island, it wouldn't make a bit of difference. What we're in the midst of right now, Matthew, is a completely, *utterly* hopeless situation."

"How do you know?"

Was that a tinge of exasperation Dekkin heard in the boy's voice? No, surely not. "How *do I know*? Have you gone daft? We've got no ship, in the *middle of the perpetually deserted Lormish Isles*. We'll never break free of the saltwater rapids. Perhaps if we were given enough time, a *lot* of time, yes, we could find a way out, but that's one thing we most definitely *don't* have. In a few days, Zage Batur and his retinue will stroll into the temple containing the Orb of Desire, entirely unopposed, and wish the lot of us out of existence. What would you call that if not hopeless?" The oracle frowned when the lorm sighed almost imperceptibly at this. "What? What is it?"

"You always say that," replied Matthew with his eyes on the section of the cave's floor lying beneath and between them, "there's no hope."

"I only say it when it's true," the immortal countered defensively.

The boy shook his head in an infinitesimal motion. "I don't know about that. It…seems like it's a constant thing, and sometimes you do it right at the outset without even trying to overcome whatever obstacle's in your path. You know, if you tell yourself something can't be helped, it's going to be quite unlikely you'll prove otherwise because you'll put hardly any effort into trying to do so. Why would you? You've convinced yourself the task before you is impossible."

"So what, you spent all that time looking for me just so you could tell me how I'm doing something wrong?" snapped Dekkin irritably. "That's not exactly what I'd say I need right now, you know."

Spurred on by the oracle's sharp tone, the boy locked eyes with and frowned down at him. "It's not an insult. It's just a little criticism. Everyone needs to be able to take a little of that, and it seems like *you* can't," the lorm muttered that last sentence sullenly.

The immortal brushed aside Matthew's sentiments with one hand in a literal, forceful gesture. "Like I said, this isn't what I need right now. Go on back to your master if you want to pretend all the world's a field of flowers and look down on those who have it hard enough already."

The boy stood there frozen for a moment, and then, surprising both Dekkin and himself, turned on his heel before storming off (or at least the closest he could get to such a movement).

* * * * *

"You finally found him?" Cornelius asked his apprentice when the lorm returned to the castaways' main camp upon the beach of their tropical prison, where Destiny's Catalyst stopped to take a break from his search for a way off the island.

Matthew nodded in confirmation.

"And where is he? What's he doing?"

"He's in a cave," answered the boy, "hiding."

"Ah"—the hero flashed the lorm before him a warm smile—"and you left him to come back here. This gladdens me greatly. Your intentions are noble, but there are many villains in this world beyond any sort of help. Zage Batur being another one, for example."

"Y-you'd say Dekkin's a villain?" Matthew asked with reservation.

"What else would you call him? He's certainly no hero."

"Those are the only two options?" inquired the boy.

Cornelius nodded. "Yes. Oh, everyone likes to say that things are more complicated than that these days. Nonsense. In this life, there are heroes, and there are villains. The path to becoming either is clear to all who stand before them. People who say otherwise are simply those who've willingly walked into darkness yet don't want to be treated as such, treated appropriately."

Protest came to the lorm's mind then, but he bit his tongue, both from his natural tendency against confrontation and a desire to avoid potentially alienating both of the two most prominent men in his life. Instead, he asked, "You and the others are still looking about for some means of escape?"

"Yes!" confirmed Destiny's Catalyst with an easy smile.

Matthew raised his brow a little. "You don't think there's a possibility it's hopeless? This is a dire situation, even by your standards."

"No evil or obstacle in this life is insurmountable," the hero declared with complete certainty. "That's my most deeply held belief, Matthew, you know that."

This was true, but spending so much time around Dekkin in the recent past had to some degree put that sort of notion out of the boy's mind. And in a small isolated corner of his thoughts, there came a whisper that told him his master's optimism was a bunch of hogwash. But the man's sentiment was, for obvious reasons, so intoxicatingly attractive that the lorm ignored that tiny voice at the back of his brain and nodded in enthusiastic support of Cornelius's ethos.

"So now that you've found the oracle, will you stay here?" Destiny's Catalyst asked his apprentice after a beat, gesturing at the sprawling camp behind him.

Matthew's gaze followed the hero's outstretched hand. The boy didn't want to abandon the immortal but, at the same time, couldn't fathom remaining by his side in the depths of that pitch-black cave when an expanse of verdant grass and shining sun lay before him if he chose to stick with Cornelius.

After a moment of indecision, the lorm looked up at Destiny's Catalyst, flashing the man a firm smile, as he answered in the affirmative with gusto.

When Matthew's first assigned task was cleaning duty about and within the many tents sheltering, hopefully on a temporary basis, his fellows, he began to doubt the wisdom of his decision but stuck with it nonetheless, taking the broom and rake proffered to him and beginning to make his way through the camp with Adam to assist him.

The young human man seemed uncharacteristically gloomy then, speaking very little and sighing heavily every few minutes. Master Hefull exuded an aura of discontent so thick that even the boy was eventually prompted irresistibly to inquire as to its source.

"I'm starting to think I made a mistake, joining the military," answered Adam readily and in a frank tone, surprising the lorm not one bit.

"Why's that?" Matthew asked anyway so as to hide this.

The human soldier paused his work and looked off into the distance pensively for a short while before he responded. "I thought if you set out into the world with a courageous heart, you could become a hero, save people. But I've done it, that first part, and since becoming a member of Her Majesty's army, I haven't accomplished a single thing. I feel so *helpless*. A hostile invasion of the capital? Kalgorite terrorists were the enemy. Of course, a fresh recruit like me couldn't do a blessed thing to stop them. Protect the queen from capture? The same. And when our ship entered the saltwater rapids, I hadn't a choice except to let the current carry it along to its doom." His gaze dropped to the section of ground directly before him. "Every problem that's arisen since I signed up has been by its nature completely out of my hands. I'm starting to think heroes aren't made by will. They're designated at birth, like your master."

Matthew was silent as Adam wrapped up his monologue and got back to work. What could the boy reply, when, to his thinking, everything Master Hefull had just said was true? The two of them spent the rest of their shift in uncomfortable silence save for the scuffing of their feet on the sands beneath them and the sound of their brooms or rakes being dragged across it. By the time they were done, it was dusk, time for dinner. The boy was ravenous after having to wait in line a half hour for his bowl of stew but still had the presence of mind to deliberately avoid sitting beside Adam, mopey as he was at the moment, and instead pick a spot directly beside Nadia.

"Matthew, I know this is a tad out of nowhere, but what does your master think of me, as far as you know?" she asked him following several minutes of wordless dining on both their parts.

The boy looked up from his food and over at her. "Uh, he likes you."

"In what way?" inquired the warlord further, leaning toward the lorm beside her a little. He raised his brow when she stared back at him with a suggestive smile. "Oh! You mean—"

She nodded. "That's right."

The boy turned his head to face forward, looking off into the distance thoughtfully. "Well, uh…"

The smile on Nadia's face grew strained. "Ah, I see."

"No, no!" the lorm assured her, moving to return her gaze yet again and raising one hand up slightly, its palm facing her. "It's just that my master has never truly talked about or done anything related to…that kind of thing."

The warlord lifted one eyebrow incredulously. "*Never?* Cornelius Arcind, *Destiny's Catalyst*, has never even *flirted* with a woman? Surely you jest or lie to protect my feelings."

Matthew shook his head in a vehement gesture. "No, I speak true! He's never pursued anyone himself in all the time I've known him. And, of course, there have been women who've approached him. But whenever that's happened he's never returned their affections. Actually, he seems entirely oblivious to the fact that they're even flirting with him."

Nadia searched the boy's face for evidence of falsehood and, finding none, replied, "Ah, interesting. Well, that's better than him selectively ignoring *me*, I suppose."

"You're…interested in Master Arcind? In…that way?" the lorm asked, a tad flustered making such an inquiry in so direct a manner, adorably enough.

The warlord answered in the affirmative. "I never made my feelings known. How could I ever think I'd have even a fraction of a chance? I'm *twice his age*, and a noblewoman I am not. But I thought perhaps…given that we're stranded, and there's a strong chance we'll all be killed in a few days…" She shrugged. "But if Cornelius is completely apathetic to the whole enterprise of romance, I suppose that puts an end to my plans."

"I…I don't think he *is* apathetic about it, truly," theorized Matthew.

Nadia furrowed her brow inquisitively. "What do you mean? What else could it be?"

The lorm shifted his weight from one side of his body to the other. "I think…it's just that no one treats him like a person. He's always *Destiny's Catalyst* to everyone else—this legendary hero—and so he gets treated like one, like a living symbol. There's always a degree of tension in the other party when he's talking to someone. And those women who have pursued him previously never bothered to try getting to know him because they were attracted merely to his *status*. I think"—Matthew paused pensively for a handful of seconds as he thought over what he was about to say—"I think he's actually very lonely because of that. It barely shows because he's *him*. But over the years, and I may be mistaken, it seems to me whenever he smiles, it's a little…strained."

"Hmm, so you think he might be open to—?"

"I'd say he's never given any sign of *not* being interested," the boy replied diplomatically.

The warlord looked ahead and to one side of herself, one eyebrow raised, to where Cornelius sat eating at the head of the table they were all sitting at. "I see."

* * * * *

As he sat alone and blind in the void of his choosing, Dekkin resolved to abstain from consuming even a single morsel of food more in the few dozen hours he had left of his life; despite how succulent the meat and fruit Matthew brought him earlier had looked, he barely was able to taste anything as he ate either, and so he figured that would be true of any other edible at his disposal.

His mind was soon very much against his will, on Matthew, and how frustrated and upset the boy had been with him when the two last talked. It was strange; the lorm had been but a pace away, and speaking as emphatically as he ever had (which wasn't much, but still), yet when the immortal revisited the memory of it, Matthew's visage and voice seemed faint, indistinct, as if he'd viewed them then from several yards away. Even despite this and much to his surprise, the oracle found his ancient heart quailed at the thought of the boy disliking him even from a distance.

But what could be done about that when the source of the lorm's resentment toward him was the latter speaking the truth? *Isn't that always the way with children?* Dekkin said to himself silently. So was this his fate, to spend the last few days of his long life with the most important person currently in it angry with him? Life was far crueler than even he had believed up until this point.

A pinprick of light appeared in the middle of that cave's darkness, however, when a thought sprang to the oracle's mind, *What if I help Matthew search for a means of escape, even though I am certain none existed within our reach? That might patch things up between us, without me having to lie to accomplish it.* Dekkin nodded after a moment of reflection. *Yes, that is the thing to do.*

Though the cave the oracle ventured into was not deep, it seemed an eternity of sightless travel passed before a dot of light became visible on the horizon, and even longer still before he was completely clear of its hard rock walls. The immortal realized then with a grimace as he looked about that he'd been so consumed with despair while picking his way through the surrounding jungle on his way to the cavern he'd not paid any attention to the route he took. Because of this, Dekkin was left to try to find his way back to the others purely via almost entirely uneducated guesswork, and as he'd been sure he would found himself after a lengthy trek on a deserted stretch of beach with Cornelius and the rest of his retinue nowhere in sight.

Swearing loudly to no one but himself, the oracle was about to turn back when he spotted something beneath the surface of the water before him—a ringfish about as long as a kresh, swimming against the current around it and making good time too. The immortal frowned at this in confusion and then watched, utterly disbelieving, as the aquatic creature continued slicing through the sea with the salt water right before it at any given time pushing directly against its front. Dekkin realized then that if this specimen before him could move in such a way *here*, there was a very real chance others of the same ilk, *many* others, could too. In fact, given this most recent development, the ringfish they'd encountered earlier probably hadn't been merely outsiders who had gotten too close to the rapids and been unintentionally caught up in them; they most likely *lived there* and had the ability to move freely around them. They'd have to in order to make the area their home. And if the ringfish populating the strip of sea containing the current that had served first as the basis of and then the wrench in, he and the others' plans to avert Zage Batur's scheme of genocide could propel *themselves* any which way through it.

Dekkin picked at random a course he hoped would lead back to the others once again, and this time, much to his delight, he guessed right.

"Cornelius!" the oracle called out to Destiny's Catalyst once the other man was within earshot.

The hero looked up from the raft he and several of his subordinates were working on building from the wood of the surrounding trees. In addition to being surprised at the immortal's appearance,

Cornelius was a tad irritated at the interruption, though he shouldn't have been; unbeknownst to him and his fellows, the only trees to be found on what they fervently hoped would not become their final resting place, and indeed on any of the many landmasses dotting the area within which the saltwater current that shipwrecked them ran were sinkwoods, a variety exclusive to the rapids, which boasted the distinction of being the only one incapable of floating in water.

"Yes, what is it?" asked Cornelius, turning to face the other man and standing up as he brushed his hands together to clean them of the sawdust clinging to their exteriors. Dekkin came to a halt a pace before Destiny's Catalyst and explained his recent discovery. The cool, neutral expression on the hero's face gradually fell away over the course of the oracle's monologue, to be replaced by a euphoric glow. "*Yes!*" he cried in ecstasy, balling both hands into fists, raising them up to a point several inches ahead of his chest, and shaking them back and forth a single time. "*By the gods, yes!* I *told* him! I *told* him everything works itself out!"

Cornelius gathered his scattered forces and then told them how their salvation had been found. The hero did this at a shout so that it would reach all the ears it needed to, but the immortal didn't even register the sound of it; he was too busy searching among the assemblage around him for Matthew. After a few false alarms (most lorms looked the same to a human, especially when viewed from the side or back), Dekkin successfully located the boy and sidled up to him.

"Hello," greeted the oracle, a tad standoffish in his manner.

The lorm only gave him a passing glance, his lips puckered slightly and his brow low, creating a pouty expression. "Hello."

A brief, uncomfortable pause followed. Looking to fill it, the immortal gestured toward Destiny's Catalyst from across several rows of listening soldiers. "I found a way off here. I came out of the cave… uh, obviously."

When Matthew gave only a noncommittal grunt in response, Dekkin sighed deeply, swallowing his pride and resigning himself to his fate. "I'm sorry, all right? What you said about me earlier…wasn't incorrect. I can be an ass sometimes, and…I was being one then. So are we square?"

The boy smiled up at him eagerly and quick enough to give away the fact that treating the oracle so coldly just then had not come without a great deal of effort on the lorm's part. "Yes! Uh, yes. We're square."

The immortal looked down at Matthew with a matching expression, then shifted his gaze so as to face forward and found much to his confusion that the crowd around them was dispersing, its members heading for the sea. "What…oh, horb it. I wasn't listening. I don't know what we're supposed to do. Do you?"

The boy shook his head in embarrassment, and the two of them shared a laugh at themselves. Consulting the nearest soldier, they found that Cornelius had ordered his subordinates to dive down to their sunk ship and salvage what rope they could from its wooden skeleton. The plan was to try to lasso passing ringfish of appropriate size with it.

Dekkin stayed behind as did most of the humans present; it, of course, made the most sense to leave the task to their Lormish fellows. Eventually the green-skinned halflings who dipped far below the surface of the water began to emerge with damp rope wrapped around their shoulders. After an hour, the ship was stripped of all it could be, and even then, there was only enough material for a few dozen of the castaways to try their hand at ringfish wrangling.

The oracle would've left to his own devices, sat back, and let some of the others do the work here, but knowing it would ingratiate him further with Matthew, he volunteered to help try to catch some of the cylindrical aquatic creatures alongside the boy. As the two of them stepped into the water, rope in hand, both had to brace themselves against the current rushing around and against their feet to maintain their balance while standing still. It was several minutes before a potential target of appropriate size presented itself to the immortal, who then swung the lasso in his grip around above his head a few times before sending it out toward the nearby ringfish. The feeling of triumph surged across his synapses as he saw the imperfect circle of rope close around its intended target, but that emotion was ripped suddenly from his mind when the large long fish before him easily slipped free of the lasso's grasp even as it tightened around the creature.

Cries of dismay from off to both sides of Dekkin were carried to him on the warm tropical wind; the others were having the misfortune of going through the exact same thing. Pausing, the oracle considered what to do for a moment, at the end of which, an idea came to him. Reeling in and untying his lasso, he rearranged and reknotted it such that the circle at the end of the rope was now bisected right down the middle by another length of cord. This, he hoped, would catch on the front of the ringfish's face, allowing the lasso to successfully ensnare the slippery sea beast. The immortal shared the concept with the lorm beside him and had the boy go off to tell the others of it as well once Matthew made the necessary alterations to his own long strand of rope.

Half an hour passed without a single ringfish coming within Dekkin's reach, and he began to fear he and the others missed their chance when he spotted a solitary fin slicing through the top of the surf just within range. The oracle brightened, swung his lasso over his head several times, released it outward…and missed. He began to let out an emphatic obscenity but, remembering the presence of the impressionable youth at his side, bit it back when it was but half-birthed. As the immortal resumed scanning the stretch of sea immediately around and directly before him, he heard whoops of victory from off to one side of himself; his method worked for some of his peers, each of whom after reeling their lasso in passed it off to another while beginning to hold their catch in place. This was, of course, good news for all involved, including himself, but Dekkin couldn't keep a little petty jealousy from bubbling to the front of his brain. His next throw went way wide as his inner feelings bled through into his outward movements, and after hours of standing in the brink, he failed to capture even a single one of his and the others' quarries.

At dusk, only three properly sized ringfish now rested in the possession of Cornelius (who had, of course, been among the few fishermen lucky enough to nab one) and his retinue, and the most recently acquired of their number had been caught several hours prior; it appeared the creatures of the rapids stopped passing the area the castaways had gotten stranded on after a certain point in the day.

The oracle couldn't lie, seeing the distraught look on the face of Destiny's Catalyst as the hero contended with this most undesirable outcome brought him no small amount of satisfaction, even as he shared in the other man's dismay.

"What do we do?" the hero wondered aloud, both hands resting on the corresponding hips. "We can't face down the Dark Lord and all his forces with a group of *three*." He raised his brow. "And we can't afford to wait any longer. We'd be lucky to arrive at the temple the *same time* as the kaglorites, even if we set out right this instant."

Cornelius may not have been used to contending with the worst-case scenario, but the feeling of such a predicament was all too familiar to the immortal, who piped up, "We have one lifeboat left. Those three could pull it. We could fit perhaps five on board."

"*Five?*" repeated Destiny's Catalyst incredulously. "That's scarcely better than three!"

"It may be our only option," Dekkin pointed out, his voice cool. "And a very slim chance of victory is still much better than a certain defeat."

The hero paused to consider this for a short while. "You may be right," he conceded immediately thereafter. "But in that case, who stays…and who goes?"

29

THERE CAME THE SOUND of clashing metal as Coria and Zage locked the shaft of her hammer and spear and the blade of his sword respectively. The queen grinned in premature triumph as she began pushing out, expecting her opponent to crumble under the massive force of her toned musculature as all of them usually did, but the Dark Lord instead held firm. When the edge of his sword pressed against the hammer and spear began to scrape down one side of its shaft, Coria brightened, thinking after several seconds of straining every part of her arms that he was weakening, only to realize too late what was actually happening. The kaglorite, with one last sideways shove of gargantuan force, dug into the calloused flesh of one of the queen's hands with the sharp edge of his weapon, making her cry out as drops of blood fell to wet the gray metal of her own and instinctively release the corresponding side of the hammer and spear from the clutch of her freshly wounded appendage.

As half of Coria's weapon began to tilt downward and to one side as a result of this, Zage used the blade of his sword to push it around in the direction it did this in and out of her grip. This all happened in less time than it takes to blink, but that still wasn't fast enough to get one over on the queen, who leaped toward the appropriate spot as soon as the hammer and spear left her other hand to take it in the grip of both once again before even touching down. She turned in midair as she did this, so as to face the Dark Lord and confirm he was doing exactly what she thought he would, slashing out at her while her feet were off the ground, before blocking the swing with the middle of her weapon's shaft.

As accomplished a fighter as Coria was, however, even she couldn't change her course as she cut through the air, and so her landing point was already set and clearly visible to her opponent, and Zage took full advantage, recovering from the rebuttal to his previous move and swinging his sword at where her left knee would be a split second hence in a horizontal motion. The queen saw it coming from quite a ways away but, as was said earlier, could do nothing but watch, cringing preemptively as she looked down in horror at her targeted knee. Fortunately for her, though, despite the fact that they were sparring with real weapons, as was the convention among Zage's people, even kaglorites didn't grievously wound those they faced in mock single combat if they didn't have to; the Dark Lord twisted the hilt of his sword at the last moment, smacking the front of her left knee with the flat of its blade rather than slicing clean through it with its sharp edge.

Coria fell to the knee upon which a dark blotch was already blossoming with a cry of agony. The pain was so strong it even made her let go of her hammer and spear with both hands, and a split second later, the point of the kaglorite's sword was a centimeter before her throat.

"I yield," she said somewhat redundantly, leaning back and bringing her posterior to rest on the coarse wood of the main deck.

Zage scowled as the queen beamed down at the wound she now kneaded with one fist. "Why do you smile so? You hurt. You were defeated, *dishonored*."

"You should know by now that humans go through life quite differently than kaglorites, Zage," pointed out Coria, gazing back up at him with the strange mixture of a grimace and grin on her face. "But besides all that, I'm just…*delighted* to have a sparring partner who can keep up with me, *beat me*, even. I'd been starting to think I'd gotten to the point where such a thing didn't exist." She bowed her head slightly. "Thank you."

The Dark Lord was about to avert his eyes uncomfortably at this before realizing the perfect pretense for looking away from her lay right in front of him. "*Boy!*" he cried over one shoulder. "*Collect weapons!*"

The kaglorite youth who'd been waiting in the wings for just such a command rushed forth to take Zage's sword from his grasp. He then moved to pick up the hammer and spear wielded by Coria, but in his hurry to do so, he tripped over his own feet while pacing toward her. As he fell forward, the sword he was holding plunged right toward the queen's stomach, point first. Her brow leaping, she quickly leaned frontward and grabbed the weapon by the blade, its sharp edges cutting furrows into the flesh of the hand she'd grasped it with but coming to a halt before it could impale her.

In an instant, the darkest scowl imaginable was upon Zage's face, and his mouth fell open slightly. "*Boy—*" he began to bellow.

"Zage, stop!" interrupted Coria firmly as she stood. "It was a mistake. I'm sure he feels poorly enough already."

"*He almost—*" the Dark Lord started roaring.

"*Zage!*" The queen fixed him with a warning glare as she said this. "*Enough.*"

Though his expression was and his voice had been far more intense than hers, he wilted at this. "Collect her weapon and get out of my sight," muttered the kaglorite sullenly to the boy before him, who nodded in a swift, jerky motion and did so with similar haste.

Coria walked over to the nearest section of railing and leaned against it as she looked out at the watery horizon before her. Zage's gaze followed her as she moved, and soon, he was by her side doing the same. "Children these days have it far too easy," he growled insistently. "If that had been me when *I* was a boy and my father had seen that…"

The queen lifted her brow curiously. "Oh, yes? You've never talked about your father before. Tell me about him." She wondered at the pained grimace this elicited in the long moment before the Dark Lord began speaking.

* * * * *

Even the rotting bits of the stolen fruit the nine-year-old Zage's father brought him tasted like the nectar of the gods in the mouth of one who hadn't eaten in a week.

"It was a good fight," Zofu Batur related to his son with a mouthful of food. "The merchants' ships nearest the western border are the most heavily guarded, as you would imagine. We were outnumbered three to one." The man beamed proudly. "Of course, such an advantage meant nothing in a battle against kaglorites." He turned his smile to the boy beside him. "You'll be joining us soon enough, Zage. You're almost a man."

"I"—his son paused and looked away, perturbation written clearly on his face as all emotions are for children of that age; after a beat, he realized his father wasn't going to let him leave any part of the sentiment he'd begun to express unspoken, and so he marshaled up a great deal of courage and continued—"I don't think I want to do that, Father."

Zofu scowled, disbelieving. "What foolishness do you speak, boy?"

Zage flinched at the man's forbidding tone but still replied, "I do not want to fight the humans or the lorms."

The boy hadn't known his father's expression could darken any further, but just then, he found himself proven wrong. "*You do not—* this must be a jest, yes?"

"N-no," insisted Zage, "fighting means people get hurt. Why would anyone *want* to fight?"

"*What, it's* because they *murdered millions of our people*," his father answered incredulously before gesturing at their immediate surroundings. "They *torched our homeland*. They *destroyed an entire* country that once looked like <u>this</u>."

The kaglorites' home base, within which father and son now sat eating, rested at the center of one of the many small areas of land unaffected by the massacre. It was also quite close to what was now called Blackbeach, the charred sands at the edge of the western ocean, so you would be forgiven for thinking the violet-skinned magicians' headquarters was constantly under attack by forces from Humania or the Lormish Isles or both, but it wasn't, *never* was, in fact. For Kuli, as it was called, was along the northern stretch of that coast, far enough up from the isles that no party setting out from there would sail over water nor survey on land far enough to find it. Barring that, the only remaining potential threat was the giants of the north, the *itrasi*, and anyone who knew anything about those ivory-white behemoths recognized that, as a rule, their species was completely apathetic on the subject of anything taking place outside their sizable borders.

"But that was so long ago," pointed out Zage. It had actually only been about three years, but for a boy such as him, that was almost half a lifetime.

"*Long ago?*" his father spat, motioning wildly in the direction he'd come from. "I just returned with the *fresh corpses* of *three men*!"

"But they were killed because they attacked people, in their homes."

Zofu was so dumbstruck by this that the rage on his face actually flickered out for a moment. His son hoped fervently it would not return, but his prayers went unanswered. The man leaned toward the boy and, grabbing him roughly by the hair at the back of his head, stood while forcing the latter to do the same. "We'll see how *passionless* you are about our *neighbors' demises* after *this*," growled Zage's father as he dragged his offspring along with him back the way he'd taken to reach the youth's side.

Someone had done the kaglorite man lying on the sterile dirt before them at the end of their journey the courtesy of covering his gaping stomach wound with bandages wrapped around his body, but this did nothing for the smell, which made the boy gag from a yard off.

Zofu shoved his son forward so roughly Zage fell. Feeling damp cloth on one of his hands, a split second before the other hit the dirt, the boy looked over to where it had touched down as soon as he stopped moving to find that it was resting right on top of the blood-soaked bandages. Zage reeled back in utter revulsion at this, but this motion was halted partway from behind by his father. "No, do not go away," commanded Zofu with a nasty smile his son was fortunate not to be capable of seeing. "This is your new bunkmate now, after all."

"Wh-what?" the boy asked, barely registering the words coming out of his mouth as he concentrated intensely on not vomiting up his long-awaited lunch.

"Why, this corpse here is going to lie right beside you as you sleep...for a *week*," explained his father. "Then we will see how much apathy you have for the liberation movement."

His son's eyes, already watering from exposure to the cadaver's rancid stench, bugged out. "*What?* Father, *no*! I...I am sorry, you are right—"

The man behind him shook his head immediately. "No, no! You have already said what you said. The damage has been done. If you are truly remorseful, good on you, but I am not voiding or even *shortening* your punishment because of that." He pointed to the corpse before them. "Pick it up, part of it anyway, as I know you have not the strength to carry it completely, and bring it into your tent."

Zage started. "Wh-what?"

His father folded his arms over his chest. "I know your hearing is as good as any other boy's. Grab the corpse and tow it until it is *right* beside your bed."

The boy looked behind him over one shoulder in confusion. "But...that is about a *mile* away!"

Zofu turned around and started walking in that direction "Then I suppose you had better start the process of transporting it soon. Do not think you can get out of this through some kind of trickery either. I will be checking your tent multiple times a night to make sure you are obeying my orders." At no point while he said all this did he turn his head, not wanting to make his voice more easily heard by his son.

Zage watched his father leave him in complete despair. The man had always been intimidating and quick to anger, as most members of his species were, but ever since the massacre scarred his son's chest and taken entirely the life of his wife, he'd grown cruel, constantly displaying what had once been his worst tendencies. But Zofu *was* his father; the boy reminded himself. Surely if he was good enough, for *long* enough, the man would change, back to the way he used to be or perhaps even better if his son followed those of his father's edicts, which were directed at him, like the one that had just been handed down to drag this heavy (for him) corpse for a mile and then sleep next to the rotting, organic hive of writhing, feasting maggots for seven days.

It was an easy decision that of whether or not to do it. Zage turned his head to face forward, approached Zofu's dead comrade, knelt, and began pulling it very gradually and with tremendous strain visible on every part of his slight frame back to camp.

That night, as the odor of death hung heavy over the boy while he lay in bed under the cover of his small tent, its front flaps closed to seal in the stench as per an addition to the conditions of his punishment. He realized there was an upside to the present situation—to fall asleep was to escape from the real world and therefore the smells within, the one currently afflicting him so pointedly to be specific. It almost made him long for slumber to take him and, as always, thrust him into a nightmare of the massacre.

* * * * *

"Ah, excuse me."

Zage looked up from the patterns he was tracing in the dirt with a long stick as he sat just outside his tent and cried out in alarm and terror. The voice addressing him had been at a very mild volume and come from a good distance away, but nevertheless, the boy was terrified, for the *look* of this man (that's what it sounded like, but who *knew* if the thing was even a *person*) was disturbingly unlike anything he'd ever seen in his short life. His skin was so *light*, a sort of beige somewhat similar to the color of sand. His eyes were *blue*, and his hair was black as night.

Zofu bolted from out of his own tent's confines at the sound of his son's startled exclamation and, seeing the strange sandman, conjured an axe out of thin air with blue magic before charging at the new arrival with a bloodcurdling battle cry.

The interloper raised both his empty hands up until they were level with his head, each of them just off to one side of the corresponding shoulder. "Stop, stop, I'm not armed. I'm not here to hurt you!"

The chief of the kaglorites didn't hear any of this over the thunderous pounding of his heart in his ears but saw that the other man had no weapons on him (within view, at any rate) and was making no move to counter the forthcoming assault on his person as its potential perpetrator rocketed right toward him. Zofu brought himself screeching to a halt, the sharp edge of his weapon's blade coming right up to the sandman's throat.

"Why have you come here, *human*?" bellowed Zage's father, spittle flying out into the open air from the other side of his lips.

Realization washed over Zage like waves on a beach. So *this* was a human! They'd been described to him before, of course, but not being old enough to take part in the raids the adults of his people carried out against them, he'd never actually seen one in the flesh. Despite the glaring differences between the intruder standing before him now and the violet-skinned, golden-eyed people he was exclusively familiar with, the boy thought to himself that this human looked more similar to them than he'd have thought.

The newcomer began reaching into one of his pants pockets, and Zofu immediately pressed the sharp edge of his weapon's blade into the soft flesh of the other man's throat a tad, causing a bit of blood to trickle down from the freshly made wound and run along its cold metal surface. "I've no intention of fighting you!" the human cried out in a panic. "Look, look!" He pulled something out of his pocket with one hand, and Zofu's entire body tensed up, though he made no further move to stop this. Looking down, the kaglorite man saw in the interloper's hand a small cloth pouch.

"What is that?" asked Zage's father, confusion dulling the sharp edges of his aggression.

The human gestured toward the fabric in his grasp with his head. "Open it up and see."

Zofu scowled distrustingly at the other man, but curiosity got the better of him in the end and so he removed one hand from the handle of his axe to untie the knot at the top of the pouch, which then fell completely open, revealing its contents to be a few dozen small brown seeds.

The kaglorite man's brow reversed itself completely, shifting from crowding his eyes to rising so high it looked like it was attempting to break free of his face. "What are those?" he inquired, though he knew what he saw.

"Seeds," answered the human. "I'm a horticulturist. I work with plants. These are vegetable seeds, ones that I've bred myself to grow in Kagloris's soil and not just in places like these!" He indicated the patch of green immediately surrounding them. "They can flourish *anywhere* in this country."

The chief of the kaglorites scowled and huffed with incredulity. "Nonsense. The soil throughout most of Kagloris"—he gestured at the charred plains beyond the pocket of verdant land wherein he and his people resided—"is totally barren. Nothing could *possibly* grow in it, and even the dirt like that which we stand upon now didn't escape the massacre unscathed. It is not hearty enough to support anything more than short grass."

"It's true," the horticulturist insisted, moving his hand with the seeds in its palm toward the other man a little in a proffering motion. "Try planting them, *please*. This could change the fate of your entire *people*."

Zofu thought on this with a frown. After a beat, he snatched up the seeds, grunting, "I know you tell lies, but I will do as you say. I'm known to fall prey to foolishness on occasion." As he closed his fist around its new cargo, a thought came to his mind, and his brow shot up. He jutted his head out toward the human, questioning through gritted teeth, "Hold a moment. How did you find our camp? <u>Who else among your people knows of this place?</u>"

"No one!" Having to stay on the defensive for so long was beginning to wear on the human; you could hear it from the exasperation beginning to creep into his voice. "No one who'd attack you or give your location away to another who would, at any rate. My superior discovered this place and only tells those he is certain will not use the knowledge to hurt you or your people, like me. We and several others are part of a secret cell within Humania's military known only to the queen, dedicated to helping with kaglorite reconstruction."

Zofu squinted suspiciously at this. The kaglorite then ordered the human interloper to be imprisoned and watched constantly, and after this edict was carried out, he increased security around camp as much as he could. But days passed, and nothing untoward occurred. And eventually, when he thought no one was watching, Zage's father went out to a field of ash just past the safe zone's perimeter and planted some of the seeds the intruder gave him.

* * * * *

This is exactly what Zage imagined when he first heard tales of heaven. True, Ravenhair, as he and the other kaglorites had taken to calling the human horticulturist on the orders of Zofu (who coined and insisted on the constant usage of the nickname in an attempt to further dehumanize his prisoner), hadn't brought but one variety of seed with him to Kagloris. But while the resulting dietary homogeneity would've bothered a human or Lormish child, perhaps, for a violet-skinned youth such as Zage, who'd grown used to only eating on a weekly basis, it was far and away beyond any of his wildest dreams, to be able to have *multiple meals a day*!

His father vehemently forbade his son from interacting in any way with Ravenhair, and for several weeks, the boy obeyed, out of fear for Zofu's wrath and also that of humans in general, which had been taught him his whole life. However, as time passed and it appeared no ill effect was seen or felt by any living in the verdant island amidst black sea, Zage and his father called home as a result of the human's presence. Curiosity began to sprout, and physically seeing (or rather, tasting) what seemed like proof of a good nature on the horticulturist's part mellowed his phobia further until, one day, as Zofu was out scavenging the ruins of yet another far-off former village within their borders, his son decided he'd have words with Ravenhair.

The human had been given the rattiest secondhand tent possible for shelter and made to pitch it near the center of camp where he could be most easily guarded.

"I'd like to see the prisoner," Zage declared up at the soldier standing just outside and with his back to its front. The boy scowled in pretend distaste as he said those last two words and kept his posture as straight and rigid as he could, just like he practiced earlier.

The guard smiled nastily down at the chief's son and stepped aside to clear the front way to their captive's quarters. "All right. But not *too much* torture, understand? He brought us those seeds. He could be quite useful yet."

"No promises," snapped Zage as he crossed the freshly unobstructed threshold, looking straight ahead and so missing the nod of approval this elicited from the soldier he was speaking to.

The human looked up in surprise from the book he was reading (fortunately for his sanity, though he was confined to his tent except in the event of a need on his part for urination or defecation and had been given absolutely nothing to help pass his time of incarceration he'd brought along with him several tomes on his chosen field of study) at the swish of fabric the passage of the chief's son stirred up from the front flaps. "Hello," he greeted the boy with caution and unease as he set the book in his hands down and to one side of himself. "You're the chief's son, isn't that right? Ah…Zage, was it?"

The boy nodded in response before immediately jumping into the matter he had on his mind. "Can I ask you something?" Ravenhair made a motion of affirmation. "Why are you helping us? My father told me all humans are evil monsters."

The human suppressed a chuckle. "Well, I wouldn't agree with that. I'd say there's a wide range of different varieties of human, just as there's infinite diversity among the kaglorites."

Zage found he was inclined to believe this. After all, as he'd noted previously, the two species were quite similar in terms of their bodies' builds and the way that they spoke. So it followed that they'd think in about the same way too. An objection came to mind shortly after the boy came to this conclusion however. "But…my people *attack* yours," pointed out the young kaglorite. "They, ah, *we* hate all humans. Why would any of you *help* us?"

"Well, some people want to help others even if those they help spit in their faces," Ravenhair replied. "Only a few, perhaps, but they exist nonetheless. My cohorts and I are among them." His face fell, and he averted his eyes as something came to his mind that made him hesitate for a moment. "Although, ah…I'll admit there's a selfish reason for it on my part."

When the human didn't elaborate, Zage asked him, "Well, what is it, this selfish reason?"

A shadow fell over the horticulturist's face at the thought of it. "My…my mother died not too long ago. She was the most important person in my life. I've never managed to make friends, and I don't get along with my father. She passed, and…it took me to a place I couldn't stay." At this, he started breathing as heavily as if he'd just run several miles. "I needed something to…get me and keep me out of it. Some sort of…extremely involving work. I still would have taken the job even if my mother hadn't died." His tone and expression when he said this were those of assurance. "But I'd be lying if I said it was an entirely, or even mostly, altruistic decision."

Zage nodded in sympathy. Three years after the fact, he was still quite shaken by the death of his own mother during the massacre. She'd listen to him when he was having trouble with something. The boy's father, on the other hand, always tried to fix whatever problems were brought to his attention immediately upon hearing of them. And this was, of course, a good thing in and of itself, but strange as it is to say sometimes issues only needed to be spoken of, not attempted to be solved. It was still quite common for his son to remember his mother and cry at the thought of her, in his tent where no one could see and quietly enough that it wouldn't be heard by anyone but himself.

"How did your mother die?" questioned Zage.

Ravenhair stirred uncomfortably. "Well, ah…she was killed, by a kaglorite."

The boy's eyes bugged out. "*What? Truly?*"

The human confirmed it with a nod. "My father is the warden of my village's prison, and many of the kaglorite prisoners of war during my people's conflict with them were sent there to be incarcerated. My mother, she helped my father with his work. She was… cruel to those kaglorite prisoners. She was in charge of the prison's kitchen and gave them caneo feed to eat almost every day. On nights when she couldn't sleep, she'd head over to the jail and make sure they wouldn't either. She'd put chunks of ice into the bathwater, make it freezing for them when they were let out to wash themselves." He shook his head at the memory of all this. "One day, she was over there and one of the prisoners got free. Beat her to death." A single tear ran down one of his cheeks from the already watery eye it shared the right half of his face with.

The chief's son scrunched up his face in utter bewilderment. "So a kaglorite killed your mother…and you still *volunteered to help us?*"

"Yes," the horticulturist answered without reservation. "I bear your people no ill will. Much as it hurts to say it, she deserved what happened to her. She brought it all on herself. If you treat people like animals for long enough, they'll start thinking that's what they truly are and begin acting accordingly. Attack, destroy—that's the basis for the entire conflict between our peoples, I believe."

The two of them talked a little while longer. That night, as Zage ate a hearty meal with his father, he recognized how much he relished its contents and remembered how Ravenhair seemed to light up when he arrived to visit the man and deflate when he had to leave.

"Father?" the boy asked Zofu, who let out a single terse grunt in response. "Do you think we could let the human out of his cell? It's been a while since he first came to us, and nothing bad's come of it."

The chief paused his dining midchew. "You would have me set Ravenhair *free, completely?*"

His son prepared for just such a response. "No, not completely. I mean that we could just give him a *bit* more freedom, let him outside some, give him other people to talk to."

A long moment passed before Zofu said, "Very well, it shall be done." Strangely enough, he had a look on his face just like that of a person delivering a death sentence to someone they dearly loved.

A few days later, Zage went to his father's tent when the man failed to show up on time at a predesignated spot to take his son scavenging like he had said he would the previous night. The boy was in high spirits, both because he was spending more time with his newfound human friend, and it warmed his small violet heart to see Ravenhair enjoy himself a little more, even while still in captivity.

"Father?" Zofu's son called out when he reached the closed front flaps of the man's quarters. "Are you there?"

"Yes," answered his father, "come in, quickly."

His son crossed the threshold before him with a puzzled frown on his face; his only surviving parent had what had seemed up to now to be a perfect memory, and the man's voice just then had sounded so *weak*, frail, as uncharacteristic as it possibly could have.

Zage turned his head to face Zofu, who he saw lying face up atop the tent's only bed in his periphery, to find his father in a pool of the blood streaming from a gaping gash in his stomach.

Zage's brow shot up as he rushed across most of the short distance between them before kneeling. "*Father! What—*" He stood and turned toward the front entrance as quickly as he'd arrived where he now was. "*I'll get the healer—*"

"No," croaked his father before the boy could start moving again. "It's too late. I've lost too much blood."

His son shook his head at first but quickly came to realize the man was right from merely a cursory view of the graphic tableau beside him. This happened much quicker than it usually would for a youth of his age, but after all, he was a kaglorite. "Wh-who did this?" he asked, beginning to sob, as he turned to face his father's head and crouched before taking one of the man's hands.

"It...was...Ravenhair." That last word came out as only a breathy whisper.

Zage was so shocked by this he started violently. "*What?* No... no, that can't be...are you certain?"

Looking back on it (something he would do over and over again for decades to come) that was, of course, a foolish question, but given the circumstances, he couldn't be much faulted for it. The obvious answer that should've followed never reached his ears, for at that moment, his father stopped breathing, turning still as stone. Zage stayed there, calling out to Zofu many times and shaking him with increasing fervor as he did so, to no avail. It seemed impossible that

Ravenhair would do such a thing…but then again, the chances of another party being responsible felt slimmer yet.

At this point, the boy's mind blacked out for several minutes, and going forward, he would have no memory of what occurred during that time. The next thing he knew, after his father's death, he was sprinting directly toward Ravenhair as the accursed human milled about in an open field under guard.

The traitor turned to face the chief's son after spotting the latter and fixed the youth with an inviting smile. When he looked closer and saw the way Zage was walking and the look on his face though, the human frowned in confusion and concern.

"Zage!" he called out. "What—" He stopped himself and bugged out his eyes when the boy conjured up a knife out of thin air via blue magic, all without breaking stride even slightly. "WHAT ARE YOU DOING? WHAT'S GOING ON?" The panic clear on his face also froze Ravenhair in place, allowing the young kaglorite to pace up to him and plunge the blade in his grip deep within the human's gut, just how the sandman had done to Zofu. Ravenhair let out a cry of agony that quickly morphed into a strangled gurgle and fell to his knees. As soon as this happened, Zage grabbed him by the back of his head and carved with mystically created knife a wide slit in his throat.

The boy didn't see or notice this, but as a geyser of blood shot out of the freshly made furrow in the human's neck, two streams of it went high, each of them landing just below one of his eyes. And as the thick red organic fluid flowed down his cheeks, Zage renounced right then and there all of what he now saw to be naive sympathy for the natives of Kagloris's western and eastern neighbors. His dear departed father had been right all along. All humans and their Lormish accessories were murderous monsters and so had to be killed, each and every one.

* * * * *

Coria's face was a rictus of horror as the Dark Lord wrapped up his tale, his tone very matter-of-fact.

There was a brief, pregnant pause immediately following the end of the story, broken when she reached over and grasped lightly one of his shoulders, saying in tearful sympathy, "Zage, I'm *so sorry*."

At first, the kaglorite merely grunted once flatly in response, but as he looked back into the queen's eyes, he softened and said, though with averted eyes, "Thank you."

Coria let go of him with the hand now touching the man and let it fall to rest at her side. "That Ravenhair did you a great injustice," she acknowledged following another moment of still silence. "But…have I done anything of the sort to you, Zage?"

The Dark Lord furrowed his brow in confusion. "What? No, of course not. As I said before, through your inaction as queen, you are responsible for some great evils, but you have yet to do something of that nature directly, to me or anyone else, as far as I know."

The queen nodded readily. "So you see that not all humans are monsters, right?"

"I see that *one* of them is not, yes," grumbled the kaglorite, his frown deepening to a scowl.

"And how many humans have you known, well, throughout your life?"

Zage thought on this for a handful of seconds. "Two. You and Ravenhair."

"So *half* of them are not evil, not deserving of premature death, is that right?" Coria continued.

The Dark Lord bristled again at this. "Well, yes, I *suppose* so, but as I said that is only out of a group of *two*."

"Exactly my point," replied the queen, jumping on this as quickly as she could. "You've only gotten to know *two* humans in your *entire life*, and *just among those two, one of them* is, by your estimation, good-hearted."

The kaglorite still wasn't getting it. "Yes, what of it?"

Coria leaned toward Zage a little. "If half of the two humans you know *aren't* monsters, doesn't that mean it's conceivable half of *all humans* don't fit that description? *And, yes,*" she continued, cutting the Dark Lord off as he opened his mouth to counter the argument she'd just made, "it's entirely possible it's not *that many*. There's no way of knowing with such a small group of people to base that of. But there are *many*, you must realize this. There are many good people among the humans and lorms too, innocent beings you'd be killing along with the evil ones if you carry out their scheme to wipe out humans and lorms entirely."

The kaglorite's mouth gaped like that of a fish as he stared in silence at her for a long while periodically opening it wider in preparation for a retort before finding himself at a loss and contracting it again. Finally, after some time, a look of concession dawned on Zage's face, and he said with great reluctance, "Yes. Yes, you are right. I know you are right."

Coria's entire body went taut with elation. "*Truly? Excellent!* So you won't do it? You won't try to use the Orb to commit genocide against my and the Lormish people?"

The Dark Lord shook his head. "No, I will not. I will wish for all of them to be killed, except for you."

First, the queen raised her brow in uncertainty, then as she looked into his eyes and saw total sincerity there, her face fell as far as it could; his response was not, of course, what she'd been hoping for. "*What?*"

"There probably are good humans out there, good lorms, but not enough for me to spare their entire race, I would say," explained the kaglorite with utter nonchalance. He followed this up with a look that was the closest his face could come to romantic. "But you I will not kill, for certain. I'll become king of most all Samu after I use the Orb, and a human woman could never be my queen, but you can be my favorite concubine."

Curiously, that second part of his declarations upset Coria much more than the first, though it was there that he affirmed and defended genocide. "Oh, *thank you much*," she replied, her voice dripping with sarcasm. "Those three little words every woman wants to hear—*my favorite concubine*!" Even she, ever the devout optimist, began then to think that perhaps the Dark Lord was beyond saving, but just as this idea took root and was about to grow, blanketing her entire brain, she had an epiphany.

"If you do as you say, you might as well kill me along with all the others," declared Coria firmly. "Because I would *never* forgive you for it."

Much to her relief, she could see plain on Zage's face that he was feeling the desired effect of her words; he may still not care for humans or lorms in general, but he did about her, quite a lot she was beginning to suspect, and so she thought, the possibility of her looking upon him with hatred might just be enough to make him change his mind.

But, of course, if her scheme came to fruition it would be after much delay and resistance, token and otherwise, from the kaglorite. "What do I care about your forgiveness?" he muttered unconvincingly. "You had best get used to the idea, of being the last purebred human left alive." He stomped off to his quarters after this, working with great effort to restrain himself from looking over one shoulder anxiously at her as he moved but failing to hold back multiple times.

The queen watched him go, so intently that she didn't pick up on the sound of approaching footsteps behind her until they were but a pace away. Coming about, she found Zuza standing before her with a slight, twisted smile. "It is no use, you know," the kaglorite said to Coria, "trying to talk him out of it."

Coria straightened. "Well, I've just looked into his eyes, and I say you're wrong. I say he's conflicted about it now, and that could very well lead to a reversal of his position on my people."

"Oh, I think *that* is *very* possible," conceded Zuza with unexpected ease, throwing off the queen. "That is not what I meant though. What I meant is that I am going to get the Orb before him and wish for *every single* human and lorm to die." Her smile widened into a grin of sadistic glee.

Coria was visibly disturbed by this, much to the other woman's delight. "We're not all bad, you know. Humans, lorms." She gestured back the way Zage had went. "What I said to him is true."

The kaglorite nodded readily. "Oh yes, I know."

"You—" the queen began without bothering to absorb the contents of this reply before stopping cold in her verbal tracks as she did, completely floored by what had been said. Thinking she'd misunderstood, she craned her neck in the other woman's direction. "What's that?"

"The popular line of thinking among my people, 'every human and lorm is an irredeemable demon,' it's hogwash, all of it," assured Zuza of the meaning behind her affirmation, so strange in the ease with which it had been coaxed from its speaker and in fact its very existence. "There are plenty of good people among those two races. When I use the Orb, when I carry out another massacre, I will be wiping out more innocent people than I've ever even met in my entire life."

This explanation did nothing to soothe Coria's puzzlement. "So…so you're going through it even knowing that?" She should've been horrified, furious over this, but the conversation had taken such a sudden left turn she was too disoriented to react properly. "*Why?* Are you just that…spiteful, *malicious*?"

The violet-skinned woman reached out to the side of herself to grasp with one hand the railing beside them and began leaning against it. "Zage told me that he informed you of my situation. I am a widower, have been for years." The queen barely managed to pull herself together enough as she sloshed about haphazardly in the viscous sludge of confusion surrounding her to nod in confirmation. "But he did not tell you how exactly my husband died." She looked at Coria without seeing her, wistful at any memory of her deceased lover even if it was that of his final days. "We were in the middle of a campaign in the heartland of Humania, he and I. The latest of ways we and our fellows had found to infiltrate the country involved approaching it from the *north*, an arduous and lengthy process, as you can imagine. At any rate, my husband and I were pacifists then, completely opposed to the ongoing war. But one does not voice such things among our people, and so we went where Zage told us to. However, we got around having to fight, *kill*, by volunteering to go on raids for supplies, just the two of us. What we did in actuality was go hunting, and then trade for the necessary amenities with those farmers, shop owners, and craftsmen willing to engage with us in such a way. We were on such a mission when we came upon a small farm, just like a hundred others we had seen in our time among the terrorists. One man alone inhabited it, and though he allowed us into his home, he was…visibly unnerved. I broached the topic of his present disposition as lightly as I could, and just as a rural farmer is wont to, he was totally honest with me; he said he had never met a kaglorite before, never been personally wronged by one, and yet he felt compelled to kill us, these strange-looking outsiders. This set my husband and I on edge a little, as you can imagine, but we believed in the fundamental good nature of all sentient beings, so we thought we would stick around and see if we couldn't get him through experience to shake free of his prejudices. The farmer, he remained visibly torn over the rest of the day's course. We ended up asking to be put up for the night after the weather took a turn for the worse before we had a chance to leave. He allowed it, and I fell asleep beside my husband convinced that this time the following day that conflicted human would be our close friend."

The lack of a quaver in her voice or tears in her eyes as she said what followed were to Coria far more devastating to observe than if either or both of those things had been there.

"I awoke to the sound of him choking on his own blood and looked over to find the farmer had stabbed my husband in the chest while the latter had been sleeping. I had just enough time then to escape myself." Zuza paused briefly for effect. "It was as I ran from the sword-slinging human giving chase after me in the middle of the night that I forged in my mind a new philosophy—there existed both good and evil in the spirits of our eastern neighbors, but for the most part, the second would overpower the first in the end. And how could one ever know for certain which moral force held the most sway over an individual person, let alone a group of them? You could not, and I have refused since the night of my husband's death to take any chances with what remains of my people. And so all humans and lorms must die."

The queen opened her mouth to say something after a pregnant beat, but the kaglorite woman before her with impatience and exasperation raised a hand to silence her preemptively. "Speak not, human. My faith in this creed has gone unshaken since the time many years ago it was formed. Nothing you could say would change that."

It was of course not in Coria's nature to obey such a command, but looking into Zuza's eyes, she saw all she needed to know that the other woman spoke true. She fretted over what to reply with instead; finally, after some time, she decided to try a different tack in her mission to prevent the coming genocide. "I'll tell Zage everything you've just said, and he won't stand for your scheme, won't let it come to pass."

The kaglorite snorted in unabashed derision. "He won't believe you. I have known him for decades. You met him last month." A grin of spiteful glee dawned on her face then. "Weep not for you and yours, Coria Roneage. This was inevitable. If the doom of humans and lorms had not been assured by the Orb, it would have come to pass at the hands of the Prime Wizard."

The queen, with her utter lack of worldly knowledge, wouldn't have known what Zuza was talking about had not one of the human woman's many drinking companions told her of it one drunken night. It was believed by the kaglorite people, and had been for decades, that at some point, one of their number would manifest magical abilities on par with those of a god, become the Prime Wizard. This was merely an old folktale however; no oracle's premonition had ever backed it up.

Then without any degree of fanfare, the kaglorite woman came about and began pacing at a casual clip back to her quarters. She stopped herself after a few steps however as a wicked inclination popped into her head. "Ravenhair did not kill Zofu, you know," she said to Coria over one shoulder. "It was suicide, with the human framed as a murderer in order to put Zage on the right path. The chief told me he would do it a short while before he did. Sometimes a lie must be told to make someone see the truth. As I said…your word against mine." With this, Zuza brought her head to face forward once again and walked off.

Another part of the queen's nature, as I'm sure you've noticed, was a refusal to give up on causes she believed in ardently, but even she had trouble as she stood alone on the ship's creaking main deck with the nighttime ocean wind buffeting her hair lightly seeing a way out of the doom currently circling low above the human and Lormish people. During her time with the Dark Lord, she learned that you could caress someone's face even with your wrists in chains, but she wasn't at all sure one, as a human in such a predicament, could face down an unencumbered kaglorite in single combat and come out on top.

30

CORNELIUS WAS, FOR OBVIOUS reasons, a shoo-in for one of the spots on the single row boat that would be carrying the incredibly meager force dedicated to preventing the Dark Lord from using the Orb for his vile machinations, as was Dekkin for his precognitive abilities. It was then decided Nadia would accompany them after a very brief period of discussion. Deciding the identities of the final two members of the party took considerably longer, and the choices at the end of the passionate debate on the subject were selected for unorthodox reasons. Adam Hefull begged Nadia privately to campaign for him to be the fourth, seeking to prove himself as always, and she vehemently refused to go along with this. However, Destiny's Catalyst then got wind of the situation and charitably gave the recent recruit the all-clear. And lastly, the oracle insisted Matthew come with them as well, not to fight, of course, but to be dropped off somewhere safe and outside the rapids before the climactic showdown. With the setting of the sun, the local wildlife on the island he and the others had found themselves shipwrecked on became quite bold and aggressive, something they'd discovered very painfully their first night there. As such, the immortal refused to allow the boy to stay in such a place for what could be an extended period before a rescue could be mounted for the lorm as well as his fellow castaways.

With that, the five of them lashed the captured ringfish to the front of the row boat and, taking aboard as much food, water, and weapons as they could, ventured forth atop the powerful current once again. It was an exhilarating ride through the remainder of the rapids because of the incredible speed of their travel, but none of them were ever in any real danger, as the aquatic creatures allowing them to steer their tiny vessel could change direction so quickly every natural obstacle in their way was easily avoided. It was only dusk when the row boat got out of the current, and the excitement during the former's journey across the latter made the time it had taken appear even slighter to Dekkin and the others.

Even after they were clear of the rapids, they kept their fishy steeds tied to the front of their vessel; after all, they needed to save all the time they could if they wanted to catch up to the Dark Lord and his retinue. When night fell, the boy volunteered to take the first watch, and as soon as this had been approved, the oracle jumped at the chance to back him up. The lorm thought as this too was accepted by all that the immortal must want to talk with him, one on one, and yet once the others were asleep, Dekkin said nothing for quite some time. When he finally did speak up, Matthew understood why it'd taken him so long to say what he did and why he'd wanted to wait for Cornelius, Nadia, and Adam to fall out of consciousness.

"You know, ah…if we pull this off, and Zage doesn't kill us all with the Orb…I'm going to pick a replacement, give them my turins," the oracle muttered to the boy with averted eyes. "And then…ah, and then…I'm…going to kill myself."

"I know," replied the lorm immediately and in a tone that made it clear he was telling the truth.

The immortal raised his brow in surprise. "You do?"

Matthew nodded. "No offense, but…you're not a very good actor. It's pretty easy to read you. Besides, I knew we wouldn't be together long even before you told me and Coria what you were going to wish for from the Orb."

Dekkin's eyes widened even further as far as they could. "*What?*" he exclaimed. This made Cornelius frown and turn over in his sleep, and the oracle kept his voice low from then on, a task that required considerable effort. "What? How could you?"

The boy's face fell drastically at the thought of his answer. "Something this good could never last."

"It was…a nice set of final days," said the immortal after a pregnant beat, his own expression moving at the start of it to match the lorm's. "Thank you."

Matthew frowned in confusion at this; hadn't they spent the last several weeks roughing it across two countries, frantically beating back death all the while?

Dekkin stared off into the pitch-black distance for a moment before he teared up and began, though he tried to choke it off, crying softly. "I'm sorry…I'm sorry I'm not strong enough," apologized the oracle as he wept.

"I'm sorry I'm not good enough," the boy replied, his own eyes filling with the water of despair. After a moment, he stood and crossed the meager distance between them before hugging the immortal, who eventually returned the gesture.

A few hours later, the two of them woke Nadia and Adam up and went to sleep themselves. Dekkin awoke at midmorning the following day and looked about with squinted eyes to find they'd entered a vast swath of thick fog. Reluctantly rising from his spot curled up on the floor of the boat, the oracle looked out ahead of their vessel while he waited for his mind to pull itself free from the mental post-slumber mire. Soon after he began doing this, a large dark shape appeared at the very edge of his and the others' vision, coalescing for them over time into the hulking wooden frame of a galleon; it was on a parallel course relative to the row boat, and the latter soon proved to be a tad faster, gaining on the former as it went along. Eventually, when Dekkin and the others were close enough for the figures of themselves and their minuscule vessel to be fully discerned by those aboard the galleon, one of its occupants walked to the back of it, looking out and down at them, and the hearts of the oracle and his fellows leaped into their throats.

The man gazing at them from above was none other than the Dark Lord Zage Batur.

31

"HE'S NOT CALLING FOR reinforcements!" Cornelius observed brightly as he unsheathed Kiam. "It's five against one!"

Idiot. What good does a sword of several feet do when your opponent is many *yards* away and unreachable for you besides? On top of that…

"He doesn't *need* reinforcements," pointed out Dekkin, fixing Destiny's Catalyst with a withering glare of disdain that the other man, his gaze fixed on Zage, didn't spot. Shifting his focus back to the Dark Lord, the oracle could only watch as the kaglorite raised up one hand, palm facing the sky, slightly, and feel his stomach drop to the row boat's floor at the thought of what was to come. Zage's outstretched hand began to glow…

Blue. Blue?

The immortal frowned up at the Dark Lord in puzzlement. *What's he playing at?* the former wondered; one moderately sized ball of red magic flung to the bottom of his party's meager vessel would be enough to sink it, ensuring for its five occupants, as far as anyone involved knew, the agony of death by drowning, which would end with their waterlogged corpses being dragged across the seabed far below them by the ocean's currents. When the kaglorite summoned a long, coiled-up metal chain into his grasp, Dekkin still didn't get it. But when Zage whipped it out toward Matthew and its end section farthest along its considerable length from the handle wrapped itself completely around the boy's slight, short frame several times, the oracle realized what the other man's plan was, and his stomach bored a hole through the bottom of the row boat before shooting straight away from the rest of the man's body through the salt water now surrounding it to touch down on the abyssal plain far beneath him.

"*No!*" cried the immortal, grabbing at the lorm only for the Dark Lord to yank Matthew out of their small vessel and the oracle's reach.

"Oh, make no mistake, Dekkin Eterden!" the kaglorite shouted as he began hoisting his newly acquired captive up with short yet frequent and consistent movements. "I will still be sinking your little ship down there!" The boy had now been pulled all the way up to the deck of the galleon Zage stood upon, and in the palm of the latter's hand not holding the former in place (as you might've guessed, the task only required one of them), the Dark Lord conjured up an appropriately sized orb of red magic. "I am simply making sure that, even as you wait to drown with no hope of rescue, you lack even the small comfort of your beloved lorm's presence!"

The oracle furrowed his brow in confusion; the way the Dark Lord was speaking, carrying himself, was so…*stilted*, his manner like that of a first-time actor performing in some small-time production of a low-brow stage play, like he didn't truly *feel* the way he wanted everyone else to think he was. But before the immortal could ponder this peculiarity for more than a split second, the kaglorite above him flung the mystical sphere in his grasp toward an open patch of the rowboat's bottom. He did this so fast and unexpectedly no one aboard the minnow to his vessel's whale had the time to block its path. As soon as the ball of red magic touched down, it seared right through the wood with a loud hiss a hole sizable enough to guarantee the tiny waterborne vehicle's demise.

As seawater poured in from the aperture beneath him to pool about his feet before immediately beginning to rise up the legs attached to them at a blistering clip, Dekkin didn't even look down, instead gazing up at Matthew and thinking only of the boy as the galleon the lorm was now a captive aboard sailed off, swiftly fading into nothingness amidst the surrounding fog.

The oracle found himself treading water by the time this happened, and an infinitesimal noise sounded in his ears, so slight he dismissed it as an imagining on his part. It repeated then a little louder, however, and kept doing so, its volume increasing gradually with each repetition until it became clear to the immortal what it was—Cornelius calling out his name as the hero swam in place beside him while attempting to hold up the rapidly sinking skeleton of their fatally perforated ship.

Dekkin shook his head, muttering dismissively, "What's the point? There's no salvaging that boat."

Destiny's Catalyst huffed in exasperation. "*Dekkin!* Please—" He stopped himself when he looked back at their vessel to find that despite his most spirited efforts only about half a foot of its length remained above water. While the rest of it was swallowed up by the sea, his mind raced as he turned over every corner of it in a frantic search for the alternative solution he was sure rested somewhere within. All they had to work with was a scuppered ship…but he realized a split second later, perhaps it could be more than that.

"Nadia!" the hero exclaimed, whipping his head around to face hers. "Dive with me. Use your halberd to tear off chunks of the boat's bottom. Try to make them as large as you can. I'll use Kiam."

A question was on the tip of the warlord's tongue, but seeing frenzied urgency in the man's face, she bit it back and, taking a deep breath, obeyed the first of his commands. She wasn't surprised to see as she began following the rest that Cornelius proved the faster swimmer, racing past her toward their vessel, now several feet underwater. Tearing his sword from his sheath as fast as the salt water currently enveloping him would allow, Destiny's Catalyst used it to carve out a rectangle roughly two feet across along each side of its perimeter from the bottom of the boat. And as their doomed vessel's offspring shot to the top of the waves above them, Nadia realized the nature of the hero's plan.

They ended up collectively cutting four rafts, one for each member of their party, from the boat as it continued its descent, and by the time her part of the task was complete, the warlord's lungs were crying out in agony. Swimming back up with movements as forceful as she could make them, Nadia's head just barely crested the surface in time for her to maintain consciousness. On a completely unsurprising note, Cornelius's breaths were barely any louder than normal even immediately after his own popped out of the ocean with a noisy splash.

"Well, now what?" grumbled Dekkin once he and the others were all sitting cross-legged atop their newly created rafts.

"*Now* we can rest while we look for a way out," Destiny's Catalyst replied in very slight irritation.

"A way out?" The oracle snorted at this and gestured all around them. "What's there to look for?"

"*At the moment*, I don't see anything, yes, but we don't know where the waves will take us." The hero's tone sounded uncharacteristically half-hearted as he said this, and on another strange note, he didn't look the immortal in the eye as he spoke.

Dekkin turned away from Cornelius in disgust, and the next half hour went by in silence and stillness, save for the leaden passage of the four rafts. The oracle grew bored before long and began scanning the immediate area for points of interest, if not mechanisms for salvation. His gaze came to settle on a pair of very long, thin, side-by-side outcroppings, about a yard and a half high, to their right, its size such that it had stretched out beside them ever since they'd left the rapids.

The immortal frowned as his eyes traced its narrow, rocky frame…and the noise of rushing water coming from that direction fell on his ears. It sounded just like…

In an instant, Dekkin's brow leaped up as high as it could, and his entire body started. "*Cornelius!*" he exclaimed as he looked back over at Destiny's Catalyst. "I think we might be able to get out of here and with some luck still stop Zage!"

The hero lit up as he returned the oracle's gaze. "*What?* That's *great!* Ho?"

The immortal pointed with one index finger toward the shelf of stone off to one side of them and the others. "Do you hear that over there, the sound of rushing rapids? It's just like the noises we heard while we were in that strong ocean current, isn't it? Perhaps between those two outcroppings, it keeps going, for who knows how long. Ben didn't mention it to us when he spoke of the shortcut, but perhaps that was because this…outstretched arm of it is too narrow for a full-size ship to pass through."

Cornelius considered this and as he did so his face fell. "Well, yes, but if it would be too narrow…" He stopped himself as he got it.

"Too narrow for a ship, yes, but it could be perfect for small little rafts like these," finished Dekkin when Adam continued casting him the look of complete puzzlement he'd donned and directed toward the other man once the latter had proclaimed the possibility of their salvation. At this, the young recruit brightened and let out a whoop of rapture.

It took an agonizingly long while for the four of them to paddle their way by hand to the nearest of the two shelves, and the oracle cursed their luck as they crept toward it, but upon their arrival, he found their fortunes had come about; the surface of the rock was thoroughly pockmarked to the point that climbing up the side of it would be quite easy. Or so he thought, at least; the immortal discovered much to his dismay shortly after beginning his ascent that it was incredibly tricky climbing with one hand while holding onto a whole (albeit diminutive) raft with the other, no matter how many perfectly sized indentations there were upon its face. At one point, when he was about halfway up, Dekkin's climbing hand slipped, and his stomach churned as he began to fall, but he managed to find another cleft in the stone to clutch with it a split second later, though he came away from the incident with nasty scrapes on the hand in question that made him swear profusely. The pain in said appendage faded from his mind completely and immediately however when he upon cresting the top of the near seaborne wall found exactly what he'd hoped to—a narrow offshoot of the ocean current he and the others had almost ridden to their doom some time ago.

Making their way down the other side of the stone above the sea proved just as if not more difficult; they couldn't drop their rafts down to make their journey easier since the current below would've whisked the wooden slabs away immediately, and with them, the only chance of survival for those who had schlepped them up to the top of the rock in question. Both of Dekkin's arms were on fire by the time he was finally able to put down and sit on his raft again, and his chest was tight from the thunderous pounding of his heart; he welcomed death but not the pain associated with one taking place in an area like that which he now found himself in. Soon all four of them were riding the rapids once again, each taking care to keep their arms and legs tucked in for whenever the raft beneath him or her listed off to one side and scraped up against one of the twin stone walls fencing it in.

Cornelius had gotten on the water at about the same time as Dekkin, which was fortunate given that the oracle had some things to ask and say to the other man. "Cornelius?" He had to raise his voice to be heard over the roar of the rushing salt water beneath them.

Destiny's Catalyst was forced to do the same. "Yes?" Just as he had ever since discovering Matthew, Coria, and Zage in the back of the immortal's wagon, the hero spoke to the other man with an air of distaste.

Dekkin noticed this and couldn't have cared less. "Do you think you can defeat the Dark Lord without the Orb?"

The hero paused for a beat (he'd never considered the question) before replying, "Ah…perhaps." Hearing his own wishy-washy tone, he corrected himself, saying confidently, "Yes, yes, I can."

The oracle nodded. "Good. Because you're going to have to."

"What do you mean?" asked Cornelius with a perplexed frown.

"Even though we're riding the rapids, we won't beat the kaglorites to the temple. We can't stop them from entering it. So we'll need to use the Orb to bring Matthew back to life."

Destiny's Catalyst scrunched up his face even further, utterly bewildered. "Dekkin, what are you *talking about*?"

The immortal didn't respond for a short while, considering whether or not to come clean to the other man about everything. But when he realized he might have to if he wanted to save the boy's life, his hesitation fell away, and he told the hero everything, from his reasons for stealing the map and key to his budding relationships with the other members of his party as they traveled together, and

SEEDS IN THE SAND

finally to the vision he'd had of the lorm in both speaker and listener's lives dying at the massive clawed paws of a duracut.

Throughout this and immediately afterward, several entirely separate emotions visibly battled for supremacy over Cornelius's mind—contempt, pity, despair, surprise. Every one of these fought viciously against the others, and together, all of them wound up eradicating themselves by the end, leaving the face of Destiny's Catalyst devoid of any emotion. "Well, you may not be a *total* villain, but you have still committed many wrongs."

"Horb off," Dekkin snapped. "You know yours is the only life in which everything always works out, right?"

To this, the hero said nothing, for truthfully, he hadn't.

* * * * *

"Are you certain this is the right place?"

The kaglorites' helmsman looked over at Zage from the object of both their attentions, removing with great effort any trace of the exasperation he felt at this question from his voice. "I have…been following the map, sir."

The Dark Lord couldn't be faulted for asking this however. After all, their destination was supposed to be a great temple, and what lay before them where *X* marked the spot instead was a square, unbroken stretch of sand about a mile across amid the azure sea surrounding as well their ship.

"It is probably hidden there somehow, my lord," offered the helmsman dubiously. "After all, if it were out in the open, everyone would know where it is, right?"

Zage considered this before nodding in affirmation. "Yes, you are most likely correct. We will just have to make land there and search the area for any trace of it."

Under the helmsman's guidance, the kaglorites' ship came ashore on the island indicated by the map, and all its passengers save for three disembarked to begin surveying it for signs of a hidden temple. The identities of the trio left behind were as follows—the two prisoners, Coria and Matthew, and one of the Dark Lord's underlings, who remained with them to keep the outsiders from escaping or fouling up his fellows' plans or both.

Zage ordered those who followed him to line up side-by-side in one corner of the island, and together, they started walking straight ahead in that fashion, combing the sand beneath them along one side of the landmass' perimeter before rearranging their formation upon reaching the opposite coast to extend out to one side of where it had been, turning around and doing the same for another strip of lifeless land. They did this for hours, to no avail. The Dark Lord was beginning to despair as, at dusk, he noted that they'd gone over far more than half the target area with nothing to show for it when he heard a victorious cry far off to one side of himself.

Running to its source along with the others, Zage walked through the crowd, which parted to admit him without being instructed to do so by anyone, and found that the owner of the voice that drew him there stubbed his toe on a stone tablet previously obscured under a layer of sand while walking. Kneeling, the Dark Lord wiped it off to find lettering etched into the rock, reading as follows:

> What is whole in your hand must not be,
> Front and side unlock simultaneously.

Beneath this verse, three oddly shaped indentations had been carved into the tablet as well.

"What does it mean?" Zuza asked him once she'd come up beside him and seen what he had.

Zage shook his head. "I have not the foggiest. I do not see any kind of keyhole in the stone."

"And what could this riddle possibly mean?" added his second-in-command, squinting down at the lettering before her once more. "'In your hand'…how could whoever made this possibly know what would be in the hand of those who came here?"

"Indeed, it would have to be something anyone who got to this island looking for the Orb would possess. Is there such an item?" The Dark Lord paused pensively with her for a moment, his arms crossed over his chest. "I suppose it is a safe bet they would all probably have the map and key." He stopped himself as revelation flooded his brain. "The key…that's *it*!"

Zuza frowned over at him as he took the object in question out of his pocket with one hand. "What? What's it?" Her eyes bugged out when Zage raised the key in his clutches up over his head and threw it down hard on the stone slab. "*Zage! What—*"

The metal frame of the key gave way upon its impact with the tablet like a wooden practice sword swung at the blade of a sharp axe, fracturing across its shaft into three tiny pieces. "What are you doing?" cried Zuza in dismay as she looked down upon the iron fragments at their feet. "You've <u>*broken the key*</u>!"

"That *was* the idea," the Dark Lord replied nonchalantly as he crouched and gathered up the metal trio now resting atop the rock before him. His second-in-command was about to continue yelling at him when he turned one of the key fragments over in his hand… and she as well as he saw that its shape was identical to that of the leftmost hollow carved into the near end of the tablet's top. It was then that she came to understand.

Immediately after, Zage had fit each of the pieces snugly into the three slots whose proportions did not now seem so strange the ground beneath all of them began to shake. The tremors grew so violent that no one was able to stay on their feet as a massive stone temple began to emerge from beneath the sand at the center of the island.

Zuza lit up as she watched this all play out before her. The Orb was minutes away for the kaglorite woman now…and there was no one anywhere close to it that had even the slimmest chance of stopping her.

* * * * *

As you can imagine, Coria had been quite surprised to see Matthew as the boy was brought aboard the Dark Lord's ship and shackled before being put right beside her. When prompted by his fellow captive, the lorm filled her in on all she'd missed relating to himself as well as Dekkin and Cornelius since her capture. As he was going through the beginning of the story, the queen was elated, thinking it would conclude with the promise of forthcoming rescue. However, her spirit was crushed by the end, when Matthew told her tearfully that there was nothing but certain doom for the other members of his small party now.

Their collective despair didn't keep them from forming a plan of escape among themselves long however. "Excuse me," the boy said up to the guard standing a pace in front of them and shifting his intent gaze back and forth between his two charges with a fearsome scowl on his face. "I have to relieve myself."

The kaglorite grunted once, taking a hand off his weapon to gesture at the door leading below decks. "Go ahead." He'd been instructed to keep a close, constant eye on the both of them but felt comfortable disobeying the edict in this case, as he couldn't imagine the lorm being able to do much of anything even when out of sight.

His mistake. As Matthew passed the guard, he pickpocketed the man, in a tiny fraction of a second and without making the slightest of sounds or touching even lightly anything other than his mark. The boy descended to the bottom deck and, after waiting as long as would be expected for someone to do what he had said he would, returned to his place beside Coria. He and she both had their hands cuffed behind their backs, so the former was able to pass the latter the ring of keys in his grasp to her without the kaglorite before them noticing.

Similarly, the queen was able to handle these objects now in her possession without fear of being discovered, though she was forced to do so in a painfully ponderous manner so as to keep the guard from hearing this. After a long while trying to unlock her bonds with several of the keys in her clutches to no avail, she struck gold, but as she did so, her heart leaped into her throat; she'd been careless, making enough noise for the kaglorite before her to hear as she turned the key. The guard raised the sword in his grip high over his head in preparation for a killing blow, but before he could even begin to bring it down, Coria's free hand darted out, smashing into one side of his face and knocking him unconscious instantly.

"Now what?" the lorm asked as the queen stood crouched behind him, releasing him from his chains.

"What do you mean?" replied Coria as she stood and his cuffs hit the deck with a metallic *klink*. "We've got to stop Zage from using the Orb!"

Matthew motioned at the portion of the island the ship they found themselves aboard had come ashore on visible to him with one of his newly unshackled hands. "But where is it? They've been searching this area for hours. And they still don't seem to have found anything."

The queen's gaze shifted to where he was pointing, and with a sinking feeling in her chest, she realized that perhaps the Dark Lord's helmsman truly had taken them to the wrong place, which was, of course, fantastic for humankind and lormkind, but unfortunate for them specifically, as they were now faced with the prospect of having to try fighting their way through a few dozen kaglorites instead of merely intercepting and outmaneuvering the terrorists in order to stop the Orb from being used for the violet-skinned magicians' nefarious purposes (since they would be killed for breaking free of their bonds should they do nothing). Coria could have, of course, taken the wheel of the ship she and Matthew were now the masters of after dumping the immobile body of the unconscious kaglorite who'd formerly guarded them and sailed away, stranding Zage and his fellows, but she didn't for a second even entertain this idea. No matter who it was, she refused to doom anyone to the slow, agonizing process that was a death by thirst.

Both their ruminations were abruptly and violently interrupted then by a quake so powerful the section of the ship they occupied resting atop the sand slid a good bit back into the water. Coria was knocked to her feet by these intense vibrations and until they ceased after several minutes kept her eyes glued to the flat deck below her she was now in a futile gesture clutching at for dear life while being shaken this way and that across the top of it. When the queen did finally look up, what she saw blew her away completely—a towering stone temple had risen from beneath the sand before her. And between her and it, she spotted Zage's party pacing rapidly toward its yawning, open front entrance.

One of them, near the front, was Zuza. The sight of the other woman put a hard metal vise around Coria's heart.

"They found it," Matthew squeaked in utter dread as he watched them go. "We're all going to die."

"Not if we stop them, we're not," countered the queen with a reassuring smile.

The boy looked up to return her gaze; if he had been anybody else, he would've been exasperated. "How? We can't catch up to them from here, just for starters."

Coria studied the considerable distance between them and the kaglorites as well as the meager span separating the violet-skinned terrorists from the temple and, realizing he was right, cursed to herself silently. "Well...ah...there has to be *something*..." She scanned the stolen ship she and he were aboard, her mind racing, and saw no solution to their present dilemma. It was then however that she remembered the existence of something she couldn't, something that just might prove to be such a mechanism of salvation—the cannon on the front of said vessel.

The queen lit up upon recalling this but then stopped short; she didn't want to *kill* Zage and his fellows. She looked out then at the building before her yet again, and shortly thereafter, an idea sprang to her mind. "MATTHEW, GO BELOW DECKS TO THE FRONT CANNON!" she ordered urgently. "LOAD IT AND FIRE IT! MAYBE WE CAN COLLAPSE THE TEMPLE'S ENTRANCEWAY, BUY OURSELVES SOME TIME!"

"Coria, I don't think the temple is made of ordinary stone," the boy pointed out lightly without moving. "If it were, anybody with a cannon could blow a hole inside, and I doubt those who built it would allow that to be possible."

The queen inspected the exterior of the building before them again and, seeing the unnaturally black and unblemished rock making it up, saw as her stomach sank that he was almost certainly correct. However, as her gaze darted here and there about the ancient stone building, she spotted something else too; its roof was topped by an overhang of what looked like ordinary, weathered gray rock, gigantic in both length and height.

"We may not be able to break off a chunk of the temple itself, but we can collapse the normal stone ahead of and above its entrance," she said to the lorm, whipping her head down and to one side of herself until it was facing his. "Get down there and fire the cannon quickly!"

As Matthew rushed to obey, Coria gazed back out at the temple and the kaglorites approaching it and blanched; they were already ascending the long, tall stairway leading up to the front entrance before the boy had gotten below decks, and she worried that Zage and the others in his party would be crushed by falling rubble immediately after their ship opened fire on the massive slab of rock up above their destination in an unfortunate episode of almost comically precise (and deadly) poor timing. Just as she was at the top of the stairs leading to the bottom level after crossing the distance between them at a sprint, however, the cannon in question sounded, like a large tower bell at the center of a vast, labyrinthine city announcing the time of an appointment of hers when she was still racing to get dressed in her bedroom.

"*No!*" the queen cried out, whipping around to face the temple. The cannonball Matthew had just fired shot forth, slamming into the rock above the ancient, previously buried building and blowing its front section to pieces that came crashing down to the stone floor beneath it...what looked like mere inches in front of Zage, walling off the interior of the Orb's resting place.

Coria balled one of her hands into a fist and lifted it up slightly in victory, but this feeling of triumph quickly faded into nothing when a new thought came to her mind, *Now what?*

* * * * *

Dekkin and his fellows truly had the best and worst luck of their entire lives, all within the span of less than a day. Coming out of the rapids' single outstretched arm, the kaglorites' galleon had been within view, beached on the far shore of a nearby island. The oracle and the others began paddling toward this landmass, their journey painfully ponderous and laborious, each of them noting as they did so that no temple appeared to rest there but, not knowing what else to do, continuing to head in that same direction. After a few hours of inching forward in this manner, Cornelius ordered the rest of his party to bring their rafts to a halt, not wanting to give away their presence to the violet-skinned magicians who could now be seen combing the area in which the temple had been said to rest. However, quickly realizing they would need to be closer if and when the fabled structure finally made an appearance, Destiny's Catalyst amended his earlier order by ditching his raft and telling the others to do the same before leading them to approach the enemy further.

As the sun set, exhaustion was pressing down hard on every square inch of the hero's arms and legs from treading water for hours, and he began to regret ordering this course of action, but shortly after he had this thought, the island before him started shaking violently, the landmass rumbling loudly in protest, and the temple, the exact middle of its back facing him and the others, rose from unseen depths. It was with great relief that Cornelius then led Dekkin, Nadia, and Adam straight ahead and ashore. They went to a spot just before the near right corner of the newly unveiled building from there before stopping and cautiously peering around it for any sign of the kaglorites, who could be heard by them before that but were far enough away that this couldn't be used to pinpoint the violet-skinned magicians' exact location. Not only was there nothing to see in that regard, they spotted something else, so good for them it seemed impossible for it to be true—there was, near the farthest section of the wall that they were now gazing down the length of, a small wide-open side door.

Thanking the gods, they slipped inside and began making their way through the corridor they now found themselves in, completely unopposed.

* * * * *

SEEDS IN THE SAND

"Zuza, stop!"

Zage's second-in-command was so furious over Coria's last-minute intervention as she stomped back to the ship to slaughter the human queen that she couldn't see clearly and everything sounded as if her ears were filled with wax, yet despite all this, she still acquiesced to the Dark Lord's command as soon as it left his lips. She whipped around to face him as he approached her, spitting as she did so, "What? Do you realize what she's *done*?"

"Yes, I do, but what would be the point in killing her personally?" pointed out Zage evenly. "If everything goes to plan, she and all her kind will be dead quite shortly anyway." His tone was unusually half-hearted as he said that last sentence, making Zuza frown suspiciously. She chose not to pursue the issue any further, however, for there was currently, she thought, a far more pressing matter at hand as she then turned to face the wall of rock separating them from the advent of a new, perfect world.

"Could we make an opening with red magic?" she asked her superior as they both scanned the obstruction before them.

He didn't answer as he didn't have to. The two of them, along with every other kaglorite, gathered outside the temple knew that, though by throwing hard several balls of the mystical crimson energy at just the right places in its base—that could be accomplished—there was no way of knowing where they would need to be hurled at specifically and in what manner.

"What else…" Zuza began before trailing off as she clutched at one side of her head suddenly.

The Dark Lord's eyes bugged out in concern, and he reached over to touch her on one shoulder. "Zuza? What's wrong? Are you not feeling well?"

That is the understatement of this and most likely any century, she thought to herself. Her whole body hurt *badly*, to a degree she'd never experienced before. Anger so strong it turned her vision red and made her cry out uncontrollably in fury was flowing through her every vein. She was a woman prone to roaring and destructive rage more often than not, but now she saw how positively mild her usual levels of wrath were in comparison to whatever had her in its clutches presently.

 The rush of emotion was like a waterfall pounding away at her brain, drowning out the sound of her thoughts. After a few seconds though, as the throbbing in Zuza's head increased so much in both frequency and violence, she was sure it would outright burst, a single mental concept punched through the middle of the thundering falls like a hearty stone outcropping jutting out into and beyond their plummeting flow from a cliff wall they ran in front of—the mission. All that mattered in life was the mission. And right now, the mission required her to find a way into the temple, a way to bust through this pile of loose stone before her.

 A strange instinct took hold of her then, and she raised both hands, completely outstretched, toward the towering mound of debris. A saucer of red magic the height of her body materialized before her and just as she marveled at the sight of this, again poking a hole in the waterfall, it expanded in all directions by about a yard. Its formation increased Zuza's agony further still, to the point that her vision blackened about the sides; there was no more room for thought. Raising the pitch of her warrior's cry, the Dark Lord's second-in-command released the magic she'd conjured up before her, and it shot forward to neatly carve a large hole right through the rubble and into the temple.

 The newly awakened Prime Witch saw then by the light of the setting sun, surprisingly enough, a group of people gathered inside, and the strangest such lot she could've possibly imagined to boot; it was the oracle and his party, those whom Zage had stranded in the middle of the open ocean and seemingly without hope of survival some time ago. Normally she would've puzzled at least a little over this, but given the circumstances, her one-track mind became even more pronounced than it had been before. The only thing that mattered was that there were humans in front of her, staring back at her in terror with their bodies running perpendicular to hers, and of course, all humans needed to die.

32

Like zuza, coria should've been surprised by what she saw, in the case of the latter, a single kaglorite off in the distance summoning up all on her own an amount of magic it would normally take hundreds of violet-skinned magicians to create, but also like the Dark Lord's right-hand woman, the queen had larger issues to contend with.

"Matthew!" she shrieked over one shoulder.

Just as his name left her lips, the boy finished bounding up the steps leading below decks and whipped his head around to face the temple as he ran toward her, spurred on by the intensity of her tone. "What is it? Did we"—he paused as he took in the sight of the tunnel burrowed through the wall of rubble before the ancient building's front entrance—"did it not work?"

"No, it did," replied Coria as she whirled about and started making for the gangplank. "Somehow Zuza was able to make that hole all on her lonesome." She stopped at the top of the long ramp leading into the surf and looked back at the lorm when she realized he wasn't following her. "Come on!" she cried, motioning for him to do so with both arms and crouching slightly at the same time. "There's still time!"

Matthew obeyed this directive as soon as it was given, as you might imagine, but he did so with a confused frown on his face. "But…what can *we* do? They've got a massive head start on us, and we're outnumbered, and they're *kaglorites*—"

"Maybe they'll get lost inside!" pointed out the queen as she descended down the gangplank with a hasty *clomp, clomp, clomp*. "I don't know! But we're not just going to stand around doing *nothing*, waiting to be obliterated!"

There was another reason for the boy's reticence to give the kaglorites chase that he wasn't voicing. *What is the point*, he thought to himself, *of saving the world when it is one in which Dekkin is dead, or at least close and doomed to it?*

* * * * *

In response to the wave of a few dozen kaglorite warriors bearing down on him, Cornelius Arcind turned to face them and drew his sword, as, of course, he would.

Destiny's Catalyst was preparing himself for what he recognized might be a bit of a tough fight when Zage called out to his magic-wielding fellows, "Leave him to me! Go into the temple and retrieve the Orb."

"You do the same!" the hero ordered Nadia and Adam when he looked over one shoulder to find they were joining him in his stand, albeit with wobbling knees on the part of the latter. "It is as the Dark Lord said. He and I will handle each other. Obtaining the Orb is up to the rest."

Zage's subordinates rushed past Cornelius as he made his way steadily toward their leader, himself advancing in an identical manner, without so much as scratching the hero skin-deep in the side with a weapon of some kind, and Destiny's Catalyst never even flinched as they did so; all of them knew kaglorite honor would not allow such a thing.

Cornelius furrowed his brow when his prospective opponent didn't conjure up a weapon with blue magic as both of them continued approaching each other. "You can't be planning to face me with naught but your own fists now, can you?" asked Cornelius of the Dark Lord when the two of them came to a halt in unison two paces away from each other.

Zage flashed him a haughty grin. "That is exactly what I intend. I want our final bout to be distinctive."

Destiny's Catalyst scowled at the other man's arrogance but nodded. After a few seconds of still silence, each of the two combatants leaped toward the other.

The hero swung the sword in his hand horizontally to start. The Dark Lord easily ducked under the weapon's arc, and Cornelius winced in anticipation of the inevitable blow he'd receive for his failure…only for nothing to come. The kaglorite before him merely stood and waited for the next attempt at assault, even taking a step back and therefore making it easier for Destiny's Catalyst to launch immediately into another attack.

The hero lashed out at Zage again and again with Kiam, downward, upward, sideways, diagonally toward the floor or ceiling, and every time the Dark Lord dodged out of the way, as flawlessly as if he had a turins stuck to his back feeding him visions of his very immediate future. After several minutes of this, Cornelius was breathing hard, and his movements slowed, but this wasn't what held his mind then. What did instead were his opponent's techniques. Destiny's Catalyst had, of course, the most experience out of anyone alive or dead with facing the head of the kaglorites on the battlefield. Thus, he was quite familiar with Zage's fighting style—full-frontal, no-holds-barred, go-for-broke offense. Another reason the hero knew the Dark Lord's proclivities in battle was that they never changed until today, that is.

Today the kaglorite was actually moving like he had something to lose. *It is almost as if,* Cornelius thought to himself as he huffed and puffed and swung away, *Zage has learned patience somehow in the weeks since our last bout of combat.* Having never fought against the Dark Lord when the other man was acting like this, Destiny's Catalyst had no idea how to counter it, and so continued fruitlessly lunging and swiping at him, every swing coming a little slower than the last.

Finally, after several minutes of this, the hero was in the middle of an attempt at a horizontal strike when the kaglorite hopped forward a little and, crouching, timed an uppercut to perfectly connect with the bottom flat of Cornelius's blade. The blow was so forceful, and Destiny's Catalyst was so fatigued that Kiam was knocked up and right out of his grip. The hero began to shift his gaze up to snatch it out of the air but saw in the bottom of his periphery Zage preparing to wail away at his stomach and brought his head back down to face the Dark Lord again.

The kaglorite unleashed a flurry of blows that Cornelius in his present state was just barely able to fend off. But while he was doing this, his sword was, of course, still out of his hands and falling to the floor, and he hadn't the time to divert any degree of attention at getting it back before it touched down. When it then inevitably did, Zage raised his forearms to protect his head as he stepped forward with his left foot and kicked the sword, sending it skittering across the floor and well out of reach by his opponent.

Destiny's Catalyst cursed his lack of insight with gritted teeth and despaired at the loss of his greatest weapon. Did he have even a slight chance of beating the Dark Lord without it? Yes, yes, of course, he did. The hero assured himself as he put up his dukes. He was the prophesied savior of the world and devoted much time to training in fisticuffs besides.

The only one hurting when Cornelius's fists connected with the kaglorite's chest and stomach was the human; Zage's musculature was so incredibly developed hitting him was like sprinting head-on into a sturdy stone wall hoping to bust through it. After half a dozen blows to the Dark Lord, none of which appeared to even make him blink. Destiny's Catalyst had several broken fingers, and those parts of his hands that weren't outright busted were bright red, unusable for picking up a fork, let alone beating someone into submission.

In the back of his mind, Cornelius knew then that he was finished, but in the heat of the moment, he didn't, of course, have the time for this realization to travel all the way into its conscious segment. So despite the fact that there was no chance of this ending well for him, Destiny's Catalyst began guarding himself, incapable of anything other than defense now.

The beating Zage delivered unto the (on his part) much-hated hero was brutal and cruel, even by the Dark Lord's higher-than-clouds standards. The kaglorite's blows had the force of the average stone battering ram; it took only a few to wear down even Cornelius's formidable defenses. And after that…Zage broke the hero's nose, busted his lip, then went downstairs, fracturing several ribs on each side, knocking the wind out of his opponent with the slam of a fist to the stomach and wrapping it all up by kneecapping the other man, in *both legs*.

The Dark Lord burst out laughing in sadistic triumph as he stood over the man they called Destiny's Catalyst, lying on the cold, ancient rock floor beneath the two of them because that's all he *could* do, his clothes wet and dripping with his own blood. The kaglorite credited the hero mentally for, even in his sorry present state, refusing to back down from his nemesis as Zage stepped over the other man and prepared to literally beat his brains to a pulp. Yes, even to the very last, Cornelius Arcind had his heroic pride.

The Dark Lord paused as he thought this. Pride. It was the most important thing to this preening idiot. Losing that…would be worse than *death*.

The kaglorite retreated further into the temple a few paces before fixing the fallen hero with a grin of twisted glee. "You know what, Cornelius Arcind? I will *not* kill you here today, not until I use the Orb to erase you and the rest of your kind from the face of Samu, at least. What I am going to do is stand here, motionless, for a few minutes. Give you an opportunity to get back at me. You would like that, would you not? Oh, but you *cannot* at the moment. Is that not right? And that is what I want you to ruminate on, Destiny's Catalyst. Your greatest foe stands before you here today, poised to carry out a genocide, and you are *powerless* to stop him."

True to his word, Zage remained still for some time after that. At first, there was a defiant flare in the hero's eyes, nigh delirious from the severe injuries he'd just sustained. A few times shortly after the Dark Lord's silent vigil had begun, Cornelius even placed a hand or two flat against the floor below him and started trying to lift himself up. But each time he attempted this, he collapsed again without even managing to raise slightly any part of his body. And after he'd done this a few times, the realization set in, churning his stomach as it did so; he couldn't beat Zage Batur. The Dark Lord had faced him one-on-one, without *weapons*, without *magic*, and come out on top.

Salty tears streamed down Cornelius's face, mixing with the thick blood staining it and the rest of his body, as the kaglorite who'd bested him came about and strode toward the Orb like a future king at his coronation.

* * * * *

Why is it always me? This was the prevailing thought in Adam Hefull's mind as he ran, for when he split off from Dekkin and Nadia at an intersection of corridors within the depths of the temple, all but a couple of the kaglorites giving chase to them chose to continue following him. Good luck as well as bad abounded for the young recruit as he tried in vain to shake his sizable tail; on one hand, none of the magically-created weapons thrown at him dealt a fatal or even severe blow, but on the other, none of them missed entirely either. After a few minutes of this, Adam had bleeding cuts across every section of his back.

The hounded human was surprised when he started hearing one of the many sets of footfalls behind him beginning to quickly catch up to their source's target; clumsy he may have been, but he was well-built from his past growing up on a farm and so wasn't losing speed even after spending some time running full tilt. Looking back, he soon recognized that he wasn't moving slow; the man who'd come to the front of his pack, his face all scrunched up in determination, was simply that fast on his feet. Adam shifted his gaze back to his front, hoping to see some mechanism for his salvation, but nothing even remotely of the sort presented itself to him. It was fortunate he brought his head about to face forward when he did, for doing so allowed him to spot a strange outcropping of mottled gray rock of an entirely different hue from the walls surrounding it sticking out and back from one of them and which would have brained him completely had he not seen it and ducked out of its way in time as he did.

The young recruit almost didn't want to look back over either of his shoulders at the coming assailant, see his doom as it approached, even if doing so would give him a better chance of averting it. After a moment though, he recognized the foolishness of this line of thinking and swiveled his head to gaze once more at the enterprising front man of the kaglorite assault force. The violet-skinned magician in question just summoned a throwing knife into one of his hands and pulled the appendage back in preparation for the blade's launch. Adam still wasn't feeling any fatigue from the several minutes of dead sprinting he'd done, but seeing that made his breathing suddenly turn fast and hard.

The kaglorite with the knife was so focused on his target however that he didn't spot the strange, small finger of stone sticking out between him and it until he'd thrown his weapon, and it dinged off its surface, falling uselessly to the ancient rock floor beneath the both of them. This small victory, this meager display of good fortune, and the sensation of through it possibly escaping quite narrowly an early grave sent a visible thrill through Adam's every vein, but what happened next—though, in part, it greatly confused him—sent his very soul to the heavens. The odd stretch of stone, upon being struck by the blade of the knife with a loud, metallic *clang*, spat out from the many holes along its surface some sort of organic spray that, once breathed in by the frontmost kaglorite moving too fast to avoid it, knocked him on his belly, passed out, in an instant.

Now Adam thought to himself as he faced forward once again, *If only there were a few dozen more of those, strategically positioned to take out the rest of the opposition.* Up ahead, he saw the corridor he and those chasing him currently occupied led into and across a vast chamber narrowing to such a degree that one would have trouble spanning it even at a careful, leaden pace. And after half a minute, during which, thank the gods, none of the other kaglorites proved to have the ability and the gumption to do what their unconscious predecessor had tried. The young recruit came out into this new room… to find that everything except the thin walkway leading across it was positively bristling with the strange, spritzing rock.

You know where this is going. Adam fell off the edge of the narrow natural bridge almost immediately after stepping onto it. *I take it back* was his last thought before he collided head-first with one of the chamber's thick stone hairs and took a face-full of its sleeping powder. Just before he lost consciousness, the young human noted that it sounded oddly enough to his failing ears like there was a cascade of such ventings sounding out all around him.

* * * * *

Dekkin was more irritated than petrified as he ran for his life from a pair of murderous, muscle-bound mages.

"You're *sure* the map didn't include the interior layout of the temple?" Nadia asked him as she batted a dagger that would've impaled the oracle through the back of the neck had it been left to its own devices out of the air with the head of her halberd.

"Positive!" replied the immortal insistently. "Do you think I'm doing this for fun?"

The warlord huffed as she leaped off to one side, dodging out of the way of a ball and chain flung at where her legs had been prior to the movement. "Well, it's not a very good map then, is it?"

"Agreed!" Dekkin affirmed. At this point, air was bursting out from behind his lips before getting sucked back up greedily into a mouth open as wide as a small apple; he hadn't exerted himself this much since before the turins was attached to his back, and his traditional robes being wholly unsuited for anything remotely like what he found himself doing now as well as dripping with his own sweat certainly didn't help matters. All this to say, he was slowing down.

Nadia recognized this and came up right beside him, sheathing her weapon and bringing both hands down and back a little, palms facing the ceiling and fingers pointed backward. "Come on, get on my back!"

The immortal furrowed his brow in incredulity. "You can't be serious."

"I am. If you keep this up, they'll reach us. We'll be forced to fight them head-on, and even I can't fend off a *single* kaglorite all on my lonesome, let alone *two*."

There was a pause, during which Dekkin remained firm in his refusal to take her up on her offer.

"It's all right. I'll barely feel the difference."

"Oh, I'm sure," replied the oracle sincerely. "It's more a matter of pride."

"How much pride can one as shameless as you possibly have?" the warlord pointed out.

The immortal considered this for a few seconds before conceding with a reluctant grimace, "Fair point," and getting on Nadia's back.

She hadn't been bluffing when she said there'd be no break in her pace as a result of this, for there wasn't. Their trek through the temple did grow more treacherous immediately after this began though since she no longer had any free hands to wield a weapon with, either offensively or defensively. Nevertheless, after a protracted, roundabout journey during which they lost their tail, the two of them finally came upon a wide, tall chamber near the back of the building, supported by gargantuan pillars of unblemished white stone and with an altar on a dais at the center of it. And upon the altar was a light-purple ball of what looked like ordinary glass but most certainly was not—the Orb of Desire.

Dekkin and Nadia should've been elated at that moment...but they weren't because of what they saw by the chamber's other doorway on the opposite side of the room.

* * * * *

Coria's plan, as she entered the temple via the front entrance with Matthew trailing closely behind her, was an unorthodox one, but such were the circumstances in which she found herself. If the kaglorites had already or were at that moment about to find the Orb, she and the boy had no chance of victory. But there was still hope if they hadn't, if they'd all taken a couple of wrong turns and hadn't gotten their bearings yet. Therefore, when after several minutes of traversing the many hallways within the ancient building (it was somehow more unnerving for them to be completely lit than entirely dark, given that the source of illumination was a supernatural one), she started hearing the sounds of kaglorite battle cries and the clattering *ting* of metal on metal and stone, she changed course, heading in the opposite direction; if the violet-skinned terrorists were close to the Orb, it was already over, but if the reverse was true, she'd find it well before they did, saving all humankind and lormkind.

The distant footfalls and exclamations faded into nothingness as the queen advanced away from them, but after some time, a single set of steps (apart from those of the queen and the boy) came into earshot up ahead and off to one side of them. Coria was about to alter course to avoid these as well, but upon growing a little closer to them out of necessity (she was halfway down a long corridor completely unbranching in that area) found as she could hear them more clearly that they sounded purposeful, those of someone confidently walking toward a destination well within sight. Blanching as she realized this, the queen began sprinting in the direction of the footfalls; Matthew had to strain his short legs to their limits in order to keep up but said not a word of complaint.

When Coria flew around a corner and saw Zuza in the distance up ahead about to walk through a doorway there, her blood somehow steamed and froze over simultaneously.

The queen thanked the gods when, as she'd hoped, the Dark Lord's second-in-command turned away from what she'd been doing to engage the other woman, a nasty grin digging a furrow into the middle of her face like a sharp knife.

As the two women raced toward each other, Coria unsheathed her hammer and spear from its sheath on her back. Meanwhile, Zuza's hands began to glow red; the kaglorite planned to wreck the human's weapon first rather than lash out against it with one of her own created with blue magic. When both were within two paces of each other, they came screeching to a halt. The queen lifted the hammer half of her weapon high over her head, and the Dark Lord's second-in-command raised both her gaze and her hands to match this movement…only to be blindsided when she was attacked not from above but head-on with a rough kick to the stomach.

Zuza growled in ire at both her opponent and herself as the magic around her hands vanished, and she clutched at her belly with them; the motion of Coria's weapon had been a feint, and she'd fallen for it completely. However, there was one fatal flaw in the queen's plan of attack that, in the heat of the moment, she hadn't had the time to think through. Immediately after it, she was left wide-open, and the kaglorite took full advantage of this, leaping forward despite the ache in the terrorist's abdomen to tackle the human to the ground.

The Dark Lord's second-in-command laid into Coria from there, and the queen was helpless to fight back, at least with her hammer and spear; there wasn't enough room to use it properly. For *her* anyway, she realized a second later as Zuza struck her hard across the face, drawing blood from her mouth.

"Matthew!" Coria called out through a mouthful of her own bodily fluids as she tossed the weapon in her grip out and away from her and her assailant. The boy, who'd been standing on the sidelines of the battle with uncertainty over whether or not he could contribute to the fight in a positive way as well as fear of what might happen to him if he tried to do so, understood immediately what was being asked of him and rushed over to pick up the hammer and spear as it hit the floor flat on one side with a light *clang*. However, as he paced over to the dueling women and raised the weapon now in his grasp over his head with the intention of impaling Zuza from above with it, the kaglorite realized what he was doing even without seeing any of this and flipped both herself and the queen upside down.

The boy shifted gears to aim for Zuza's legs after this happened, but clever girl, she tucked them in, shielding them behind Coria's. The Dark Lord's second-in-command had a fistful of fabric from the back of the queen's shirt in the grip of one hand and pressed down on it, keeping the other woman from rising and escaping or more effectively fighting back. With her other hand, Zuza began summoning a wickedly sharp dagger with blue magic. As such, with both appendages entirely occupied, the kaglorite left herself open to assaults on either of her sides by the other woman, and Coria took full advantage of this but to no avail; Zuza made not a sound even as the queen's toned fists pounded on her left and right.

Once the slight weapon was in her grip, the Dark Lord's right-hand woman lifted Coria up a foot, whirled her around, and pressed the blade of the knife to the other woman's throat. "Drop it or I kill her!" she ordered Matthew.

"Don't do it!" exclaimed the queen, the muscles in her neck flexing as she spoke and, the skin over them and under the edge of the dagger coming up against the latter as a result, letting it draw blood. "If we let her get the Orb, we're all dead anyway."

Zuza nodded. "This is true. But dying from a slit throat is a far worse end than being wished out of existence, is it not? Not only that"—she smirked—"the boy's spent too much time around Cornelius Arcind. He thinks there's still some way to keep the Orb out of the hands of my fellows and I *and* save you." The lorm opened his mouth to protest before freezing at the realization that she was absolutely right on all counts.

The smug smile never leaving her face, the kaglorite hauled herself and her captive to their feet and dragged the latter toward the doorway she'd been about to walk through before the two of them had locked eyes, keeping her gaze on Matthew casually all the while. "I want you to see something, *Your Highness*." The venom in her voice was so palpable Coria was surprised it didn't take physical form and drip onto the floor before beginning to eat its way through the old stone. The queen gazed out attentively as Zuza shoved her head into the frame of the rectangular opening…and her heart nearly burst in despair when she saw, a minute's walk away, and yet many worlds removed from her, the Orb of Desire on its altar.

"That's right!" the Dark Lord's second-in-command crowed. "You were *so close* to *total victory*…" She jerked Coria around and pressed down on the other woman's throat further with the edge of her dagger, eliciting from that segment of flesh a fresh stream of blood. "And yet in the end, you failed. And now with that thought in your mind, you'll die, painfully."

Matthew started at this and, though Zuza couldn't see this, raised his hands slightly in protest. "Wait! You said—"

The kaglorite raised her weapon high in the air; it pointed directly facing the queen's jugular. "I lied."

33

THERE CAME THE SOUND of approaching footfalls off to one side of Zuza, and she whipped her head around to face it, letting the knife in her grip hang motionless in the air (for now, at least). The Dark Lord's second-in-command was on high alert as she did this, thinking a comrade of Coria's might be the one coming up to her but relaxed once she saw that it was, in fact, the man himself.

"Zage!" she called out in excitement. "You are just in time to watch me kill Her Highness."

Her superior was visibly uneasy as he continued walking up to her. "What would be the point of that? I am about to wish her and the rest of her kind into nothingness."

Zuza nodded, still smiling. "Yes, but would you not say the wretched human curs' queen deserves special treatment?" She returned her gaze to the prey in her grasp. "Come now, watch me cut her throat."

The Dark Lord's eyes bugged out and he extended one hand out toward her slightly, palm facing her. "*No!*"

His right-hand woman paused once more and fixed him with a disapproving frown. "Zage, I know that for reasons I cannot even come close to comprehending you have grown attached to this woman, but she *must not live*. Samu will not become a paradise until *all* humans and lorms have vanished off the face of it. You know that."

Zage nodded slowly, the motion seeming to take as much effort as if there were pulleys attached to the top and bottom of his head trying to raise it up while he lowered it and bring it down as it was lifted. "Yes." His eyes darted back and forth. "Ah...no. Zuza, no. We cannot kill her and especially not the human race as a whole."

It was as if he'd suggested they roast Zuza's son alive and eat him for supper. "*What?* What are you *talking about*, Zage?"

The Dark Lord came to a halt a pace away from his second-in-command and drew himself up. "Coria is a good woman, Zuza, undeserving of an early demise. And if there is one such human, the *first* I ever got to know well, there are many. Because of that, we cannot kill them off. It is *wrong*. Put down the knife. It is time we made peace with the humans and lorms."

Zuza, scowling in disappointment, turned her head back to face the queen's. "This woman has beguiled you, made you lose your senses. Well, if *you* will not do it—"

"No!" cried out Zage, and in a fraction of a second, he conjured up his own dagger with blue magic and thrust its blade into the path of his right-hand woman's as she tried bringing it down to impale Coria through the throat.

C*LANG!* The point of Zuza's knife was halted mere inches from its target. She gritted her teeth in frustration before glancing over into the room before her...and seeing that Nadia Torum had ascended the steps to the Orb's altar, and now held the mystical artifact in both hands.

Dekkin's mind raced as he stood right behind and off to one side of the warlord; if they used the Orb to save Matthew from death, Zuza would try to kill Coria, and might succeed at it too, but if they protected the queen with the artifact, there was a very real chance the boy would die at the gargantuan paws of that duracut the oracle had seen in his vision.

Nadia lifted the artifact in her grasp up into the air slightly, shaking him from his ruminations. "*Wait!*" he cried, holding up both hands to chest level out in front of it with their palms facing the warlord; though not having eyes in the back of her head, she couldn't see this. "I...I don't know what our wish should be."

"*I do*," replied Nadia immediately, her eyes on the Orb. The immortal opened his mouth to ask her what she meant by that when he became aware of a most curious sight off in the distance and at the edge of his vision: as the warlord held the artifact in both hands, Zuza was staring out at the other woman…and smiling.

Dekkin furrowed his brow in confusion at this, and had he known then the reason behind this seemingly odd occurrence, his stomach would've churned; the Dark Lord's second-in-command was looking upon Nadia Torum in such a way because it was the other woman who had been the one to approach her and Zage about an operation to smuggle them and their fellows across the Lormish Isles, over Humania's eastern border, and further still to the royal castle in Cobaltus, and the prized map and key stored deep and secure in its depths.

"Do it, Nadia Torum!" Zuza cackled emphatically. "Slaughter them all, the humans and lorms!"

It was at this point that the oracle understood, partway at least, what was happening, and he began taking a step toward the warlord to, against all odds, try to wrest the Orb from her grip but stopped himself when Nadia brought one of her hands down to the hilt of the halberd sheathed at her side in a threatening gesture. The immortal wasn't put off by the prospect of an early grave, as I'm sure you know, but he didn't want to be killed in so gruesome a manner in front of Coria, and without someone to take up the mantle of oracle nearby besides. But it didn't matter if he was killed in an attempt to stop Nadia, did it? If he did nothing, he would perish all the same.

"I will not," said the warlord to Zuza, then evenly, making Dekkin stop once more. When the Dark Lord's right-hand woman scrunched up her face in puzzlement, Nadia continued, "I will not kill every human and lorm. I will destroy the entire world."

"*Why?*" the oracle asked, raising his voice to be heard over the assorted exclamations of shock and dismay coming from the others.

Now it was Nadia's turn to appear perplexed. "Why? I would have thought you'd understand better than anyone, Dekkin Eterden. It's the right thing to do. I've known that ever since I was a little girl. Growing up, I thought everyone did. And when I found out they didn't, almost *all* of them didn't, I was appalled." The immortal opened his mouth to reply, though what exactly even he didn't know, when he was cut off by the warlord. "But enough talk. It's time for all this to end." She swiveled her head back to face her outstretched hand, and Dekkin did the same as he prepared to try to stop her from speaking her desire with the Orb in her grasp...only for both of them to find, much to their collective surprise, the artifact was no longer there.

Matthew was a lorm, and as such, he both took up very little space and could move near-silently when he wanted to. With this in mind, he snuck all the way up to Nadia's side without anyone, friend or foe, noticing and, a second before the warlord's gaze fell back to what had been until very recently its location snatched up the Orb.

Now the boy held it high over his head, and the oracle upon seeing him leaned toward the lorm, opening his mouth to tell him what to wish for, only for it to turn out that he was too late; before a word escaped his lips, Matthew called out, "I wish Dekkin Eterden was happy again, forever!"

"No!" shouted the immortal in utter anguish and with hands outstretched toward Matthew. And in all the commotion he and everyone else present had failed to notice it at first, but now the increasingly discernible quaking of the floor beneath their feet and pounding *boom*s of a duracut's footfalls became too prominent for anyone under any circumstances to ignore.

The Orb crumbled into a handful of dust in the boy's hand, but as you can imagine, neither he nor anyone else was terribly concerned with this at that moment. Another key element of the situation, which was forgotten in the face of the near-certain death now fast closing in on them was, on Zuza's part, Coria; the kaglorite woman let her go as the two of them and Zage raced to the others, knowing it was foolish to think that, together, they'd have any more of a chance against the approaching giant beast than they would alone but going to the room's other occupants anyway. Nadia, for reasons unknown to us or any of our characters other than the woman herself, proved to be immune to the panic setting in for the rest. As soon as all the chamber's current inhabitants were together, both Dekkin and she took off, the former ahead and off to one side of the others and the latter, oddly enough, in the direction of the duracut's now-thunderous footfalls.

When the massive creature finally made an appearance, it was through the frame of the towering doorway in one of the walls between where Dekkin and Nadia entered the room and the others came in, which had gone ignored by all of them up until now in spite of its considerable size because of the numerous, more pressing factors that had been at play previously. It was a tropical duracut, the subspecies native to the isles, and so its skin was turquoise and, though it remained hard as diamond, smooth to the touch. In addition to this, gills were positioned on either side of the beast's head.

All this went unnoticed by Dekkin and the others, of course, given that a creature of that size was now barreling toward most of them as it let loose a deafening roar. Nadia unsheathed her halberd as she moved to intercept it, planning on taking down the animal single-handedly. This may seem foolish, and indeed it was, but if you were the warlord and had in the past won all the seemingly impossible battles she had, you very well might think as she did that you had a chance of felling the dread beast. As it was, the probability of such a thing was about zero; Nadia came to a halt a few seconds away from the duracut and raised her weapon high over her head in preparation for a first strike that never came, as the racing creature slammed into her on its way to the others without even noticing, sending her flying through the air to land sprawled and unconscious some distance off to one side.

CLING! The sound of a thin metal blade forcefully striking stone rang out. To the humans, lorms, and kaglorites present, it was little more than a soft tap on their eardrums, but for the duracut intent on slaughtering them all, the noise was hot needles jabbing into its own. It came skidding to a halt, its thick and elongated claws making a piercing *screech* as they scraped across the rock floor, some distance from its targets, and cried out in agony before whipping its massive head around to face Dekkin, who was now crouched at a standstill and with his dagger drawn and in hand.

"RUN!" the oracle shouted at the others still conscious as the beast turned to face and started bolting toward him. It wasn't much of a plan (this diversion would after all only buy them perhaps a dozen seconds), but it was the best he could think of with the very limited time and resources at his disposal. As the immortal stared down the beast coming to violently wrench the very life from him, many thoughts raced through his mind in a brief moment.

His demise fast approached. Soon he would be freed from the pain and anger that had been his constant companions all throughout his lengthy yet incomplete tenure as oracle. He would feel, *be* nothing. It was a euphoria-inducing thought. And yet joy was not the only emotion swirling in his heart just then. This surprised Dekkin, and he frowned as he tried to place the thoughts and resulting feelings that were disrupting his ecstasy.

Part of it, he realized after a split second, was concern for Matthew, in the quite unlikely event the boy managed to escape the clawed clutches of the duracut now rushing toward him (to say nothing of the alternative). The lorm was certainly a tad more assertive than he had been when he'd first met the oracle, but he had a long way to go yet. He needed someone to prod him on either side whenever he wavered from the proper path, as all children did. And what of Coria as well? Destiny's Catalyst wouldn't let her go off on her own at this point; she'd have to return to the royal castle she dreaded so deeply. And from there, none of her options were even remotely attractive—stay and live out a life of misery or try to escape again and, even if you manage it, be forced to remain in solitude until death for fear of being seen and recognized.

There was more too, though it was something the immortal couldn't put into words. It was a feeling that came over him when he looked to one side of himself at Matthew and Coria, who looked so…*right*, standing next to each other and looking intently back at him like that, even when they were doing so in abject horror. What was it? Rather like…when he pictured a world in which the duracut before him didn't exist, one where he and the boy and the queen could go on being with each other, there came a…desire—a desire for the future, something Dekkin hadn't felt in centuries.

He wanted their time together to keep going.

He wanted it more than he wanted the nothingness he'd craved for so long.

He didn't want to die.

He wanted to live.

The oracle's eyes bugged out as he came to this realization, and a fraction of a second later, his heart throbbed in utter despair when his focus returned to the outside world, specifically the savage beast out for his blood within it, and he saw that he would die in about two seconds. *The gods who made this world, if they even actually exist, were sadists indeed,* he thought bitterly. The last thing the immortal soon-to-be dead said to himself before closing his eyes (he didn't want to see the end of all his meager happiness coming) was that his previous mental statement would've served quite fittingly as his last words.

Dekkin may not have been able to see it, but he could still hear the duracut's booming roar as it continued its approach before… descending? The oracle frowned and opened his eyes to find Zage crouched just ahead of him, with the latter's back to him and both hands laid flat on the floor out before the rest of both their bodies and a yawning chasm before the two men, and the vicious beast the immortal thought would be his executioner falling into the pitch-black abyss within it, its mouth open wide as it wailed in furious protest.

The Dark Lord had been watching along with those directly around him as Dekkin moved to sacrifice himself, and when the kaglorite shifted his gaze over to Coria, finding a rictus of tortured anguish upon her face, his response was of the sort most common for him—rage. Zage glared ahead then at the object of his wrath, the duracut approaching the oracle, the filthy creature who'd hurt the queen's heart so. And much to his surprise, despite the fact that he was as angry, he thought, as he could possibly be, the fury in his gut kept building; all of a sudden, every part of his body felt blisteringly hot, and his chest hurt like a sharp metal stake had been driven through it. Without thinking, the Dark Lord sprinted to the oracle's front, evaporating several square yards of stone in a single, short effort, awoken as a Prime Wizard.

34

RELIEF. ANOTHER EMOTION DEKKIN Eterden had been a stranger to up until several minutes ago, when Zage leaped in front of and saved him from the rampaging duracut. Now though, his body was flooded with the feeling, and he found he quite enjoyed it. Less than a half hour prior, he'd been in a hellish pit of despair, a common enough occurrence for him, and now he was safe and happy, surrounded by people he'd come to realize he loved.

This newfound and unusual emotional state was not, he was fairly certain, the result of the Orb, for immediately after Matthew tried to use it, the oracle hadn't felt even the slightest difference in his mood; only later had the change, motivated by his rescue and self-realization, come about. So after everything its many pursuers had done to try reaching and using it, the artifact had been nonfunctional all along. None still lived who could call themselves an expert in magically crafted objects, but it was the theory of all who were present for the boy's attempt at using the Orb that it was simply so old it had lost its mystical power.

By the time anyone thought to look back at where Nadia had been when she'd been last seen, she had long since awoken and vanished without a trace, save for a single scrap of fabric she left behind in her wake. When Coria walked over and picked up the cloth, her eyes took on a haunted quality during her examination of it, so much so that Dekkin, despite desperately wanting to know the cause of it, figured the answer was most likely, based on her expression, highly personal, and let it be.

SEEDS IN THE SAND

Zuza stood down once the dust settled over the whole affair following the duracut's deadly fall and the attentions of the immortal and his fellows turned to her. "We have such a long history together, and there is still a place in my heart for you," she said to Zage through gritted teeth. "So I will leave you be, retreat, for now. But mark my words, traitor…when next we meet, I will hold nothing back." Under different circumstances perhaps Dekkin and the others would've used this chance to take on the former Dark Lord's second-in-command while they had her alone, but as it stood, kaglorite honor required Zage to let her go and regroup with her forces, and no one else fancied a tad the prospect of facing off against a Prime Witch in their present state and with such minuscule numbers at their disposal, even with one the male equivalent on their side.

An aspect of the whole situation that went unnoticed by all immediately around the Orb before the duracut was felled was the absence of the other kaglorites there; surely, Dekkin and the others thought, at least a few of them should've found their way to the towering chamber within which it had lain. A search began, ending with the discovery that Adam Hefull, of all people, knocked out all the missing persons (excluding those who followed Dekkin and Nadia and then merely gotten lost), sacrificing his own consciousness in the process. Cornelius clapped the young recruit on the shoulder once the latter had awoken, promising marked advancement in the ranks of the human military as a result of his actions. Strangely enough, though Adam accepted this with a nod and a smile, his expression was somewhat half-hearted and uneasy.

Once the unconscious kaglorites came to and their twin lost fellows found, all of them were informed of the splintering of their people's leadership and given the option to pursue peace with the humans and lorms beside Zage or return to Kagloris and pledge to continue the fight against those two peoples with Zuza. Surprisingly enough, about two-thirds of them chose the former option. The rest were given along with their newly minted leader a few rowboats from the lower decks of the galleon they and the brethren they now found themselves opposed to had stolen to get to the temple, and several ringfish were wrangled for the purpose of pulling the small watercraft.

That night, as Zage sailed west back to Humania along with the others in the illegally obtained merchant vessel, he noticed as he stood by one of its railings on the main deck and looked out at the surrounding, isle-dotted sea that Dekkin was watching him pensively from a distance. The kaglorite turned to face the other man, raising his brow quizzically, and in response, the oracle, though at first he averted his eyes, walked over to the former Dark Lord.

"Hello," the immortal greeted uncomfortably after coming to a halt directly beside Zage.

"Hello." The awkward air around them went entirely unnoticed by the kaglorite.

It hung about them for a short while as neither man spoke any further before Dekkin finally broke the silence, saying, "Thank you, for saving me back there."

"Think nothing of it," replied Zage sincerely.

The oracle paused before continuing. "And I'm sorry for how I treated you while we were together. I…I have a history with your people, not that that's any excuse for how I behaved."

"I figured," the kaglorite replied evenly. "Do tell, if you would like. I am curious."

The immortal deliberated some before relating his tale, though it was only for a very small amount of time.

* * * * *

Dekkin spent almost the entirety of his first century as oracle in complete isolation. For the first few years of that time, he traveled in search of the most secluded living space he could find. He had no concept of what north was back then, but that was the direction he ended up going in for the most part. When he reached the border of what would later be dubbed Humania, he was astounded to find there a salty pond so vast he couldn't see the end of it, beyond the shore before him. Since knowing how to swim wasn't a given in that day and age, the oracle figured finding a spot of land in the middle of the azure waves would do quite nicely in terms of trying to locate an area he could call home which few could ever possibly reach.

So he took a knife he brought with him upon leaving his tribe's settlement and carved up a few nearby trees to make a raft before setting sail, bringing no food or water with him (for why would he?). Days passed as he paddled forward by the light of the sun and allowed his makeshift watercraft to drift as he slept at night, and when he decided he'd waited long enough, he started looking for the nearest landmass. The first one he came upon was so perfect it was almost comical—a tall, forbidding finger of sharp rock sticking up out of the ocean like a needle through cloth. The immortal beached his raft there and found the seaward stone pillar's interior was riddled with passageways and small rooms carved into it over time by surrounding harsh weather. Climbing up almost to the top of it over the course of a few hours via the slopes inside, some of them with very mild inclines and others so steep he was forced to double back and take an alternate route to proceed, Dekkin discovered a diminutive room with no view of the outside world there and metaphorically planted his flag right there.

For the next several decades, he never once got out of bed or the stretch of hard floor he'd designated for resting, anyhow. This was a sort of self-styled prison the oracle had chosen for himself, one which would've driven most people mad after a week, let alone well over fifty years, but for him, it was as close to heaven as he thought he could get at that point. He was simply happy that he wasn't at a funeral for one of his loved ones, knowing all the while that it would be just a single such instance of what would become legion. At first, he had his disheartening thoughts to contend with, but over time, they gradually faded away, and he was left with blessed, silent, pure black.

As you can imagine, after over a handful of decades spent in this manner, the abrupt sound of footfalls in the distance below him one day gave Dekkin the greatest scare of his life. He sat up, feeling like his heart was bending his ribs as it pounded ferociously, and his stomach sank as he realized the one fatal flaw of his maritime lair he'd missed when making the decision for it to such; by the time someone else's footsteps could be heard from his room, there was no way to escape the other person from there. With nothing else to do, the oracle had no choice but to simply sit and wait an interminable amount of time for his visitor to show himself or herself.

Much to his satisfaction, when the intruder, a young human man, rounded the corner into the immortal's room, he cried out, "Malun!" and jumped back instinctively, visibly shaken quite badly at the sight of the other man. Otusir, as the newcomer was called, turned out to be a master thief, looking for an isolated spot to stash his stolen goods. He was very disappointed when Dekkin told him he couldn't use the immortal's living space for such a purpose, but his attention was swiftly and completely directed elsewhere rather quickly, for it was then that he first spotted the turins on the other man's back.

At first, Dekkin refused to explain it and himself and what he was doing out there in the middle of the ocean, for the conversation thus far had already thoroughly exhausted him, but when Otusir persisted in pestering him for answers, he eventually caved and related his entire life story. By the end, in which the oracle had resigned himself to an entirely empty life, the thief sitting across from him averted his eyes and swallowed noisily.

"That's...quite a tale," Otusir said after a long, uncomfortable pause between the two of them. "You truly...can't live as a person anymore?"

Dekkin shook his head immediately with a vehement motion. "Of that, I am certain, absolutely. I'm no longer a man. I'm an oracle."

The thief considered this, visibly confused. "But...why does that mean you can't live *at all*? You lost what you were, sure, but you also *gained* a new identity, that of an oracle. Why don't you live as one?"

"What do you mean?" It was the immortal's turn to be perplexed, as well as bitter and incredulous. "What did I *gain* from having this...this *parasite* put on my back?"

Otusir shifted his weight from one side of his body to the other. "Well, you can *see the future* now. Live forever. *What did you gain?* You've practically become a god on earth. So why not act like it?" He lifted his brow as a thought came to his mind. "With your powers, Dekkin, you could unite the world, under *your* rule. Perhaps you'll never be happy again, but your life could still have meaning, the greatest meaning there is."

The oracle pictured then lording over a utopia he himself had created with his bare hands and compared this with the prospect of going back to an empty, centuries-long rest.

Given how he'd felt an hour ago (or rather how he hadn't felt anything), it surprised him how easy it was to reverse his position.

* * * * *

The thirty-odd tribesmen Dekkin approached watched as a vicious storm blew all around them, wetting their stained tunics and whipping their long, unkempt hair about, just as the oracle had said it would two hours prior, when there had been nothing visible in any direction save for clear skies. After a few moments of silent (on their part, anyway) awe, all the human hunter-gatherers assembled around the immortal turned to face him, almost in unison and knelt, their heads bowed low.

Dekkin came to call the group of followers he'd now in one fell swoop amassed the kingdom of Humania. He'd never been very good at coming up with names for things.

* * * * *

"Do you yield?"

Novisime An looked up at Dekkin Eterden as the oracle asked this question or rather was forced to when the sword tips at his throat began to rise, forcing him to move his head to match their movements lest he be cut. They were in the middle of what had been a vast battlefield and was now a mass grave. Novisime's faction had been the final holdouts in the immortal's quest for a unified people across the continent. By the time this rival for power was in Dekkin's sights, the oracle's forces outnumbered those of the other man by a factor of thousands, of course, but conquering Master An's meager compliment of warriors had nevertheless been a costly and irritatingly onerous affair, for they called the sizable landmass' eastmost area of land, that which was upon and beyond the natural bottleneck where what would one distant day be called the Peacepath rested, home. And so when the oracle made over land his initial attempt at conquest, his men found as their first and for many final battlefield a stretch of earth only able to fit a handful of them standing side by side, one wherein Novisime's warriors were therefore able to contend with the much larger army, given that only an infinitesimal fraction of them could fight at one time. In the end, the immortal was forced with gritted teeth to order a retreat and commission the construction of a vast fleet of ships to go around the continent's eastern boundary from the other side of the bottleneck in order to face off with the enemy in an area open enough to allow the advantage of their superior numbers to be fully utilized.

It took an excruciating amount of time given how close final victory was at hand, but in the end, it was done…and when Dekkin's soldiers came ashore following their maritime voyage, the battle, if such a one-sided affair could even be called such, went exactly as the oracle had planned.

This brings us to the scene of the immortal demanding surrender from his rival, surrounded by corpses that when living made up the other man's army and with his foe being held at swordpoint by those fighters who'd proved accomplished enough to be allowed a place in the god on earth's royal guard.

Novisime flashed the architect of his defeat a bitter rictus at this request, but with the sharp metal tips of enemy blades hovering an inch from his jugular, he had no choice if he wished to stay alive but to acquiesce. And so he did, though he spat the affirmation with great reluctance even in spite of this.

Dekkin smiled in haughty victory. Humania was now complete.

* * * * *

"Oh, you can't still be going on about that!" Primos Roneage exclaimed in exasperation in Cobaltus's throne room. "Survey what's beyond the sea. There's *nothing* out there! And certainly not any *new forms of men*, as you suspect."

King Dekkin, exasperated himself at the other man, suppressed a frown. "That is precisely what I am 'still going on about,' as you say." He should've known this would happen. Oh, it was undoubtedly the right call, to spend the first few decades after his final victory improving living conditions throughout Humania and solidifying his hold over the realm, stamping out the handful of budding insurrections that inevitably cropped up at the start of any newly united people's history. But by doing that for so long (or rather what a normal person would classify as *so long*), it would, of course, lead to complacency, outright aversion to the concept of exploration outside the kingdom's borders.

But there is hope, the oracle thought to himself as he stood and walked over to look out at the surrounding city through a stained-glass window of appropriate height. A city—the concept had been completely foreign to all and inconceivable to everyone but himself when he first envisioned the idea over twenty-five years ago. When the immortal described the scale of building the capital for his newly unopposed kingdom as he saw it all that time ago, the small army of carpenters he hired to realize it had, even in spite of his supernatural and royal status, burst out laughing in his face before they could stifle the exclamations.

And even after Ritall was completed and its first citizens moved into the city limits, there had been growing pains—people who'd once lived in rural farmland complaining about all the noise a life in such a metropolis contained, unfortunate souls having never passed through a settlement with more than three roads getting hopelessly lost amid the city's expansive labyrinth of main streets, side streets, and alleyways both thin and wide. Yet eventually, everyone settled in. If that was possible, selling Dekkin's subjects on his plan to seek out new land and new life would be child's play.

And if all else failed, well, he was an eternal, absolute monarch, after all. "Make it so, Primos," the king instructed with firm insistence as he turned away from his view of the adjacent road just beyond the window he positioned himself before to face his chief subordinate, who nodded in affirmation even as he grimaced uneasily.

* * * * *

Six years after the eastward expedition was sent out, and neither returned or even sent a message to confirm their continued survival, even King Dekkin, with his unnaturally long-term method of thought, was beginning to give up hope he'd ever see those brave men and women again. Admittedly, part of what was rankling him that morning had to do with something both entirely unrelated and intimately connected to this conundrum—the cramped living quarters he was currently occupying. Once it was time to send the explorers on their way eastward, the oracle ordered the center of Humania's government to be moved to the border town of Yinit so that he and his court could be closer to the action he had been so sure was just around the corner. This humble settlement was, of course, not equipped to handle this, and so the immortal was forced to call the most luxurious (and yet still constrictive and pedestrian by his standards) hotel room within it home upon first moving in along with the others he brought with him. But, of course, Dekkin could've commissioned the construction of a royal estate fit for himself and his people the minute he set foot in Yinit, and though it would've taken some time to build, eventually he would've had appropriately regal temporary quarters, for leisure, rest, and matters of state. He didn't, for he felt it would be bad luck to make as if he and his court might be spending a great deal of time in town before the expedition returned from their journey.

Time passed however, and this superstitious reasoning had done nothing to ensure a hasty or even moderately lengthy conclusion to the endeavor of outreach the oracle started all those years ago.

Or so he thought until he heard and felt the *clomp, clomp, clomp* of clothed feet pounding briskly across the second floor of the inn accommodating him and his inner circle to his room's closed door. The immortal stood even before Primos flung it open to slam against the wall in its path, crying out, "THEY'RE BACK! YOUR HIGHNESS, *the expedition has returned, and they come with people of an entirely different species!"*

As King Dekkin and his chief adviser bolted down the stairs to the hotel's lobby, they could both hear an excited clamor just outside it, and the former smiled to himself in satisfaction; now that his extended plan was coming to fruition, all the complaints he received from the citizens of Yinit, both directly and otherwise, about the spatial and material strain his presence placed on the small coastal village had now been forgotten, he knew, in the face of the scheme's success.

They were already standing just before the hotel's front door when that area came into view for the oracle and his right hand, one human man in his midthirties who was one of the explorers sent out all those years ago and…someone…alien. The seemingly male ambassador and the immortal assumed most if not all the former's people had dark-purple skin and hair, and his irises shone luminous gold like those of King Dekkin's statue at the center of Cobaltus's largest city square. Even a man with as much life experience and such a cool temperament as the oracle was put off by this novel sight, but his soul was soothed by the easygoing smile the violet man was flashing him.

The human standing beside the foreigner snapped to attention when his king came to a halt before him and his charge. "Sir!"

The immortal nodded in distracted acknowledgment. "Not to seem cold, Addus, but…what took you and your fellows so long?" Concern leaked onto his face. "Are the rest of your party all right?"

"Yes, sir," replied the explorer, his head solemnly bowed. "My apologies, Your Highness. We had to travel a great distance to find another people as you requested. There is a large island chain to the immediate east of Humania, and several times one or more of us swore we saw something in the distance as we passed through it, a sort of green-skinned fishman, but every time we tried making contact, we failed to track one down. It wasn't until we reached the vast jungle beyond that we found what we'd been assigned to"—he lifted his head and gestured toward the ambassador at his side—"the kaglorites."

King Dekkin turned his attention to the man with the golden eyes. "Your people call themselves kaglorites then?"

As soon as he'd said this, the oracle realized it was very likely the other man didn't speak English well or even at all, but just as he cursed himself for not realizing this, the latter responded, "Yes, Your Highness." It took the immortal some effort to understand what was being said, for the kaglorite spoke with a heavy accent the like of which he'd naturally never before encountered.

"We've started teaching them our language," Addus explained rather redundantly. He motioned toward the man beside him once more. "Zeho here proved to be the fastest learner, and so he was chosen to represent his people in Humania."

King Dekkin nodded. "Well, Zeho, it is so good to meet you. What is it like, your homeland?"

"It is a land of plenty," answered Zeho, his smile widening at the thought of it. "Very dangerous as well, in places, but my people are strong and united." He shifted his weight from one side of his body to the other. "We want for nothing…that we know of. I'm sure there could be much trade between our two nations, of all the things each one doesn't know it needs."

As the oracle shook the kaglorite ambassador's hand, his soul soared; the dream that the thief planted in the immortal's head so long ago was that much closer to being complete. Just as Otusir said, Dekkin still wasn't happy, didn't walk about without a weight on his chest like he had back in the forest with Seren and Anter, but he found it easy to rise every morning given the immense amount of *purpose* his life now had. Also, his duties as king kept him so busy with affairs of state that, while darkness still lurked within his skull constantly, most of the time, he was able to successfully distract himself from it, on the best of days almost quash it, for a little bit at least. And in those moments of stillness when there was nothing to occupy his mind…well, he just had to muscle through those until the next round of obligations and conundrums. Yes, his right wrist was bandaged from when he'd slit it several nights ago in a fit of despair…

SEEDS IN THE SAND

But the hand attached to that wrist was now grasping that of another, sealing however unofficially an unprecedented alliance mutually beneficial for the entirety of both their peoples.

* * * * *

What had once been meager now rose to scrape the sky. This was the central running theme among the settlements along Humania's western border—all of them had been diminutive villages before the kaglorites became King Dekkin's allies almost fifty years prior, but the explosion of trade between them and his subjects following this turned all those conveniently located outlying towns into bustling metropolitan fountains of commerce. Yes, as it turned out, the world wrapped around, something no one in the country had even conceived of before some of the violet-skinned magicians began showing up in western Humania from what had previously been thought of as the opposite side of Kagloris far earlier than their brethren who'd set out at the same time across what was now known as the Lormish Isles for the eastern section of human territory.

Of these formerly backwater communities, none started so small and prospered as much as Kociden, making it King Dekkin's favorite one to visit when he was in the area for one reason or another. And as he stood within it one morning gazing out over the dozens of packed docks stretching out from it into the ocean like fingers he saw the poster children for the area's economic boom. Talon Panvitae's father was a fisherman and his father before him and so on and so forth. Now the latest in this previously unspectacular family line was one of Humania's wealthiest merchants, with a fleet of ships numbering in the dozens to his name.

And that wasn't the only way the man's life epitomized the sea change that enveloped his home country's west coast. Beside him, both hands resting on her pregnant belly, was his daughter, Lainey, and her kaglorite husband, Zike. The oracle smiled at the sight of those three (three and a half?) as he always did.

"*Zeli is dead!*"

The ear-piercing, anguished cry rang out across the docks and the city adjacent to them. The immortal started at the sound of it, as did most others within earshot and whipped his head around to face its direction, his heart hammering in his chest. The loud, impassioned voice's owner was a violet-skinned male, standing just past the gangplank of a large docked ship and shaking with fervor, his eyes as wide as they could be. The immortal saw in the other man's face that what had been said was the truth, and his stomach sank; Zeli was, *had been* he supposed, the strongest wizard in all of history, and as such was, *had been*, one of Kagloris's most beloved and revered residents. It was no surprise his demise would produce such a response from one of his kinsmen.

There was something else though, something *strange*, about the way this makeshift town crier was carrying himself—a tautness that suggested...*rage*.

"The great warlock Zeli is dead, <u>and it was the humans that killed him!</u>" he said then.

Dekkin's blood, and indeed that of every human who heard this, froze over in a split second. Could it be true? Surely not. But if it wasn't, who was Zeli's killer? What kaglorite would assassinate a man of his or her own kind, and one of such high stature besides?

Kociden was deathly quiet for a moment, though thoughts were racing so wildly through the oracle's head that it didn't seem like it to him. Then the announcer raised up one of his hands slightly, palm facing the sky, and summoned a ball of red magic. Turning to his right to face a human merchant vessel, he hurled it at a spot on its hull below the surface of the water. It soared through the air and into the drink before boring a hole through the wet wood of the ship... and as the waterborne vehicle began to sink, all hell broke loose.

The immortal and, in fact, the entirety of the human race had never seen kaglorites display a negative emotion stronger than annoyance before just then, so naturally those within earshot and view had been deeply shaken by the scream of despair and display of wrath that kicked off this incident...but what was to come next was beyond even their wildest imaginings.

Volleys rose up from every area of the docks and those buildings and streets closest to them before plunging down to sear through the walls of nearby ships and houses, collapsing some of the latter instantly. That alone was almost unbelievable to Dekkin…and then flashes of blue magic began springing up all across his field of vision, and from their luminescence, deadly weapons were conjured up. The man who started the whole affair was the first to kill, in his case, a soldier who'd been drawn to him by his emphatic exclamations and approached with intent to restrain once he'd first summoned magic, doing so quickly enough to cut off his route onto shore. The oracle blinked hard as he stared at this, thinking with certainty that he was in a dream but opening his eyes after he closed them to find an all-too-real corpse hitting the deck it had stood upon just three seconds ago, when it hadn't been one.

"How could you do this?" The immortal's gaze darted to face the direction of this voice, part of a multitude rising up and merging to form a cacophony of torment, anger, shock, and dismay. It was Zike yelling at his wife with her right elbow clutched in one of his hands. "WE'VE BEEN YOUR *friends* FOR <u>decades</u>. WE'VE DONE *nothing* to <u>any of you.</u> WHY WOULD YOU BETRAY US LIKE THIS?"

The violet-skinned man already had a naturally deep voice, and having it cry out at you from less than a pace away was, of course, alarming.

"D-darling, what are you talking about?" Lainey managed after a short, startled pause on her part. "*I* didn't do anything—"

"OF COURSE YOU DID!" bellowed her husband. "YOU'RE A HUMAN, SAME AS THE ONE WHO KILLED ZELI! YOU <u>had</u> TO HAVE KNOWN!" You wouldn't have thought the kaglorite's face could've darkened any further than it already had, but alas, it did, most disturbingly.

"You're evil," Zike said.

The noise surrounding them all was such that Dekkin had to strain his ears to hear the other man then even in spite of the comparatively lower but empirically normal volume of the latter's voice. "All of you, you can't be trusted." He removed the hand gripping Lainey and summoned a dagger into it. "You can't be left alive, lest you do something like this again."

He stabbed his wife then right in the center of her engorged belly.

Lainey first screamed in agony, then whimpered in despair as her attention turned to the unborn child within her, already dead by its father's blade, and finally, she wept looking up at her killer, the man she loved, until she perished in a pool of her own blood on the hard stone beneath her.

Dekkin disassociated at this point, and by the time he came back to reality, Kociden was a complete, smoldering shambles. The battle had ended, but not before every single kaglorite and more than half of the humans present within its borders had met a grisly end. He furrowed his brow as he heard someone call out his name, the other person's voice seeming as faint to him as if it were coming from an ant perched on his earlobe. It wasn't until Primos came up beside and violently shook him that he realized he hadn't returned to the real world fully.

"Your Highness, we must *leave now*!" was the first thing his adviser said after the oracle turned to face the former and found his hearing finally and completely restored.

The immortal looked away from the other man and back at the carnage amassed before him. "To what end?" he muttered near-inaudibly.

Dekkin couldn't see it, but Primos looked stricken with bewilderment at this. "To what? It's…it's *dangerous* to stay here, my liege, *very dangerous*. You must *realize this*—"

"I care not for myself," interrupted the oracle in a monotone. "You know this."

His right-hand man was forced to pause and consider how best to reason with a person who'd clearly lost it entirely. "Well…yes, but"—he brightened a fraction at the inception of an idea on his part—"but we must leave here to *make plans*, to *fight back*, to *avenge those who've fallen here*."

The immortal shook his head a mere centimeter in either direction. "What would be the point?" He gestured toward the corpses and piles of burnt rubble beyond and on either side of him and the other man. "Why should I work toward the betterment of this world at all, if each of my plans, hundreds strong, can be decisively foiled in the span of five minutes?" A solitary tear welled in one of Dekkin's eyes before falling down his cheek, smearing some of the ash that came to rest there. "I lived through all the pain, for *this*. What was it all *for*? Why should I?" He paused as the answer came to him. Without another word or gesture, the oracle came about and began marching away from the docks.

Primos lit up in relief at this and began following his king close behind as he always did, but his face fell once more when the immortal turned right away from his residence and any other place he could logically be going. The adviser sped up to walk directly beside Dekkin and, with confusion and concern, asked, "Y-Your Highness, what are you doing? Where are you going? There's nothing of use in this direction."

The oracle laughed for the first time since Master Roneage met him, and the latter didn't care for the sound one bit; it was so caustically bitter it might as well have been a shouted expletive. "Oh yes, there is. There's something of great use, a good distance up ahead. It's a dagger of stone, sticking out of the middle of the ocean." The immortal looked over then at Primos, suddenly irritated. "Oh, stop following me so, you simpering fool. I resign. I relinquish the throne."

His adviser's eyes grew as big as dinner plates. "*What?* What are you talking about? You can't do that!" He proceeded to protest the issue further and at great length, but after a half hour of this being met with stony silence, he finally realized the cause was hopeless. "What shall be done with the office of king then?" Primos's voice was a squeak laced with despair that made it clear he hadn't the foggiest idea of how to proceed as the two of them crossed a point along Yinit's perimeter.

Dekkin shrugged. "Do what you want with it."

The oracle did end up returning to his former prison (oh, my mistake, his *home*) and wasted away for years on end yet again. When next day, out of curiosity, he drank some Destiny Water, he received a vision of the world's destruction and cracked a smile for the first time in decades.

35

THE KIDNAPPER, THE RUNAWAY, the terrorist, and all the rest of their party received a hero's welcome upon arriving in Cobaltus following a couple of months more of travel. Or rather they were told at that time that they would, shortly thereafter, that a ceremony celebrating their safe arrival was scheduled for later in the day, but Coria's chief adviser, Samuel, rather ominously requested that they be secretly brought to the castle beforehand for a special briefing.

When the cripple wheeled himself into his private office, right on time, of course, the queen shot to her feet from where she'd been sitting before his desk and, flashing him a wide and inviting smile, said, "Hello!"

Her adoptive brother nodded once as he rolled into position on the other side of the heavy wood construction. "Hello."

Coria remained on her feet for a beat before realizing how awkward it was to do so when the person she was addressing couldn't stand and sat back down. "I'm glad you called for this meeting, brother. I was hoping you could inform me of the current goings-on of the kingdom."

"*You* want to be told those things?" Samuel asked incredulously.

The queen's spirits took a strong hit from the tone of this question, but she still answered, "Y-yes, that's right."

"Well, I can't say I see what the point of that would be," stated the cripple evenly.

Coria furrowed her brow. "What do you mean? I'm the queen." At a knowing look from Samuel, she continued, "Brother, I know I've been…shirking my duties since I took the throne. But I've decided I'm ready to truly rule now"—she smiled warmly—"with your help along the way, of course."

The eyes of the man in the wheelchair widened. "Are you serious?"

She confirmed it with a quick nod. He sat back in his seat. "Ah, well, this is quite a surprise. But I'm afraid you won't have occasion to utilize this newfound sense of responsibility. I came upon a new turn of phrase recently that I believe applies here." He squinted and brought one hand to the bottom of his chin. "What was it? Ah, yes, too little, too late."

Coria's mouth fell open slightly in confusion. "What do you mean?"

Samuel sighed heavily. "Somehow it would seem word of the true reason behind your disappearance got out among the general public. They're calling you the Runaway Queen, and demanding that you be removed. Tensions are running so high I'm afraid if the crown remains on your head, you'll lose both by the end of the night."

The blonde woman paused in pensive dismay. "Who could've distributed the information to that many people so quickly?" When the handicapped man before her flashed a smug sneer, she put two and two together. "*You?* But…*why?* We're *family*. We've *worked together* for—"

"Oh, we've *worked together*, have we?" spat Samuel, more angry than derisive now. "When did that happen? Because all I remember is you passed out on the floor of a pub while *I* handled *everything*." He shook his head vehemently. "No, your time as royalty is *ended*. The ceremony later today isn't just to welcome you and the oracle home. Its other purpose is to serve as the commencement of a new government."

"A new government?" Coria repeated, totally lost. "Don't you just mean a new ruler? Aren't *you* to be Humania's new king?"

Her adoptive brother motioned in the negative. "The whole mechanism is being replaced, though I will be in power until such a thing has taken place. Henceforth we shall be a representative democracy."

The now-former queen was visibly taken aback by this; proposals for such a thing had been rampant since well before even her birth (she'd even backed a few of the campaigns in the hopes their success would absolve her of royal duties), but she'd never thought there was a good chance of them being realized in any way. "A representative democracy," said Coria, still a tad dazed by all this. "So the king or queen will be...voted into office."

"No," the handicapped man responded, "a council of five shall be the ruling party."

She nodded distractedly. "I see." The inkling of an idea for how to retain her position sprouted in a distant corner of her mind. "And are you certain this is the correct path to take? How do you know this elected council will do any better of a job than I would were I to remain queen?"

Smugness overtook Samuel's face once again. "Oh, I'm quite certain it will be. Perhaps I'm a bit of a psychic, like your friend Dekkin over there." He pointed at the oracle with one of his index fingers. "Because I feel quite sure *I* will be one of the council members, and let's say...*two* of my closest associates, which I believe"—he mockingly pretended to count fingers—"would ensure that my will would be carried out in all things. Just a feeling, that."

Coria scowled at the implication. "You won't get away with this. I won't let you. I'll tell everyone of what you just said to me—"

"And you think your former subjects will be quite receptive to accusations flying from the lips of a deserter and a privileged one at that?" asked her adoptive brother rhetorically, visibly drinking in all this.

The former queen struggled to draft a reply but came up with nothing.

"Coria." Samuel leaned forward in his seat, sincerity striking in its dissimilarity to the qualities of his previous expressions dawning on his face. "I won't deny I'm enjoying every moment of this, but that doesn't mean I'm not a fit ruler. You'll see. I've run things ever since your coronation, after all. I pledge to you that Supremacy will flourish under my guiding hand."

The blonde woman before him squinted, uncomprehending. "I'm sorry, the…what was that?"

"You haven't heard?" The man in the wheelchair started before saying this. "Humania and the Lormish Isles are becoming a single governmental unit. A most welcome development long overdue, in my opinion. Together, they shall be known as the Supremacy." He raised one hand up slightly, palm facing the ceiling and its fingers pointing ahead and to one side of himself at the end of the motion. "With the threat of the kaglorites still alive and well under Zuza and Nadia Torum now wreaking havoc for reasons unknown, Samu has never been more lacking in stability. This unification is designed to combat that. It'll begin in concert with the election of the first council."

There was a short pause as Coria took in all this new information. Finally, after about half a minute, she broke the silence, saying, "I see." She drew herself up then. "Well, on the subject of kaglorites, I also want to talk to you about how Zage and the other defectors are to be treated. I don't want any form of discrimi—"

"Oh, yes, yes," interrupted Samuel with an impatient wave of his hand. "They will be welcomed into the Supremacy and given treatment equal to that afforded its human and Lormish citizens."

The former queen's eyes bugged out in utter disbelief. "Truly?" she squeaked out in shock, and her adoptive brother confirmed it with a nod. How could the same man who had engineered the massacre all those years ago respond to a call for kindness upon kaglorites in such a way? But staring into Samuel's face, she detected not a bit of deception there. *And true, a man like him could, of course, probably lie about anything quite convincingly,* she thought, *but considering also how open he'd been about his devious machinations prior, I'll opt to take what he said on the subject of Zage and his fellows at face value. One shouldn't question miracles, after all.*

* * * * *

"You have to tell him *now*," Dekkin insisted.

Matthew nodded uneasily. "Right, but...could you?"

"*No*," replied the oracle firmly, shaking his head in disapproval. "I'm not doing it for you. This is something you need to handle yourself, *by* yourself."

The boy thought on this for a moment before affirming it, albeit with a slight grimace. He increased his pace to catch up with Cornelius as the two of them along with Dekkin and Coria headed for the celebration and commencement ceremony taking place in Cobaltus's main city square. With legs like his, naturally short because of both his race and prepubescent age, the lorm found he had to almost flat-out run to catch up with Destiny's Catalyst, though the man was well within his view even before the boy began to do so.

"Master," Matthew began after a nervous pause on his part as he panted once he was directly beside the hero.

It took Cornelius a few seconds to register this, and when he did respond, it was only via a distracted grunt. The man hadn't been himself ever since his landslide defeat at the hands of the now-former Dark Lord.

"Master, I"—the boy stopped himself, considering one last time if he truly wanted to turn toward and walk down the branch in his path up ahead of him now; looking back at the immortal after a while gave him the confidence to go through with it—"Master, I-I'd like to...resign as your apprentice."

Much to the lorm's surprise, Destiny's Catalyst started at this, his previously half-shut lids flying wide-open. "*What?*" said the hero as he whipped his head around to face the lorm's. "Are you serious? Why?"

"Well"—Matthew began with averted eyes—"I...I didn't choose to start traveling with you four years ago. It was decided for me. And I went along with it. Because I didn't know of anything else I would've rather done. But"—he smiled slightly and glanced back at Dekkin—"now I do. And you know, you...you don't truly *need* me for any good reason. You...can handle things completely alone, 99 percent of the time. And in those few instances where you can't, whatever you're facing that's proving to be too much for *you* is, of course, far too powerful for *me* to turn the tide in any way. So"—he shrugged—"I'm not doing it anymore."

Cornelius's eyes darted back and forth frantically as he listened to this monologue, and upon its conclusion, he replied immediately, "*But*...but, Matthew, please don't go. I...I for the first time in my life, I don't know who I am. Ever since I was born, you know, I've been told that I'm Destiny's Catalyst, the one destined to slay the Arsonist, a hero who always wins. But"—deep shame flashed across his face—"at the temple, I...I lost to my personal nemesis *badly*. I don't...I don't know." His tone became pleading. "Please don't leave. Don't take away another part of my identity."

"But, Master Arcind..." the boy began, standoffish, before pausing.

"What?" asked Cornelius, breaking the extended silence. "What is it?"

The lorm swallowed loudly. "Master Arcind, I don't mean to put you down. And I'm not angry about it. But...you've never taken what I specifically want into account ever. And yes, you haven't been unkind." He looked over at Destiny's Catalyst with a look of assurance on his face and his hands slightly raised and outstretched in the direction of his words' recipient, palms facing the man, as he said this last part, "But...nonetheless, you've never shown concern for what I as an individual feel. W-why...why, then should I do so for you now?"

To this, the legendary hero had nothing to say, and after several seconds of silence between the two of them, Matthew slowed down, returning to Dekkin's side.

* * * * *

That night, the oracle dreamed he was back in the same desert he'd visited in the throes of slumber a couple of times before, with the deformed man he'd encountered on those past, purely mental occasions. Looking to one side of himself, the immortal spotted the same tree atop a distant dune and instinctively began advancing toward it, with his companion following close behind. He pressed his lips together tightly as he passed dozens of seeds either resting in the middle of the surrounding arid sands or tumbling down an incline across them, but once he'd crested the desert hill, he did something he hadn't during his past visits. He walked over to stare down at its side opposite to the one he had traversed to reach its peak. It was there that he saw an oasis, ringed by fully-grown, towering trees, with innumerable saplings and amoebic seeds standing and resting respectively in the soft grass at their bases.

"There's water even in a desert," said the man behind Dekkin then, and the oracle's eyes began to well up with tears of rapture.

* * * * *

Dekkin, Matthew, Coria, and Zage sat at a table in one of Cobaltus's most obscure pubs at noon the following day, having their lunch with the hoods of their tunics up to decrease the chances of their being recognized by the other patrons or the employees working there. None of them had the foggiest idea where they would go or what they would do from here, but the oracle found personally that he didn't care on either account, so long as the four of them were together. After spending so many years entirely numb, the immortal was discovering he'd lost the ability to identify some of the emotions that were now coming over him for the first time in decades. Most forceful and mystifying among them was how he felt when he looked at Coria or talked to her or listened as she did so. When he was with her as she smiled or laughed or simply was still and silent, it was like he was shooting straight up into the clouds, faster than an arrow loosed from a taut bow, but always with the knowledge that at a bad look from her, he'd plummet down, burrowing into the planet's core. It was heaven. It was hell. Another emotion, which Dekkin could place but not ascertain the reason behind its existence, was the jealousy he felt whenever the former Dark Lord looked at or spoke to her.

A lull in the conversation that had been taking place between the four of them came about after a while, and into it, the oracle inserted the question that had been at the front of his mind since its initial appearance. "What was on that scrap of cloth Nadia left behind?" he asked the former queen. "The one you picked up, back in the temple."

Coria's face fell instantly, and she looked in conflict with herself as she sat like an unmolested stone, without movement or sound, for a moment. Finally, with a heavy sigh, she reached into one of her pants pockets, saying, "I didn't want to burden anyone else with it, but…I suppose given what it is, I must." She pulled out the patch of fabric and slapped it down on the surface of the table they were all seated at. The immortal hunched over to get a good look at it.

And the world stopped and froze over.

Seeing the design before his eyes, Dekkin's mind was shot back in time several decades to the day when he'd for the first time in so long induced a vision. Within it, the oracle was on his stomach, face-down, with an unseen person standing crouched over him, holding down and pressing his soft flesh, clothed and otherwise, into hard subterranean rock.

When the immortal heard a third party walking past him, he cried out as best he could with his mouth being ground into solid stone, "Don't do this! You'll destroy the world. You understand, the *whole world and everyone in it!*" The only response on the part of these words' recipient was to take off the robe he or she had been wearing and toss it back to land a few feet to one side of Dekkin's head. The oracle managed to wrench his head free from the grip of the one above him just long enough to look over at the discarded article of clothing. It was dark wherever he and the others were, certainly no place directly under the sun, and only some of the area around the immortal was illuminated by a single fire burning somewhere far ahead and off to one side of him. All that to say, most of the robe was in shadow, preventing the oracle from seeing how large it, and therefore the person who'd been wearing it was. However, one thing he could just barely make out in the split second before his head was forcibly jerked back into place facing the floor was an emblem upon it, that of a miniature mock-up of Samu completely ablaze. Shortly thereafter, there came the sound of a deafening explosion, and a few seconds later, Dekkin was wrapped entirely within its fiery embrace.

A design identical to that of the emblem was upon the scrap of cloth Nadia left behind.

About the Author

NOAH DOSIER IS A novelist and playwright. He lives in Sycamore, Illinois.

Printed in the USA
CPSIA information can be obtained
at www.ICGtesting.com
LVHW091227210124
769165LV00001B/37